D0844816

Class, Race, and Inequality in South Africa

Class, Race, and Inequality in South Africa

Jeremy Seekings and Nicoli Nattrass

Yale University Press

New Haven and London

Published with assistance from the Louis Stern Memorial Fund and the
John K. Castle Publications Fund of Yale University's Program in Ethics,
Politics, and Economics.

Set in Adobe Garamond and Stone Sans types by The Composing Room of
Michigan, Inc.
Printed in the United States of America.

Library of Congress Cataloging-in-Publication Data

Seekings, Jeremy.
   Class, race, and inequality in South Africa / Jeremy Seekings and Nicoli Nattrass.
     p.   cm.
   Includes bibliographical references and index.
   ISBN 0-300-10892-3 (hard cover : alk. paper)

   1. Income distribution—South Africa.   2. Apartheid—Economic aspects—
South Africa. 3. Social classes—South Africa. 4. Labor market—South Africa.
5. Education and state—South Africa. I. Nattrass, Nicoli. II. Title.
   HC905.Z9I5149 2005
   306.3'0968—dc22   2005008316

A catalogue record for this book is available from the British Library.

The paper in this book meets the guidelines for permanence and durability
of the Committee on Production Guidelines for Book Longevity of the
Council on Library Resources.

10 9 8 7 6 5 4 3 2 1

Contents

Acknowledgments

This volume was conceived in 1995–96, when Nicoli Nattrass served on South Africa's Presidential Commission to Investigate Labour Market Policy and Jeremy Seekings taught a course on South African society at the University of Cape Town. How, we debated, should labour market and welfare policies be reformed (or transformed) to address the challenges of poverty and inequality? It probably goes without saying that the final volume looks nothing like the volume imagined at the outset and, indeed, contains curiously little of the work we collaborated on initially in the late 1990s. The ensuing years saw an explosion in qualitative and quantitative research on many aspects of our topic. And new data became available about the continuities and changes that followed the end of apartheid. The book reflects new research by other scholars and ourselves. Previous versions of some of our arguments did find their way into print, in a series of journals, edited collections, and working papers.

The final version has benefited from comments made at many conferences and seminars, by students subjected to successive drafts, and by friends and colleagues. Research was facilitated with financial support from the University of Cape Town's University Research Committee and the Ernest Oppenheimer Memorial Trust (which financed a short stay in Oxford). From 2001 onward we benefited from the generous support for UCT's Centre for Social Science Research from the Andrew Mellon Foundation. Our stays in Oxford and (twice) at Yale University provided valuable opportunities to write and rewrite. Ian Shapiro facilitated publication by Yale University Press. We are grateful also for the detailed comments made by the press's two referees, Alan Jeeves and Gavin Williams, as well as by David Featherman. Thanks also to Allison Stevens for her help with proofreading and indexing.

We like to think that we have presented some original work herein, but our work has been based on the wealth of valuable analysis conducted by many others before us. As we hope is evident, we build on earlier work by "radical" and "liberal" scholars, as well as more contemporary work by economists and other social scientists who are now hard to label. Any attempt at naming them (you) all would risk inadvertent omission, but we hope that our debts to the work of other scholars (including present colleagues) is readily apparent in the pages that follow.

Authors' Note

Racial terminology in South Africa is a complicated matter. In this book we use the terms most widely used in South Africa in the recent past. "African" refers to people classified by the apartheid state as "native," "Bantu," or "black." "White" refers to people classified as European and later as white by the apartheid state. "Indian" refers to people who were brought to or came to South Africa from the Indian subcontinent and were sometimes classified as "Asiatic" by the apartheid state. "Coloured," referring mainly to people in the Western Cape, designates those who did not fit the other categories: some were descendants of the indigenous Khoi and San who inhabited the Western Cape before the arrival of either white or African people; others are the descendents of "Malay" slaves, brought from Indonesia and elsewhere by Dutch colonists; others are descendents of relationships between white and African people. We use "black" to refer to African, coloured, and Indian people collectively.

For the reader's convenience, we offer the following comparison of South African currencies to the U.S. dollar.

R1 in 1940 was worth R88, or about US$15, in 2004 prices
R1 in 1950 was worth R57, or about US$10, in 2004 prices
R1 in 1960 was worth R40, or about US$7, in 2004 prices
R1 in 1970 was worth R31, or about US$5, in 2004 prices
R1 in 1980 was worth R11, or about US$2, in 2004 prices
R1 in 1990 was worth R3, or about US$0.5, in 2004 prices
R1 in 1993 (the time of the PSLSD survey) was worth R2, or about US$0.3, in 2004 prices
R1 in 2000 was worth R1.2 or, about US$0.2, in 2004 prices

A wage of R8 per month in 1950, for example, would be worth about R5,500, or slightly less than US$1,000 per year, in 2004. An annual salary of £300 in 1950 would be worth R34,200, or a little more than US$6,000, in 2004. An income of R2,600 per year in 1950 would be worth about R150,000 or US$26,000, in 2004.

South Africa used pounds until the 1960s; the rand was introduced at the exchange rate of two rand for one pound, so that £1 in 1940 was worth R176, or about US$30, in 2004 prices; £1 in 1950 was worth R114, or about US$20, in 2004 prices; and £1 in 1960 was worth R81, or about US$14 in 2004 prices.

Finally, South Africa has changed its nomenclature for school grades several times. The current system of grades supersedes standards, which superseded forms.

2005 grades	standards	forms
grade 1	sub-A	
grade 2	sub-B	
grade 3	standard 1	
grade 4	standard 2	
grade 5	standard 3	
grade 6	standard 4	
grade 7	standard 5	
grade 8	standard 6	form 1
grade 9	standard 7	form 2
grade 10	standard 8	form 3
grade 11	standard 9	form 4
grade 12	standard 10	form 5

Class, Race, and Inequality in South Africa

Chapter 1 Introduction: States, Markets, and Inequality

The relation between public policy and economic inequality has been the focus of considerable research in recent years. The foundation for much of this work is Esping-Andersen's *Three Worlds of Welfare Capitalism* (1990). Esping-Andersen identified three distinct patterns of state intervention in advanced capitalist countries. In each case, the state intervened with social and (to a lesser extent) labour-market policies to reduce inequality, but the form of that intervention differed in terms of the scale of public expenditure and the extent to which the state displaced the market and the family in determining the incomes and welfare of its citizens.

Esping-Andersen's work (and related work) focuses primarily on the varieties of welfare capitalism existing in the "North" (including Australia and New Zealand). Most emphasis is placed on the way the state redistributes income using welfare and labour-market policies, with relatively little attention being paid to the way it shapes the growth path—and thus the overall level and pattern of income—with broader economic policies. Some recent work within this tradition draws on the "varieties of capitalism" literature (Hall and Soskice

1

2001) to emphasise that different welfare state regimes are "embedded" in different production regimes, that is, "different patterns of relationships between enterprises, banks, labour and government" (Huber and Stephens 2001, 5). But this particular research agenda focuses more on describing the different types of capitalism than on explaining their distributional impact.

"Northern" research into the way the state affects distribution is in sharp contrast to the "development" literature, which explores the distributional implications of particular economic growth strategies in low- and middle-income developing ("southern") countries. This emphasis is partly because there is generally little direct redistribution from rich to poor via the government budget in developing countries. But it is also a product of substantive research by development economists dating back to the mid-1970s showing that growth strategies have profound effects on who gets what in these societies (for example, Adelman and Morris 1973; Chenery et al. 1974; Lewis 1976). Whereas Esping-Andersen and others take the market-generated distribution of income largely as given and concentrate instead on how welfare states redistribute that income, development economists emphasise the relation between growth and distribution. As we demonstrate in this book, understanding the nature and trajectory of inequality in a particular country requires a sound grasp of how the state affects both the distribution of income via its labour-market and economic growth policies and the redistribution of income via the budget (most notably via welfare and educational spending). Put another way, analysis must encompass the direct and indirect ways in which the state shapes distribution.

South Africa is a particularly valuable case study for testing such a combined approach because it is a middle-income developing country and it has a set of labour-market and welfare institutions that, in important respects, mimic those in advanced capitalist countries. But South Africa's usefulness as a case study for understanding inequality extends beyond this. First, no other capitalist state (in either the North or the South) has sought to structure income inequalities as systematically and brutally as did South Africa under apartheid. Explicit racial discrimination affected earnings and income directly and blatantly. Black people and white people with the same qualifications were paid different wages for performing the same job, especially in the public sector. As late as 1979, for example, the starting salary for an African nurse in the public sector was two-thirds that of a white nurse with the same qualifications. Prospects for promotion also depended on race, with the result that the average African nurse's salary was about half the average white nurse's salary during the 1960s (Marks 1994, 173–74). The maximum salary for African secondary school teachers and police constables was only half that of those classified as white (Knight and McGrath 1977, 258). Similarly, black old-age pensioners received less from the state than did their white counterparts. In the late 1960s, the maximum pension paid to an African person was a mere one-seventh of the maximum payable to a white pensioner.

More important, state policies affected inequality by limiting the opportunities open to the black majority of the population. People were dispossessed of or denied access to property simply because of their racial classification. Business opportunities were curtailed. Discriminatory expenditure on education meant that black people entered the labour market with big disadvantages. The "colour bar" prevented them from getting the better-paid jobs, even if they had appropriate skills and experience. And discriminatory public expenditure on health services meant that black people suffered from inferior health. In many ways, therefore, an individual's income and welfare under apartheid were dependent on his or her official racial classification and hence location in a racial hierarchy.

Second, and unsurprisingly, inequality in the distribution of income was extreme in South Africa throughout the apartheid period. At the end of that era, when cross-national data were becoming more readily available, South Africa recorded one of the highest levels of income inequality in the world. Available data are nowhere near good enough to distinguish among the countries competing for the unenviable title of having the most unequal distribution of income, but South Africa is clearly right there alongside the more unequal Latin American countries (Brazil, Paraguay, Guatemala) and some other African countries including Zimbabwe and Lesotho (see, for example, World Bank 2001). In these societies, the top decile of households received almost one-half of national income, and the top two deciles together almost two-thirds. South Africa's poor, however, are unusually poor (relative to the rich, that is): average household incomes in the bottom income decile were just one-hundredth of the average household incomes in the top decile. This is a larger ratio than that of Brazil, where the ratio stood at "only" 1:50 (Psacharopoulos et al. 1997, 144). In most southern societies the ratio for expenditures varies between 1:10 and 1:20, with a few societies (including Bangladesh and Egypt) having ratios as low as 1:7 (World Bank 2001, 282–83).

The third reason for the value of the South African case is that democratisation brought to power (in 1994) a government with a clear public commitment to, and a political interest in, mitigating inequality. One might thus have expected a subsequent significant reduction in overall inequality. Yet income inequality in South Africa is proving resistant to change and may in fact have worsened since the end of apartheid (see Chapter 9). We argue that this is because no significant policy shifts have occurred to stem the rise in unemployment. This highlights the importance of labour-market and economic policies in understanding how the state affects income distribution.

The fourth aspect is surely the most surprising. Compared to other developing countries, South Africa has long had—and continues to have—a very high level of redistribution by means of the government budget. This entails a progressive and efficient tax system, an exceptionally generous system of public welfare provision (based on noncontributory old-age pensions), and pro-poor spending on public health services and public education. If inequality is measured after taxation, cash transfers, and the benefits in kind of public services, then South Africa ceases to be at the top end of the international inequality league. This redistributive aspect of government spending under apartheid has not been adequately explored in the South African literature, which, understandably, has focused mainly on the racially discriminatory and exploitative aspects of apartheid. As we show in this book, however, the way in which the state affected income inequality during and after apartheid cannot be understood with reference to racial policies alone.

The South African case illustrates how labour-market, welfare, education, and economic policies combined to structure the pattern of income in society, sometimes exacerbating inequality, at other times reducing it. We show that, under apartheid, the basis of disadvantage shifted from race to class. The deracialisation of public policy in the late apartheid and post-apartheid periods thus had a very limited impact on inequality. By the 1990s, South African society was thoroughly divided by class. Intraracial class differences persisted or deepened even as some black South Africans seized the opportunities provided, belatedly, by deracialisation. Put another way, under apartheid, discrimination within classes (by race) exaggerated the effect of inequalities between classes. With the decline of discrimination within classes, interclass inequality has become the driving force of overall inequality.

State policies played and continue to play a major role in the reproduction of inequality, in interaction with exogenous changes in South Africa and the world economy. We develop the concept of a "distributional regime" to describe the ways in which the apartheid and post-apartheid states intervened in the economy to shape patterns and levels of inequality. By "distributional regime" we mean not only the direct and readily visible ways in which states affect income inequality, such as taxation and cash transfers in the form of old-age pensions and other grants, but also the indirect or more opaque ways, in-

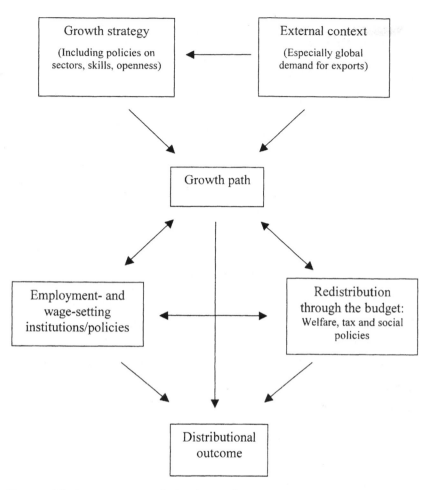

Figure 1.1. The key components of a distributional regime

cluding policies affecting education and the labour market and, more generally, the rate and path of economic growth (or what is termed, in the context of "developing" economies, "development"). Figure 1.1 summarises the key components of our analytical framework. Following Esping-Andersen, we analyse labour-market and welfare policies as being closely linked, both being designed according to a common organising principle. This "labour-welfare nexus" affects distributional outcomes directly by affecting incomes and opportunities and indirectly by influencing the growth path, which ultimately also affects the level and distribution of income. The growth path is also shaped by the broader economic growth strategy and the general economic environment.

Our central argument in this book is that the distributional regime in South Africa has long served to privilege one section of the population while excluding others, but the composition of the privileged group and the basis of privilege has changed over time. Initially, under apartheid, insiders and outsiders were defined primarily in racial terms. The apartheid distributional regime provided full employment for white people (by means of a combination of racially discriminatory labour-market, industrial, and educational policies) while channelling cheap African labour to unskilled jobs in the mines and on farms. But the very success of this regime in advantaging white people allowed the basis of exclusion to shift from race to class: white South Africans acquired the advantages of class that allowed them to sustain privilege in the market and ceased to be dependent on continued racial discrimination. The consequence of this was that some classes of black South Africans could become insiders while others remained largely excluded from the benefits of prosperity. The distributional regime was never as neatly exclusive as apartheid discourse suggested; even under apartheid it extended some benefits to the poor, and since 1994 it has had more universalist ambitions. But the underlying bases of distribution remain fundamentally inegalitarian. The reason why extreme inequality has persisted after 1994 is, above all, that the distributional regime of the late apartheid period has been reformed (primarily through deracialisation) rather than transformed or rejected in favour of a more egalitarian one.

This book is about South Africa. But the country is analysed as a case study of distributional regimes in societies that industrialised—and democratised—later than did the European and other advanced industrialised democracies of the North. The analysis of inequality under and after apartheid might shed light on the factors shaping inequality in other societies that have been spared the terrible ordeal of apartheid. We are not suggesting that South Africa at any given time is an ideal type of any category of distributional regime, but we do suggest that, across time, it has shared key features with a number of other societies. Further research is required to establish whether these cases constitute a discrete model of distributional regime.

STATES, MARKETS, AND INEQUALITY IN THE NORTH

In analysing apartheid and post-apartheid South Africa in terms of distributional regimes, we build on Esping-Andersen's canonical work on more advanced industrialised societies.[1] Esping-Andersen identifies different forms (or "worlds") of welfare capitalism in the advanced capitalist countries according to the ways in which the state affects distribution using a combination of social policies (including especially the public provision of welfare by social insurance or social assistance) and labour-market policies. His 1990 study was organised around the concept of "welfare-state regimes." Use of the term "regime" was intended to emphasise the relations among social policies, employment, and the social structure in general (Esping-Andersen 1990, 2). In later work he prefers the simpler term "welfare regime," which reduces the emphasis on the state: "A welfare regime can be defined as the combined, interdependent way in which welfare is produced and allocated between state, market and family" (Esping-Andersen 1999, 34–35). He also considers labour-market policies, primarily with respect to the maintenance of full employment. Full employment (during the golden age of postwar capitalism) meant that the public provision of welfare could be largely confined to the young (in schooling), the elderly (with old-age pensions) and the sick (via the public health system). Unemployment was contained by means of Keynesian macroeconomic policies and public-sector employment policies (which increased the demand for labour) and social and tax policies that affected labour supply. Such policies constituted different kinds of "labour market regimes," each corresponding to a different kind of "welfare-state regime" (Esping-Andersen 1990, 141–90; 1994, 169–71).

The three worlds of welfare capitalism are characterised by their welfare-state and labour market regimes. "Liberal" welfare regimes entail modest financial provision to targeted (generally means-tested) individuals in a limited array of situations. Public provision is residual in that the state only fills gaps left by the market, but its targeting means that it is nonetheless redistributive. The modal liberal welfare regime is the United States. By contrast, the social democratic welfare regime is much more generous and universal and aspires to cover (that is, socialise) all risks, with the result that it is much more redistributive and egalitarian. The state actively assumes roles—such as child care—played hitherto by the family and seeks to minimise the role played by the market. Full employment in such regimes entails very high participation rates, not merely low unemployment rates. The social democratic regimes are found mostly in Scandinavia, with Sweden treated as the modal regime (although Goodin et al. [1999] places the Netherlands in this role).

The conservative welfare regimes of continental Europe (Austria, France, Germany, and Italy) share some features with each of the other two kinds. Like the social democratic regimes, they are generous. But they are unequally generous, with differentiated benefits; support is "mutualist" rather than redistributive. The basis is insurance, not assistance. These regimes emphasise the roles played by families: public policies buttress rather than undermine familial roles. Women are discouraged from working, so that full employment entails a low participation rate. Each of these regimes has its origins in different political and ideological contexts: liberal regimes where liberal traditions were strong and liberty was the fundamental value, social democratic regimes where politics revolved around class and social equality was the fundamental value, and conservative regimes where corporatist or Catholic traditions were strong (and liberal and socialist traditions weak) and the fundamental value was social cohesion (Goodin et al. 1999). Table 1.1 shows the key characteristics of each of Esping-Andersen's regimes (based on Esping-Andersen 1999, 85). "Degree of decommodification" refers to the extent to which the state provides income to citizens as a right independent of the market value of their labour as a commodity. Esping-Andersen also refers to "defamilialisation," that is, the extent to which the state assumes roles played by close kin (such as care for children and the elderly).

The final row of table 1.1 reflects the extent of direct redistribution by means of taxes and transfers. Esping-Andersen is not very concerned with this, but other scholars have paid it careful attention, using cross-national data from the Luxemburg Income Study. Korpi and Palme (1998) showed that there was a close relation between the size of the budget for redistribution (the public welfare budget) and the extent of income redistribution via transfers and direct taxation (leading to reduced inequality in the distribution of income, as measured using the Gini coefficient). The social democratic welfare regimes tended to spend and redistribute more than the conservative welfare regimes of continental Europe, which in turn tended to spend and redistribute more than the liberal welfare regimes (see also Huber and Stephens 2001; Milanovic 1999; Przeworski and Gandhi 1999; Bradley et al. 2003). The differences between the three kinds of regime are evident also in the analysis of longitudinal data by Goodin et al. (1999).

The "three worlds" typology has, however, been criticised on a number of grounds. Many criticisms concern the categorisation of nonmodal cases, including Australia and New Zealand, Japan, the Mediterranean cases (Italy, Spain, and Portugal), the Netherlands, Britain, and even France and Belgium (Esping-Andersen 1999, 86–94). The precise categorisation of individual cases is of little concern to us. More pertinent are criticisms that the typology fails to address other determinants of inequality, such as gender differences and household or family dynamics. Some welfare regimes reduce individuals' dependence

Table 1.1. Esping-Andersen's typology of welfare regimes

Type	Liberal	Social democratic	Conservative
Role of the family	marginal	marginal	central
Role of the market	central	marginal	marginal
Role of the state	marginal	central	subsidiary
Dominant mode of solidarity	individual	universal	kinship; corporatism; etatism
Dominant locus of solidarity	market	state	family
Degree of decommodification	minimal	maximum	high (for breadwinner)
Extent of redistribution	low	high	medium

on kin as much as (or more than) on the market; in others, families continue to play a leading role in caring for children and the elderly, and male breadwinners are assumed to support dependent women.

Although Esping-Andersen (1999) recognises these weaknesses in his earlier work, he is less willing to concede that his typology, as Castles charges, underestimates the importance of labour-market policies designed to influence wages (and thereby earnings). He thus miscategorises some countries that achieved distributional goals by regulating workers' earnings rather than supporting incomes via state welfare transfers. Castles has shown that in Australia, the material well-being of the citizenry was secured primarily by the regulation of earnings, especially through the wage arbitration system (Castles 1985, 1996; Castles and Mitchell 1993; see also Esping-Andersen 1999, 89). Indeed, perhaps the most important of the state's social policies was assistance with housing for working people. The result was, in Castles' phrase, a "wage earners' welfare state," that is, a welfare state that sought to ensure a certain standard of living for Australians as (male) wage-earners (and their dependents) rather than as citizens.[2] Esping-Andersen (1999, 90) concedes that the Australian and New Zealand cases differed from other liberal welfare regimes, although they differ less so now, in the aftermath of market-oriented reforms. But he is unwilling to recognise these as a distinct world of welfare capitalism, arguing instead that they still form, in essence, a variant of the liberal welfare regime. Other comparative scholars (for example, Huber and Stephens 2001) are, however, persuaded by Castles' arguments and use his "four worlds" typology.

The three worlds typology was developed for, and continues to fit reasonably well, the advanced industrialised countries of Europe and North America. It fits less easily the later industrialising countries of southern Europe, Japan, Australia, and New Zealand (see Esping-Andersen 1999, ch. 5). It fits even less easily the countries of Latin America and East Asia that industrialised still later or the post-Communist countries of central and eastern Europe. In an edited collection including chapters on each of these three groups, Esping-Andersen and his contributors avoid developing his typology (Esping-Andersen 1996). There is, indeed, no mention of welfare *regimes*. Instead, he discusses the *trajectories* that these cases are following. Most (including Chile) are following a liberal, market-oriented strategy. Others (for example, Brazil) have taken tentative steps toward universalism (along what he later calls a "proto-social-democratic path"; ibid., 267). A third group (in East Asia) has followed the Japanese lead in combining great emphasis on both the family and employment-related welfare; public provision is residual, although the model relies on a de facto job guarantee. In his 1999 book Esping-Andersen briefly examines Korea and Taiwan along with Japan but does not mention Brazil, Chile, or Poland.

A typology in which welfare capitalism is categorised into regimes in the countries of the North but into trajectories in those of the South is clearly incomplete. Northern regimes are themselves in flux (as Esping-Andersen shows). And there is no reason to believe that the paths being followed by southern economies will lead them to the same regimes as did the paths already followed by northern economies. (The assumption that southern economies had to replicate the growth experiences of northern ones was roundly criticised in development studies). Late-industrialising countries such as South Africa, Brazil, India, and Korea are clearly capitalist. They might not spend anywhere near as much on public welfare as the liberal welfare regimes of the North, but their spending is not insignificant, and they generally invest heavily in other areas of social expenditure, especially public education. In a few cases, including South Africa, the state's social policies are, by some measures, highly redistributive. Southern states may have made clear decisions to rely more heavily on market or family and may have directed state policies in these directions.

Unfortunately, there is little research concerning the experience of welfare capitalism in southern societies. Perhaps levels of capitalist development and state intervention have been considered too low to warrant analysis in terms of welfare capitalism. Certainly, most studies of the incidence of taxation and public expenditure in the South reveal a picture of very limited—if any— redistribution from rich to poor. The data are patchy, uneven, and rarely comparable. Lecaillon et al. (1984) summarise a set of studies conducted between 1963 and 1973 (in Hong Kong, India, the Philippines, Sri Lanka, Chile, Colombia, Panama, Puerto Rico, and Iran), and there are more recent studies of Chile (Foxley 1979; Mujica and Larrañaga 1993; Engel et al. 1999), Colombia (Selowsky 1979), Malaysia (Meerman 1979), the Philippines (Devarjan and Hossain 1995), Peru (Escobal et al. 1993), Venezuela (Márquez et al. 1993), the Dominican Republic (Santana and Rathe 1993), Brazil (Von Amsberg et al. 2000; Camargo and Ferreira 2000; World Bank 2001), and South Africa (McGrath et al. 1997; Van der Berg 2001b, 2001c). The Inter-American Development Bank (IADB 1998) collated evidence for Latin America. In general, because public expenditure is often captured by nonpoor groups, Gini coefficients are not reduced by anywhere near as much as in the industrialised democracies of the North. Even taking into account the benefits in kind from social spending (especially public education and health), Gini coefficients are rarely reduced by more than 5 to 7 percentage points, which is substantially less than in the North. A glaring exception to this—as we examine further below—is South Africa.

DEVELOPMENT AND INEQUALITY: THE EXPERIENCE OF DEVELOPING COUNTRIES

The analysis of distribution in the South has generally focused instead on the consequences of particular development paths, the very issue that is sidelined in Esping-Andersen's institutional typological approach. The foundation for this work was Kuznets's argument that the relation between development (measured in terms of per capita GNP) and income inequality took the form of an inverted U: inequality initially rose and later fell as an economy developed (Kuznets 1955, 1963). Such a "Kuznets curve" trajectory of inequality over time is consistent with the Lewis model of development, in which structural change (away from agriculture and toward industry) serves as the engine of growth (Lewis 1954). In this model, underemployed "surplus" labour is drawn out of agriculture and into higher-paying industrial jobs as industrialisation and urbanisation ("development") progress. The model assumes that the marginal product of rural labour is zero and hence that labour can be drawn out of the agricultural economy at subsistence wages with no loss of agricultural output. Urban firms thus face an unlimited supply of labour from agriculture at a subsistence wage. Because average urban incomes are higher than average rural incomes, inequality initially increases as urbanisation and industrialisation begin to take place.

The steady supply of labour to industry at subsistence wages enables firms to earn high profits, which, when reinvested result in increased employment, income, and output. When all surplus labour is absorbed from agriculture, urban wages rise above subsistence levels as a result of two forces. First, rural households are no longer prepared to release household members at subsistence cost because as each additional household member leaves, agricultural production will fall (that is, the marginal product of rural labour is no longer zero). Higher wages are needed to compensate rural households for this opportunity cost. Second, falling agricultural output in the face of growing demand for food in the cities results in higher food prices and in a corresponding upward pressure on urban wages. These higher wage costs erode profitability, investment, and growth. As growth slows down in the latter stages of development, inequality falls because most workers are urbanised and because rural-urban income differences are lower as a result of higher food prices (which boosts agricultural incomes relative to urban incomes). The simple Lewis model thus traces out an inverted U-shaped Kuznets curve for the relation between development and inequality.

This stylised explanation for a Kuznets curve relation rests on the assumption that rural incomes are shared (and hence there is no rural inequality) and that a single wage is paid to urban workers (and hence that there is no urban inequality other than that between workers and capitalists). Inequality is thus entirely the product of urban-rural income differentials and the level of urbanisation. As soon as one allows for the possibility that inequality is driven by factors other than urban-rural differentials, however, then there is no necessary reason why inequality should eventually decline with growth (Lewis 1976; Adelman and Morris 1973; Anand and Kanbur 1993a, 1993b). For example, where labour markets do not adjust smoothly to changes in supply and demand, an additional source of inequality could arise—namely, that between the unemployed and the employed. As is argued in more detail in later chapters, the role of unemployment in driving inequality is particularly strong in South Africa.

According to the Harris-Todaro model, rural-urban migration will occur even in the presence of urban unemployment as long as the urban-rural differential is sufficiently high to make it worthwhile for the migrant to queue for a job (Harris and Todaro 1970). The greater the degree of "dualism" (that is, the differences in average productivity between urban and rural jobs), the higher the level of urban unemployment and the higher the overall level of inequality (Garcia-Penalosa 2000, 5–6). If urban wages decline in the presence of unemployment then the degree of dualism will fall, and hence inequality may decline also (although this will depend on the contribution of wage inequality to overall inequality).

In short, different growth paths have different implications for inequality and its trajectory over time (Adelman and Morris 1973; Lewis 1976). If technological change increases the demand for certain categories of skilled workers, then their wages will rise relative to others', thus increasing wage inequality. If this encourages people to invest more in education and training, however, then the supply of skilled labour will increase, thus lowering the skills premium and hence lowering inequality over time. Changing patterns of competition will also affect the pattern of wage earnings. For example, entrepreneurs in firms or sectors facing increased international competition (perhaps as a result of a fall in tariff protection) will find their earnings under threat. The wage gap between such sectors and others will thus rise.

Economic growth in developing countries usually starts in particular sectors and regions and then spreads out across the economy through a set of backward and forward linkages. Where the "spread effects" of growth are small, the fruits of growth remain concentrated and inequality is likely to rise. This is typically the case where the leading sector is mining. Where growth is heavily dependent on skilled labour, wage differentials are likely to rise (thus increasing overall inequality), but where a large part of the growth impetus comes from sectors that are large employers of unskilled labour (such as agriculture and construction) then growth is likely to be more equalising (Griffin 1989; Morley 2000).

During the 1950s and the 1960s, when postcolonial countries (particularly in Africa) embarked on ambitious development strategies, industrialisation was the overriding concern. Policy makers prioritised growth and structural change in order to reduce dependence on primary commodity exports (which, as the dependency school of development correctly argued, were vulnerable to long-term declines in the terms of trade). The fact that development was associated with rising inequality (Adelman and Morris 1973; Chenery et al. 1974; Lipton 1977), largely because industrialisation increased urban-rural differentials and widened wage inequality, appeared to be of secondary concern to policy makers.

Development strategies varied (Griffin 1989), but most governments adopted a basic slate of interventions: tariff protection and other forms of support for emerging industry, large-scale capital-intensive projects (including those in agriculture), regulation of financial markets, and use of state-controlled marketing boards and other instruments to siphon off agricultural profits to fund development initiatives elsewhere. National leaders saw the state as a "developmental state" responsible for overcoming the legacies of colonialism and underdevelopment (Mkandawire 2001). But in most postcolonial cases the developmental state was also a weak state in the sense that it rested on a narrow social base and was overly reliant on export and import taxes for its revenue. Cooper argues that this turned the African developmental state into a "gatekeeper state," where the focus of political contestation became control over the gate between the domestic and the international economies and where rent-seeking undermined developmental and democratic aspirations (Cooper 2002). Government jobs, contracts, subsidies, and protective policies were used to shore up political support. Resources and supportive policies became concentrated in urban areas (where politically powerful interests tended to congregate), thus further widening urban-rural differentials (see also Lipton 1977).

As growth slowed in the 1970s and then stagnated in the 1980s and 1990s, the failure of the bold development project became manifest. Attempts to recast development strategies—such as the joint International Labour Organisation (ILO) and World Bank "Redistribution with Growth" project (Chenery et al. 1974; Jolly 1976)—were overtaken by the oil shocks, debt crisis, and loss of development of the 1980s. As developing countries descended ever more deeply into economic stagnation, development economics as a discipline lost credibility and influence. It was thus unable to offer any effective resistance to the pro-market, antigovernment intervention structural adjustment packages designed and sponsored by the World Bank and the International Monetary Fund (IMF), which sought to correct policy-related distortions (including tariffs, marketing boards, food subsidies in urban areas, caps on interest rates, and excessive wages and employment in the public sector). This shift effectively removed most of the policy armoury of a developmental state.

The experience of structural adjustment has been mixed. Most problematical from the point of view of longer-term growth is the fact that investment has not improved sufficiently to generate sustainable accumulation—even in countries regarded by the IMF as successful adjustors (Akyuz and Gore 2001). Because investment is the crucial component of any growth engine, this is cause for serious concern. It does not bode well for either future growth or sustained reduction in poverty and inequality.

Structural adjustment resulted in severe economic hardship for many people, although the extent to which the burden of adjustment was borne by those who were relatively advantaged beforehand (including government employees, urban workers, and subsidised and protected capitalists) and how much was borne by the very poor (unskilled labourers, the unemployed, subsistence farmers) varied from case to case. Some previously disadvantaged groups, such as small rural producers whose output prices had been depressed by use of marketing boards and other policies biased against agriculture, benefited from rel-

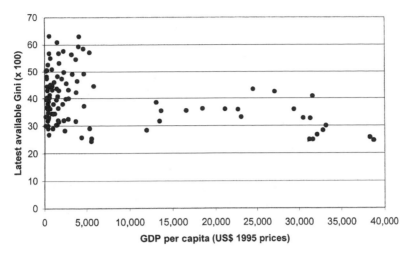

Figure 1.2. Per capita GDP and inequality. *Source:* World Development Indicators.

ative price realignment under structural adjustment (World Bank 2001). But those with low and insecure incomes suffered from the decline in demand. Research on the impact of structural adjustment in Latin America indicates that inequality declined in some cases such as Brazil but rose in others such as Mexico (World Bank 2001, 55); overall, the impact was mildly regressive (Morley 1995, 2000; Stallings 2000). In any event, it is now widely accepted that better sequenced and designed policies could have provided more of a cushion for the poor during the process of structural adjustment (Collier and Gunning 1999), and there is renewed concern within the international development institutions to ensure that adjustment and growth are carried out in ways that are "pro-poor" (World Bank 2001). In many respects, this new policy agenda resonates with the "redistribution with growth" literature from the mid-1970s, although it is more concerned with reducing risk and ensuring that markets (particularly in rural areas) work in favour of the poor.

Given the many different development strategies (Griffin 1989) and possible relations between growth and inequality, it is not surprising that the cross-sectional international evidence is more ambiguous than suggested by Kuznets (Anand and Kanbur 1993a; Bruno et al. 1998, World Bank 2001).[3] As can be seen in figure 1.2, there is no obvious cross-sectional relation between the level of per capita GDP (a proxy for level of development) and inequality (measured by the Gini coefficient for the distribution of income or expenditure). There also appears to be no systematic relation between growth and inequality

(Bruno, Ravallion, and Squire 1998; Dollar and Kray 2000). If, however, the question is recast in terms of the relation between growth and poverty, then the answer depends in part on the choice of method of measurement of poverty. According to Dollar and Kray (2000), the growth elasticity of the per capita income of individuals in the poorest quintile was about one for their sample of eighty countries. This means that the income of the poor rose on average at the same rate as the national income. The experience across and within countries, however, can differ widely. Ravallion and Datt (2002) have shown that the (absolute) poverty-reducing impact of growth varied across different states in India: states with initially higher literacy, farm productivity, and rural living standards and with lower landlessness and infant mortality benefited the most (in terms of poverty reduction) from a given increase in growth. Such conclusions point to the importance of targeted welfare, educational, and sectoral (particularly agriculture) policies for pro-poor growth (World Bank 2001).

In Latin America the major drivers of persistent inequality are unequal access to assets and very high rates of return to education and skill. We argue that similar forces are at work in South Africa, although unemployment plays a greater role in affecting poverty and inequality than it does in Latin America. Whereas in the latter case, low-wage employment in agriculture and the informal sector provided some kind of cushion for the poor, state policies in South Africa sought deliberately to undermine informal employment, encourage greater capital intensity in agriculture and industry, and undermine the African peasantry. Such policies were instituted in response to labour shortages, but they were so successful at constraining the options of Africans to earn a living by any means other than formal employment that, when employment slowed and stagnated from the mid-1970s onward, open unemployment was inevitable.

The Lewis model assumes that an "unlimited" supply of labour is available from agriculture for industry. Such conditions did not hold in sub-Saharan Africa (Lewis 1976; Karshenas 2001). Easy access to land governed by communal tenure arrangements and low population density in that region meant that those who wanted to farm could do so. The result was an extensive system of agriculture that was constrained not by availability of land but by the labour that could be mobilised to work it. Under such conditions, urban manufacturing firms in sub-Saharan Africa were forced to pay substantially higher wages than their counterparts in Asia, which benefited from a Lewis-style supply of low-wage surplus agricultural labour (Karshenas 2001, 323–25).

The South African state responded to this constraint on development by transforming the agrarian relations that underpinned it, that is, destroying the African peasantry and coercing Africans into wage labour by means of taxation and restricted access to land. Africans were removed from productive land and resettled in overcrowded "native reserves" (or "bantustans," as they were later called), where the productivity of land steadily declined. A supply of surplus labour was thus created by a process of forced proletarianisation. The decline in peasant production might have resulted in a rise in the price of food, imposing a new constraint on development. This problem was circumvented by the creation of a highly subsidised, capital-intensive commercial agricultural sector run by white farmers (and financed in part by mineral revenues).

This peculiarly South African solution to the sub-Saharan African problem of labour shortages proved, in a tragic sense, too successful. Deagrarianisation, driven by political as well as economic concerns, eventually resulted in the growth of the wage labour force outstripping the demand for labour from industry, mines, and commercial farms, while the subsistence and peasant farming sectors were too weak to provide any alternative means of earning a living. And although it was theoretically possible for manufacturing to have become more labour-intensive as the supply of labour increased, this did not occur. The labour-market institutions that encouraged greater skill- and capital-intensity remained in place (in a deracialised form), and tax policies and strategic considerations further encouraged capital intensity. The result was massive unemployment from the mid-1970s, continuing, indeed, worsening, in the post-apartheid period. The roots of post-apartheid South Africa's unemployment problem thus lie firmly in the development model pursued by the apartheid state. As we show in this book, undoing the legacy of the past entails far more than addressing racial imbalances. It requires a fundamental reorientation of the growth strategy and of the role of the state in shaping distribution.

Extending Esping-Andersen's analysis to South Africa or other southern societies suggests that different worlds of welfare capitalism are characterised by packages of functionally interlocking welfare, labour market, *and* "growth path" policies. Because the scope of our analysis extends further than welfare and full employment policies, we refer to apartheid as a "distributional regime," that is, a regime that combined (often uneasily) welfare, labour-market, and growth path policies in ways that shaped and reshaped distribution in South Africa. This approach to the study of apartheid differs from previous approaches.

APARTHEID AND INEQUALITY

Apartheid is generally understood as comprising a set of racially discriminatory policies and enforced racial segregation. It covered three main areas: political apartheid, social apartheid, and what might be called labour-market apartheid. Racial restrictions on land ownership were linked to the broad category of "political apartheid," because it was tied to the delineation of the native reserves, and to that of labour-market apartheid, because separation from the land was an integral element in freeing workers for white employers.

The term "apartheid" (Afrikaans for "separateness") burst into political prominence during the 1948 election, won by the National Party. The National Party government later tried to sanitise its policies by renaming them "separate development," but the apartheid label stuck. The period between 1948 and 1994—when the National Party finally lost power after South Africa's first democratic elections—was not a homogeneous one, however, nor were there complete breaks in many areas of public policy in either 1948 or 1994. There were important continuities between the pre-1948 policies of segregation and post-1948 apartheid policies. The division between the periods of "grand" and "reformed" periods is blurred, as is the division between the reformed apartheid and post-apartheid periods. Table 1.2, which charts the key developments in policies concerning political, social, and labour market apartheid, does not periodise the rise and decline of apartheid in terms of exact years.

The core of the system was *political apartheid,* in the form of a racially restricted or segregated franchise. When the Union of South Africa was established in 1910, one of the new country's four provinces (the Cape Province) retained its nominally and incompletely nonracial franchise; African and coloured men who satisfied property and literacy tests could vote in provincial and national elections. But in the rest of the country, only white men had a role in electing legislatures. (In 1930, white women were given the vote throughout South Africa; coloured and African women were not franchised even in the Cape Province.) In the 1930s, African voters in the Cape were put onto a separate voters' roll and thereafter were only permitted to elect white representatives to Parliament. Nonetheless, in 1948, there remained some direct representation at the national level of coloured men and indirect representation of African men from this one province.

Under apartheid, the segregation of the franchise was completed. African men in the Cape who satisfied the property qualification finally lost even indirect representation in Parliament in 1959. Thereafter African people were only

Table 1.2. The principal features of apartheid

	Pre-Apartheid	Apartheid	Late Apartheid
Political			
Franchise	White men and (starting in the 1930s) women; Coloured men (important in the Cape Province); African men (property-based franchise, Cape only) removed from common voters roll in the 1930s	Coloured voters removed from common voters roll in the 1950s (and later lose indirect parliamentary representation); African voters lose indirect parliamentary representation; franchise expanded in bantustans	Independence for some bantustans; elected local government structures for urban Africans given increased responsibilities but not powers; Indian and coloured people given vote in tricameral parliament
Social			
Racial segregation	Widespread segregation of urban Africans	Legislation including Population Registration Act, Group Areas Act, Reservation of Separate Amenities Act ("petty apartheid"), Prevention of Mixed Marriages Act and Immorality Act initially aimed at segregating coloured from white	Moves away from petty apartheid
Spatial policy	Reserves for rural Africans (1913 Land Act); Native Urban Areas Acts restricted residential rights of African people in cities and towns via pass laws	Forced removal of c. 3.5 million people (1960–82); coloured and Indian families removed primarily within urban areas under Group Areas Act; Africans removed from towns, white-owned farms, and "black spots" into bantustans; limited consolidation and development in the bantustans (decentralisation policies, Physical Planning Act, and so on); urban residential rights for Africans restricted further; starting in the late 1960s, restrictions on new housing for Africans outside bantustans	Retreat from separate bantustan development (including eventual reduction in decentralisation incentives); resumption of urban development in African townships

continued

Table 1.2. (*Continued*)

	Pre-Apartheid	Apartheid	Late Apartheid
Welfare and social spending	Starting in the 1920s, social assistance and social insurance for poor white and coloured workers, mothers, and the elderly; welfare extended to Africans and Indians in the 1940s, with moderate discrimination in benefits; slow expansion of public education (including that of African children in the 1940s)	Massive urban development in African townships in the 1950s but no development in the 1960s; education for African children of poor quality and poorly funded (with racial discrimination in spending), but primary schooling for African children expanded rapidly in 1960s; increased racial discrimination in welfare rights and benefit levels	Starting in the 1970s, increased social spending on Africans (with reduced racial discrimination in welfare rights and benefits, with parity in benefits achieved in 1993); massive expansion of secondary schooling for African children (1970s–80s); welfare and health care for whites shifted from state to market; development permitted in African townships

Labour

	Pre-Apartheid	Apartheid	Late Apartheid
Colour bar	Colour bar in mining (1926 Mines and Works Act); "Civilised labour policy" starting in the mid-1920s; closed-shop agreements favouring white unions	Colour bar strengthened in manufacturing (with job reservation determinations)	Colour bar "floated upwards" from the late 1960s onward; disappeared in manufacturing by the end of the 1970s and in mining in 1986
Collective bargaining and wage-setting	1924 Industrial Conciliation Act institutionalised collective bargaining at industry level; African workers excluded from the definition of "employee"; 1925 Wage Act set up the Wage Board to set minimum wages for all; Wage Board increased minimum wages for African workers in the 1940s	1953 Industrial Conciliation Act removed African workers' right to strike and limited their representation to works committees; white unions' control of "apprentice committees" and industrial councils ensured that no African artisans were trained outside the homelands until 1975; Wage Board allowed unskilled wages to decline in the 1950s	Growth of the independent African trade union movement starting in 1973; rising wages; the Wiehahn reforms (1979) gave African trade unions access to the industrial conciliation machinery
Allocation of labour supply	Poll taxes, hut taxes, and various spatial measures restricting Africans' access to land; influx control (Stallard principle)	Pass laws and labour bureaux strengthened, resulting in "displaced urbanisation" in bantustans	Pass laws abolished in mid-1980s; influx control ineffective

allowed representation by entirely segregated institutions: separate legislatures in the reserves or bantustans and separate municipal institutions in towns outside of them. When bantustans were forced into supposed independence (starting with the Transkei in 1975), their "citizens" lost South African citizenship, whether or not they lived within the bantustans. Coloured men in the Cape Province were removed from the common (that is, nonracial) parliamentary voters' roll in the mid-1950s, and lost indirect representation in the South African Parliament in the late 1960s. Their removal from municipal voters' rolls was largely completed in the early 1970s. Thereafter coloured (and Indian) South Africans were represented by segregated institutions at the national and the municipal levels, although they never lost their citizenship. The establishment of supposedly autonomous segregated local authorities, bantustans, and (in 1983–84) the Tricameral Parliament (comprising segregated chambers for coloured, Indian, and white voters) had the veneer of equality, but real power remained in the hands of white voters alone. Coloured and Indian as well as African men and women only obtained full franchise rights in 1994.

South Africa was not alone in restricting its franchise during these decades. In the United States, as is well known, African American citizens were denied the vote by a variety of means until the civil rights movement of the 1960s. In Brazil, universal adult suffrage was first used in a presidential election in 1989. Prior to that, voters had to satisfy a literacy test. Bethell (2000, 8–9) estimates that the proportion of the adult population in Brazil that was eligible to vote was only about 35 percent in 1945, rising to 75–80 percent in the early 1980s. South Africa under apartheid was different in that the franchise was explicitly linked, not to literacy or property, but to racial classification.

Social apartheid also distinguished South Africa from many other undemocratic countries. Government policies that segregated society along racial lines included residential segregation (systematised under the Group Areas Act), the segregation of workplaces and public amenities ("petty apartheid"), the criminalisation of mixed marriages and sex across the colour bar, and a host of other discriminatory measures. The grand vision of complete social segregation was never achieved, and many of the petty apartheid measures were dropped in the 1980s. But the spatial dimensions of apartheid policies proved more long-lasting. The pass laws controlled access by African peoples to urban areas, resulting in the segmentation of the African workforce between those with access to urban jobs and those excluded from the towns and limited to migrant labour or low-wage work in commercial agriculture. The apartheid state hardly attempted to promote separate development in the homelands, with the result that large parts of the country degenerated into poverty under the weight of population pressure and economic decline.

The third major pillar was *labour-market* apartheid. Racial discrimination in the labour market characterised South Africa for almost all of the twentieth century. This included various measures to create a supply of cheap African labour (poll taxes, hut taxes, and various measures to restrict Africans' access to land) and to limit the occupational mobility of Africans (the colour bar, restricted access to collective bargaining, limited education and training). By reserving skilled jobs for white people (by means of the colour bar) and allowing white workers to control the industrial wage-setting machinery, the state raised the incomes of white workers while shielding them from unemployment.

In each of these areas, the National Party introduced reforms during the 1970s or 1980s. The eruption of protests in urban African areas and recalcitrance about "independence" among notable bantustan leaders (led by KwaZulu's Mangosuthu Buthelezi) reopened the question of political rights for African people. Economic growth and social stability required a retreat from petty apartheid and increased state expenditures on public health and education. When skilled labour shortages began to bite hard in the late 1960s the colour bar was allowed to "float" upwards, allowing some upward occupational mobility for African workers. The movement into semiskilled occupations facilitated the emergence in the 1970s of an independent African trade union movement, whose militancy pushed the state into conceding that African workers should be allowed to participate fully in the industrial conciliation machinery. The pass laws were finally abolished, although the state attempted to maintain influx control into the towns using other mechanisms.

It has become conventional to divide the literature about the relation between apartheid and capitalism into "liberal" and "radical" (or revisionist) approaches (Posel 1983; Nattrass 1991).[4] The liberal approach focused on racism and its economic costs, the radical approach on capitalism and the relation between economic and political interests. The antagonism between proponents of the rival views stemmed primarily from their contrasting implications for political strategy. In the liberal view, what was good for big business was good for democracy, and capital should be a major—if not the primary—player in the struggle for democracy. In the radical view, however, capital was a partner in apartheid; democratisation required the overthrow of capitalism as well as apartheid.

The political differences may have been immense, but the liberal and radical views differed little in their perception of actual patterns of distribution in

South African society. They agreed that apartheid served to raise the wages and incomes of white South Africans, at least in the short and the medium terms, while depressing those of black South Africans. Furthermore, scholars in both schools agreed that labour-market policies (combined with prior land policies) were central to this distributional outcome. Indeed, Marxist scholars went to great lengths to demonstrate that white workers were paid more than they produced and enjoyed a share of the surplus value produced by black workers (Davies 1973), which was a point that liberal scholars took for granted, albeit outside of a Marxist theory of value. The fact that there was substantial agreement between liberal and Marxist scholars on the effects of apartheid on the interracial distribution of wage income is probably why little research concerning distribution was conducted.

Liberal and radical scholars differed with respect to two points concerning distribution more broadly. First, they differed with regard to the "functional" distribution of income: that between capital (profit) and labour (wages). Liberal scholars argued that apartheid policies generally eroded profitability although profits might have been raised in certain sectors or for short periods of time (for example, Horwitz 1967; Lipton 1986). Radical scholars asserted that apartheid policies sustained high profits, with the payoff to white workers more than compensated for by savings in wages paid to black workers (for example, Saul and Gelb 1981). Subsequent empirical analysis of profit rates revealed a trend of declining profitability from as early as the mid-1950s, thus undermining some of the radical claims about the functionality of apartheid for capitalist development (Nattrass 1992, 1994b). Second, liberal economists argued that apartheid, by eroding profitability, retarded economic growth, implying that the long-term growth in incomes of white working and middle classes was also constrained. For many analysts, this argument seemed implausible in the face of rapid economic growth in the 1960s. But as Bromberger (1983) and Moll (1991) pointed out, South Africa's growth rate was not as high as those of other developing economies even in the 1960s. Indeed, the slowing economic growth rate in the 1970s and 1980s encouraged radical scholars to shift away from their earlier, functionalist formulations and to argue instead that apartheid had contradictory implications for capitalism and that its functionality eroded over time (Saul and Gelb 1981; Gelb 1987; Wolpe 1988).

The debate between liberal and radical scholars is thus something of a red herring in terms of the analysis of distribution in South Africa (except with respect to the functional distribution specifically). Neither camp paid much attention to inequality or the social structure, with the result that the social scientific study of these topics remained curiously underdeveloped in South Africa. This is not to say that these topics have been ignored entirely. As we shall see, there is rich historical scholarship concerning the social and economic changes that shaped inequality, and social scientists have written at length about the consequences of the social structure. But prior to the 1990s, there were very few studies that focused directly on inequality or the social structure. References to income distribution, for example, were few and far between in books and articles. Many scholars referred to the extreme level of income inequality in apartheid South Africa, but almost none actually examined income inequality itself.

Besides not being a priority either in political terms or in terms of intellectual dispute, the study of distribution was also constrained by the lack of data about incomes. Presumably for the obvious reasons, the state did not publish such data. The official Population Census, conducted every ten years, collected no data about African incomes despite providing sophisticated statistics for other economic indicators; moreover, the census recorded income data for white South Africans in terms only of broad income ranges (Archer 1971; McGrath 1983). In addition to the census, the state collected data about income distribution among white South Africans in its surveys of family expenditures (in 1955 and 1966). But for coloured, Indian, and especially African people the only data were for small urban samples, collected intermittently from the early 1960s by the Bureau of Market Research at the University of South Africa (UNISA). In the *Oxford History of South Africa,* the leading liberal economist D. Hobart Houghton complained about the dearth of reliable statistical information about income distribution and the fact that racial earnings data were difficult to obtain. He was thus unable to do more than identify three "tiers" in society: white people at the top; coloured, Indian, and urban African people in the middle; and rural Africans at the bottom (1971, 43).

There were considerable data about average wages by race, broken down by economic sector, but almost none for incomes as a whole. Most studies of the economy or society therefore focused on racial inequality in average wages. A few studies attempted to gauge shares of total income by race, generally by estimating the distribution by race of national income. Unfortunately, the African share had to be estimated as a residual, subtracting the incomes of white, coloured, and Indian people from total personal income. Even if this was done on the basis of sensible if crude assumptions, estimates of the African income share were very sensitive to errors in the estimation of other racial groups' shares (McGrath 1983, 130–31). The share earned by the African population was consistently estimated at about 20 percent between 1910 and 1970, whereas the share earned by white people was estimated at between 70 and 75 percent of the total (as summarised in ibid., 123). Taking account of estimated population shares, this meant that the average income of white people was about ten to twelve times that of African people—as was recognised by the official Tomlinson Commission for the Socio-Economic Development of the Bantu Areas Within the Union of South Africa (see Union of S.A., 1955a and discussion in Houghton 1976, 166). There were, however, almost no data about *intra*racial distribution, making it very difficult to measure overall inequality.

Perhaps because there were so few data, social scientists seem to have avoided theorising about inequality in South Africa. The first attempt to examine the character of inequality in South Africa seems to have been Knight's application in 1964 of the Lewis dual economy model. Knight (1964, 289) suggested that South Africa comprised "a highly developed capitalist sector and an underemployed peasantry in subsistence agriculture, which provides an elastic supply of largely unskilled labour to the capitalist sector." The population could be divided into three groups: a profit-receiving capitalist group, a fully employed skilled white group paid high wages (in part owing to high productivity and in part comprising a monopoly rent derived from the inelastic supply of skilled labour that itself was due to racial discrimination), and an unskilled, underemployed black group paid low wages (because of the effectively unlimited supply of cheap labour). Knight's analysis was echoed in later work by Archer (1973), who described South Africa as a case of "perverse dualism." Knight and McGrath (1977) referred to the malevolent hidden hand of the market (see also Devereaux 1982).

This brand of non-Marxist political economy was undertaken primarily by economists but largely ignored in mainstream social science. Simkins (1976, 1979), Nattrass (1977), and McGrath (1979a, 1983) pioneered new standards in empirical research on inequality, interrogating much more fully than hitherto the available data to measure the extent of inequality. Their work remained constrained, however, by the grave limitations of the data.

In the early 1970s Marxist and neo-Marxist scholars mounted a sustained challenge to the prevailing liberal interpretations of South African history and society. The pioneering work of Johnstone (1970, 1976), Wolpe (1972), Legassick (1972, 1974), Davies et al. (1976), and Morris (1976a, 1976b) placed the study of capitalism at the core of South African studies. In subsequent work, however, Marxist structuralism became less a source of insight into the dynamics of South African society than a badge of intellectual and political correctness. Non-Marxists, including scholars drawing on Weberian and Ricardian approaches to political economy, were dismissed as "liberals" (as were some scholars working within a neo-Marxist framework). The empirical work of Mc-Grath, Simkins, Bromberger, and others was largely overlooked in what became an ever more theory-driven approach.

Marxist social scientists seemed little interested in either the size distribution of income or the social structure. Insofar as they were concerned with the distribution of income, they focused on the functional distribution (between profits and wages). This reflected the priority attached to capitalism as a productive system. More curiously, there was remarkably little social scientific work on the class structure itself. Most Marxist studies have focused on the political behaviour of different classes rather than the class structure per se.

Marxist approaches rapidly became hegemonic, but they were far from homogeneous. In response to the empirical weakness of much (but not all) of Marxist structuralism, and especially to its apparent neglect of the agency of the black rural and urban population, there arose an alternative Marxist approach that has generally been labelled "social history." Using archival sources and oral testimony, these scholars provided richly textured accounts of struggles over proletarianisation, on the land and in the towns, and of the political consequences of the transformation of South Africa's economy and societies. Among the scholars in this vein whose work covers mid- and late twentieth-century South Africa are the historians Van Onselen (1996), Delius (1996), Bonner (1995), and Glaser (1994), the sociologists Bozzoli (1991) and Posel (1991), the anthropologist Murray (1992), and the political scientist Lodge (1983).

The differences between the structuralist Marxist social scientists and the neo-Marxist social historians were set out in a later debate between Morris (1987) and Keegan (1989). Morris accused the social historians of setting up a "new dogmatic orthodoxy eschewing broad schematic explanation in favour of micro-historical analysis. With its built-in political justification—the 'views of the masses' were finally being reflected—it altered both the epistemological foundations of left social and political analysis and the conceptual terms of debate" (Morris 1987, 8). The so-called social historians focused on the experiences of the ordinary person but (Morris charged) were unable to analyse the "totality of contradictions and forces structuring the lives of the 'ordinary person in the street'"—contradictions and forces which individuals themselves are often unable to comprehend (ibid., 9). Morris insisted that he accepted the value of micro-studies but demanded that these be "informed by the wider structural relations and social forces fashioning the society" (ibid., 11). The social historians were guilty, Morris concluded, of theoretical poverty amidst their headlong flight into empiricism (ibid., 14). In response, Keegan argued that "a more adequate, conceptually sound history, which is attuned to theoretical issues and problems, is not possible without innovative new methodological approaches." The social historians, he wrote, had broken free of the "massive limitations" implicit in the kind of evidence used by "abstract structuralist writers of the 1970s" and were "exploring new ways of uncovering the past" (1989, 3).

Both camps generated powerful insights into aspects of South African history and society, but overall patterns of inequality and the social structure were topics that they generally neglected. The structuralist Marxists sought the big picture, but their work was driven too much by theory that soon proved to more limiting than it was illuminating. The social historians did conduct careful empirical studies, but their research was almost exclusively qualitative. In addition, their concern with localised case studies often led to difficulty in discerning the bigger picture. They employed class as a major analytical tool but generally worked without any careful empirical analysis of class structure itself. Discussion of the class structure remained schematic and devoid of evidence. Neither structuralist Marxists nor social historians conducted careful research of a quantitative kind, nor did either school make much use of work done by liberal political economists.

An antipathy among broadly Marxist scholars to quantitative research is not unique to South Africa. The leading American neo-Marxist sociologist, Wright, has noted that this attitude has long characterised Marxist social science: "Left-wing scholars, especially Marxists, are generally sceptical of quantitative analysis and have traditionally relied primarily on historical and qualitative methods in their empirical research." He attributes this scepticism in part to the fact that Marxists have been especially concerned with topics that "are not easily amenable to precise measurement and quantitative treatment" but in significant part also to "a general hostility by many Marxists to anything that smacked of 'bourgeois social science.'" Wright thus identified his own objectives in his major book *Class Counts* as "demonstrating the usefulness of class analysis to non-Marxists *and* the usefulness of quantitative analysis to Marxists and other radical scholars" (Wright 1997, 545–46, emphasis added).

Wright's recent arguments have been slow to find converts in South Africa. In the 1970s, South African Marxists' attempts to study the size of particular classes were generally focused on the "atypical" classes that defied a crude identification of class and race—the white working class (Davies 1973, 1979) and the African middle class or petty bourgeoisie (Wolpe 1977). Preliminary work on the occupational class structure by Simkins and Hindson (1979) went largely ignored, perhaps because it employed a Weberian emphasis on skills. In the 1980s, amid revolt and confrontation, almost no work was done on the dimensions of class and inequality in South Africa. Most recently, innovative work on class by Crankshaw (1997a) has been largely ignored. Crankshaw plotted the changing occupational division of labour under apartheid and the changing racial composition of different occupations, focusing on the "advancement" of African workers. Upward occupational mobility underpinned changes in the distribution of wages and incomes, and inequality became increasingly a function of occupational class rather than race. Crankshaw's study was made possible by his manipulation of the government's Manpower Surveys, but his study was also constrained by his source. The Manpower Surveys cover only the population working in the formal sector, excluding farm workers and domestic workers. Subsistence farmers, other self-employed workers, and the unemployed also fall outside of his focus on the workplace. He was therefore unable to examine the class structure of society as a whole. Nor was he able to trace out the broader social changes underpinning South Africa's process of class formation. By using a wider range of data sources and considering the entire population, rather than only some workers, we provide a more comprehensive picture of the changing nature of South Africa's social structure during and after apartheid.

Like Wright, Crankshaw approaches the study of class from a broadly Marxist perspective, but he recognises the importance of using operational class categories that have much in common with Weberian understandings of class. "As is usually the case in sociology," Wright notes, "the empirical categories of analysis are *under*determined by the theoretical frameworks within which they are generated or interpreted" (Wright 1997, 37; emphasis in original). Crankshaw employs an eclectic blend of approaches to class that is rooted in Marxist, Weberian, and labour process theory. In this type of instrumental approach, class categories are employed insofar as they inform a broader understanding, rather than being constrained within a theoretically predetermined approach. Such an instrumental approach characterised some of the early Marxist work in South Africa (most notably that of Johnstone [1976]) but then fell into decline. It has also become widely espoused internationally, not only by the preeminent Marxist scholar Wright but also by the preeminent Weberians Goldthorpe and Marshall (1992).

Apart from work by Crankshaw and ourselves, class appears to be in danger of falling off the map of South African studies. It is remarkable how quickly South African social scientists seem to have abandoned class analysis once the political context changed. The retreat was most notable among scholars who had been at the forefront of Marxist scholarship before they moved into prominent positions advising the post-apartheid state. To be sure, there remains a rump of radical political economy, sustained by writers such as Bond (2000) and Marais (2001), but its attention has become fixed on the intimacy between the new political elite and global capitalism (as represented by the chimera of investor confidence and the more tangible World Bank and International Monetary Fund). This is often insightful, but it is political economy without class analysis. On the rare occasions when radical scholars have considered class politics more broadly (for example, Adler and Webster 1999), they have remained trapped within the traditional Marxist concern with the relations among state, capital, and labour with regard to production and have been reluctant to consider either broader issues of distribution or social cleavages in society as a whole. Class analysis is in a parlous state in post-apartheid South Africa.

In contrast to the study of class, the study of inequality has been transformed rapidly by the availability of entirely new data sets. Research into inequality took off in the 1990s in the face of the combination of newly available data from countrywide household income and expenditure surveys (initially donor-funded), unprecedented demand for data about poverty for policy-making, and technological change due to the proliferation of personal computers (Seekings 2001). The first countrywide economic survey of households was conducted in 1993 by the South African Labour and Development Research Unit at the University of Cape Town, together with the World Bank, under the title Project for Statistics on Living Standards and Development (PSLSD). The PSLSD survey covered a sample of about eighty-five hundred households. From October 1994 onward the government's Central Statistical Service (since renamed Statistics South Africa) conducted an annual October Household Survey with a much larger sample of households. In 1995 the October Household Survey was combined with a detailed Income and Expenditure Survey. The October Household Surveys were discontinued after 1999, replaced by twice-yearly Labour Force Surveys and (in 2002 and 2003) a General Household Survey. In 2000, a second Income and Expenditure Survey was conducted, in conjunction with one of the Labour Force Surveys. The consequence of this rash of surveys is an abundance of survey data.

These data sets have been used primarily by economists. Most of this research has been highly technical and very narrowly focused. In this book we use extensively the detailed and valuable research by scholars such as Leibbrandt, Woolard, Klasen, Moll, Case and Deaton, McGrath, Whiteford, Knight, Kingdon, and Wittenberg, together with our own work with the data sets, to try to piece together the bigger picture of inequality in South Africa at the end of the apartheid era. In particular, we direct attention to the importance of unemployment in driving inequality and poverty. Ours is the first major empirical study that incorporates unemployment into a broader historical analysis of the class structure and the policies that shape it.

We believe that it is especially important to highlight the importance of unemployment because the interests of the unemployed are easily overlooked in struggles over policy. The black middle class clearly stands to gain from policies of affirmative action, and the black industrial working class stands to gain from policies that raise the wages of the employed. Both classes have major influence on policy-making (the former because of the close social and economic links between the political elite and the emergent black middle class, the latter because of the role of the Congress of South African Trade Unions in the ANC Alliance). By comparison, the unemployed, and especially the rural unemployed, have very little influence on policy-making. Their votes are important, to be sure, but the South African electoral system serves to weaken even this leverage (see Nattrass and Seekings 2001b).

In this book we do not examine the politics of inequality or of policy making in South Africa (except for a brief discussion in Chapter 10). We are concerned more with the design of public policy, its interaction with exogenous processes of economic change, and the outcomes in terms of inequality than we are with why some policies were chosen and implemented rather than others. The politics of distribution and redistribution is an important topic and one that is integral to recent scholarship concerning the welfare state regimes of the north and growth path policies in the south. We omit it simply because to include it would require that a long book be further lengthened.

A recently published book with a title indicating some overlap with our own is Terreblanche (2002), and for this reason alone it deserves mention. Terreblanche's *A History of Inequality in South Africa, 1652–2002* is a political tract aimed primarily at getting white South Africans to "acknowledge explicitly that they have benefited from colonialisation, segregation and apartheid" (4). It touches on some of the more recent determinants of inequality (racial discrimination, rising unemployment, and the growth of the black middle class). His argument that inequality in post-apartheid South Africa is now a product of "systemic exclusion" (of the unemployed) resonates with our own and other academic work on the importance of unemployment as a key determinant of inequality and poverty.

Unfortunately, Terreblanche's analysis is of limited relevance for the scholarly exploration of distribution either during or after apartheid. First, his conceptual framework lacks rigour. Despite his focus on the "systemic" aspects of inequality, he never shows how "the system," beyond the obvious impact of discriminatory regulations and institutions, actually functions to drive inequality. Second, the book fails to engage adequately with the large body of academic work in the field. As Dollery complains in a book review, Terreblanche "simply neglects vast swathes of scholarship that present a contrary perspective to his own line of argument. It is almost as if he has made a conscious effort to ignore the voluminous literature on the historical relationship between capitalism, as it has been manifest in the South African milieu, and apartheid. The great 'South African debate' between the traditional or 'liberal' approach . . . and the competing 'revisionist' or Marxian perspective . . . that occupied scholars of South African history for more than thirty years, may as well not have taken place for all the attention it receives" (Dollery 2003, 596).

Third, the book fails to engage with the newly abundant empirical data about inequality in South Africa. The combination of a weak conceptual underpinning, failure to engage with existing scholarship (or provide adequate citations) and neglect of empirical research effectively renders the book unusable for academic purposes and we discuss it no further. (For a more detailed critique, see Seekings et al. 2003, 57–63).

APARTHEID AS A DISTRIBUTIONAL REGIME

In this book, our concern is not simply to chart the changing character of inequality in South Africa but also to explain these changes—and especially the limits to change—in terms of the underlying distributional regime, that is, the character and consequences of public policies affecting distribution directly and indirectly. Our analysis of apartheid as a distributional regime builds on the important work that Marxist and other scholars have done on public policy. Marxist scholarship concerning inequality and class might have been very thin, but Marxist and other political economists have contributed invaluable studies of selected areas of public policy. These writers focused on the design and operation of institutions that affected the labour market, most notably legislation concerning collective bargaining (including rights to collective action, closed shop agreements, and the state's policing of wage agreements); measures such as hut taxes and forced removals designed to stimulate a supply of labour to the mines, farms, and factories; and measures designed to keep the cost of that labour cheap so that profits could be sustained (including, it was argued, the influx control system that underpinned migrant labour). Marxist scholars argued that these interventions served to structure markets in ways that promoted capitalist development, white prosperity, and black poverty (see overviews in Posel, 1983, 1993; Nattrass 1991; and Chapter 4 below).

Marxist or radical scholars emphasised these interventions, which were seen as underpinning the profits of capitalists (or particular factions among them) more than they underpinned the incomes of the National Party's white electoral base. Indeed, most of these interventions preceded apartheid; they date from the period of the minerals revolution in the second half of the nineteenth century. Some scholars, influenced by underdevelopment theory, also emphasised restrictions on land ownership in the 1913 Natives Land Act, which constituted a further form of direct state intervention that long predated apartheid. But these critics of racial capitalism tended to concentrate on the relation between wages and profits, and most neglected to analyse more fully the ways in which the state shaped the overall growth path of the economy. This left them vulnerable to the retort that the state's interventions served to retard economic growth and profit levels in the long term (see Moll 1990; Nattrass 1990). Marxist scholars also paid inadequate attention to public policy outside of the workplace, including policies concerning public education and welfare.

The apartheid state did introduce a welfare system, but it was one that discriminated along racial lines, with poor white people in particular benefiting (see Chapters 3 and 4). Nonetheless, distribution in society was certainly affected by the payment of old-age pensions to elderly black people (albeit racially discriminatory), by the provision of public education to black children, and by the provision of public health to black people when sick. McGrath (1983) calculates that there was probably limited redistribution from white to black South Africans via patterns of government taxation and expenditure (as we shall see further in Chapter 4). In other words, even under apartheid, the final distribution of income was significantly more egalitarian than the market distribution of income. The state also intervened directly in the labour market, at times setting minimum wages for low-paid workers via the Wage Board.

But provision of limited welfare to black South Africans quite rightly attracted less attention than the racial discrimination that permeated the welfare system and other direct state interventions in distribution. The state discriminated along racial lines when it raised some people's incomes and depressed others by means of statutory job reservation, that is, the reservation of certain occupational categories for specific sections of the population in terms of a colour bar. It discriminated in its own employment practices, favouring some sections of the population rather than others. It used its power as a consumer to support the profits of specific sections of the population by discriminating in the awarding of state contracts. It restricted income-generating opportunities (for example, in trading and farming) for large sections of the population in much of the country. Such actions shape distribution in ways that go far beyond the impact of the tax and transfer system. These interventions were emphasised by liberal critics of racial discrimination.

The approach we employ in analysing inequality and the social structure thus combines elements of the liberal and the Marxist analyses of the apartheid era, while adding also some elements neglected by both. We ask what kind of distributional regime South Africa had in the apartheid period and what kind it has now. We discuss the changing nature of inequality and outline the process of class formation between the 1940s and the 1990s, and we assess the ways in which the apartheid and post-apartheid states shaped distribution with their various welfare, labour-market, and other policies.

We analyse critically the workings of labour markets and show how government policy shapes processes of class formation and inequality in post-apartheid South Africa. Our work on labour markets falls soundly into a well-established radical tradition of studies of the ways in which state policy serves to divide the labour force—although our emphasis is not merely on the differentiation of workers (as in Hindson 1987 and Posel 1991) but on the entrenchment of inequality between a stable, permanent urban working class and a set of marginal classes, some precariously employed, most unemployed. Our discussion of the apartheid and post-apartheid distributional regime owes much to the writings of radical scholars of South Africa as well as more liberal political economists. We do not see the class structure and prevailing pattern of inequality as inevitable but rather emphasise the wide range of state policies that serve to share class formation and the distribution of income. We discuss trends with respect to welfare policies that have been almost completely neglected within both academic traditions, and we then move beyond his framework to include the impact of the growth path on distribution. In particular, we show how labour-market policies (and their transformation from the 1970s onward) helped shape a growth path that became—and remains—profoundly incapable of absorbing large amounts of unskilled labour, thus entrenching if not exacerbating inequality.

Clearly, both race and class were important in shaping "who got what." Race served as a mechanism for establishing barriers to entry into privileged occupations, that is, as a mechanism for selecting who gets to be privileged. It also served as a mechanism for reinforcing high differentials between earnings in different occupations. Race thus served to shape the class structure and to allocate positions within it. Race was especially important for previously poor white people, mostly Afrikaans-speaking, who benefited greatly from discriminatory welfare, job protection, and especially public education. But inequality should not be reduced to race alone. Most rich people were not rich simply because they were white; most enjoyed higher incomes because being white helped to ensure that they secured the better opportunities and positions within an inherently inegalitarian economic structure. Increasingly, white people were able to maintain their economic privileges by using the advantages they inherited and ceased to depend on active racial discrimination.

Public policy in apartheid South Africa differed from that in most of the advanced capitalist countries in at least two respects. First, labour-market policies were especially important within the distributional regime. Indeed, liberal as well as revisionist studies of public policy generally focused on labour-market policies and, with important exceptions, neglected the distributional effects of tax and social expenditures. In this respect, South Africa's form of welfare capitalism was similar to Australia's. Of course, the citizenry in South Africa excluded the bulk of the population (although Australia also threw up barriers to inclusion with its "white Australia" immigration controls, which were not dissimilar to apartheid influx control). Second, the South African case emphasises the importance of a range of policies that are largely neglected in comparative studies. Macroeconomic, industrial, and trade policies shaped the growth path of the economy in ways that had clear distributional consequences. These growth path policies, as we shall call them, structured the distribution of employment opportunities to a far greater extent in South Africa than in the advanced capitalist economies. Policies favouring some sectors rather than others and capital- rather than labour-intensive forms of production had profound effects on the distribution of income. In this respect, South Africa had much in common with other semi-industrialised economies in Latin America and elsewhere.

The distributional regime of apartheid served to buttress the standard of living primarily of white South Africans, at least in the short and medium terms. But white South Africans were not the *only* beneficiaries of *every* policy within the regime. State spending, for example, was massively biased toward the white population, but at the same time there was a low level of net redistribution

through the budget from white to black South Africans. As apartheid was reformed, the level of such redistribution rose, such that on the eve of democratisation it had reached a level that was very high by comparison with other middle-income countries (although still low by comparison with the advanced
capitalist countries). The budget could be redistributive because it was never
the primary mechanism for supporting white peoples' incomes in the short or
the medium term (with heavy public spending on education for white children
being important in the longer term only). Rather, the state underpinned the incomes of its white constituents with policies designed to boost their wages and
to ensure full employment among them. The system of industrial bargaining,
the colour bar, and protected employment were central pillars of this strategy.
The welfare system served as a safety net to catch any poor white people who
could not benefit from such a favourable labour market. A strategy of import-
substituting industrialisation (ISI) also boosted the incomes of skilled industrial workers in the short and medium terms. The major losers in this distributional regime were unskilled Africans in rural areas. In the 1950s they were
confined to low-productivity, low-wage sectors of the economy. In the 1970s
and 1980s, having been removed into effectively landless conditions in the bantustans and denied access to good education, they were sentenced to long periods of unemployment in an economy that provided fewer and fewer jobs for
unskilled labour. The benefits to a minority of the population under the
apartheid distributional regime were to some extent premised on the exclusion
of the growing number of rural poor and unemployed.

Our analysis of apartheid emphasises two factors above all others: the relation
between the supply of and demand for unskilled labour and the skills (and hence
market strength) of poor white South Africans. We argue that the distributional
regime of the early apartheid period was defined by policies that were adopted in
response to shortages of unskilled labour and the weak market position of poor
white workers. The distributional regime of the late apartheid period, in contrast, was defined by policies adopted in a very different context of a surplus of
unskilled labour and a newly strengthened market position of poor white workers. It would be wrong to see the distributional regime as changing in response to
purely exogenous conditions, however. The transformed context was itself the
product of the policies adopted in the early apartheid period. The crucial features of public policy at that time were those that led to high levels of unemployment, on one hand, and the educational policies that gave poorer white
South Africans much stronger positions in the labour market, on the other.

Our periodisation of the distributional dimension of apartheid differs from much existing work on other aspects of apartheid. We identify an important break or shift in the middle of the apartheid period, in the early 1970s, rather later than the early 1960s as often noted in studies of other aspects of apartheid (such as Bonner et al. 1993). The shift of the early 1970s was marked by two simultaneous processes. First, mechanisation on and forced removals from white-owned farms, growing landlessness in the reserves, and slow employment growth in nonagricultural sectors resulted in the shift from labour shortages to massive, open unemployment, for the most part displaced to the reserves. Second, the state's support for poorer white people, especially by means of education, resulted in almost all white people having the skills that equipped them to command earnings that were sufficiently high to obviate the need for massive public welfare. The state could therefore retreat from welfare provision, leaving its white constituents to resort to the market for provision against ill health and old age (with private medical aid schemes and retirement funds). At the same time, many key features of the distributional regime of apartheid were abandoned during the 1970s, 1980s, and early 1990s. By 1994, very few areas of public policy were overtly discriminatory on racial grounds. The transition to a distributional regime that we might label "reformed apartheid" was uneven, as some policies were reformed earlier than others. But the overall shift was considerable. Apartheid became less a system of market regulation and mitigation than a coercive mechanism for controlling dissent among the many unemployed who were in effect excluded from the market. Table 1.3 summarises the key features of the pre-apartheid, early apartheid, late apartheid and post-apartheid distributional regimes, and figure 1.3 points to the continuities between the apartheid and post-apartheid regimes.

Apartheid might be thought of as a system for determining who got what that started off much like the Australian wage earners' welfare state but was transformed into a salary earners' welfare state. It did this initially and most obviously by means of labour-market policies that ensured that certain forms of employment were well paid and others poorly paid. Social security policies plugged gaps with the provision of largely means-tested support for certain categories of people who were not participating in the labour market, and unemployment insurance provided for the short-term unemployed. But both of these declined in importance for white South Africans under apartheid. It was the highly discriminatory public education that served not simply to reproduce inequality in the labour market but, more important, to ensure especially rapid upward mobility (in terms of occupational and social class) among the children born into poorer white families. Growth path policies structured the economy

Table 1.3. The Periodisation of Distributional Regimes in South Africa

	Pre-Apartheid	Early Apartheid	Late Apartheid	Post-Apartheid
Redistribution through the budget (taxation and transfers)	Tax mostly paid by the rich; limited redistribution to African and poor people	Tax mostly paid by the rich; redistribution to poor whites, especially Afrikaners, and to Africans (to a limited extent)	Taxes mostly paid by the rich; redistribution to urban Africans and to the poor in general as pensions and education expand	Taxes mostly paid by the rich; improved redistribution to the poor via expansion of services
Welfare policy	Racially exclusive in the 1920s and 1930s; racially discriminatory in the 1940s	More racially discriminatory—but retained universal access with respect to pensions (but not UIF)	Less racially discriminatory; coverage extended; pension becomes a major instrument for redistribution	Removal of racial discrimination; extension of UIF and child grants; erosion of the real value of the pension
Education	Racially discriminatory (but less so in 1940s)	Racially discriminatory; improvement in white education laid the basis for upward class mobility of poor whites (particularly Afrikaners)	Massive expansion of schooling for black children, but quality of schooling remains low and expenditure discriminates by race	Removal of racial discrimination in expenditure; expenditure becomes pro-poor; rise of class-based distinctions (private schools and so on)
Wage-setting labour market policies	Centralised bargaining for white workers; minimum wage-setting by Wage Board in unorganised sectors (and for African workers—but determinations very low until the 1940s)	As before; 1953 Industrial Conciliation Act denied Africans the right to organise in trade unions; Wage Board failed to protect African wages in the 1950s	Uneven deracialisation of wage-setting institutions, resulting in partial inclusion of organised African workers in centralised bargaining system	Complete deracialisation; strengthening of unions and centralised bargaining by Labour Relations Act and other legislation; extension of minimum wage-setting to unorganised sectors

continued

Table 1.3. (*Continued*)

	Pre-Apartheid	Early Apartheid	Late Apartheid	Post-Apartheid
Employment-setting labour-market policies	Job reservation in mines; African peasantry undermined; "civilised labour" policies in mines and manufacturing; influx control restricted urban African population (but relaxed in the 1940s)	Increase in job reservation in early period (but colour bar "floated up" from the mid-1960s); Afrikaners benefited the most; influx control extended and tightened; 1952 Urban Areas Act introduced insider-outsider distinction. White unions prevented Africans from training as artisans.	Uneven deracialisation; attempt to coopt a stabilised urban African labour force. Relocation of surplus people from commercial farms and urban areas to bantustans (rather than promoting labour-intensive production to absorb the unemployed)	Removal of last vestiges of labour-market discrimination, extension of employment protection, and strengthening of industrial bargaining; affirmative action; employment equity; skills development
Growth strategy	Import-substituting industrialisation (with tariff protection linked to civilised labour policy); mining and agriculture rely on cheap African labour and remain labour-intensive	Continued ISI policies; labour shortages in the postwar boom coupled with capital subsidies, overvalued exchange rate, and racial restrictions on employment (e.g., Physical Planning Act) slow growth and further encourage capital intensification, including that in agriculture; small business and informal sectors undermined by Group Areas Act and labour-market policies	Negative real interest rates, rising wages encourage greater capital intensity; oil shocks cushioned to some extent by rise in gold price; international opposition to apartheid and desire to boost self-sufficiency (arms, SASOL) boosted average capital intensity; some limited trade liberalisation in the 1980s and early 1990s	Trade liberalisation and compliance with GATT, WTO, and so on; labour-market and industrial policies encourage high-wage, high-productivity sectors and activities rather than labour-intensive ones; sound fiscal and macro policies assumed to encourage investment (results disappointing so far)

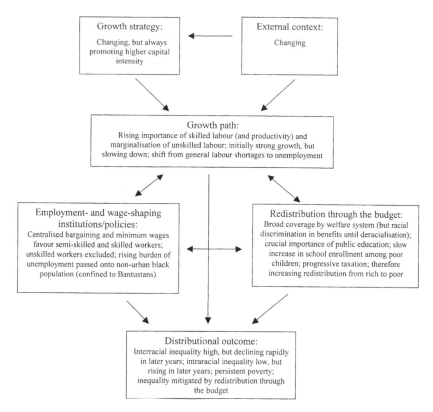

Figure 1.3. The continuities between the apartheid and post-apartheid distributional regimes

so as to strengthen further the earning opportunities for some (mostly but not only white people), but they did so at the cost of rising unemployment. The distributional regime was certainly responsive to the demands and needs of capital, but it was also responsive to political pressures conveyed via the racially exclusive institutions of apartheid. As white people moved up the occupational ladder, so public policy came to be aimed at maintaining and raising the standard of living of salaried people. By means of a deepening of racial discrimination across a wide range of policies, the early apartheid state served to maintain deep economic inequalities. Policies that confined growing numbers of people to unemployment while allowing the expansion of opportunities for working people allowed the late apartheid state to generate new lines of stratification in society that served to entrench a high level of inequality. The deracialisation of public policy has broadened the distribution of benefits from South Africa's form of welfare capitalism—creating a new, nonracial wage-earners' welfare state—but has not transformed the system in the ways necessary to overcome inherited patterns of stratification.

In some respects, welfare capitalism under apartheid resembled the liberal model identified by Esping-Andersen. Welfare policies were means-tested and modest, and there was little decommodification. But, as in Australia, the state's interventions in labour markets were crucial. At the same time, welfare capitalism under apartheid had important corporatist characteristics. Racial discrimination and exclusion served to maintain a strict hierarchy of racially classified groups. Although racism might have been specific to South Africa, it shared its corporatist hierarchy and inequality with many countries in Latin America as well as continental Europe. Welfare benefits, and especially the benefits in kind of public education, were highly unequal. Indeed, they were so meagre for the poor that the poor were forced to rely on familial systems of welfare, especially the remittance of migrants' wages to poor rural kin. Labour-market policy served to increase inequality, in contrast to its inequality-reducing effects in Australia. The South African model of welfare capitalism thus entailed a fusion of disparate elements.

A crucial component of our analysis is the importance of unemployment. The apartheid distributional regime had its origins in periods of unemployment (the 1920s and 1930s) and full employment (the 1940s), and the initial period of "grand" apartheid (in the 1950s and into the 1960s) was one of reasonably full employment. This explains some of the paradoxes of this regime, including the maintenance of an unusually extensive welfare system, in comparison to other middle-income countries. The period of "reform" of apartheid was one of rising unemployment. The deracialisation of labour-market and welfare policies occurred at the same time as rising unemployment in part because a growing shortage of skilled workers coincided with a growing surplus of unskilled labour. Contrasting trends in the demand for skilled and unskilled labour were not unrelated. Both were rooted in the growth path policies pursued in the apartheid period, policies that resulted in deagrarianisation in rural areas at a time of capital-intensive industrial growth and tight restrictions on the informal sector. The importance of growth path policies in South Africa marks a clear contrast between the South African model of welfare capitalism and the typologies applicable to the countries of the North.

OVERVIEW OF THE BOOK

This book provides an analysis of the changing nature of inequality and the social structure in South Africa between the mid-twentieth century, when the

National Party was elected with apartheid as its platform, and the beginning of the twenty-first century, when the African National Congress was ensconced in office having contested and won two democratic general elections. The book thus covers about five decades of South African history, the bulk of which constituted the apartheid era. Apartheid was infamous across the world, of course, because of systematic racial classification and discrimination. We argue in this book, however, that this era saw a fundamental shift in the social structure. Until 1960s, race was clearly the basis of inequality in South African society. Race largely determined class. In the 1970s and 1980s, however, race and class ceased to be coterminous. The decline in racial discrimination in the second half of the apartheid era, and further deracialisation after its end, have not led to reduced levels of inequality. By the 1990s, it was class rather than race that was the basis of inequality. As in any capitalist society, a key class division was that between those who owned capital and those who did not. But there were other, important class divisions along lines of skill, authority, and, increasingly, simply access to employment.

Chapter 2 explores the nature of South African society at the outset of the apartheid era, in the late 1940s and early 1950s. At that time South Africa was still a largely agrarian society, albeit one in which the rural population had become less and less dependent on agricultural production and more and more dependent on remittances sent by migrant workers. Two-thirds of the population lived in rural areas; most of those living in urban areas were recent immigrants from the countryside. Although the bulk of the countryside was reserved for white ownership, many African families struggled to retain some access to the land and grew crops and kept cattle and other livestock. Dependent at the same time on migrants' earnings, many households had one foot in the countryside and the other in the fast-growing towns. It is not surprising that the themes of journeying and urbanisation predominated in literature. In terms of the distribution of income, society could be divided into three broad strata: rich white households at the top, Indian, coloured, and urban African households in the middle, and rural African households at the bottom (with considerable variation between different rural areas). Our analysis suggests that race thus broadly coincided with class at this time, except that the African population was becoming increasingly heterogeneous, as people moved into the expanding working class. The chapter concludes with an analysis of the kind of distributional regime that the National Party government inherited in 1948.

Chapter 3 traces the fundamental transformation of society during the apartheid period, focusing on processes of class formation and the ensuing combination of continuity and change in the pattern of inequality. The middle class expanded with the growth of semiprofessional and routine white-collar employment. Urban African workers began to move up the occupational ladder, and the urban African population as a whole grew and put down roots in town. Deagrarianisation continued on a massive scale, with the result that peasant agriculture all but disappeared. This transformed South Africa into a society that was unusually dependent on wage labour. By 1975 there were clear indications of a growing differentiation within the African population, although race remained a driving force behind inequality. As new occupations opened up for African people, some were better placed than others to seize the opportunities. Education grew in importance. Intraracial differentiation became more pronounced in the 1980s, and the share of total income earned by white people began to decline after half a century of stability. The chapter concludes with a brief discussion of alternative trajectories that South Africa might have followed: the route of land reform, which would have slowed the process of deagrarianisation, and the route of uncontrolled urbanisation as the rural poor flooded into cities to get better access to better-paid jobs in the formal and the informal sectors.

Chapter 4 provides a new interpretation of apartheid as a distributional regime, integrating analyses of education, welfare, labour-market, and growth path policies so as to assess how the apartheid state shaped the distribution of incomes in society. We show that the main way in which it initially sought to underpin the incomes of white families was by means of interventions in the labour market that gave protected employment to poorer, less-skilled workers and increased bargaining power to the more highly skilled white workers. The pass laws served to provide low-productivity employers with low-wage workers. However, the state also invested heavily in public education for white children in order to ensure that the weak position in the labour market of unskilled white people was not replicated through the generations. The state also promoted a capital-intensive growth path of import substitution that ensured high wages for more skilled workers as well as protected profits for employers. This distributional regime was reformed fundamentally later in the apartheid period, in large part because of intended and unintended consequences of earlier policies. Better education ensured that most white South Africans had skills that could command high wages in open labour markets, without direct intervention based on racial discrimination. The higher earnings and incomes of white families meant that the private welfare and health care industries could assume roles that the public welfare system had previously played. At the same time, the rapid growth of unemployment among unskilled African workers posed a social and political threat. Influx control now sought primarily to restrict urbanisation in order to maintain political control of the towns, confining most poverty and unemployment to remote "rural" areas. In short, government policies now sought to protect the market rather than subvert it via direct interventions as before. Employers' interests were provided for by accelerating public investment in black education and by the gradual floating upwards of the colour bar. The deracialisation of public policy meant that some African people enjoyed newly opened opportunities and rising incomes. But the maintenance of a growth path that was unfriendly to unskilled labour and of a public welfare system that entailed no support for the long-term unemployed ensured that widespread poverty and deep inequality continued.

Chapter 5 explores the rise of unemployment late in the apartheid era. We examine critically existing series of data about unemployment, noting the conceptual confusion surrounding the issue, and we identify the major causes of its growth. We argue that open unemployment manifested itself with dramatic effect from the early 1970s onwards as a result of the combined pressures of an economic slowdown, government policies that favoured capital intensity, and increased labour supply (in large part due to the collapse of subsistence agriculture and removals of African peasant farmers from white farms).

Our analysis of inequality through most of the apartheid period is bedevilled by a lack of good data, but the rush of surveys conducted in the 1990s allows us to analyse distribution at the end of the apartheid period in considerable detail. In Chapter 6 we use the 1993 PSLSD survey to analyse inequality at apartheid's end, identifying who was poor and who was rich, where and how they lived, and why earnings and incomes varied so greatly. The incomes of the richest 10 percent (or top income decile) were, on average, one hundred times larger than the incomes of the poorest 10 percent (or bottom income decile). The poor lived predominantly in rural areas, but agriculture was of marginal importance only. Most poor households were poor because they had no members in employment; if they did include working members, they were likely to be confined to low-wage jobs in agriculture and domestic service. Unemployment was thus a key factor in determining overall inequality, whereas education was increasingly important in determining inequality of wages within as well as between racial groups.

Data from the PSLSD and other surveys can also be used to map the class structure, as we do in Chapter 7. Whereas the analysis by Crankshaw (1997a) was limited to individual people in employment (and excluded major economic sectors), our use of household surveys allows us to analyse the class positions of the entire population and to take into account household composition as well as individual occupation. Chapter 7 includes some discussion of the methodology of using household survey data to map class, in order to emphasise the contingency of class analysis on the assumptions made and methodology employed. We end up with a nine-category class structure, with three classes defined on the basis of income from entrepreneurial activity of wealth, five classes defined on the basis of occupation, and a residual class. In this scheme, most households in the "core working class" have incomes above the median but below the mean for South Africa as a whole, meaning that the class is both unprivileged relative to the higher classes and privileged relative to the poorer half of the population.

The value of any mapping of the class structure is, we suggest, indicated primarily by evidence that the categories are "consequential" in terms of other attitudinal or behavioural variables, that is, that class "counts" (as Wright [1997] puts it). Surveys conducted in South Africa provide few data that allow us to demonstrate the consequentiality of class, but in Chapter 7 we are able to show that our class categories are consequential in several important respects, at least in the sense that there are clear correlations between class and some other variables. Thus class is closely correlated with household income, with living conditions, with some attitudes, with some indicators of health and, perhaps most important of all, with children's education (which raises the likelihood of class status being transmitted between generations).

One of the shortcomings of the class analysis in Chapter 7 is that it does not address the role of unemployment in structuring incomes and opportunities. If class is defined in terms of entrepreneurial activity, wealth, or employment, the unemployed cannot be classified individually. If they are dependent members of households that also include working people, then (in our analysis) their class position is defined by those other household members; that is, these unemployed persons have what are generally termed "mediated" class locations. If the unemployed live in households in which no one is working, however, they fall into the residual category. Chapter 8 places the spotlight on unemployment and asks whether some or all of the unemployed should be conceptualised as a distinct underclass. We argue that some of the unemployed can be viewed as an underclass in that they suffer particular disadvantage in terms of access to job opportunities in a society in which incomes depend overwhelmingly on wage employment. This disadvantage arises from the fact that access to employment depends primarily on networks of family and friends; unemployed people living in households in which other people work are therefore in a much better position to secure work than are those who live in households where no one works. A large part of the residual class discussed in Chapter 7 can thus be identified as a distinct underclass. We also show that this members of this underclass have lower incomes and inferior living conditions than members of the classes defined in Chapter 7. In terms of attitudes, however, the evidence suggests that there is a difference between unemployed people in general and employed people with respect to key issues.

Chapters 9 and 10 turn to the post-apartheid period. Chapter 9 examines what we know about trends and patterns in inequality after 1994, using not only census data but also the frustratingly uneven evidence from the plethora of household surveys conducted by the official South African statistics agency (Stats SA) as well as by university-based researchers. Overall, although income distribution seems to have changed little, it probably became slightly more unequal in the 1990s. At the same time, the share of total income received by African people has continued to rise and the share received by white people has continued to fall. The former is close to passing the latter, if it has not passed it already. Declining interracial inequality is driven by the upward mobility of some African households into the top income deciles. By 2000, there were about as many African people as white people in the top income quintile. Declining interracial inequality continued to be accompanied by rising intraracial inequality. The gap between better-off African people and poorer African people continued to grow, rapidly.

Trends in the labour market explain rising intraracial inequality among African people. Upward mobility among a minority continued to be driven by movement into higher-paid occupations. For a larger number of people in formal employment, wages and hence incomes rose in real terms. But rising unemployment meant that poverty persisted and even deepened. By 2002 the unemployment rate had risen to 30 percent (by the narrow official definition) and 40 percent by the more appropriate broad definition. Flux in the labour market as some workers were retrenched and others found jobs meant that there was a fair amount of flux in incomes also. But preliminary evidence suggests clear stratification into distinct classes: some African people enter the labour market with clear advantages in terms of human and social capital (that is, education and contacts), greatly improving their chances of finding employment, especially well-paid employment. It is the unskilled, especially those who also lack contacts, who face the bleakest future in terms of unemployment and poverty. In short, the post-1994 evidence indicates clearly a continuing shift in inequality from race to class in South Africa.

Chapter 10 considers the post-apartheid distributional regime. We argue that, in important respects, post-apartheid South Africa is weighed down by the legacy of apartheid. By this we do not simply mean that deep inequalities persist, nor that there remains a relation between race and class in that almost all of the poor are African. Rather, we mean that the post-apartheid distributional regime includes aspects of its predecessor in the form of policies that serve to perpetuate deep inequalities. The post-apartheid state inherited a distributional regime that was inappropriate to the kind of society that South Africa had become. In apartheid South Africa, as in many other capitalist societies, the state had adopted labour-market and welfare policies that benefited disadvantaged voters, mitigating poverty and inequality among the enfranchised citizenry. But the restricted franchise meant that the beneficiaries of such policies were the poorer white citizens, who were not, of course, the poorest members of society. Indeed, the policies were premised on privilege in that a *minimum* standard of living for white South Africans was secured by limiting the claims of poorer black South Africans. The possibility of near exclusion on racial grounds allowed for the development in South Africa of a welfare system that was a grotesque caricature of its counterparts in the advanced capitalist countries. Inequality remained limited only as long as the African poor could find some kind of employment or could practice subsistence agriculture.

The formal deracialisation of public policy in the last years of apartheid has not transformed an essentially inegalitarian system into an egalitarian one. To be sure, access to privilege under apartheid was defined in racial terms, but key policies served to entrench class differences regardless of race. The deracialised mix of labour-market and welfare policies inherited by the newly elected democratic government offers significant benefits to many poor households, but it also continues to provide privileges to a deracialised section of the population at the expense of the very poor. Deracialisation has meant, in effect, that a system designed to protect poor white people in the industrial working class has been extended to protect, most of all, the now predominantly African industrial working class. But that group today, like the white working class of earlier decades, is far from being the poorest section of society. Under apartheid unemployment grew, and South Africa had a massive labour surplus. Amid very high unemployment, those with jobs have come to be a relatively privileged group. A system of labour-market and welfare policies that assumes full or almost full employment serves to reinforce such relative privilege rather than provide for the very poor, and such a system, we show, displays clear continuities from the apartheid distributional regimes.

It is crucial that the government has promoted economic growth along a path that was not, in the short or (prospectively) the medium term, pro-poor. The favoured growth path entailed rising productivity, wages, and profits for workers and firms in the formal sector, or what we call a "high productivity now" strategy. But employment has fallen and unemployment risen. The AIDS pandemic might be reinforcing these pressures for increasing inequality. The post-apartheid state inherited a public welfare system that was exceptional in the South in terms of its reach and generosity. The deracialisation of that system has been completed, but its basic shape has not been changed. As was the case in the apartheid distributional regime, the public welfare system in post-apartheid South Africa makes no provision for the many poor people who are not old enough for the pension nor young enough to qualify for child support. There is no provision for the long-term unemployed, nor for people who have never been employed. Whereas the apartheid distributional regime was premised on full employment, its successor operates in the context of extremely high unemployment. The post-apartheid state also redistributes massively in the form of spending on services to the poor, including especially public education. If the value of services provided in kind is added to cash transfers and the effects of taxation, the Gini coefficient is reduced to just 0.44. But the value of these public services is questionable: spending large sums on the teachers in schools attended by poor children need not—and apparently does not—entail corresponding improvement in the educational opportunities facing those poor children. Chapter 10 concludes with a brief discussion of why democratisation has not led to a more fundamental transformation of the distributional regime.

Finally, in Chapter 11, we consider what a more egalitarian distributional regime might credibly entail in the South African context. We identify three features of the distributional regime that inhibit the reduction of inequality: labour-market and other policies that encourage growth along a path that favours a small group of economic "insiders" while excluding the poor; spending on public education that fails to improve significantly the educational opportunities open to poor children; and the lack of any welfare provision for people who are poor because they are unemployed. Acknowledging real political constraints, we argue that a transformed distributional regime would require a social accord between state, capital, and labour, with the goal of expanding employment. Welfare reform (perhaps via a basic income grant) and public works programmes should be linked to wage restraint and consent to the reform of policies that inhibit employment growth, especially for unskilled workers. The value of educational spending on the poor needs to be addressed by increasing the accountability of teachers, principals, and education bureaucrats.

In Chapter 11 we draw parallels with the recent experiences with social accords in Ireland and the Netherlands. The relevance of parallels with the North reflects characteristics of South Africa that are unusual in the South: a strong labour movement, declining employment and rising unemployment, no peasantry, and a small informal sector. South African society is deagrarianised to an extent that is unusual among middle-income countries. And though South Africa might be one of the first post-agrarian societies in the South, it will certainly not be the last. Its experience in transforming a distributional regime inherited from an inegalitarian past will provide lessons for other southern societies in the future.

There are many important and related topics that we cannot address even in a book of this length. Inequality is, for the most part, reduced to income inequality alone. But a full analysis of inequality should address the many inequalities that characterise societies. We have little to say about inequalities within households, for example, including those of gender. These are clearly important, but we rely primarily on data about households that provide few clues as to what is happening within them. The study of families, households, and the complexities of individuals' social and economic relationships with other individuals is one of the most exciting areas of social science in South Africa. In the future, much more will be said about these other inequalities. Finally, we say little about the politics of inequality. We do not set out to explain in detail why or how the South African state adopted some policies rather than others. We are more concerned with analysing the consequences of policies that were adopted. As ever, there is much more research that should, and, we hope, will, be done.

Chapter 2 South African Society
on the Eve of Apartheid

Apartheid policies of systematic racial discrimination and segregation had a deep and enduring influence on inequality in South Africa. But inequality predated apartheid, and the core components of its distributional regime predated the system itself. By 1948, the state had developed a set of policies concerning welfare, the labour market, and the growth path that structured patterns of inequality. State polices shaped but did not determine the massive social and economic changes in South African societies. The nation at this time was still a largely agrarian society, albeit one in which a large part of the rural population had become dependent on remittances sent by migrant workers. The economy was essentially capitalist and increasingly industrial, but large numbers of African people strove to retain access to land and cattle and to preserve features of an agrarian society. They endeavoured to retain some control over how and when they participated in the market and resisted complete proletarianisation. This was to have important implications for the development of inequality and the social structure during the apartheid period. In this chapter we examine the character of South African society at the onset of apartheid and discuss the ways social and economic changes were affecting inequalities and the way state policies shaped inequalities, directly and, by shaping the broader social and economic changes, indirectly.

DEPICTIONS OF SOUTH AFRICAN SOCIETY

Novels and films often provide vivid images that can help us understand what society was like in the past. In the middle of the twentieth century, South Africa was typically portrayed in dualistic terms. This dualism was not that of race alone but also involved the contrast between the bustling society of the fast-growing towns and the surrounding countryside. The great novels and films of the time focused on this deep gulf and on the personal journeys of individuals who sought—or were compelled—to cross this divide. In such stories were captured the broader social and economic changes of the time.

A positive spin was put on town and countryside in the 1949 film *Jim Comes to Jo'burg* (which, incidentally, was the first film made in South Africa with African actors playing African parts). The film opens with scenes of idyllic, almost timeless rural life. An African man, in supposedly traditional dress, stands on the stone walls of his homestead, gazing out over fertile cornfields. Fat cattle pass the thatched huts, and a man ploughs a field with an ox-drawn plough. Happy children smile at the camera. Young men hunt impala in the bush. An (African) voice-over completes the picture:

> This is the story of a native boy in Africa, the story of one of my brothers. His name is Jim Jabulani Twala, but we shall simply call him Jim. This is the country where he was born and grew to manhood, where he lived in the freedom of the wide hills and valleys, tending the crops and herding the cattle. It was a simple life, and a good life, and Jim was happy. But to many of us there comes a time when we feel the urge to leave our villages and to travel to the city. Often the young men go for a year, sometimes two years, or even more, so they can earn money and then return to their people, and buy cattle, and marry. Sometimes it is just a state of restlessness and adventure that sends them travelling. So one day, . . . Jim said goodbye to his parents and set out to go to Johannesburg.

Jim's journey to the city has a fairytale quality as the country bumpkin overcomes adversity to find love and success. On arriving in Johannesburg, he is mugged by a gang of *tsotsis* (criminals) but befriended by a night watchman who helps him find employment, first as a garden-boy and later, after his white employer sacks him for incompetence, as a waiter in a nightclub. At the nightclub he is discovered to have a wonderful singing voice, falls in love with a young woman singer (played by an emerging star, Doris Rathebe), and foils a break-in by the very men who had mugged him earlier. The film ends with Jim and his girlfriend recording songs in a studio, under the management of the white man who had fired him earlier, thus achieving commercial as well as romantic success.

Both the countryside and the town are portrayed in *Jim Comes to Jo'burg* in generally cheery terms. The countryside is home to a prosperous and happy peasantry. The town, although a place of mild danger, is primarily a world of opportunity: jobs are easy to find, white people may be short-tempered but are neither brutal nor obviously racist, and love and success are easy to attain.

Very different views of rural and urban life were portrayed in the great novel of the time, Alan Paton's *Cry, the Beloved Country* (1948). Paton's novel is also a story of a journey from the countryside to the city of Johannesburg, but the journey is overshadowed by material and moral destitution. To be sure, the novel opens in the green and rolling hills of the southern Drakensberg, overlooking "one of the fairest valleys of Africa." But immediately, Paton dispels illusions: the hills and valleys below are overgrazed and overcultivated, eroded and crossed by deep *dongas* (ravines):

> The great red hills stand desolate, and the earth has torn away like flesh. The lightning flashes over them, the clouds pour down upon them, the dead streams come to life, full of the red blood of the earth. Down in the valleys women scratch the soil that is left, and the maize hardly reaches the height of a man. They are valleys of old men and old women, of mothers and children. The men are away, the young men and the girls are away. The soil cannot keep them any more. (1948, 4; see also 21–22)

The men and the young women, driven by failing crops, a lack of cash to pay taxes, or insufficient land, have gone to the city. "All roads lead to Johannesburg," Paton writes (not once, but twice: 10, 52). Once people have gone they are rarely heard of again.

Paton's novel revolves around an African priest's journey to Johannesburg to find his sister and his son. His sister went to the city in search of her migrant husband, who had not returned home. The son had gone to look for his aunt. On arrival in the city, the priest—like Jim—is cheated by a tsotsi. But this is no isolated incident. Crime and deceit hang over the novel. The priest eventually finds both his sister and his son. She has become a prostitute, brewing beer and living in squalor. He is in jail, charged with murdering a liberal white man after being led astray by amoral companions. The son is convicted, sentenced to death, and then executed.

Notwithstanding this picture of gloom, Paton finishes on an upbeat note. The father of the murdered white liberal is a conservative farmer who lives very close to the African priest's church. The murder of his son serves as an epiphany for the farmer, who takes it upon himself to improve the lives of the "native" people in the area. He employs a young African "agricultural demonstrator" to teach the people how to farm more productively. The novel ends with the prospect of a prosperous peasant society as the people build a dam, implement measures to conserve the soil, use improved seeds, and aim for smaller but improved herds. For Paton, the countryside holds out the prospect of a life free of the decadence of the town.

Jim Comes to Jo'Burg and *Cry, the Beloved Country* were both the products of white liberalism. *Mine Boy,* written in 1946 by the black author Peter Abrahams, painted a different picture of migrancy and urban life. The central character, Xuma, comes to Johannesburg "from the north," just as Jim did in the film. But, unlike Jim, Xuma is driven by rural poverty; when he arrives, his trousers are torn, his shirt is tattered, and his shoes are broken. He finds lodging in the Malay Camp and work in the mines. Neither place is pleasant: the streets of the Malay Camp are dark and dirty, with puddles of muddy water; people drink, gamble, and fight; the police brutalise residents while checking their passes or clamping down on illicit beer-brewing; work in the mines is hard and dangerous, with fatal disease and underground accidents; most of the white miners are racist. In contrast to Paton's vision of urban life, however, Abrahams's Johannesburg contains the seeds of hope. In the Malay Camp and in the mines, people achieve some humanity despite the appalling conditions; people live, laugh, and love, and create a resilient vibrancy. Moreover, the future lies not in some imagined rural idyll but in the towns, where individuals hold out the possibility of a common humanity that transcends racial boundaries and African people stand up for their rights.

All three accounts focus on the central theme of social change as people are drawn from rural lives on the South African periphery to the surging urban and industrial centres of the Witwatersrand and elsewhere. Life is profoundly different in the towns, in terms of both work and leisure. Society is being remade; cultures and values are being transformed. The process is brutal: people are driven to migrate to the towns by the worsening conditions in the countryside as much as by the opportunities in the towns, and the latter often entail great hardship and danger.

How accurate are these images of South African society? Are they corroborated in the work of social scientists and historians? Consider first the overall demographics of South Africa. According to the 1946 census, 11.4 million people lived in South Africa, of whom 2.4 million were classified as European (that is, white), 1.2 million Coloured or Asiatic (that is, Indian), and 7.8 million as Native (that is, African). The population was growing by slightly more than 2 percent per year, so that the population had grown by more than one million by the time of the 1951 census. Almost two out of three South Africans lived in the rural areas, with 4.4 million living in cities and towns as against 7 million in the rural areas, despite the rapid urbanisation that had occurred during the early 1940s. A majority of coloured, Indian, and white people lived in urban areas, but only one-quarter of the African population lived in the towns or cities. More than one-half of the economically active population worked in agriculture (in the commercial and the subsistence sectors), and many workers in urban areas were migrants who remitted part of their income to dependents remaining in rural areas. The journey from countryside to town was a crucial part of the lives of most African men (but few African women) but, overall, South African society was still overwhelmingly rural in 1950.

RURAL SOCIETY

The rural population in 1950, overwhelmingly African, was divided into two parts. Slightly more than half of the rural African population lived in the "reserves," the remainder in the "white" farming areas. The reserves were areas set aside for African settlement under the 1913 and 1936 Land Acts; they comprised about 15 percent of the country. In novels and on film, these reserves were often portrayed as prosperous rural paradises; even Paton represented them as potentially prosperous. The idea that a resilient peasant society existed (or could exist) in the reserves was attractive to many white elites. It served as an important pillar of segregation (prior to 1948) and apartheid (thereafter), in that subsistence agriculture was seen as integral to "tribal" life and custom. It provided justification for the low wages paid by capitalist employers of migrant workers, especially the mines (although the mines already recognised that the rural economy was in a parlous condition: Crush et al. 1991, 55, 68–69). It also provided supposed justification for the lower old-age pensions paid by the state to African people in rural areas and for restrictions on urban settlement ("influx control") that ensured that Africans were only "temporary sojourners" in town.

But life in the countryside was far from idyllic, as was made evident in a series of official investigations in the mid-1940s. The Lansdown Commission (Union of S.A., 1944c) found evidence of overpopulation relative to production in the reserves, resulting in widespread malnutrition and dependence on migrants' remittances (as depicted by Paton). These findings were underscored in reports by the Social and Economic Planning Council. The council found that "in practically no areas do the Reserve inhabitants as a whole produce sufficient food for the most elementary requirements of health" (Union of SA 1946, 49). The Lansdown Commission calculated that agricultural production of an "average" family of five in the Transkei or the Ciskei met only one-half of the *minimal* needs of such a family. Even the average family was dependent on migrants' remittances.

These assessments have been broadly corroborated by Simkins, whose careful collation of data led him to conclude that "taking the reserves as a whole, one finds that their inhabitants were far from able to provide for their subsistence requirements from agricultural production as early as 1918" (1981c, 264). For the period 1918–55, agricultural production in the reserves on average provided for slightly less than one-half of the food requirements of the resident population and slightly less than one-third of total subsistence requirements. Simkins notes important variations between reserves in different parts of the country. Some districts in Zululand and the Transkei were, in the aggregate, not far from being self-sufficient in terms of food production. But, overall, the reserves were not home to a thriving peasantry. Men were not going to the cities simply to secure the resources to buy the cattle they needed in order to get married, as was implied in *Jim Comes to Jo'burg;* rural families needed the remittances of migrant workers in order to survive.

One of the few case studies of life in the reserves focuses on Keiskammahoek, a summer rainfall area that was later to become part of the Ciskei. Houghton supervised an income and expenditure survey in 1949, a year in which there was a severe drought. The value of subsistence agriculture amounted to only 20 to 25 percent of the average family's cash income. Half of the cash income came from remittances sent by family members who were living and working elsewhere in the country. Without remittances, Houghton and Walton (1952, 183) noted bluntly, "the vast majority of the families would starve." More than half of the working-age men were migrants. There were, therefore, between two and three times as many women in the middle age cohorts (ibid., 32–35). So many adult men (and some women) were absent that the average family was unable to utilise fully its three acres of land (the problem was compounded, Houghton and Walton suggested, by a lack of equipment, skills, and initiative). Almost all of the work in the fields was done by women who had stayed behind, who also gathered firewood and collected water. "The District is at one and the same time both overpopulated and lacking in sufficient labour to make even normal use of the available resources" (ibid., 183). In an exceptionally good year, subsistence agriculture contributed perhaps one-half of the average household's nutritional requirements. But in a bad year, when drought struck, it contributed less than one-twentieth (ibid., 177).

Not only was Keiskammahoek poor overall, but it was also characterised by a high degree of inequality. The average family had four head of cattle, seven or so sheep, and a few goats. But one in three households had no cattle; fewer than one in three households had six or more head. Two of three households had no sheep. Houghton and Walton (1952, 97–99) provided examples of well-to-do, average, and poor families. The illustrative well-to-do household was headed by an elderly teacher who was paid a salary that on its own amounted to six times the average household income. He employed a herdboy to tend their cattle, horse, and sheep. The average family relied on remittances from family members—typically, it seems, three—working as migrants in Johannesburg. The poor household, comprising a widow and three children, had almost no income; the two older children had migrated to the cities, but only one ever sent anything back, and then only small sums. The family was heavily indebted and relied on neighbours' charity to supplement the meagre old-age pension. As the Lansdown Commission had recognised, subsistence was "but a myth" for some households in the reserves (Union of S.A. 1944c, 17).

Iliffe argues that the general causes of poverty in the reserves were those that had prevailed in Africa historically: the poor were "the incapacitated, aged, orphans, and solitary women," that is, people who had no access to jobs (Iliffe 1987, 126). In the reserves, able-bodied people could generally find some employment locally, albeit poorly paid work such as casual work on road gangs or cattle herding. More important, they could migrate to towns, mines, or (in some parts of the country) farms and remit some of their wages. As early as 1936, according to one official report, half of the male population of working age in the reserves was working and living elsewhere (Union of S.A. 1944b, para. 33). Poverty thus arose either because there were no able-bodied family members or because those who had migrated to the cities ceased to send remittances. Although the pattern of poverty was typical of Africa, poverty was exacerbated by the ways in which the changing nature of South African society entailed newly accentuated processes of household disintegration.

Keiskammahoek may have been especially impoverished, particularly in a year of drought. But even the crude data collected by the Lansdown Commission confirmed that households in the reserves were heavily dependent on cash income and suggested that there was widespread inequality between house-holds. The sale or consumption of agricultural produce (including stock) was valued, in the aggregate, at little more than one-third of the total income of 374 *kraals* (homesteads) surveyed in different parts of the country. Inequality was indicated by the fact that, although there were more than ten head of cattle per kraal on average, the proportion of kraals owning no cattle ranged from 10 to 30 percent on reserves in different parts of the country (Union of S.A. 1944c, appendix J). The Social and Economic Planning Council reported that in seven Transkei districts, perhaps 44 percent of households had no cattle and 20 percent had between one and five cows (Union of S.A. 1946, 23). Another government commission reported in 1948 that one in three families in the Ciskei had no arable land, and as many as 29 percent of married men owned no cattle (Native Laws Commission, quoted in Wolpe 1972, reprinted in Beinart and Dubow 1995, 76). As these reports emphasised, poverty underlay high infant mortality rates and poor health. Soon afterward, the government's Tomlinson Commission described inequality in the reserves as "very striking," with the richest one-eighth of households earning almost one-half of the total income (Union of S.A. 1955a, 98). Seventy-five percent of households in the Northern Transvaal reserves had no cattle, as had 63 percent of households in reserves in Natal and Zululand (Simkins 1981c, 274).

Some districts in the reserves were relatively prosperous in terms of agricultural production. Simkins (1981c) points to some areas, including Pondoland and parts of Zululand, that were able to meet three-quarters or more of their needs from agricultural production. Beinart (1992, 178) notes that the best series of maize harvests in the history of Pondoland occurred between 1956 and 1964. Perhaps the makers of *Jim Comes to Jo'burg* had these areas in mind. But such areas were very atypical, and even in them it is likely that production was distributed very unevenly.

Overall, although the peasantry was fast disappearing in the reserves, agricultural production remained one important source of income for many reserve households. But it had not disappeared yet: many households were only able to survive because migrants' remittances and local wage income were supplemented by production (as the Chamber of Mines argued in order to justify paying wages that were below what was needed to support an entire family). Efforts to preserve an agrarian way of life were reflected in livestock ownership. As much as one-third of the country's twelve million cattle were crowded into the reserves, as was one in ten of the country's nearly forty million sheep (Union of S.A. 1944b).

The reserves accommodated about one-half of the rural African population but accounted for only a small fraction of the area of South Africa. More than three-quarters of the country (with about 85 percent of the farmland) was reserved for white ownership. The bulk of this was divided into 117,000 white-owned farms producing, primarily, cattle (for beef and dairy products), sheep (for wool and meat), and maize. The 1940s had been years of rising incomes for commercial farmers, owing to rising demand and the state's policy of maintaining high producer prices by means of parastatal (semipublic) marketing institutions. In addition, white farmers had easy access to subsidised credit via the parastatal Land Bank. Landowners began to invest in tractors, with the total exceeding twenty thousand in 1946, and to bring larger acreages under cultivation. But prosperity was shared unevenly. Some farms were highly capitalised enterprises. Others struggled, barely able or unable to pay wages to the African workers they needed. Incomes varied greatly, although after 1948 the new National Party government raised maize prices (via the marketing boards) and hence incomes for many struggling farmers.

A total of between 2.2 million and 3 million African men, women, and children were resident on white-owned farms in 1950 (Union of S.A. 1952a; Simkins 1984b, 54). Slightly more than half a million adult men and about 180,000 adult women were employed on the farms, together with 100,000 boys and 50,000 girls under the age of sixteen (Union of S.A. 1952b). In addition, a large number of casual labourers were employed, mostly on a seasonal basis (especially during the harvest, since most harvesting was done by hand). Apparently there are no data for 1950, but the figure for casual labour in 1960 was almost 600,000 (Greenberg 1980, 423). Some of these workers would have been drawn from neighbouring reserves and others from the farms themselves. In addition, perhaps 100,000 permanent employees (and another 100,000 casual employees) were coloured or Indian.

Official statistics described all employees as farm "servants," but the men typically worked in the fields while the women served as domestic workers inside the farmhouse. Wages were low in comparison with urban wages; they were especially low in remoter parts of the country such as the Western Transvaal (Van der Horst 1949, 125–26). A large portion of farm workers' earnings was paid in kind. Such payments amounted to about one-third of all payments countrywide and one-half or more in some areas (Union of S.A. 1952b). In many areas, wage-earning farm workers were allowed to graze their livestock on the farms or were given land on which they could grow their own crops.

Many African families on the farms were not simply or primarily paid farm workers. The late 1940s was a period of acute labour shortage in white farming areas. Many farmers, especially those with smaller farms, were unable or unwilling to offer wages that could compete with those paid by urban employers and instead acceded to the demands of African households for access to land in return for their labour. Three relationships predominated. The first, illegal since 1913 but nonetheless practised in parts of the Western Transvaal especially, was sharecropping, whereby white landowners allowed African farmers the use of land in return for a share, usually one-half, of the produce (hence "farming on the halves"). Its illegality means that there are no records of how many sharecroppers remained by 1950. The second relationship was cash tenancy, or "squatting," whereby African households paid a cash rent for the land they used for grazing or cultivation. Again, there do not appear to be any aggregate data about the prevalence of this practice (although in the 1960s, when the state clamped down on squatting, the Department of Native Affairs claimed to have traced 170,000 and resettled a growing number of them: RSA 1968).

Almost certainly the most prevalent relationship was labour tenancy. A labour tenant secured access to white-owned land in return for providing labour to the landowner, typically for three months (in the Transvaal) or six months (in Northern Natal). Men typically worked in the fields and women in the house. Sometimes they were paid in addition to getting access to land; in other places children provided unpaid labour; and in still other places nobody was paid, the land alone sufficing. In principle, what distinguished labour tenants from farm workers was that the latter were employed permanently, and the former for part of the year only. Labour tenancy was attractive to African households not only because it secured access to land but also because it gave them some control over where they worked for part of the year. Some labour tenants therefore migrated to the towns for the part of the year when their labour was not used by the farmer, thereby earning wages substantially higher than those available on the farms. In practice, the boundary between labour tenancy and employment may not have been so clear, because paid farm workers were often given access to land and labour tenants were often paid for their labour. In the 1930s and 1940s, labour tenancy was almost ubiquitous (Jones 1949; Keppel-Jones 1949, 196–97; Schirmer 2003, 5–6).

Later, from 1956 onward, farmers were required to register labour tenants, and so there are some data about its prevalence (although even then it was possible to hide the real number by identifying some as permanent paid farm servants: Schirmer 1994). Prior to 1956, however, there are no aggregate data. Given that the number of *registered* labour tenants peaked at 164,000 (in 1964), it is unlikely that there were fewer than 200,000 in the early 1950s. It is unclear whether labour tenants were included in or excluded from the employment data from the Agricultural Census provided above; Mager (1999, 29) provides an example of one labour tenant who was recorded as a farm servant. In the Barberton district, 14 percent of the African farm population consisted of labour tenants in the mid-1950s, and this figure probably excludes their dependents (Mather 1997, 67). Given that about two out of three labour tenants were in the Transvaal and that the total number of employees categorised as "Native" on farms in that province was recorded at 294,000 in 1950, it is certainly possible that there were as many labour tenants as full-time paid farm workers in the Transvaal in 1950. Even in parts of the Cape, such as the Border (Mager 1999, 21–41), African families continued their struggle to retain access to white-owned land.

In some parts of the country, including the southern Orange Free State, many white-owned farms were neither occupied by their owners nor rented to white tenant farmers. Such farms were occupied by African families, but the relationship between them and their landlords is unclear. Ostensibly, most such African families were headed by paid farm workers or supervisors, but many no doubt used whatever autonomy they enjoyed to preserve their own livestock. A belief that white families were leaving these areas led to fears of *"die beswarting van die platteland"* (the "blackening" of the farmlands) and the appointment of a Commission of Enquiry (the Du Toit Commission) that reported in 1960. The commission's report illustrated the extent of African occupation of farms (or rather the "reoccupation of the land": Platzky and Walker 1985, 120–21).

African households were able to retain access to land and resist proletarianisation because they had two things that landowners were short of: labour and oxen (for ploughing, in the era before tractors replaced oxen). Moreover, many landowners had a surfeit of land. African labour tenants and sharecroppers were able to seek out better contracts with landowners by leaving unsatisfactory employers. Van Onselen (1996) provides a detailed account of the fortunes of one sharecropper, Rabonela "Kas" Maine, who lived on a series of farms in the hot, dusty plains of the southwestern Transvaal. Almost every year Maine would have to renegotiate a contract with a landowner; fifteen times in the thirty years prior to 1950 he had moved in search of a better deal. Schirmer (1994, 1995) provides evidence that labour tenants in the Lydenburg district in the Eastern Transvaal also voted with their feet.

The significance of independent agricultural production by African farmers depends on the point of view. Viewed in terms of aggregate production, it was minor: African households on white-owned farms accounted for perhaps 10 percent of total South African maize production (including maize consumed by farmers as well as maize sold), with a further 10 percent produced by African farmers in the reserves and the other 80 percent produced by white farmers. The equivalent figures for cattle ownership were probably about 10 percent, 30 percent, and 60 percent, respectively (Union of S.A. 1950a, 834; Simkins 1981c, 1984a). Countrywide, there were many more wage labourers than labour tenants or sharecroppers. But from the point of view of the African households, independent production remained important. Simkins (1984a) calculates that agricultural production by African households outside of the reserves contributed about one-fifth of the total income of all African households in these areas (Simkins's figures probably include production on "black spot" farms, that being the official term for African-owned freehold land acquired before the 1913 Land Act prevented African land ownership outside of the reserves). If about half of this production was accounted for by one-fifth of the households, then there were probably more than half a million African people living in households that still primarily farmed for a living, albeit on land they did not own and that they farmed in return for their labour. Such independent producers were not spread evenly across the countryside but rather were concentrated in specific areas. In the district of Barberton, for example, Africans owned almost as many cattle as their white landlords (Mather 1997, 74).

Sharecroppers and labour tenants could strike extraordinary success. Kas Maine enjoyed his most lucrative farming season ever in 1948, the year that the National Party was voted into government and just before the making of *Jim Comes to Jo'burg*. For that year's harvest, Maine employed twenty-five labourers to supplement his family's labour. After paying his landlord his share and paying the labourers, Maine was left with 1,000 bags of sorghum, 570 bags of maize, and more than 200 bags of sunflower seed; these he sold for three hundred pounds, the equivalent of the annual salary of a teacher. He also had 8 horses, 12 donkeys, 60 head of cattle, and 220 sheep (Van Onselen 1996).

This was an exceptional year for Maine, and he may have been unusually successful as a sharecropper, but he was not entirely alone (as Simkins's data show). Keegan (1988) describes the lives of several other farmers who were sharecropping south of Johannesburg. For Lucas Nqandela, the years of World War II were the best period of his sharecropping career, although this period of relative prosperity ended abruptly in 1945. For Ndae Makume, however, farming remained lucrative up until the mid-1950s: Ndae Makume had only one span of oxen, and so he had to cooperate with other families when ploughing.

In good years, he harvested 160 or so bags of maize; he combined this farming with building work. The survival of Maine and Makume as sharecroppers was in part due to their productivity; less productive families were evicted much earlier.

It should not be forgotten that while some sharecroppers and labour tenants were desperately hanging onto the land, the living conditions of Africans living on white farms were usually appalling. White farmers were often oppressive and generally exploitative. Even where labour tenancy persisted, landlords demanded more and more labour from their tenants, with the result that children were kept out of school; physical brutality was commonplace. Living conditions for white farmers had improved immensely during the previous decades: they enjoyed electricity, running water and sewerage in the home, boarding-school education for children, private tennis courts, cars and (for a few) aeroplanes. For the vast majority of black families, however, conditions were "essentially the same as they had been a hundred years before": "Workers continued to live in wattle and daub huts, in shacks and (a more recent development) in compounds. They had no electric light; water came from an outside tap, or, more commonly had to be fetched by bucket from some distance away; and lavatories, if they existed, were of a pit type. . . . Bicycles, radios, and occasional old cars were the sole evidence among the vast majority of farm workers that the country was becoming wealthier" (Wilson 1971, 158–59). Indeed, in some respects life was clearly worse. But the value of sharecropping and labour tenancy to African households was not simply economic. Access to land enabled families to keep cattle, and cattle remained the cornerstone of a culture and society that African men sought to preserve.

If sharecropping and labour tenancy were crucial to the preservation of an agrarian way of life, then that way of life was under threat. Keegan (1988) relates how Lucas Nqandela was pushed into paid farm work as early as 1945, while Ndae Makume prudently diversified by learning building skills and then developed a lucrative building business. As these two examples indicate, sharecroppers could move into the non farm social structure at very different levels. Nqandela's descent into the proletariat was far more common that Makume's move into an upwardly mobile middle class (with Makume's children becoming teachers).

White farmers sought political power in order to restore their power over African labour and especially over sharecroppers and labour tenants. In the 1948 general election the National Party campaigned with the slogan "Die kaffer op sy plek en die Koelie uit die land" (the African in his place and the Indian out of the country, using very derogatory terms; Van Onselen 1996, 305). Winning sixty-three of seventy-one parliamentary seats in rural areas, the National Party sought ways of solving the labour shortage in farming areas without farmers' having to pay higher wages. The squeeze was to be put on sharecropping and labour tenancy. All over the country, complex relations of paternalism were giving way to the simpler relations of apartheid. As Van Onselen writes, Afrikaner landlords were making "the difficult, embarrassing, painful and at times downright treacherous transition from paternalism and the social intimacy of its quasi-kinship relationships to the emerging discourse of apartheid with its deeply alienating emphasis on racial distance" (ibid., 211).

Very few, if any, African families, within or outside the reserves or farms, could depend on independent farming alone. Most depended on remittances sent by migrant workers. For sure, many young men were pushed into migration in part by their need to raise cash for marriage. But most were driven also by the pressing need for cash for the subsistence of their families. After describing conditions in the Natal reserves, Brookes and Hurwitz noted, "No wonder that the question 'Why leave the reserves to work in the towns?' evokes the simple, if grim, reply 'Starvation'" (1957, 84). No one actually starved, but this was only because almost everyone had access to remittances. Nonetheless, taking into account the more successful labour tenants, sharecroppers, and reserve farmers, perhaps 15 percent of the total population of South Africa was sufficiently involved in independent farming to warrant the label "peasant."

URBAN SOCIETY

Migration from countryside to city is the central theme of the film *Jim Comes to Jo'burg* as well as the novels *Cry, the Beloved Country* and *Mine Boy*. All three accounts were produced after an extended and unprecedented period of growth of the urban population. Influx controls were relaxed during World War II, largely because of the extraordinary need for labour in industry and commerce. Between 1936 and 1951 the population of Johannesburg rose from slightly more than 500,000 to almost 900,000 and that of the Witwatersrand as a whole from about 1 million to more than 1.6 million. The 1951 census found that the African population of Johannesburg had doubled as immigrants had arrived from the maize farms of the Orange Free State and the Transvaal. Rapid urbanisation was not unique to the Witwatersrand. The African population of Durban doubled between 1943 and 1949 alone (Maylam 1996, 16). But, in absolute terms, urbanisation on the Rand dwarfed that in other cities.

During the first half of the century, a clear majority of African people in cities such as Johannesburg had lived in hostels or servants' accommodations in the backyards of employers. These locations, including places such as Sophiatown and Alexandra (in Johannesburg) and Lady Selborne (in Pretoria), had been home to a minority of the urban African population. Sapire describes the Brakpan location as a "veritable island surrounded by single men in compounds" (1987, 374). But neither the state nor employers built new hostels or houses during the period of rapid immigration, with the result that the existing ones were soon bursting at the seams. Overcrowding, poor living conditions, and the absence of amenities all contributed to high levels of violence, as was evident in *Mine Boy.*

High rents charged by the location's landowners together with overcrowding led to land invasions and the proliferation of shack settlements, which the authorities largely accepted for want of any better alternative. By 1950, a substantial proportion of the urban African population was living in shack settlements: upwards of 100,000 people on the Rand (Bonner 1995, 121), 50,000 people in Cato Manor in Durban (Nuttall 1996, 178), and perhaps as many as 150,000 coloured and African people in Cape Town (Goldin 1987, 69). Living conditions in these shack settlements were poor. But they were cheap and had the additional advantage of being largely unregulated by the South African Police, being administered and policed (sometimes severely) by local leadership (see, for example, Edwards 1996).

In the film, Jim finds work in Johannesburg as a domestic working in the garden and the house of his employer, then as a waiter, and eventually as a nightclub singer and recording artist. The first part of this progression is not far-fetched. In East London, at least one in three people in the African labour force was in domestic work, living at the employer's residence, in the mid-1950s. Domestic work inside the house had, however, largely shifted from being a male to a female preserve (Gaitskell et al. 1984; Cock 1980, 250; Reader 1961). African men continued to perform largely unskilled labour, but they shifted into the better-paying sectors of manufacturing and commerce. By 1950, 267,000 African workers were employed in manufacturing and 100,000 in commerce (Greenberg 1980, 423–26). At this time much of industry was very labour-intensive, with little machinery. Common jobs included those of messenger, packer, and cleaner, in addition to manual labourer. Mining employed almost as many people as manufacturing, but only a minority of these were South African. During the war, rules governing the reservation of semiskilled jobs for white workers had been relaxed because so many had been drawn off into the armed forces, but after the war job reservation was tightened again and African workers once again confined to unskilled work. In Durban, four of every five African men were recorded as labourers or domestic servants in the 1951 census (Nuttall 1996, 177).

Jim's story also is not atypical in the ease with which he found work after having been sacked from his first job. African workers may have been unskilled. But there was no shortage of work, and even the unskilled could move easily from job to job. Turnover in employment was high, and municipal officials complained routinely about "job-hopping" by "native" labour. Such job-hopping entailed a form of struggle. As Nuttall writes, "Thousands of unskilled workers sought to improve, and retain some control over, their working conditions not by direct confrontation with capital, but by incessant job searching" (1996, 194; see also Bonner 1995; Reader 1961). But it was a form of struggle that undermined the prospects for union organisation, perhaps depressed wages, and impeded the development of a stable or settled urban working class.

Although the urban African population was booming, it was unevenly urban in the social and the cultural senses. Most African people in the towns were first-generation immigrants, and they retained a rural orientation. As Bonner (1995, 118) puts it, urban life remained for them highly "conditional." They held onto the hope of returning to rural areas, where they would be free from the pressures of pass laws, curfews, and so on and from the moral decadence of the city life. Many sent remittances to their dependents in rural areas. Immigrants formed ethnic associations, one of the purposes of which was to police the behaviour of migrants in the towns and prevent them from "forgetting home" and becoming too "assimilated" into urban life.

Urban politics at this time reflected the shallowness of the African population's roots in the cities. The most important political movements of the era were squatter movements, led by populist leaders such as James "Sofasonke" Mpanza in Soweto (Bonner and Segal 1998, 20–24). The Sofasonke and similar movements were based among the recent immigrants. Tellingly, the ANC's first major campaign in urban areas—its Defiance Campaign in 1952—targeted six "unjust" laws including several of an unambiguously rural flavour: laws concerned with livestock limitation and the reform of rural administration.

Where Jim's story is atypical, even far-fetched, is his easy mobility into the world of the emerging African middle class. To be sure, there was a self-conscious African middle-class, but it was very small, and there were few opportunities for entering it. There is no agreement as to what precisely constitutes the "middle class," and the available data have been widely misused, giving rise to widely divergent assessments of its size. The most thorough analysis of the first available Manpower Survey—conducted in 1965, sixteen years after Jim went to Jo'burg—suggests that only 10 percent of African employees in the sectors covered (which exclude farm and domestic work) could be considered middle-class using the broadest possible definition (Crankshaw 1997a; 1996a, 635–36). Jim represented the possibility of upward mobility, a black version of the "American dream," not a common reality.

The urban middle classes were, of course, overwhelmingly white. For white people, and to an increasing extent coloured and Indian people, too, the cities and towns were now clearly home. White people were in the process of shifting out of industrial-sector employment into service-sector employment. Already in 1951 the number of white workers in commerce and finance was almost equal to the number in manufacturing (RSA 1994, 7.5). The general trend in the class structure of the white population is evident in the analysis by Davies (1979, appendix 1), although he unfortunately provides no data for the period between 1946 and 1960. Using occupational data (that is, for working individuals, not households), Davies found that the "bourgeoisie and traditional petty bourgeoisie" (owners of farms and businesses, the self-employed, and managers) accounted for 26 percent of the economically active white population in 1946 and 23 percent in 1960. The "new petty bourgeoisie" (which encompassed supervisory, professional or semiprofessional, and bureaucratic occupations) accounted for 45 percent of the white population in 1946, rising to 60 percent by 1960. The proportion in skilled, semiskilled, and unskilled blue-collar work was in decline, from 29 percent in 1946 to 17 percent in 1960. The proportion of white workers described as labourers was tiny: less than 2 percent in 1946 and only 1 percent in 1960.

With white people occupying the higher positions in the division of labour and African people occupying the bottom positions, coloured and Indian people filled intermediate positions. This racial hierarchy was especially clear in Cape Town, with its substantial coloured population and especially strict controls on the influx of Africans. Among African workers, 90 percent were employed in unskilled work, 8 percent in semiskilled work, and only 2 percent in skilled work. Among white people, in complete contrast, 1 percent were employed in unskilled work, 6 percent in semiskilled work, and 93 percent in skilled work. Coloured workers occupied a clear intermediate position: 30 percent in unskilled work, 48 percent in semiskilled work, and 15 percent in skilled work (Van der Horst, cited in Goldin 1987, 96). As these figures indicate, there were still as many unskilled coloured workers in the Western Cape as there were unskilled Indian workers in Natal. Indeed, certain occupations, such as street-cleaning in Durban, were informally reserved for coloured or Indian workers. But many coloured and Indian families were beginning to enjoy upward mobility through the occupational class structure.

In Cape Town and Durban, growing numbers of coloured and Indian people were moving into middle-class occupations and better-off residential areas. The result was a growing consciousness of social class. Walmer Estate, in Cape Town, was home to "upper-class Coloureds with electric stoves, refrigerators and Venetian blinds on their windows" (as Richard Rive wrote cuttingly, as quoted in Bickford-Smith et al. 1999, 130–34). The new middle class looked down on the coloured working class in places such as District Six (in Cape Town). The working class, although poor, was distinctively urban in ways that the bulk of the African working class was not. Even recent immigrants to the town recognised that they had left the rural areas for good. The result was the development of clearly urban "communities" in District Six and elsewhere (ibid., 130–141).

CLASS AND THE DISTRIBUTION OF INCOMES

The complex articulation of urban and agrarian societies makes it difficult to sketch clearly the shape of the class structure. There is little problem with coloured, Indian, and white households, which can be easily defined in terms of their position in the labour market. But many African households had one foot in the labour market and the other on the land. Most African men spent part of their life as migrant workers and the rest on their land. Scholars seeking to apply class labels have wrestled with the fact that the African population was incompletely dispossessed of its land and incompletely proletarianised.

What is clear is that there was a close correlation between race and class. White people held a near monopoly of skilled labour and middle-class occupations. Coloured and Indian people were moving into semiskilled occupations (although many were still employed as unskilled workers in towns and in the countryside). African people remained confined to the combination of unskilled wage labour and subsistence agriculture.

The paucity of data about incomes makes it difficult to plot the relation between class structure and income distribution. The state did not collect aggregate data about the distribution of incomes, so any analysis has to proceed by means of a mixture of calculation and guesswork. Our analysis rests on two pillars: macrolevel data, especially the estimates made by McGrath and Simkins in the early 1980s, and micro-level data from records on earnings and the occasional local survey.

Most estimates with regard to income distribution under apartheid focus on interracial inequalities. The official Tomlinson Commission estimated that the average income among white South Africans was ten times that of African people, eight times that of coloured people, and five times that of Indian people in 1952 (Houghton 1964, 166). McGrath estimates that disparities were slightly larger (1990, 95). Taking the more conservative Tomlinson estimates gives racial average incomes per capita per year of R631 (for white people), R133 (Indian people), R86 (coloured people) and R63 (African people). These would correspond to annual household incomes of about R2,500 (for white households), R660 (Indian households), R430 (coloured households), and R315 (African households), assuming average household size of less than four members in white households and about five members in others.

In order to move from these figures for average incomes by race to a picture of the overall patterns of inequality we need data about *intra*racial inequalities. Unfortunately, there are no coherent data about these for the early apartheid period. But we can collate data from different sources and, on the basis of plausible assumptions, identify broad income strata within racial groups. A useful way of examining the way households fit into the overall economic hierarchy in society is to disaggregate society into income deciles. A decile is simply one-tenth of the overall population. The richest income decile is thus the richest one-tenth of the population, and the poorest decile is the poorest one-tenth. Our goal in this section is to suggest what kinds of households comprised each income decile in 1950. In Chapter 3 we show how patterns of inequality had changed by the late 1970s, and in Chapter 6 we conduct a much more thorough examination of high-quality data for 1993.

Unfortunately, no data exist for the incomes of different deciles in society for 1950. The best we can do is to suggest possible average incomes for each decile on the basis of plausible assumptions about the overall pattern of income distribution. Our starting point is what we know about the distribution of incomes. McGrath and Whiteford (1994) assert that the overall distribution of income (as measured by the Gini coefficient; see further Chapter 6) changed little between 1975 and the early 1990s. In addition, a series of studies suggest that racial income shares changed little between the second decade of the century and the 1970s (Devereux 1983, 4). Given the close correlation between race and class, and hence income, up to the 1970s, it is likely that the overall distribution of incomes changed relatively little across this period. It is therefore likely that the deciles' shares of income were not very different in 1950 than they were twenty-five years later. Given this assumption, and given that average income per capita in 1950 was about R180 per year and the average household income (for the average five-member household) about R900 per year, we can speculate that the approximate average household incomes in each income decile would be as set out in the middle column of table 2.1.

These estimates cannot be easily reconciled with the available microlevel data, examined in detail below, which suggest lower incomes across a wide range of deciles. Put bluntly, the microlevel data do not indicate the existence of enough households to fill the higher decile categories. Differential household sizes might explain some of this divergence. White households were smaller than African households (and rich white households were the smallest of all). The 1955 Survey of Family Expenditure found that the average white household in the larger cities had 3.6 members, with a modal size of four (Union of S.A. 1958). Simkins (1984b, 238 ff.) estimates that the average African household in 1960 had more than 5 members. Thus, although white people made up slightly more than 20 percent of the population, they composed more than 25 percent of the households. Taking this into account helps reconcile the micro- and macro-level data. In the absence of a full explanation, however, we are compelled to the adjust microdata estimates of income upward and the macrodata estimates of decile incomes downward.

Taking this mismatch into account, what kinds of households are in each decile? The paucity of good data means that we can only use class categories in a general, descriptive sense, not in the precise analytical senses used in Chapters 7 and 8 below. But the available data for incomes points to two major dividing lines. The first lay between what might be described as the skilled working class and middle class, which were overwhelmingly white, and the unskilled working class, which was overwhelmingly African. The second fault line occurred between the urban African households (that is, in the unskilled working class) and the bulk of African households in rural areas. Within the latter there was considerable inequality, but almost all had very low incomes in comparison with urban African households.

Consider first the incomes of white people, who made up the bulk of the skilled and white-collar occupational classes. The best data available regarding the distribution of incomes among white South Africans is for 1954–55, from the Survey of Family Expenditure (Union of S.A. 1958). In the ten principal cities and towns, the average family income in 1955 was about R2,200 per year

Table 2.1. Approximate composition of income deciles, 1950

Income decile	Approximate average household income per year (macro-level data), in rands	Approximate class and racial composition
1	R40	Poorest African households in reserves (usually without members of working age)
2	R135	African households in reserves and on white farms (including labour tenants)
3	R195	African households in reserves and on white farms (including labour tenants); migrant African mine workers
4	R252	Coloured and Indian farm workers; richer rural African households; poorest urban African households
5	R360	Urban African households (unskilled, including domestic workers); richest rural African households; poor urban coloured and Indian households
6	R480	Better-off urban African households (including police, nurses); coloured and Indian working classes
7	R645	African professionals, teachers; the occasional African sharecropper; coloured and Indian middle classes
8	R945	Poor white people; coloured and Indian middle classes
9	R1,590	White working class
10	R4,250	White upper and middle classes (including self-employed)

in 1950 prices. Incomes were heavily dependent on the earnings of male bread-winners. Only one in four wives was contributing to family income, and their average contribution amounted to only 7 percent of total family income. Earnings and family incomes varied between occupational classes. Families headed by the self-employed had the highest average incomes (about R3,800 per year). Managers and other administrative officials had an average family income of R3,300 per year. Families headed by those in professional and technical occupations (including especially engineers, designers and draughtsmen, teachers, and doctors) had an average annual income of about R2,600. The white working class had annual family incomes of between R1,400 and R1,800. White-collar workers such as salesmen, bookkeepers, and clerks had family incomes higher than this but lower than those of professionals. In smaller towns, the white upper classes (managers and professionals) had lower family incomes than their big-city counterparts, but the white working class had incomes comparable to their counterparts'.

The top decile of all South African households would thus have comprised households headed by white men in self-employment or in managerial and professional occupations. The white working class would have filled decile 9. The very poorest white South Africans would have been in decile 8. These would have been families without members in employment, whether because of age, infirmity, or the desertion or death of the former breadwinner. The state provided financial support to almost one hundred thousand white people via old-age, war veterans', or disability pensions. In 1950 the government's old-age pension was set at just R168 per year, a very low level compared to earnings. Most retired white people would have had access to occupational pension schemes (including the government's schemes for public-sector workers); in 1946 only one in three white persons of pensionable age was receiving the means-tested government old-age pension. Furthermore, many retired people did not live on their own. Because the means test applied to individual rather than household income, income from a government pension was often a contribution to, rather than the sum total of, household income. The 1955 Survey of Family Expenditure found that the *average* family income among retired people was more than R1,600 per year (in 1950 prices). Only a very small number of white families was poor. About seven thousand received child maintenance grants. In general, as we shall see below, job reservation and discriminatory public sector employment provided for high employment rates among white people and kept most white workers out of unskilled occupations. This, combined with minimum wage legislation, ensured that the incomes of white South Africans would rarely have dropped below the level of decile 8.

If the eighth decile provided a floor for white South Africans, it provided a ceiling for African people. The highest incomes that African people could reasonably hope to attain would have put them in the seventh decile, but no higher. Consider Kas Maine, for example. His peak harvest of 1948–49 earned him R600. Even allowing for additional income of other members, the Maine household at its peak would only have reached decile 7. An African teacher might get into decile 7 more regularly. But there were not many occasions when sharecroppers would have reached the top half of the income hierarchy, and there were not many African professionals (such as doctors) or even semiprofessionals (such as teachers and nurses).

Most urban African households would probably have fallen into deciles 5 and 6. Research conducted by the South African Institute of Race Relations

(Wix 1951) found that the "average" African family on the Witwatersrand had an income in 1950 of R25 per month (R300 per year). The institute derived the family income from estimates for the income of different members of the family. The male breadwinner's earnings were put at about R17 per month (or R200 per year), the woman's earnings at about R6 per month, and children's contributions at R2 per month. Houghton (1960) found that the average annual income in East London was very slightly higher in 1955, at R72 per capita or about R360 per household (in 1950 prices). In Durban's Baumannville location, the median annual household income in 1954 was also, in 1950 prices, about R360 (Brookes and Hurwitz 1957, 47–48).

The institute's figures for the Reef are based on more detailed data about earnings that are consistent with other evidence. Consider the earnings of male workers. Most African workers were unskilled and were paid at or near the minimum wages determined by statutory bodies (see below). Minimum wages on the Reef (including a significant cost-of-living allowance) were between R16 and R22 per month, or R190 to R260 per year (Wix 1951). The median wages in commerce and industry in East London in 1955 were about R25 per month (Reader 1961). Wages appear to have been slightly higher in Johannesburg than in Pietermaritzburg and Durban. Brookes and Hurwitz (1957) give examples of a garage hand earning R16 per month in Durban in the early 1950s, by which time typical wages in Johannesburg has risen to R22 to R25 per month (see also Van der Horst 1949, 134). In manufacturing, the average earnings of African workers countrywide was R232 per year in 1950, whereas in construction the average was R204 (Houghton 1964, 289). The few people in nonmanual employment were paid more: police constables earned about the same, nurses rather more, and teachers much more (about R600 per year).

Employment opportunities were more limited for women and children. The institute reported that washerwomen, who collected laundry from several different houses, typically earned about R8 per month in total. Domestic servants who lived out earned much the same (Wix 1951). The institute did not estimate earnings from activities such as beer-brewing or prostitution. Domestic workers who lived on their employers' properties earned less in cash but received food, accommodations, and other benefits in kind. Many children were available for work; Hyslop (1993, 396) reports that only one in three African children of school-going age was in school in the early 1950s. Children could earn small amounts from work such as caddying at golf clubs.

There is indirect evidence that a significant minority of households had higher household incomes than the institute's "average" family. This is indicated in debates about rents for municipal housing in Soweto and elsewhere in the early 1950s. Low-income families qualified for reduced "sub-economic" rents. In 1954 the government set the limit for sub-economic rents at a monthly income of R30 (R360 per year). The Johannesburg municipality felt that a monthly income of R40 (R480 per year) was a better limit. There was presumably a sizeable proportion of families with incomes above these limits. A survey carried out in Soweto in 1956 found that only 20 percent of families had incomes below R20 per month, or R240 per year (Bonner and Segal 1998, 49). In Meadowlands, in Soweto, 55 percent of households had monthly incomes above R30 in 1956. In Moroka, also part of Soweto, the average income was R30 per month (de Gruchy 1959). But few households with incomes high enough to disqualify them from sub-economic rents would have had an unskilled breadwinner. In the mid-1950s African workers campaigned intermittently but unsuccessfully for minimum wages of one pound (R2) a day (about R500 per year), which was regarded as a radical (even idealist) demand.

Brookes and Hurwitz (1957, 47–51) make the point that such findings about household incomes exclude any consideration of illegal earnings, especially from beer-brewing (the importance of which is so evident in Abrahams's *Mine Boy*). Allowing for such earnings raises incomes and reduces poverty rates substantially. A minority of households in urban locations would have fallen into the fifth income decile in South Africa as a whole, with most households falling into the sixth and a few into the seventh decile.

There was, thus, a deep gulf between the incomes of urban African households and the incomes of white households. This was in part due to direct wage discrimination. Unskilled white labourers were paid more than double the wages of their "native" counterparts (Union of S.A. 1948, 25). But racial inequality was also due to the very different incomes of skilled and unskilled workers, which converted into racial inequality because of the formal and informal colour bar. The Social and Economic Planning Council (ibid., 30) cites evidence (unfortunately, from the late 1930s only) about wage differentials for the skilled and the unskilled in South Africa compared to other countries. In comparison with European, North American and Australasian countries, South Africa had the lowest unskilled wages and the highest skilled wages and hence by far the highest differential.

There was a similar gulf between the incomes of urban African households and the much larger number of rural African households (which made up half of the population of South Africa). Consider first the incomes of African households in the reserves. Simkins (1981c, 263) calculates that the value of agricultural production by these households was about R7 per capita per year in 1950. Most households received a substantial share of their income from remittances from absent family members. Lipton (1977, 80) estimates that the average household income was about R100 per year, with a little more than half coming from agriculture. These figures are consistent with Houghton's data for Keiskammahoek, where the value of agricultural production was clearly lower than in many other reserve areas. Houghton and Walton concluded from their survey that the average Keiskammahoek family has a cash income of about R80 to R90 and income in kind worth about R14, giving a total income of about R100 per year. Almost one-third of family income came from outside the reserve (1952, 6). For similarly sized households, therefore, the average urban African household had an income probably three times larger than that of the average household in the reserve. The gulf between urban and rural incomes is also evident from a calculation made by Simkins (1984a, 270): the average wage for African workers in industrial employment (excluding mining) was five times the average value of agricultural production in the reserves by a family of five people.

Income in the reserves was, however, distributed very unequally. Houghton and Walton's study of Keiskammahoek is the only detailed study available. Although the average household might have fallen into decile 2 of the country-wide income distribution, many households would have fallen into the poorest decile. The example of a poor family dependent on the old-age pension of the grandmother falls clearly into this bottom decile. From 1944 (when pensions were introduced for elderly African people) to 1950, the value of the pension for an African in the rural areas was R12 per year (set at half the value of the pension of African people in the cities); in 1950 pensions were increased by one-quarter. Not only was the pension set at a low level, but many elderly people who were eligible did not receive them at all. Simkins (1984b, 260) estimates for 1960 that fewer than half of the elderly African people who were eligible for pensions actually received them.

Average incomes on white-owned farms were much the same as in the reserves. Simkins (1984a) calculates that the average income (from all sources) of African households on white-owned farms was R21 per capita per year in 1950, that is, about R100 per year for a five-person household. About one-fifth of this came from agricultural production and four-fifths from employment (including wages and in-kind payments). Lipton (1977) reports that average annual incomes in the Eastern Cape were about R72, half of which was paid in kind. The 1950 Union Yearbook (Union of S.A. 1950c, 325) records that farm workers' wages (including in-kind contributions) were about R60 to R70 per year. A detailed study of farms in two Eastern Cape districts in 1957 found that average family income (including cash and in-kind income) was about R210 per year; only a small portion of this consisted of cash; the bulk was in kind or in the form of grazing rights and land for farming (Roberts 1958). Earlier studies of farmworker households showed that household incomes were boosted by the work of women and children in the fields or the houses. The actual cash wages of the male breadwinner might amount to only one-fifth of the overall household income, including payment in kind (Keppel-Jones 1949, 201–2). Some members of families resident on the farms also worked as migrant workers elsewhere, at least for part of the year, so some households had some remittance income.

Although wages and incomes were much lower in rural than in urban areas, the cost of living was higher in the latter. This was primarily because of the high cost of accommodations and transportation in town (Wix 1951; Reader 1961; Bickford-Smith et al. 1999, 123). In about 1950, rents were commonly about R1.50 to R2 per month, whether in private accommodations in the locations or in municipal housing. Only in the shack settlements were accommodations cheap. Transport, too, could cost almost R2 per month.

In summary, the income hierarchy in South Africa around 1950 divided into neat racial and demographic blocks. Almost all of the rural African population—half of the country's total—would have been in the bottom five deciles. The urban African population (about 17 percent of the country's total) would have ranged across deciles 5 and 7. The coloured and Indian population (together comprising about 10 percent of the total) would have ranged perhaps from decile 4 (in the case of coloured and Indian farm workers) to decile 9. The white population would have been concentrated in the top two deciles, with some poor whites falling into the eighth decile. The scanty extant data thus suggest that Houghton (1971, 43) was right to identify three broad strata in South African society: rich white households at the top, coloured, Indian, and urban African households in the middle, and rural African households at the bottom (with considerable variation between different rural areas). Race thus broadly coincided with class, except that the African population was becoming increasingly heterogeneous as people moved into the expanding urban working class.

We should note that an analysis performed in terms of households obscures inequalities within them, especially along lines of gender. As Van Onselen's biography of Kas Maine shows, patriarchal heads of household sought to monopolise control over the family's resources. In addition, many of the poorest households were headed by women or comprised primarily women and children. In a society and economy in which there was work for almost anyone who was prepared and able to migrate to it, the poor were generally those who could not work, whether because of age, infirmity, or the legal or social obstacles to migration facing rural women. In Keiskammahoek, 38 percent of heads of household were widows (Houghton and Walton 1952, 55); these households were especially prone to poverty.

Finally, the importance of household composition meant that it is probable also that incomes varied dramatically across the life cycle. Inequality of incomes across lifetimes would have been lower than inequality of incomes at any point in time. Individual African men and women might grow up in households in the poorest deciles, then, during their peak working years, be in households in higher deciles, before reverting to lower deciles after they had ceased to work.

THE PRE-APARTHEID DISTRIBUTIONAL REGIME

The patterns of inequality discussed above were in large part due to the process of economic development and only to a small extent to the *direct* interventions of the state via taxation, public welfare, and other social policies. Public expenditure on welfare accounted for only one-twentieth of total government spending and less than 1 percent of GDP in the 1930s, although much larger sums were invested in public expenditure (Union of S.A. 1943b). At the outset of apartheid, provision of public welfare was very much residual, with the welfare regime having "liberal" features. But the state intervened actively with labour-market and growth path policies, building a generous welfare state for better-paid wage earners, that is, for a privileged minority defined largely by race (and gender, given that the wage earners were male breadwinners). And the entire economy was built on developmental foundations that underpinned extreme inequality. Pre-apartheid inequality was profoundly shaped by the pre-apartheid distributional regime.

The foundations of this regime were laid in the nineteenth and early twentieth centuries, as historians of Southern Africa have long made clear. Colonial settlement entailed not only the political subordination of the indigenous African population but also the taking of most of the land (and mineral rights), active discrimination in order to restrict African competition in agricultural markets, the imposition of taxes to compel rural African peasants to seek wage employment, and other actions intended to secure for white farmers cheap and unfree labour. In the early and mid-twentieth century, South African employers were constantly complaining of labour shortages. As in other parts of Africa, the labour supply was not unlimited, as imagined in the Lewis model (and the Kuznets curve, as we saw in Chapter 1). To the extent that South African employers were able to obtain cheap labour, it was largely because of this history of massive and brutal state interventions. This laid the basis for a highly unequal growth path.

Policies that secured a supply of cheap, unskilled labour not only were necessary for growth but also helped determine who got what in the growing capitalist economy. Opportunities for African farmers were severely curtailed. Farmers such as Kas Maine were unable to prosper on a sustained basis because, above all, they were unable to invest in land. Investment in livestock was too precarious in the absence of secure access to land. Land policy, and to a lesser extent policies concerning agricultural marketing and credit, prevented African farmers from competing with white farmers and limited their earnings.

More important, overall, were the policies that determined who got what in the industrial and urban sectors. The pre-apartheid distributional regime was characterised by labour-market, welfare, and growth path policies that privileged one section of the population ("insiders") while disadvantaging the rest ("outsiders"). The key components of the distributional regime were constructed in the ten or so years from 1924 onward as the state adopted policies that buttressed the incomes of poor and working-class white voters and their families (and to a lesser extent coloured voters and their families also). In the mid-1940s the distributional regime was modified somewhat as the state deracialised some of these policies, extending a range of benefits to African (and Indian) people. The difference between the late 1920s and early 1930s and the late 1930s and early 1940s was not simply that different political parties dominated the government. In addition, there was an important shift in the employment situation: the first period was one of labour surplus (high unemployment during the Great Depression), the second one of growing labour shortages (amid the subsequent boom). The policy framework that emerged reflected both contexts. By 1948, the general relation between state, market, and family in the provision of welfare had been established: the apartheid distributional regime was a slightly modified version of the regime that the National Party inherited in 1948.

The public provision of welfare in South Africa dates for the most part from the 1920s. Prior to the 1920s welfare was provided primarily by churches, with very limited help from the state. Organised white workers in some sectors had secured industry- or firm-specific disability insurance schemes, but the state's involvement was limited to poor relief, that is, ad hoc grants in cash and in kind that were administered by magistrates or by state-subsidised charities (Bottomley 1990; Iliffe 1987, 115–23; Duncan 1995, ch. 3). Funds for medical services to the poor came from the poor relief budget. The major exception to this picture of limited state involvement was public expenditure: schooling for white children was free in three provinces (and in the fourth, the Cape, from 1920 onward). In the early 1920s state spending on social services amounted to a little more than 5 percent of GDP. Two-thirds of this went to education, with much smaller amounts going to health and social security (Union of S.A. 1943b, 97).

Two factors led the state to accept greater responsibility for maintaining living standards: the militancy of the white working class and the "poor white" problem, which mainly entailed unemployment among unskilled, Afrikaans-speaking immigrants to towns from rural areas. Throughout the industrialised world, the urban, industrial working class was a powerful force in the expansion of the welfare state in the twentieth century. Using both the power of the vote and power in the streets and on the shop floor, the working class secured the deepening of what the British sociologist T. H. Marshall called "social citizenship," that is, the range of rights "from the right to a modicum of economic welfare and security to the right to share to the full in the social heritage and to live the life of a civilised being according to the standards prevailing in the society" (1992, 8).

In South Africa, working-class power was demonstrated dramatically in the Rand Revolt of 1922, when the army was deployed to suppress mine workers who rebelled against the mines' attempts to replace them with cheaper African workers (Davies 1979, 145–75), and in the 1924 general election, which returned a coalition of the socialist Labour Party and the (Afrikaner) Nationalist Party as the "Pact Government." In both cases, it was the *white* working class that mobilised against white economic elites. By means of the ballot box and the threat of revolutionary struggles in the streets, the white working class in South Africa secured a considerable measure of social citizenship—but on a racially discriminatory basis. White workers mobilised under the slogan "Workers of the World Unite for a White South Africa." Social citizenship was to be largely confined to them.

The well-being of white workers was secured primarily by labour policies that ensured raised earnings. The first major legislative concession to white workers came just before the 1924 election, with the Industrial Conciliation Act. The act provided the machinery for collective bargaining at the industry level between representative trade unions and employers associations. Bargaining covered the setting of a minimum wage in areas covered by industrial councils. The act gave official recognition to white and mixed trade unions but excluded most African workers from the definition of "employee," thereby barring them from the collective bargaining machinery. White workers were thus in a position to negotiate binding minimum wages for all grades of work, while the mass of unskilled African workers had no say in the negotiations. Furthermore, trade unions were empowered by the act to negotiate agreements with employers that restricted employment to trade union members only. Because African workers were not able to join trade unions, white unions were able to impose colour bars via the closed shop. Craft unions in building, construction, and mining made particular use of this provision (Van der Horst 1981, 43–44). The colour bar was reinstated and reinforced in the mining industry in the 1926 Mines and Works Amendment Act. White workers used statutory job reservation and discriminatory collective bargaining legislation to secure privileged jobs and incomes. The government established the Department of Labour, largely to protect the interests of white workers.

Unskilled white workers required additional intervention. They formed the core of the "poor white problem." The decline of sharecropping among white farmers resulted in migration to the towns and high rates of unemployment and poverty. By the late 1920s one-sixth of the white population (most of whom had once been small farmers and sharecroppers) was estimated to be "living in great poverty"; almost all were Afrikaans and unskilled (Iliffe 1987, 117). The Pact Government formulated a "civilised labour policy," defining "civilised labour" as "the labour rendered by persons whose standard of living conforms to the standard of living generally recognised as tolerable from the usual European standpoint," in contrast to "uncivilised labour [, which] is to be regarded as the labour rendered by persons whose aim is restricted to the bare requirements of the necessities of life as understood among barbarous and undeveloped peoples" (quoted in Van der Horst 1942/1971, 250). Evidence of what constituted a civilised standard was heard by a government commission in 1925: "The term 'civilised' would appear to be a variant of 'living' or 'reasonable' as applied to a European in South Africa. So far as we were able to follow the witnesses who used the term, they meant by it the standard represented by the highest wage earned by a skilled artisan in one of the higher wage centres of the country. If this be its meaning, it is obviously a misnomer; for the level of real wages in such countries as Belgium, Germany, and Italy is only half that of the white artisan in South Africa." The question facing the commission, it seemed, was: "Is a Native servant essential to a civilised existence?" (quoted in ibid., 254).

In practice, the civilised labour policy entailed measures to bolster employment among unskilled white workers combined with measures to raise their earnings. The government replaced black workers with white workers at higher wages, especially on the railways and in the harbours. Between 1924 and 1933 the number of white labourers employed by these industries grew fourfold, rising from less than 10 percent to 40 percent of the total (ibid., 251). The Pact Government also used preferential tariffs and access to government contracts to reward firms that employed a high ratio of civilised to uncivilised labour. This treatment notwithstanding, the global recession of 1929–32 resulted in high unemployment among white workers. Registered unemployment among white and coloured workers together reached 188,000 (or 22 percent) in September 1933; the total number of poor white people reached 300,000 (O'Meara 1983, 37). The state responded in the short term with massive public works programmes paid for by general government revenue (Wilson and Ramphele 1989, 317–8). More important in the medium term were the civilised labour policies, which ensured that when the economy resumed its growth, white workers would be the first to benefit. In the mid-1930s the economy recovered rapidly, with industrial employment rising by a massive 14 percent per year. During 1936 about 140,000 white and coloured workers experienced unemployment, but for an average (among white workers) of only fifty-six days; the overall unemployment rate was thus less than 3 percent (Smith and Byron 1941). The privileged position of white workers during this boom was reflected in the declining proportion of black workers in manufacturing. The ratio of black to white labour in manufacturing fell from 1.76 in 1923–24 to 1.43 in 1938–39 (Archer 1989).

The Pact Government also ensured that employment did not entail low wages by setting minimum wages for workers not covered by collectively bargained agreements. The Wage Board, established according to the 1925 Wages Act, set wages for all workers (black and white) who were not covered by industrial councils, but it pursued the interests of unskilled African workers with different degrees of vigour over time (Nattrass 1990). Its initial policy was to set wages in predominantly white occupations so as to be in line with the civilised labour policy and to set minimum wages in African occupations at subsistence level. Later, by setting high minimum wages for more skilled occupations, the state prevented the more highly skilled black workers from undercutting white workers by accepting lower wages for the same jobs; without the incentive to cut costs, few employers would employ black workers rather than white workers at the same wage rate. This system served as a subtle colour bar.

Radical scholars have argued that "there was no dramatic increase in wage rates" for white workers under the Pact Government; "the workers' state (even the white workers' state) was a myth" (Davies et al. 1976, 11). The state remained dependent on the gold mines for tax revenue, and the Pact Government was wary of intervening (Yudelman 1983). But the effects of the Pact Government's policies should be assessed with respect to employment as much as wages. As revisionist scholars (including Davies et al.) acknowledge, there was increased employment for poor whites. Given the recessionary conditions at the end of the 1920s and the early 1930s, protected employment was a major gain. Furthermore, one might expect that the employment of unskilled white workers would depress *average* wages for white workers. The fact that average wages did not drop showed that labour-market policies protected wages as well as employment.

By making tariff protection conditional on firms' employing adequate quantities of civilised labour, the Pact Government set South Africa on a Latin American—style growth path of inward industrialisation, in which industry was given tariff protection as compensation for paying higher wages. This enabled firms to pass some of the costs of higher wages onto consumers in the form of higher prices. Although this injected inflationary pressures into the economy, the monetary authorities never allowed it to get out of control. This contrasts sharply with the Latin American experience, in which destabilising swings in demand erupted regularly as governments tried to satisfy competing claims with expansionary policies (Dornbusch and Edwards 1990; Haggard 1990). By focusing on labour-market and trade policies to protect a relatively small elite of white workers (rather than attempting to support the incomes of the entire working class, black and white, as was the case with regard to Latin America), the apartheid state was able to channel income into white hands without losing control of the macroeconomy.

The white working class was not the only constituency to benefit from the Pact Government's initiatives. White farmers, who were overwhelmingly Afrikaans, also benefited handsomely. Previous governments had favoured agriculture, but small farmers were especially advantaged by the Pact Government, which sought to move poor white people back onto the land (Morrell 1987, Schirmer 2003, 2–3). The state moved to subsidise production, support domestic prices, and protect farmers from international competition with tariffs. Farmers were provided with cheap credit, export subsidies, and preferential railway tariffs. A massive parastatal system for marketing produce was used to maintain high producer prices, with the cost passed onto consumers. As a result, consumers paid local prices that were higher than world prices, and agricultural exports declined despite the economic boom of the 1930s (Jeeves and Crush 1997, 5–12; Schirmer 2003). State interventions, especially those affecting the marketing system, served not only to boost farmers' incomes but also to protect them against risk.

The Pact Government also took the first steps in establishing a more comprehensive public welfare system, and further progress was made by its successors. The existing piecemeal and fragmented system, dependent on magistrates and charities, was seen to be incapable of coping with the severity of the "poor white problem," especially with the onset of recession. Welfare became the state's responsibility. The 1928 Old Age Pensions Act provided for noncontributory old age pensions, subject to a means test, for white and coloured men aged sixty-five or older and to white and coloured women aged sixty or older. In practice, many white families were covered by superior private occupational retirement schemes, and only a small proportion of the white population was dependent on the government's pensions (Van der Berg 1997, 486). Most white pensioners thus received pensions related to their former earnings; only the poorest were compelled to resort to the ungenerous public system. A Department of Social Welfare was established in 1933 (initially within the Department of Labour). In 1936, pensions were introduced for blind white and coloured people. The following year, these groups became eligible for disability grants, child maintenance grants were introduced (also on a discriminatory basis), and provision for the temporarily unemployed was introduced with the contributory Unemployment Insurance Fund (UIF). Although nonracial in design, the UIF excluded "native labourers" by setting the minimum income restriction for participation sufficiently high to exclude African workers (Meth and Piper 1984). Free medical services were introduced. The state also introduced subsidies for low-cost housing for poor white people. Faced with racially mixed slums, the government adopted further legislation that enabled it to expropriate an entire area; black residents could be removed to segregated residential areas, and white residents could be rehoused in sub-economic housing (Parnell 1989, 265–67).

Most of these new welfare programmes took the form of means-tested social assistance, not social insurance (the UIF was the exception). In other, not dissimilar societies at the time, such as Brazil's, immigrant workers in urban or industrial employment secured welfare reform in the form of employment-related social insurance. There appear to be two major reasons why the South African state opted for social assistance instead: it was favoured in Britain and its dominions (especially Australia and New Zealand), and there was concern for poor white people who would not be covered by social insurance schemes based on contributions made while formally employed.

The consequence of these policy shifts was rising public spending on redistributive programmes. Although public expenditure remained more or less steady as a proportion of GDP during the 1920s and 1930s, there was rapid growth in social security (which rose threefold as a share of GDP) and assistance to farmers. Education, however, remained the largest item of social expenditure (Union of S.A. 1943b).

The labour and welfare system developed in the 1920s and 1930s was focused on white households with a well-paid male breadwinner. Labour market policies ensured that unemployment was generally low and wages high, so that adult men had jobs with so-called civilised wages. The Wage Board assumed that the wage was a family wage. Welfare policies provided a safety net for households that did not have a male wage earner, whether because of temporary unemployment (via unemployment insurance), sickness or disability, old age, or the need for the nonworking mother to look after the children. The model assumed that a woman's place was at home; there was no assistance for working mothers. Nonetheless, it would be wrong to see the policies as the product of struggles by the male working class only. Du Toit (1996) shows how Afrikaner nationalist women fought and achieved modest victories against the presumption that poverty could only be due to unemployment. Child allowances were secured, social workers were subsidised, and the Department of Social Welfare was separated from the Department of Labour. The allocation of any money to welfare reflected the recognition that poverty had various causes. The nascent South African welfare state did not simply follow what Skocpol (1992) has called the "paternalist" model, in which benefits were provided only for working men as heads of household with dependent women and children.

The new labour and welfare system provided major benefits to the privileged insiders, but could only do so by excluding outsiders. Born in the 1920s and 1930s, the policy framework was concerned in large part with a lack of employment at wages deemed to be civilised. Protecting jobs *and* wages required that outsiders bear the burden of unemployment during periods of slow growth or recession. During the depression of 1929–32, especially, the burden of poverty was passed to retrenched African migrants from rural areas, as the 1932 Native Wages Commission found, and Africans were the last to benefit from renewed growth in the mid-1930s. Similarly, the provision of generous welfare benefits to a needy few could only be financed if the overwhelming majority of poor families were not allowed to press claims. The division between insiders and out-siders was drawn primarily along racial lines. Policies served to boost the earn-ings of white workers and provided protection for white families in times of need. The level of grants and pensions going to white people was roughly dou-ble that going to their coloured counterparts. Africans and Indians were almost entirely excluded from benefits. Africans were excluded from the old-age pen-sion on the grounds that their position and lifestyles did not warrant it. A gov-ernment commission later reported that Africans in rural areas had been "ex-cluded from old-age pension mainly on the assumption that Native custom makes provision for maintaining dependent persons," while "urban Natives were excluded in consequence, regardless of their needs, owing 'to the difficulty of applying any statutory distinction between them and other Natives'" (Union of S.A. 1943a, 20, quoting an earlier government inquiry into pensions). Simi-larly, child maintenance grants were not paid to rural African mothers because of "the fact that under Native law it is the natural duty of the head of the kraal or guardian-at-law to support any minor belonging to his kraal or under his care"; indeed, "the granting of maintenance by the state will probably lead to an eva-sion of the responsibility" (ibid., 61). The assumption underlying these plans was surely that peasant agriculture and migrant remittances together were suffi-cient to support Africans. Thus the state promoted the model of a household headed by a male breadwinner among white citizens and the model of a famil-ial, peasant-based household among its African subjects.

Not all state officials agreed that the boundary between insiders and out-siders should be drawn along strict racial lines. The first chairman of the Wage Board declared that the board's aims included safeguarding "civilised standards of living for all classes of workers irrespective of race or colour" (quoted in Van der Horst 1942/1971, 253). The inclusion of skilled African workers within the ambit of civilised labour was a chronic source of dispute. The pro-exclusion ar-gument had been set out clearly by the architect of influx control and residen-tial segregation, Charles Stallard, in 1923: "To exempt from the pass and regis-tration laws the most skilled and educated native is to expose the white population to the most deadly competition which the black race is capable of offering, and to ensure the ultimate abandonment of the most hopeless portion of the white race to the most competent portion of the black race" (quoted in Parnell and Hart 1999, 372). This argument underpinned the push for com-plete segregation and systematic discrimination. The opposite argument emphasised the growing number of permanently urbanised or "detribalised" African people, who were generally more educated, had better-paid jobs, and (it was assumed) were cut off from rural support networks. A small group of liberal politicians and intellectuals sought to redefine the boundaries of civilised labour so as to include this minority of African people (along with most or all coloured and Indian people). They were to achieve brief prominence during the 1940s amid a blossoming of proposals for welfare reform. Ultimately, however, they enjoyed little real power and could not compete with the power of the white working class, particularly when the latter combined with farming interests under the umbrella of a growing pan-class Afrikaner nationalism. The black poor, of course, were marginalised politically and economically.

During the 1940s the highly racialised set of labour-market and welfare policies was reformed, albeit to a limited extent. These reforms followed from a wave of enthusiasm for broad state involvement in the provision of welfare that swept through South Africa. The wartime prime minister, J. C. Smuts, promised a more humane postwar order. This was not purely idealistic: the rapid growth of manufacturing meant that the urban African population grew, generating new concern about African poverty and productivity, and urban industrialists comprised a powerful lobby opposed to the high cost of skilled labour. Sustained economic expansion and a shortage of unskilled as well as skilled labour pushed employers and bureaucrats to consider how to raise productivity.

In 1943 the government appointed a committee to investigate social security. The Social Security Committee was clearly influenced by the Beveridge Plan, undertaken in Britain in 1942, and it sought a similarly comprehensive and unified social security system under the auspices of the state (Seekings 2000). The proposed system would comprise primarily a set of contributory (but state-subsidised) social insurance schemes with limited social assistance. The contributory scheme provided a wide range of benefits, whereas the noncontributory scheme offered only means-tested old-age and disability pensions. The proposals thus provided for provision against risk more than for redistribution from rich to poor. Indeed, the committee argued, the low level of development of South Africa meant that "income redistribution even when pushed to extreme lengths cannot at this stage eliminate poverty" (Union of S.A. 1943a, 6). The first of the two schemes was intended to cover white, coloured, and Indian people together with "urbanised" African people and some better-paid African farm workers. Benefits would be determined according to the race and the residence of the claimant, on the grounds that these reflected differences in the cost and standard of living (except that highly paid coloured, Indian, and African people would be allowed to enjoy the same benefits and pay the same contributions as white people; ibid., 27).

The cost of proposals amounted to about 7 percent of the net national income (ibid., 10). Contributions would only cover one-third of the total expense. A subsequent government report estimated that the marginal tax rate on an income of one thousand pounds per year would have to rise from the current 5 percent (approximately) to between 20 and 30 percent (Union of S.A. 1943b, 89). About 40 percent of the subsidies would go to white beneficiaries, more than one-third to African beneficiaries (mostly to the urbanised minority), and slightly less than one-quarter to coloured and Indian beneficiaries. The system would be modest compared to those introduced in Australia, New Zealand, and Britain, but it was exceptional in the developing world. The 1940s were times of worldwide concern with welfare, but in most of Africa, Asia, and the Caribbean, colonial states made agricultural development and the strengthening of agrarian society their priorities. It was only in isolated cases, including South Africa and parts of the Caribbean, that the state opted for pensions, recognising that the peasant economy and agrarian society were irretrievably disintegrating (Seekings 2003e).

Another government commission proposed similarly radical but expensive reforms to the public health system. A national Department of Public Health had been established long before, following the great flu epidemic of 1918. But resources were concentrated on hospitals, run by the provinces, while preventative services were neglected. Very high rates of tuberculosis and infant mortality among African people led to growing calls for a more systematic approach to health care. The wartime government appointed a National Health Services Commission, chaired by a reforming doctor, Henry Gluckman. The commission's report called for a unified health service, with extensive primary preventative services offered by four hundred health centres across the country, all financed by general tax revenue (Union of S.A. 1944a). These recommendations were "remarkably innovative," "revolutionary," and in line with, if not in advance of, those of similar commissions in the United Kingdom and elsewhere (Marks and Andersson 1992, 132, 155; see also De Beer 1984). It was estimated that this proposed National Health Service would cost 3.5 percent of GDP (Union of S.A. 1943a, 10).

Criticised by the opposition National Party and fearing a political backlash, the government scaled down the proposals substantially. Nonetheless, three major welfare reforms were introduced. First, under the 1944 Pension Laws Amendment Act, means-tested old-age pensions were extended to African and Indian people. Second, under the 1946 Unemployment Insurance Act, unemployment insurance was provided for most urban workers (except domestic workers, mine workers, and public-sector employees). The system was contributory, with contributions and benefits linked to income. Blindness and disability pensions were also extended to African and Indian people. Third, the government allocated much larger funds for the education of African children, abolishing the earlier restriction on spending to the value of taxes levied on African people. In 1943 school-feeding schemes were introduced for all children (although funding was racially biased). These reforms entailed a major shift in the coverage of the public welfare system. Furthermore, some saw them as a stepping-stone toward a fully comprehensive welfare system through which the state guaranteed a minimum income for all. Although no National Health Service was set up, the state did move toward greater coordination of health services and established fifty health centres.

The new welfare system was "residual" in at least two senses. First, the state only provided assistance when the private sector failed to do so. Thus most (white) citizens were expected to provide for their old age and for sickness via occupational pension schemes and private medical expenditure (or, increasingly, medical insurance). Second, the welfare system revolved around what the Social Security Committee had called "collective provision against the risk of want only in *the non-productive periods of life*," that is, childhood, sickness or disability, temporary unemployment, and retirement (Union of S.A. 1943a, 6, emphasis added). The system assumed that the government would use other policies to ensure that such "non-productive periods" did not include long spells of unemployment:

> To achieve Social Security in its real sense, it would be necessary to create favourable conditions of employment under which a minimum number of people would find themselves in need of direct assistance from the State. . . . The Government therefore aim at the creation of general economic conditions which will provide for a stable level of productive employment for all classes of the community. . . . There will, however, always be a residual problem relating to those individuals who, despite a general improvement in living conditions, are unable to maintain themselves according to certain simple standards, and it is mostly in respect of these individuals that the proposed arrangements are necessary. These arrangements . . . must not, however, be taken as derogating from the Government's over-all policy of large-scale employment, which is the only real and lasting basis of social security—in the broader sense. (Union of S.A. 1945, 3)

The importance of full employment for welfare was recognised also by capital, labour, and the representatives of the African population.

Assumptions about employment contributed to the welfare system's uneven coverage of African people in rural areas. Rural workers were excluded from unemployment insurance on several grounds. It was argued that they did not face involuntary unemployment; many experienced periods when they did not work, typically in between contracts or seasons, but this was voluntary joblessness in that they chose not to take up the offer of work that was always available. Insofar as rural people did face needs during periods of joblessness, they faced low costs because they paid nothing for housing and could grow most of their own food. The elderly and the disabled were, of course, exceptions to this, notwithstanding customary practices of sharing resources. The 1943 Social Security Committee had acknowledged that "Natives in the Reserves have shelter and can eke out an existence so that they do not need the *elaborate* cash benefits indispensable for a civilised community" but concluded nonetheless that *"nominal"* payments in cash and kind were "essential" for the elderly and the disabled. "It is true that Native custom provides for the maintenance of those who are old, ill, or orphans; but overcrowding of the Reserves, primitive farming methods and low unskilled wages make this increasingly difficult" (Union of S.A. 1943a, 6; emphases added). On white-owned farms, also, the breakdown of labour tenancy and increasing reliance on wages had exposed African people to poverty if or when individuals were unable to perform paid farm work.

The inclusion of Africans in the old-age pension and unemployment insurance schemes was strongly opposed by the National Party, then in opposition to the government. It was especially hostile to the Unemployment Insurance Act, which was to feature centrally in its election campaign in 1948. Some of their criticisms were explicitly racial. The NP protested against using white workers' contributions to pay benefits to unemployed African workers. It wanted separate funds to be set up for each racial group. But it transpired that African workers actually contributed to the fund more than they received in benefits in 1947–48 (as did all racial groups, allowing the fund to accumulate strong reserves during a period of low unemployment). When the NP came to power, it excluded (in effect) all African workers from the unemployment insurance system rather than establishing racially segregated schemes.

A more important criticism was that the provision of unemployment insurance for African workers encouraged "idleness" among them and actually increased unemployment. Members of parliament from the NP reported that the Unemployment Insurance Act was known as the "Loafers Act." As one MP, F. E. Mentz, put it: "It is now really a joy for the native to be unemployed" (*Hansard* 1947, col. 2094). This general view was shared by the National Party's constituents among white farmers and workers—and by the gold mines. The mines complained that their attempts to recruit workers from among the Africans waiting to claim unemployment insurance benefits had been unsuccessful because the benefits were so favourable relative to earnings: "At a time when so many employers are in need of Native labour, it is illogical that large numbers of Natives should be able to draw unemployment benefits and live in idleness at the expense of the state" (*Hansard* 1949, col. 6519). One of the first acts passed by the NP after its election in 1948 excluded African workers from the unemployment insurance system. The NP was opposed to the extension of old-age pensions to African people on the same grounds: that the payment of pensions had the effect of allowing pensioners and their dependents to remain idle rather than earn wages.

The relation between full employment and unemployment insurance was, in one sense, deeply ironic. The establishment of the UIF was premised on the state's capacity to maintain a high level of employment by means of other policies; unemployment insurance provided for temporary need. At the same time, the UIF was unpopular among employers and employees in part because the late 1940s had been "good times with comparatively full employment" (as the NP Minister of Labour put it—*Hansard* 1949, col. 6525). Racist beliefs about "native psychology" had rational underpinnings: white workers might have feared that the UIF would facilitate African competition for their jobs (by funding prolonged job search), while some employers clearly feared that the UIF tightened an already tight labour market, leading to wage increases. Scaling down the UIF was made easier by the weakness of opposition, itself due in part to the poor prospect of unemployment among white and African workers.

In other areas, too, the wartime government acted to raise the incomes of many African households. Even in the late 1930s, with a time of renewed economic growth, the colour bar was increasingly circumvented as white workers conceded African advancement in certain occupations in return for higher wages. Industrial action by African workers also prompted the Wage Board to raise minimum wages in many unskilled categories for the first time since 1928. During the war, the wages of African workers rose faster than those of white workers (Union of S.A. 1951b, 47). Faced with labour shortages, the wartime administration further authorised African people to work in skilled positions, and the number of pass law prosecutions declined dramatically (Siebert 1975, 56). African workers enjoyed stronger bargaining positions. Wage increases were controlled, but the government boosted the earnings of the unskilled and reduced the differential between high- and low-paid work, in part with "cost-of-living allowances" (Steenkamp 1962, 95). The Wage Board committed itself to increasing unskilled and semiskilled workers' wages on the grounds that they were "insufficient for the maintenance of a healthy existence" (Union of S.A. 1941, 31). When compulsory arbitration of industrial disputes was introduced in 1942, the Wage Board was often the arbitrator, resolving most disputes in favour of black workers (Siebert 1975, 50).

The wartime government headed by Smuts was remarkable in a number of respects, the importance of some of which would only be fully revealed many decades later. But there remained strict limits as to what this government would do to improve the postwar order. It was deemed unacceptable politically to impose high costs on white taxpayers (Duncan 1995, 88). Most dramatically, when African mine workers went on strike for higher wages in 1946, the government employed considerable force to suppress them (O'Meara 1975). As scholars in the radical tradition have emphasised repeatedly, this government (like its predecessors) sought to strengthen the country's capitalist economy. Welfare and labour-market reforms were seen as improving the efficiency of this capitalist economy, and not primarily in terms of the endowment of rights per se. But capitalism is not homogeneous with respect to distribution. The version of capitalism promoted by the Smuts government was a more inclusive form of welfare capitalism than its predecessors.

Chapter 3 Social Change
and Income Inequality
Under Apartheid

South African society was transformed during the four decades of apartheid. Processes of class formation remade town and countryside. The economy grew rapidly with industrialisation and the growth of services (including those in the public sector). A large, settled urban African working class was formed, and a significant African middle class emerged. As important, large numbers of African families lost access to land and became entirely (rather than primarily) dependent on wages. Throughout this period inequality remained at a high level. In the 1950s and 1960s this was clearly due in part to the direct effects of public policies of systematic racial discrimination and segregation. When, in the 1970s, the state began its slow retreat from direct racial discrimination in public policy, interracial inequality began to decline—but the overall level remained largely unchanged. Inequality under apartheid was not the product of public policy alone but rather resulted from the interaction of public policy and the dynamics of capitalist development. Marxist scholars have rightly emphasised the power of capitalism as a motor of social change, but they have focused too narrowly on the ways in which public policy was supposedly functional to the development of capitalism. Moreover, in neglecting Weber in their homage to Marx, they have underestimated the growing importance of education and skill in economic and social differentiation. In this chapter we examine the ways in which capitalist development transformed the social structure and patterns of economic inequality in South Africa.

There was nothing inevitable about the path of capitalist development in South Africa. At the start of Chapter 2 we considered two novels and a film that held out different images of South African society in the late 1940s. Each of the different visions they offered might (in some sense) have come about. The vision implicit in *Jim Comes to Jo'burg* was of a society that was semi-meritocratic: rural-born young men enjoyed opportunities for considerable occupational mobility, although these opportunities remained bounded (Jim might become a successful recording artist but would never be the owner of the recording company). For Paton, South Africa's future rested on the development of an African peasantry that adhered to classic middle-class values. In Abrahams's bleaker vision, South Africa's future lay in the communities built by immigrants in the towns. The first of these visions might have been achieved with a decline in racial discrimination, the second with land reform, and the third with unfettered urbanisation. Each path would have resulted in a distinctive social structure and corresponding pattern of inequality. There are examples from other parts of the world of countries that went down each of these paths. South Africa went down none of them because of the particular character of public policy. In Chapter 4 we examine in detail the ways in which public policy shaped inequalities under apartheid. For now we focus more on the changes in the social structure than on the policies that shaped them.

The power of capitalist development and, beginning in the 1970s, the retreat from overt racial discrimination combined to transform patterns of inequality in South Africa. At the outset of the apartheid period, race was clearly the key factor in inequality. There were highly rigid racial barriers to better-paying employment or opportunities for lucrative self-employment for African (and, to a lesser extent, coloured and Indian) people. Access to employment and land was tightly controlled. In the 1970s the racial barriers began to be less restrictive, in large part because new employment opportunities opened up for better-educated African workers. Education and skills became increasingly important in the determination of earnings and household incomes. Throughout the 1980s and into the 1990s, education and skills became ever more important, determining not only earnings but increasingly whether people found employment at all. As race and class ceased to be coterminous, class grew in importance.

DEAGRARIANISATION

The transformation of South African society after 1950 was not simply or primarily due to the further institutionalisation of policies of racial segregation and discrimination. Rather, it reflected broader processes of social change, processes that were profoundly shaped by state policy but not by the racial and labour policies most commonly associated with apartheid (by liberal and Marxist scholars, respectively). Overall, what had been a largely agrarian society became something else, although it is not easy to label what it became. One process that can be labelled easily is "deagrarianisation," which transformed rapidly the South African countryside. Within twenty years of Kas Maine's bumper harvest in the 1948–49 season, the last vestiges of an independent African peasantry were all but eliminated, both on white-owned farms and in the reserves. Without access to land, African families were unable to preserve their cattle holdings. The loss of land and cattle led to massive social disruption, with the effect that even rural society bore little resemblance to the agrarian society of the first half of the twentieth century. Landless African households were kept out of the towns by influx control legislation; urbanisation was thus displaced to the reserves. At the same time, however, there emerged for the first time a settled urban African population that had urban residency rights under influx control laws. The result was a new pattern of poverty and inequality: inequality became more intraracial and not simply interracial.

This transformation began on white-owned farms. Buoyant demand for agricultural products meant that landowners sought to utilise more of their land themselves, while mechanisation enabled them to do so without relying on the oxen, ploughs, or family labour of African households. In 1946 there were a mere 20,000 tractors in South Africa. By 1950 there were 48,000, by 1955, 87,000, and by 1960 almost 120,000. The number continued to rise, passing 150,000 by the end of the decade. The number of motor lorries also more than tripled between 1946 and 1960. Conversely, the number of horse-drawn wagons on white-owned farms declined from more than 100,000 in 1946 to fewer than 44,000 in 1955 (Houghton 1964, 65). Not long after complaining about labour shortages, many farmers declared African families to be "surplus" to their needs. At the same time, intensified racial hostility made it harder for white landlords to avoid either law or social pressure and allow African farmers access to land or markets. The *beswarting* (blackening) of the white-owned farming districts was deemed a threat to white society and power. The introduction of combine harvesters in the 1960s further reduced landowners' dependence on African labour (De Klerk

1984). The state showed great determination in this onslaught against labour-intensive forms of production (Marcus 1989, 58–69, 80–85). Sharecropping, already illegal, was stamped out; labour tenancy proved only somewhat more resilient, becoming illegal countrywide in 1980. African people were denied access to land outside of the reserve, and those that were "surplus" to white farmers' needs were removed to the reserves, by force when necessary.

Independent production declined steadily in importance for African households on white-owned farm land. Simkins (1984a) estimates that the total value of agricultural production peaked in 1953, while income from paid work on farms rose steadily. But rising population meant a steady decline in production per capita. In the aggregate, the proportion of total income derived from agricultural production declined from about 20 percent in 1950 to less than 15 percent in the early 1960s and less than 10 percent by the end of the decade.

These figures are given a human face in Van Onselen's biography of Kas Maine. For Maine, the decline from success to poverty was rapid. In the winter of 1949, immediately after his spectacular harvest, Maine and the other "rich 'kaffirs' who owned spans of oxen" were summoned to a meeting; a state official told them that sharecropping would no longer be tolerated; they would have to sell their oxen or move to the reserves; henceforth, labourers would be employed only to drive the tractors and trucks that were replacing their oxen. Van Onselen writes: "For 'rich kaffirs' the old order had suddenly given way; for those who remained behind what little there was left of paternalism served only to grease the slippery slope of proletarianisation" (1997, 212; 1996, 314–15). Maine desperately but unsuccessfully sought to defy the changes, moving from farm to farm. But by 1956 his once-large herds had shrunk to two horses, two donkeys, twenty head of cattle, and twenty-five sheep and goats. Unable to continue sharecropping in the ever-harsher economic and political climate, Maine moved first to one of the "black spot" farms—African-owned freehold land acquired before 1913. Later he was forced on, again, into an arid reserve, taking with him only five horses and four head of cattle.

Mechanisation also transformed production on the few black spot farms. Ownership of or access to land did not necessarily mean that it could be farmed, because few families had sufficient oxen for ploughing, and tractors were expensive. According to Petrus Pooe, who farmed at Magopa in the 1960s and 1970s:

> The only group of people who are capable of producing enough from the fields are those who have tractors. In fact the tractor owners are the people who are making

money here. If they plough for you, out of ten bags you, the owner of the land, get one bag. Some of them do get sympathetic with their clients. If you are lucky you might get as many as two bags. Beyond that you get nothing. What I am saying is that we have the land, but we are incapable of putting it to use. Only those with tractors can. In order to survive as a farmer you must have a tractor. Apart from its being expensive you also have to hire a driver if you buy one. (quoted in Keegan, 1988, 124–25)

Mechanisation thus not only accentuated inequality between white and black people in the South African countryside but also accentuated inequality between African households.

Maine's move to a reserve was typical of the time. More than one million people, about one-third of the resident African population, were removed from white-owned farms to the reserves; half a million people were removed from black spots as they, too, were cleared (Platzky and Walker 1985, 10–11).[1] As table 3.1 shows, the proportion of the African population living in rural areas outside the reserves fell from about 35 percent in 1950 to about 25 percent in 1970 and about 20 percent in 1980; the proportion in the bantustans rose from 40 percent through the 1950s to more than 50 percent by the late 1970s (Simkins 1983, 53–57; 1998, 6). African families from white-owned farms were very vulnerable. Most had no right to seek work in towns, and most had no claim to land in the reserves (F. Wilson 1975a, 175).

Many of the families cleared from white farms were former labour tenants. Labour tenancy had survived as long as it had because white landowners, faced with labour shortages, were prepared to give up the use of some of their land in order to secure labour. The state responded by building a system to allocate African labour to the struggling farmers who were unable to compete successfully for labour in the open market and later by encouraging the replacement of African farm labour by machinery (as we shall see in Chapter 5). In 1956 the state began to regulate closely the number of labour tenants. They had to be registered, and farmers could be ordered to eject "excessive" tenants. The system proved difficult to operate, however, because some farmers were not cooperative and could disguise labour tenants as farm workers. In addition, labour tenants themselves continued to play farmers against each other in their search for better access to land. The failure of partial regulation led the Nel Commission of Enquiry to recommend in 1960 the complete abolition of labour tenancy: Africans should have no alternative to paid work, at whatever wages white farmers offered (Schirmer 1994). At the same time, the advent of the tractor (together with the provision of prison labour to farmers) was reducing farmers'

Table 3.1. Distribution of the African population, 1950–85

	Farms (%)	Reserves (%)	Towns (%)
1950	35	40	25
1960	32	39	29
1970	24	48	28
1980	21	53	26
1985	12	53	35

Source: Simkins (1983, 1998).

need for labour tenants. The number registered peaked at 163,000 at the end of 1964 (RSA 1966). Thereafter, the number of new labour tenancy contracts registered each year declined.[2] From 1968 onward the state began to abolish labour tenancy in selected districts. In the 1970s it remained legal in Natal only, and then only until 1980. It was these former labour tenants who formed the bulk of the "surplus" population removed from white farming districts. Illegal labour tenancy persisted but on a much smaller scale than hitherto (see further Williams 1996).

The decline of labour tenancy represented the continuation of the long, slow process of proletarianisation outside of the reserves. Many Africans continued to live and work on the farms. Indeed, the absolute number of Africans on white-owned farms actually rose slightly in the 1950s, 1960s, and 1970s: it was the surplus population caused by natural demographic growth that was removed. The African households that remained on white farms were still dependent on agriculture, but now they were fully proletarianised, entirely dependent on wages (and in-kind payments) from their employer. Society in these areas thus remained agrarian, but in a different sense than before. African society could no longer revolve around land and cattle. Economic change precipitated social disintegration, as patriarchs no longer had control over the resources that had allowed them to hold multigenerational families together. Young men who escaped to the mines or the towns became ever less likely to return, and farmers would often evict retired farm workers whose children were not working on the farms (Schirmer 1994; Murray 1992, 214–18).

Deagrarianisation was most evident in the reserves, where a rapidly growing proportion of the population lived. Forced removals from the farms combined with natural population growth and tightened controls on emigration to the cities, with the result that average population density in the reserves almost doubled between 1955 and 1969. The total value of agricultural production remained steady, but the value per capita fell rapidly. By 1967 agricultural production accounted for only about one-quarter of the reserve population's food requirements and one-sixth of total subsistence requirements (Simkins 1981c; see also Lenta 1981, 23).

The effects of this are summed up in the title of a chapter concerning this period in Delius's history of Sekhukhuneland: "The Cattle Are Gone." The population of Sekhukhuneland (in the Northern Transvaal) soared as former labour tenants were evicted from white farms. The first to arrive were permitted to bring some cattle with them and often secured access to fields. By the 1960s, however, new arrivals were required to sell all livestock except poultry and were given quarter-acre building plots only. The importance of cattle declined even where households had nominal access to land, because the expansion of schooling meant that boys were no longer readily available to herd cattle at "cattle posts," that is, grazing areas distant from villages. As the cattle post system collapsed, the remaining cattle were kept in the villages, leading to erosion of the local veld and increased vulnerability to drought and disease. Inadequate supervision also led to a rising incidence of stock theft. "By the 1980s, only a minority of households in the region still had stock and the herds that remained were dominated by goats and sheep" (Delius 1996, 146). A detailed study of two villages in the area found that only one in four households owned any livestock; only one in ten owned cattle in the one village, and one in six in the second (Baber 1998, 292–95). Lacking oxen, and without the means to hire tractors, families with access to land could rarely plough it. Many supposedly rural areas were, in practice, thoroughly urban. QwaQwa represented an extreme form of this postagrarian "rural" area (see Slater 2002).

Removals from white farms were less important in the case of Transkei than on the highveld. But in the Transkei, too, the population doubled between 1946 and 1985. Total cattle holdings—for which there are good data—remained broadly stable, but a growing proportion of households had no cattle at all. In the 1940s perhaps one-third of African households in the reserves had no cattle. By the late 1970s, perhaps one-half had none, with at most 15 percent owning ten or more head (Beinart, 1992).

The state, seeking to maintain agricultural production in the reserves and thus a peasantry of sorts, had for several decades implemented piecemeal "betterment" policies. These involved primarily the control of livestock and the reorganisation of land use. In the 1940s the state had begun to look at dividing the population of the reserves into a class of supposedly viable peasant farmers and a class of landless wage labourers, and this idea was pushed by the Tomlinson Commission (Union of S.A. 1955a). The commission's brief had been "to conduct a comprehensive inquiry into and to report upon a comprehensive scheme for the rehabilitation of the Native Areas with a view to developing within them a social structure in keeping with the culture of the Native and based on effective socio-economic planning" (ibid., xviii). This emphasis on the "development" of peasant agriculture was not specific to South Africa; historians have described the dispersion of colonial agricultural officers across East Africa as a "second colonial occupation" (Lonsdale and Low, cited in Freund 1984, 194). In South Africa, however, the reserves were already unlikely locations for a thriving peasantry (as the government had recognised in the 1940s, prompting welfare reform). The Tomlinson Commission recognised that the "Bantu areas cannot carry their present population as full-time farmers" (Union of S.A. 1995a, 113) and proposed relocating half of the reserve population to villages. The remaining half, it was proposed, would be given individual tenure in place of the existing communal tenure and would develop into a class of viable peasant farmers. The government did implement a watered-down version of betterment planning, including some villagisation, but held back from following the course of private ownership recommended by the commission (De Wet 1995, ch. 3; Ashforth 1990, ch. 5). Instead, it implemented policies of forced removal from the white farms, further undermining agricultural activity in the reserves.

The proliferation of research in rural areas in the 1980s allows us to detail the kind of society that emerged from these processes of change. Remittances sent by absent family members were already important by 1950, as shown by Houghton and Walton (1952) for Keiskammahoek, but in the subsequent decades they became ever more important. Studies of the Transkei in 1982 showed that more than two-thirds of the income of poor and middle-income households came from remittances; about one-sixth, on average, came from old-age pensions and the remaining one-sixth from wages in local jobs; the contribution from agricultural production was insignificant (F. Wilson and Ramphele 1989, 62–63). Social and economic change accentuated inequality in the reserves. In one area of the Transkei, the average monthly income of the top 10 percent of households was fifteen times that of the poorest 10 percent. Income was so low among the poor that "it becomes difficult to afford food apart from simple mielie-meal, samp and porridge, clothing is a luxury, and schooling cost impossible—thus ensuring that the legacy of abject poverty is passed on to the next generation" (T. Moll 1984, 38). Only in a few areas did subsistence agriculture remain significant. One such area was Mahlabatini, in Kwa-Zulu, and even there remittances were more important than agricultural production (F. Wilson and Ramphele 1989, 70–71). Some people prospered, including especially some shopkeepers and other businessmen who benefited from a growing, if poor, market (Sharp 1994). Workers in government-subsidised bantustan industries or who commuted to white towns fared better than most, but such opportunities were scarce and the wages were generally low (Slater 2002).

Simkins estimated changing patterns of income distribution in the reserves between 1960 and 1980. He concluded that income inequality had risen but that a large majority of households actually had rising absolute incomes during this period. The clear losers were the poorest 5 percent, who "were destitute in 1960 and remained so in 1980," and households from the fifth to the fifteenth percentile, which "suffered a deterioration in absolute terms since 1960 because of increasing landlessness and unemployment" (Simkins 1984b, 259). Households between the fifteenth and the thirtieth percentiles had higher absolute incomes, but their incomes had declined relative to the median, whereas the top 70 percent of households had rising absolute and relative incomes. For most households in the reserves, if not all, the shortage of land meant that agriculture made a declining contribution to income. But for many households this was more than compensated for by rising income from other sources, especially remittances and pensions.

Other studies suggest that these years saw an explosion in migrancy rates and presumably therefore a big increase in remittances to rural areas. The number of officially registered migrants from the Transkei rose from less than 30,000 in 1968 to 425,000 in 1978. Thereafter, however, migrancy—and remittances—declined. In the 1980s, more rural men worked in areas close enough to their homes to commute. Typically, these jobs were low-paying. Longitudinal data from Venda indicate a sharp drop in the 1980s in the share of income coming from remittances sent from outside the bantustan. This contributed to rising inequality within Venda and in other rural areas (Leibbrandt and Woolard 1999).

Social and economic change was reflected in changing patterns of rural politics. Popular grievances and demands changed, as did the repertoire of actions on which people drew. In the 1940s and 1950s, popular politics in the reserves was generally defensive in that people resisted the imposition of betterment regulations and new administrative structures. In areas such as Sekhukhuneland, which rose in revolt in the 1950s, men (and women) sought to keep one foot in an agrarian society while keeping the other in the industrial sector as migrant labour. In Delius's words: "A determination to hold the market and the white state at bay, and a last-ditch defence of land, livestock and chieftainship, lay at the core of the 1950s struggle." The prospect of economic benefits from betterment seems to have mobilised very few rural people in support of change. In the 1980s Sekhukhuneland again rose in revolt, but now it was led by the "comrades," young men out of school and out of work. "The comrades in 1986 barely mentioned land or cattle, and were profoundly critical of chiefly rule. Their primary concern was not with autonomy but with changing the terms of their participation in a common society. . . . In particular, the comrades were determined that unskilled and migrant labour, which had so often been the lot of their less-educated parents, should not be their fate. At the very least, their imagined future depicted them in white collar jobs" (1996, 221). This directs our analysis to parallel changes in urban society.

THE TRANSFORMATIONS OF URBAN SOCIETY

Economic growth and technological change were motors of social change in the towns as well as in the countryside. Between 1950 and 1980 the economy more than tripled in size. Even in per capita terms—that is, taking into account the steady growth of the population—the economy grew by about 75 percent (RSA 1994, 21.5–21.6). Agricultural production grew, but the spectacular growth lay in the industrial and service sectors. In manufacturing, for example, employment tripled between 1950 and 1980 from fewer than half a million to almost one and a half million workers (ibid., 7.4). The industrial and service sectors not only grew but were also transformed by technological change. Just as tractors transformed the countryside, so new machinery transformed factories, building sites, mines, and offices. These economic changes wrought a transformation of the class structure, which in turn had far-reaching political implications.

The official Manpower Surveys provide an indication of the shifting class structure (see table 3.2). Unfortunately, the first year for which there are survey data is 1965, and the Manpower Surveys exclude agricultural and domestic employment. In the sectors that are covered, however, there is a clear shift between 1965 and 1992 (Crankshaw 1997a). The proportion of employment in unskilled occupations declines markedly, whereas there is a rise in the proportion of jobs in managerial, supervisory, professional, and semiprofessional occupations (the latter including primarily teaching and nursing). For people with the skills,

Table 3.2. Structure of employment (as covered by
Manpower Surveys), 1965 and 1992

	1965 (%)	1992 (%)	Change (%)
Top and middle managers	2.5	4.4	216
Professionals	1.2	3.1	360
Semiprofessionals	6.4	12.1	237
Routine white-collar workers	17.8	16.5	65
Routine security personnel	2.4	4.6	247
Supervisors	0.9	3.5	599
Artisans and apprentices	6.2	5.1	46
Semiskilled operatives	29.7	27.1	62
Unskilled manual workers	28.5	18.1	13
Unskilled menial workers	4.5	5.6	123
Total	100.0	100.0	78

Source: Data provided by Owen Crankshaw.

qualifications, racial classification, or pass law status to be able to secure employment in the expanding, better-paying classes, the period was one of rising prosperity. For people competing for the stagnant number of unskilled jobs, the period was one of continuing or deepening hardship.

The period after 1950 was one of unprecedented prosperity for white South Africans. The white population became almost entirely urban and employed in white-collar rather than blue-collar occupations. The proportion of Afrikaans-speaking white workers in agricultural occupations fell from 30 percent in 1946 to 16 percent in 1960 and 8 percent in 1970. The proportion in blue-collar and other manual labour remained stable through the 1950s but fell rapidly in the 1960s and 1970s. Conversely, the proportion in white-collar employment rose from 29 percent in 1946 to 65 percent in 1977. This was a period of widespread upward mobility into the middle and managerial classes (O'Meara 1996, 138). English-speaking whites also benefited from occupational change, if they benefited less from state patronage specifically. Upward mobility continued through the 1980s (Lipton and Simkins 1993, 9). Real per capita incomes among the white population more than doubled between 1947 and 1975 (McGrath 1990, 95). "Low density suburbs with modern detached houses in gardens, some with swimming pools, proliferated," and car ownership rocketed (Beinart 1994, 174). Not everyone benefited equally. McGrath (1983) found that inequality grew within the white population at the same time as inter-ethnic inequality declined. Even among Afrikaners, inequality changed little (Steenekamp, cited in Giliomee 1999, 89).

These economic changes also brought prosperity to most of the urban coloured and Indian population. Semiskilled, skilled, and white-collar employment grew rapidly as the economy expanded, and most coloured and Indian workers were able to move into better-paying occupations. The class composition of the Indian population was transformed as Indians moved into middle-class occupations (Lipton and Simkins 1993, 9). With regard to the coloured population, the number of workers in unskilled jobs (outside of agriculture) rose slightly in the twenty years after 1965 but the number in semiskilled and artisanal employment doubled, and the number in semiprofessional employment (primarily teaching) and in routine white-collar jobs tripled (Crankshaw 1997a, 144–50). Employment for women changed especially rapidly. Employment in domestic service declined in importance, but more and more women found jobs in factories and offices. The number of coloured and Indian women employed in routine white-collar jobs grew from about eleven thousand in 1965 to almost one hundred thousand by 1985 (ibid., 159). Not everyone shared in this prosperity. Goldin (1987, 174) estimates that as many as one hundred thousand coloured farm workers were made redundant by mechanisation, especially on the wheat farms of the Boland. Although they, unlike most African families, were able to move from the farms to the towns and cities, many experienced unemployment there because they lacked the skills for the better jobs and were unable to compete with African labourers for unskilled work.

The 1960s saw coloured workers move into better-paid job, but also saw many coloured families fall victim to forced removal by the state. As many as six hundred thousand coloured and Indian people were forcibly removed under the Group Areas Act (Beinart 1994, 147). Although employed in more highly skilled and better paid-jobs than their African counterparts, many coloured and Indian working-class families lived in run-down and crime-ridden areas. This provided conditions in which radical civic organisations emerged and briefly flourished in the late 1970s and early 1980s. In the mid-1970s, reformist National Party leaders recognised that the support of coloured and Indian South Africans was crucial to any successful counterrevolutionary project. The government therefore sought to encourage a nascent process of embourgeoisement of these groups, investing heavily in housing, infrastructural development, health facilities, and schooling, as well as promising a degree of inclusion within the framework of representative democracy (Goldin 1987, 178–89).

Upward occupational mobility among coloured and Indian people was based on improved public education. The 1960s and 1970s also saw a rapid expansion of secondary and tertiary education for these groups (although not on the same scale as among African people, as we shall see). In 1960 there were fewer than 40,000 coloured and Indian students in the top five years of school. This number grew sixfold by 1983, when it stood at almost 235,000. The number of students in standard 10 rose from about 1,500 to 20,000. The number of coloured and Indian students at residential universities rose from fewer than 2,000 in 1960 to more than 14,000 in 1983 (SAIRR 1961, 1962, 1971, 1983).

One dramatic reflection of these processes of economic and social change among coloured families was greatly improved health. Urbanisation, better schooling, and rising incomes contributed to a decrease in the infant mortality rate among coloured children of 9 percent per year between 1970 and 1985. As Eberstadt notes: "Hardly any other population on record has to date enjoyed such a rapid and sustained pace of improvement in child survival" (1992, 160). Fertility rates also declined.

The growing, changing economy brought huge changes to the urban African population also. Despite influx control, this population grew steadily during the postwar decades. From about 2.2 million in 1951 it increased to 3.4 million in 1960, 4.4 million in 1970, and 5.6 million by 1980 (Simkins 1982b). This growth was accompanied by change in just about every aspect of life: schooling, work, household structure, living conditions, culture and leisure activity, and politics. Between the 1940s and the 1970s the urban African population was transformed from one undergoing urbanisation to one that was clearly urbanised. In 1950, as we have seen, most urban men and women had been born and raised in rural areas, only later migrating to the towns. Such first-generation immigrants only slowly began to think of themselves as settled urban residents rather than migrants (Bonner 1995). By the 1970s, however, much of the urban population had put down deep roots. This shift was especially dramatic on the Witwatersrand, which accounted for more than half of the urban African population.

This transformation was in part the result of government policies. In the 1940s, newly urban workers invaded land and established squatter settlements. The state responded by setting up "site and service" schemes (in which residents received a site with sewerage and other infrastructure but no actual house) and then (in the 1950s) building tens of thousands of small brick houses ("matchbox" houses) in new townships like Soweto. These accommodations were for families, not for single male migrants (see Bonner and Segal 1998, 28–31). Men brought their wives from rural areas to the towns or formed relationships with women already in the towns; either way, the ties between these first-generation urban immigrants and their rural kin weakened. The growth of manufacturing employment served to erode these ties further. Whereas mine workers were paid monthly and employers organised remittances to migrants' areas of origin, factory workers were paid weekly (making it harder to spare cash to remit), and employers operated no such remittance system. In the towns, people began to incur new expenses. As one person put it, "This kind of house whispers to you that it needs more furniture" (quoted in Bonner 1995, 122). The changes in society were also reflected in leisure activity as people formed new urban-based churches, football clubs, youth gangs, and so on. Bonner detects in the new townships in the late 1950s the emergence of "a new sense of common identity . . . which overrode many of the ethnic and social divisions which had characterised the previous two decades." This "gradual process of coalescence" was manifested "in the political ferment of 1959–61" before being "masked by the blanket of repression that was thrown over South Africa in the following decade" (Bonner 1995, 128–29).

The forced removal of the old pre-apartheid locations (such as Sophiatown) and the clearance of shack settlements served to consolidate the rise of this new, urban working-class society. Life in the new townships was very different than anything that had gone before. Apartheid policies thus had a complex effect on the towns: the pass laws, tightened formally in 1953 and in practice in the 1960s, served to keep the vast majority of the population outside of the towns. At the same time, however, a settled urban population grew steadily.

During the 1960s and 1970s these immigrants put down deeper and deeper roots in the urban areas. The core of this urban population held the coveted "section 10 rights" defined by the 1945 Blacks (Urban Areas) Consolidation Act (and subsequent amendments thereto). African people qualified for these rights to permanent urban residence by being born in urban areas, by working therein for a specified length of time, or by being the dependent spouse or child of a qualified urban worker (see further Chapter 4). African people without an indication of these rights in their pass books were not permitted to remain in urban areas for longer than seventy-two hours. The whole system of influx control served to limit the number of unauthorised people in the urban areas. But at the same time it allowed an ever-growing number of people to abide there legally. This resulted in growing segmentation between urban "insiders" with stable access to urban jobs and facilities, those dependent on migrant contracts, and those who were in urban areas illegally (and hence most vulnerable to exploitation; see Chapter 4). Curiously, there are no aggregate official data for the precise number of African people with section 10 rights (as the government's own Riekert Commission noted [RSA 1979, 17]). Estimates put the number of qualified adult urban workers at 1.5 million in 1970, with most of the 1.8 million youngsters under the age of twenty and an unknown number of spouses and unemployed also qualifying (ibid.; Nattrass 1979, 79).

The key new urban constituency was the fast-growing number of second-generation residents born or socialised in urban areas. There do not seem to be any data concerning the number of urban-born residents, but official census data provide a breakdown according to age and hence date of birth. These data suggest that the growth of the urban population between 1960 and 1980 was almost entirely the result of natural increase, with the number of births far exceeding the declining number of people in oldest age cohorts. The proportion of the African population living in households (that is, excluding hostels) in metropolitan areas that was born after 1950 grew from one-third (in 1960) to one-half (in 1970) and two-thirds (in 1980). By 1980 there were more than half a million people aged between ten and twenty years and a slightly lower number aged between twenty and thirty years in metropolitan households (calculated from Simkins 1983, 71–72). It is likely that most of these were urban-born and that almost all of them grew up in that environment. They comprised South Africa's first substantial, fully urbanised generation of African people. Their experiences of childhood and adolescence were very different from those of their parents.

These urban adolescents experienced a massive expansion in primary and, later, secondary schooling. This expansion occurred in two distinct periods. First, from the mid-1950s onward there was a massive increase in the provision of primary schooling for African children. The effect of this was to raise adult literacy rates among urban African people from 21 percent in 1946 to 60 percent by the mid-1960s (Bonner and Segal 1998, 61). Second, from 1972 onward there was a massive expansion of secondary schooling in urban areas (Hyslop 1999, 151). Secondary school enrollment rates among African children rose from a mere 4 percent in 1960 to 16 percent in 1970 and 35 percent in 1980 (Pillay 1990, 34). By 1980, secondary education had been transformed from "the prerogative of an elite" into "a mass phenomenon" (Bundy 1987, 312). In greater Soweto, for example, there were only eight secondary schools until 1972. By 1976 there were twenty, with three times as many students as in 1972. By the end of 1984 there were fifty-five. A growing proportion of urban youth was in secondary school, and they spent increasing amounts of time there. Not only did they grow up in an environment very different from their parents', but they were also educated to a greater degree than any previous generation.

The result of this was the emergence of an urban school-based culture and consciousness. As Glaser has shown, secondary schooling provided the space for the development of an entirely new set of radical, urban political identities very different from the rural-oriented and generally more ethnic identities of the previous generation:

> By the mid-1970s, high school students were uniquely placed to assume political leadership in Soweto. Secondary schools, which cut across narrow, street-level identities, had a unifying influence. They drew together literate youths, with similar experiences and grievances, on a large scale. High schools, with their core of intellectually inquisitive students and their ready-made network of extra-mural associations, were receptive to the Black Consciousness ideology. . . . School students, with energy and independence, and brimming with a self-belief inspired by Black Consciousness, occupied the political vacuum left by the outlawed [African National and Pan-Africanist] Congress movements. (Glaser 1994, 4–5).

The student-led revolts of 1976–77 demonstrated the importance of this new generation.

There was also a marked expansion of tertiary education. In 1960 there were fewer than 800 African students at university (excluding the University of South Africa, UNISA, which offered correspondence courses). By 1983 there were about 20,000 (and a further 12,700 enrolled in UNISA). Most of this expansion occurred during the 1970s (SAIRR, 1962, 1971, 1983). The political importance of African university students bore no relation to their meagre number: it was university campuses that provided the main recruiting ground for the black consciousness movement, and it was university graduates who took radical ideas back into schools and townships as teachers, as doctors, and in drama groups (Glaser 1994; Seekings 1989).

The expansion of urban schooling was accompanied by the continuing transformation of urban employment. The number of African workers in unskilled employment declined, and the number in semiskilled, skilled, clerical and administrative, and professional employment rose. This was in part due to technological change (in the context of rising wage pressure). Thus the construction sector was transformed by the introduction of bulldozers, front-end loaders, tipping trucks, trench diggers, powered hoists and barrows, cranes, conveyor belts, and pumps. Crankshaw reports that the African workforce in manufacturing was reduced by 10 percent by the introduction of forklift trucks, cranes, and other handling equipment in factories (1997a, 54–57). The changing occupational structure of employment was also due to economic change as the service sector grew.

African workers advanced steadily up the occupational ladder (ibid.). Until 1960 almost all African workers had been unskilled, but by 1980 unskilled labour accounted for less than half of African employment in the Johannesburg area and between one-half and two-thirds in other areas of the whole Pretoria-Witwatersrand-Vaal area. This decline accelerated in the recessionary 1980s. In the sectors of the economy where white workers had secured the protection of a colour bar (see Chapter 4), it was relaxed, or floated, upwards as white workers themselves moved up the rising occupational ladder. In 1965 only 13 percent of supervisors or foremen were African; by 1985 the proportion had risen to 36 percent. During the same period, African workers' share of skilled jobs rose from 0 to 7 percent. Even when the share did not rise, as was the case with semiskilled employment, the rising number of jobs in total meant that there were between one and a half and two times as many semiskilled African workers in 1985 than there had been twenty years earlier. In sectors where there was no colour bar—especially in the service sector—African workers moved up the occupational ladder even faster. Thus the number of African workers in routine white-collar employment tripled between the mid-1960s and the mid-1980s. The number of African school teachers quadrupled in the same period.

Upward occupational mobility was primarily intergenerational in that newcomers to the labour market entered occupations beyond their parents' reach. In Soweto more than 50 percent of the respondents in a 1981 survey were in occupations ranked higher than the ones held by the heads of the households in which they had grown up. One in three was in the same occupation, and only 17 percent were in lower-ranking occupations (Schneier 1983).

As African workers moved into more highly skilled jobs, average wages rose (Hofmeyr 1994; Crankshaw 1997a). A steady rise in manufacturing wages in the 1960s was followed by a sharp increase in the early 1970s such that average manufacturing wages doubled in value in real terms (that is, taking inflation into account) in the two decades (see Chapter 5). Most of the children who were born in the 1950s and went through secondary school in the late 1960s or 1970s thus entered the labour market at a time of new occupational opportunities and rising real wages. More and more women also entered paid employment. With immigrants' wives and adult children working, the average number of wage earners per family in Soweto grew from 1.3 in 1956 to 2.2 only twelve years later (Bonner and Segal 1998, 57).

The African residents of townships such as Soweto were subject to chronic harassment (especially about passes) by the police and systematic discrimination in wider society, but at the same time many of them enjoyed a rising standard of living and expected that improved schooling would lead to further material improvement in the future. Urban culture reflected these changes. The cornerstones of this new culture were the new mass-circulation newspapers (such as the Golden City Press in Johannesburg), bottled alcohol and shebeens (bars), the rise of soccer and other sports, black musicians (including Dolly Rathebe, the female star of *Jim Comes to Jo'burg*), and growing consumerism, fed by intense advertising (Bonner and Segal 1998, 57–65; Beinart 1994, 181–87).

This changing urban population was not homogeneous. New occupational opportunities resulted in upward occupational mobility for African people in the aggregate, but they did not have equal access to the new opportunities. Employment in occupations such as clerical work was expanding so fast that many clerical (and semiprofessional) employees had grown up in households headed by semiskilled or unskilled workers. But the chances of people from such backgrounds moving into clerical work were much lower than the chances of people from relatively privileged backgrounds (Schneier 1983, 45–46). The occupation of the previous generation had a clear influence on the relative probability of the following generation moving into a higher-ranked occupation. Respondents who grew up in households headed by professional, semiprofessional, or white-collar employees were many times more likely to move into these occupations than respondents who had grown up in households headed by manual labourers. Conversely, the children of manual labourers were many times more likely to follow that path than were the children of professionals, semiprofessionals, or white-collar workers. The settled urban population in turn had far better access to the better-paid occupations and were far more upwardly mobile than migrants in hostels. These findings point to clear processes of stratification being reproduced across generations. Migrant workers who grew up in rural households were likely to have had less skilled and less well-educated parents than were urban workers, to have been less well-educated themselves, and to have moved into relatively bad jobs when they entered the labour market. Thereafter they were relatively unlikely to have moved into better jobs. There was less intergenerational mobility among hostel dwellers than among township household residents, and intragenerational mobility was also more restricted. Comparing studies conducted in 1981, Schneier found that "only 7 percent of the hostel dwellers were upwardly mobile from one generation to the next as compared with 27 percent of the Soweto sample and 23 percent of the household residents in the [Cape Town] townships" (1983, 107). Legal status in towns—in terms of section 10 rights—had "a powerful influence on the occupational opportunities available to work seekers, and to the chances of upward mobility from initial occupation. Individuals who have no rights to permanent residence in an urban area will not only be more likely to be employed lower down on the occupational hierarchy than permanent residents but their chances of promotion are far slighter" (Schneier 1983, 109).

Hostel dwellers were likely to remain in much the same occupational category for life; insofar as they were upwardly mobile, it was likely to be within manual employment, moving, for example, from unskilled to semiskilled or from semiskilled to skilled employment. A high proportion of urban household residents, by contrast, moved from manual to nonmanual occupations; those whose first job was in unskilled manual employment were likely to move into semiskilled and skilled employment much faster than were migrants. Schneier suggests further that migrants "are likely to be the ones to bear the brunt during periods of high unemployment when they may be removed from urban areas to their respective homelands" (ibid., 109).

The opening of new employment opportunities in the towns thus exacerbated emerging class inequalities in the African population. The fact of having section 10 rights alone meant that urban African workers were likely to be in better jobs and be paid higher wages than were migrant workers with identical educational and other qualifications. Scholars such as Hindson (1987) and Posel (1991) have argued that state influx control policies implemented in the 1950s and 1960s produced a differentiated labour force. This differentiation was further accentuated with the expansion of occupational opportunities in the 1970s and 1980s.

Research conducted in Soweto in the mid-1960s found that Sowetans were very conscious of class and status: "Most residents divided Soweto's population into three or four classes: a thin layer of professionals and businessmen who constituted a sharply defined elite; a middle-class of semiskilled workers, drivers, policemen, clerks and so on who adopted a more urban western lifestyle with its associated middle-class trimmings and who made up about a quarter of the population; and the 'ordinary working people,' many of whom were children or grandchildren of immigrants. The latter group could be further subdivided into the 'respectable poor' and the dissolute" (Bonner and Segal 1998, 58). As the economy continued to change in the 1970s and 1980s, more and more township families made the transition from respectable poor to middle-class.

In most parts of the country, however, these emerging urban working and middle classes were thrown together and confined to overcrowded and inadequate living conditions. Little housing had been built since the early 1960s, and municipal infrastructure and services were appalling. Few townships were electrified, and many continued to use a bucket system for sewerage. Such neglect was based in the government's strategy of concentrating development in the bantustans. In the mid-1970s state officials came to recognise the folly of this strategy, especially in light of the 1976–77 uprisings in Soweto and elsewhere. The uprisings were led by students protesting against the iniquities of "Bantu Education," but they were fuelled by discontent with living conditions in town (as the government-appointed Cillie Commission found). The state has already begun to reconsider its urban policies (Chaskalson 1989), but the uprisings greatly accelerated the pace of reform. Crucially, the state recognised that the urban African population needed improved housing and services. It began to allow the private sector to build new urban housing and local government to develop urban infrastructure in white South Africa. In 1979 the government-appointed Riekert Commission further recognised the claims of urban Africans. The result was that they were ever more clearly divided into insiders and outsiders.

The apartheid state may have embraced urban development, but it required that it be financed by revenue raised in the townships themselves. Development, which was slow and uneven, therefore meant increases in the rents and service changes that served as local taxation or in substantial bond payments to banks and building societies (Seekings 1990). Discontent with rising municipal rents and service charges was exacerbated when the economy slid into recession beginning in mid-1981. In most urban areas unemployment rose, and a rising proportion of the urban population was pushed into poverty (although, at the same time, a large proportion of urban African households continued to enjoy rising real incomes because of continuing upward occupational mobility). Worst hit by the recession were areas that depended on heavy manufacturing, including the Vaal Triangle, East Rand, and Port Elizabeth—Uitenhage, where a majority of households suffered declining real incomes. The recession left a growing number of young men out of school and out of work but available for forms of direct action that other people might have balked at (Seekings 1993; Ntsebeza 1993).

Upwardly mobile, educated youngsters lived with their unskilled or semi-skilled parents; rich and poor households lived alongside each other, and the employed and well-paid were neighbours to the unemployed and poor. This provided fertile ground for the growth of civic organisations that took action concerning material grievances such as rent increases and inadequate infrastructure or services and overtly political grievances concerning democracy and freedom. Secondary schools provided similarly fertile ground for school-based organisations such as the ANC-aligned Congress of South African Students (COSAS), and their graduates moved into leading roles in trade unions and in township-based "youth congresses." The continued expansion of semiskilled employment in manufacturing provided the basis for the fast-growing independent trade union movement that cohered, in 1985, into the Congress of South African Trade Unions (COSATU). At the same time, the growing ranks of unemployed and poor people in urban areas provided many more recruits for any revolutionary movement (Seekings 1993).

Just as urban politics in the 1940s and 1950s bore the imprint of the first-generation urban residents' rural roots and experiences of urbanisation, so urban politics in the 1970s and 1980s was fundamentally shaped by second-generation residents' experiences of growing up in and being confined to segregated townships. In the mid-1980s townships across the country exploded in revolutionary protest. The revolt was led by activists articulating demands for full inclusion in some kind of common society. They employed tactics such as strikes and boycotts that drew on the strength they derived from their integration into the modern economy and state system. The leaders generally were educated at high school or university, and many had clear middle-class aspirations. At the same time, a substantial section of the urban population was economically marginalised as well as politically subordinated and was drawn to more violent and destructive forms of action.

Urban society changed even faster in the 1980s, in part because popular struggles reduced resistance by the state. The African middle class began to grow rapidly. By 1990 African people filled 11 percent of professional jobs, 41 percent of semiprofessional jobs, 31 percent of routine white-collar jobs, and 19 percent of skilled blue-collar jobs (Crankshaw 1997a). Much of this emerging middle class lived in new housing developments on the edge of or apart from the old townships. With the breakdown of racial segregation, some African families moved into formerly white, coloured, or Indian areas. The flipside of these changes was the growth of shack settlements as state controls collapsed in the face of popular revolt. They were home to the urban poor, typically unskilled and semiskilled manual labourers. Crankshaw (1996a, 1997c) analyses the growth of class and residential differentiation among urban African people. In a case study of Bekkersdal (Crankshaw 1996b), he found that the average income of households in a private housing development was more than double the average income of households in old, council-built township housing, which was in turn higher than the average household income in backyard shacks or in the informal shack settlement.

Not all urban areas experienced upward mobility under apartheid. Influx control meant that much urbanisation was displaced into the homelands (Simkins 1982b; Murray 1992, 206). Once land ceased to be available for new arrivals, as we saw above, ever more people were packed into settlements such as Botshabelo, east of Bloemfontein, and in QwaQwa, on the border with Lesotho. The population of QwaQwa rose from 24,000 in 1970 to 100,000 in 1975, 200,000 in 1980, and perhaps as many as 500,000 by the late 1980s. The population of Botshabelo rose even more rapidly, from 64,000 in 1979 to an estimated 500,000 only seven years later (Murray 1992, 237). These settlements were not officially urban, but they were urban in all other respects. Some of the residents of such new settlements commuted long distances to work. Some found work locally in the public sector, in low-wage manufacturing firms lured to the area by government subsidies, or as shopkeepers and taxi drivers. For most, however, chronic unemployment meant chronic poverty, as we shall see in Chapters 5 and 6.

CHANGING PATTERNS OF INEQUALITY

The apartheid era was long enough to witness significant class formation and change in the social structure. Overall, the "middle classes" expanded with the growth of semiprofessional and routine white-collar employment (as well as, on a smaller scale, managerial and professional employment). The character of working-class employment changed with the growth of semiskilled jobs and the contraction of unskilled jobs. The last vestiges of a smallholding peasantry vanished in the face of forced removals and population pressures in the reserves. The racial composition of these classes began to change, also, with African advancement into sections of the middle class. Furthermore, a substantial proportion of the African population was now thoroughly urbanised in that many African adults had been born, socialised, and schooled in the cities and towns. Even in supposedly rural areas, many people lived in conditions of "displaced urbanisation" far removed from the agrarian society of earlier times.

How did all of this affect patterns of income distribution? Work by McGrath and Simkins, together with surveys conducted by the Bureau of Market Research (BMR) at the University of South Africa and by other researchers, allows us to plot the overall distribution of incomes in the mid- and late 1970s and match this to what we know of the class structure with greater precision than we were able to obtain for 1950 in Chapter 2. McGrath (1983) found that the income share of Africans hardly changed during the 1960s, holding steady at about 20 percent of total South African income. But it rose thereafter, reaching 25 percent in 1980. The BMR's estimates by race for shares of personal disposable income suggest a more marked upward trend, also starting in the early 1970s (BMR 1989). One factor in the initial shift in income shares was the increased proportion of the population that was African. The average or per capita income of African people barely rose relative to that of white people (although the relative per capita income of coloured and Indian people did rise steadily; ibid., 11).

The first good estimates of the Gini coefficient for the distribution of income are McGrath's estimates for 1975. These indicate moderate levels of intraracial inequality and a high rate of interracial inequality. The Gini coefficient for the income distribution as a whole was 0.68. For African people only it was 0.47, for white people 0.36, for coloured people 0.51 and for Indian people 0.45 (McGrath 1983, 319.)

More recently, McGrath and Whiteford reexamined and extended McGrath's data to analyse the distribution of income in terms of income deciles. McGrath and Whiteford's estimates for the income shares of different income deciles in 1975 are set out in table 3.3. Their analysis of the racial composition of each income decile is set out in table 3.4. Although there remained a close relation between race and income decile, there was evidence of upward mobility by an elite of higher-income Africans. By this estimate, they comprised one-half of decile 8, and a very small number moved into decile 9.

Taken together, this work allows us to identify the approximate income range and composition of the different income deciles. Table 3.5 presents this information, showing incomes in 1975 prices (which were almost three times 1950 prices because of inflation, especially in the early 1970s).[3] Surveys conducted by the BMR enable us to examine in more detail income distribution in different parts of the country. The BMR had been founded in 1960 to conduct surveys among black South Africans, paying particular attention to income and expenditure patterns. Their surveys were organised by race. (Surveys from 1975 or thereabouts are summarised in table 3.6 below.)

Between 1950 and 1975 the overall distribution of incomes displayed elements of both continuity and change. On one hand, there had yet to be much change among the races in income share. Most white South Africans retained their privileged position, with class and race broadly coinciding. On the other, social change had transformed the geographical and class composition of different deciles. The forced removals of Africans from white farms to the reserves had the effect of raising the proportion of households in the lower deciles

Table 3.3. Estimated income shares, 1970–80

	1970 Simkins (%)	1970 McGrath (%)	1975 McGrath (%)	1976 Simkins (%)	1980 Devereux (%)
Deciles 1 to 4	4		5	7	8
Deciles 5 and 6	7	26		8	12
Deciles 7 and 8	12		24	14	20
Decile 9	77	74	22	71	60
Decile 10			49		
Total	100	100	100	100	100

Sources: McGrath (1978, 1983); Simkins (1979); Devereux (1983); McGrath and Whiteford (1994).

found in the reserves. In 1950 the African population on farms was almost the same as that in the reserves. By the early 1970s, twice as many people lived in the reserves (excluding the towns within them) as on the farms, as we saw in table 3.1 (Simkins 1983). The absolute number of low-income households in the reserves was now much higher than the number on farms. In addition, the distribution of incomes within most of the major demographic categories used above had shifted, with increasing inequality. As discussed above, Simkins suggests that forced removals to the reserves had led to widening inequality there as incomes rose for some but remained stagnant or declined for others. In urban areas, a rising proportion of African households had incomes that placed them in deciles 7 and 8, higher than some white households whose incomes were in relative decline; some urban African households were reaching decile 9.

The long boom of the 1960s had raised white South Africans' incomes across the board, but some had benefited much less than others. In 1975 some poor white households would have fallen into the middle deciles. McGrath estimated that 8 percent of white households were in decile 6 or lower, and another 8 percent were in decile 7 (McGrath and Whiteford 1994, 41). The government's 1975 Survey of Household Expenditure, conducted only in white households, found that only 5 percent of white households in major urban areas had incomes below R2,000 per year in 1975 (RSA 1978, 5), which would have put them at the bottom of decile 7 or lower. But incomes would have been lower in small towns and rural areas than in the cities. Even among major urban areas there were significant variations. In Johannesburg, Cape Town, and Pretoria, about one-half of all white households had incomes below R10,000 per year, but in the Vaal Triangle the proportion was almost three-quarters. And in Port

Table 3.4. Racial composition of income deciles, 1975

	Decile 1 (%)	Decile 2 (%)	Decile 3 (%)	Decile 4 (%)	Decile 5 (%)	Decile 6 (%)	Decile 7 (%)	Decile 8 (%)	Decile 9 (%)	Decile 10 (%)
African	87	87	86	86	90	86	75	51	7	2
White	2	2	2	2	2	3	8	26	83	95
Coloured	10	10	10	11	6	7	12	16	7	2
Indian	2	2	2	2	2	4	6	8	3	1
Total	100	100	100	100	100	100	100	100	100	100

Source: McGrath, cited in Whiteford and van Seventer (2000, 15).

Table 3.5. Approximate composition of income deciles, 1975

Income decile(s)	Approximate annual income range	Approximate racial and geographical composition	Approximate class composition
1 and 2	Less than R499	About two-thirds of households were African households in the reserves and about one-third were African households on white-owned farms.	Rural households without migrants sending remittances, especially female-headed households; farm workers in remote areas
3 and 4	R500–R999	About one-half of households were African households in the reserves, about one-quarter were African households on white-owned farms, and about one-quarter were a mix of urban African households and poor coloured households.	Rural households with migrants sending remittances; farm workers in less remote areas
5 and 6	R1,000–R1,899	About one-third African households in the reserves, one-third urban African households, and the remaining one-third a mix of other households.	Unskilled and semiskilled urban African workers; richest rural African workers
7	R1,900–R2,499	A mix of coloured, Indian, urban African, and reserve African households. A few poor white households.	White households without working members; coloured and Indian working class; skilled African workers
8	R2,500–R4,999	About 40 percent of the households were urban African households, about 40 percent were coloured, Indian, and white households, and a small proportion were African households in the reserves.	Most white pensioner-headed households; coloured and Indian middle class; African middle class
9	R5,000–9,900	Most of the households in this decile were white.	White working class and lower middle class
10	R10,000 and above	Almost all of the households in this decile were white.	Professional, managerial occupations; self-employed whites

Note: Poorer households were larger, and so there were more people in the poorer deciles than in the richer ones.

Elizabeth—Uitenhage, the average income was only two-thirds that in Johannesburg (BMR 1979, 27, 29).

Poor white households were typically ones without working members. Fully 87 percent of white households in major cities with incomes below R2,000 per year had heads who were not economically active. Among households with incomes between R2,000 and R4,000 per year, the proportion was 39 percent. The average income in households headed by pensioners was only R3,600 per year, much less than half the average for white households as a whole (RSA 1978). Two white pensioners, living on their own and with no other income except the government old-age pension, would have had an income of only R1,500 per year, placing them exactly on the median for South Africa as a whole, that is, on the dividing line between the fifth and sixth income deciles.

The Survey of Household Expenditure shows a close relation between occupational class and household income among white households. The small proportion of households headed by the self-employed had the highest average incomes (of almost R15,000 per year). Those headed by salaried workers in professional, technical, administrative, and managerial occupations had an average income of R11,600 per year. Those headed by clerical and sales personnel and production and transport workers had an average income of less than R8,000 per year. In all of these households, the head's salary or wages contributed the lion's share of income, but other family members (usually the working wife) contributed small sums, and many households also received small sums from sources besides wages and salaries.

The top decile in South Africa as a whole, therefore, comprised white households headed by male breadwinners in professional, managerial, and related occupations or in self-employment. Decile 9 comprised white households headed by men in lower middle-class and working-class occupations. Some poorer white households, generally comprising pensioners or single mothers, were in decile 7 or lower.

Most coloured and Indian households were still in deciles 7 and 8. A minority, benefiting from upward occupational mobility, had moved up into decile 9. At the same time, some Indian and many coloured households in rural areas remained in the poorer deciles. Household income was closely related to education and occupation. Men earned much more than women. Skilled and white-collar workers earned considerably higher incomes than semiskilled workers. The lowest incomes were earned by farm workers and unskilled workers in urban areas (although unskilled Indian workers in Durban, for example, were paid more than unskilled African workers in the same city). The low wages paid on farms were surely a major cause of the high rate of voluntary migration to the cities. Public welfare was also increasingly important for the coloured and Indian poor. Indeed, the poorest coloured and Indian households were typically those that had no one in employment and that depended on welfare. Three of four elderly coloured and Indian people, that is, a total of about eighty-three thousand people, received government old-age pensions. Another forty-three thousand coloured and Indian people received disability grants, and forty-one thousand received child maintenance or foster-care grants.

The dimensions of inequality and poverty within the coloured population became clear in research conducted in the late 1970s and early 1980s and presented at a 1984 conference about poverty funded by the Carnegie Foundation. Case studies of essentially agricultural districts in the Karoo revealed high rates of unemployment and low wages among coloured workers (Morifi 1984; Archer and Meyer 1984; Horner and Van Wyk 1984; Buirski 1984; Wentzel 1984). In these districts, employment opportunities were generally limited to farm and domestic work. Opportunities for higher incomes were generally limited to occupations such as teaching and nursing. Public welfare was very important. Opportunities were only slightly better in towns with more diverse sources of employment such as George (Levetan 1984) and Worcester (Yosslowitz 1984). It is not surprising that there were high rates of out-migration, temporary and permanent, to the cities, where there were more jobs and higher wages. Large numbers of coloured households outside of Cape Town would have been in the poorer half of the population.

Inequalities were increasing within the urban African population. Many households had risen to deciles 7 and 8 by 1975. The BMR's surveys found that average household income in selected townships on the East Rand, on the West Rand, and in Pretoria was about R2,000 per year in 1975;[4] in Johannesburg, incomes were slightly higher (BMR 1976a, 1976b, 1976e). Households with average incomes in these areas would have been in decile 7. In Johannesburg, as many as one in three African households had incomes putting them in decile 8 or higher; perhaps one in seven was in decile 5 or lower, and approximately one in six was in decile 6.[5] Rising inequality reflected in large part increased dispersion of earnings as African men and women moved into better-paying occupations. Across the Witwatersrand, the small but growing number of professionals earned on average two and a half times the earnings of unskilled labourers, who still made up more than half of the workforce. White-collar, skilled, and semiskilled workers' earnings fell in between these poles. In the early 1970s, professionals' earnings had risen in real terms whereas unskilled wages had declined. There remained persistent poverty in urban areas, as measured by the proportion of African households with incomes below variously defined poverty lines (see also Pillay 1984). But, even accounting for the higher costs of accommodation and so on in urban areas, there was much less poverty there than in rural areas.

The poorer half of the population in 1975 lived mostly in African households in rural areas, either in the reserves or on white-owned farms. McGrath (1984, 5) estimated that average incomes among African households on farms (R670 per year) were lower than those in the reserves (R925 per year). He suggested that 45 percent of African households on white farms had incomes below R500 per year, compared to 40 percent of households in the reserves. Incomes below R500 per year put these households to the bottom two income deciles.

Some details about the reserves can be added from surveys conducted by the BMR between 1977 and 1979 in Venda, Bophuthatswana, the Transkei, and Kangwane. The results of these surveys are summarised in table 3.6. By deflat-ing the income data to take into account inflation between 1975 and the date of each survey, we can plot the approximate distribution of incomes in each of these bantustans. In the Transkei in 1979, most households were in the bottom two income deciles. About 80 percent of households were in the bottom four deciles countrywide. Incomes were markedly lower in some districts, such as Cofimvaba and Tsomo, than in others, such as Bizana (BMR 1981). Incomes in Venda were probably much the same as in the Transkei (BMR 1978b; the figures for Venda in table 3.6 have not been adjusted to 1975 prices). In Kangwane and Bophuthatswana incomes were higher (BMR 1978a, 1980); in Bophuthats-wana's case this was probably due to the bantustan's proximity to Pretoria and other towns where there were more opportunities for better-educated people to find relatively well-paid employment.

Local studies from the early 1980s help indicate the kinds of households that fell into in each decile. In Nkandla in KwaZulu more than half of the house-holds were in the bottom two national income deciles, and 40 percent were in the third and fourth deciles. Only a tiny proportion belonged in a higher in-come decile. The poorest households were those that had no migrants or that had migrants who were unemployed, especially if they had no pensioner, ei-ther; many of these households were headed by women. Migrants' remittances constituted 40 percent of aggregate cash income and almost half of total in-come (including income in kind); old-age pensions constituted about 30 per-cent of cash income, or a quarter of total income (Ardington 1984, 37–41, 45). In the Lower Roza area in the Transkei, Moll (1984, 37) found that "the worst

Table 3.6. Income distribution in selected areas by race, c. 1975

Annual income (R)	Approximate income decile(s)	Urban coloured, 1975 (%)	Urban Indian, 1975 (%)	Urban African, 1975 (%)	Urban African migrants, 1975 (%)	Venda African, 1977* (%)	Bophuthatswana African, 1977* (%)	Kangwane African, 1978* (%)	Transkei African, 1979† (%)	Farms (African) 1971† (%)	Urban white, 1975 (%)
0–499	1 and 2	1	0	16	4	33	12	8	54	44	
500–999	3 and 4	6	3		39	46	26	26	27	38	
1,000–1,499	5	15	5	41	34	12	26	29	9	13	5
1,500–1,999	6	13	7			4	15	16	4		
2,000–2,499	7	11	12		23	4	14	14	3	5	
2,500–2,999	8	10	11	26					2		11
3,000–3,999		18	23	10		3	7	7	1		
4,000–4,999	9	10	14	4							55
5,000–9,999		16	25	3							
10,000–14,999	10										20
15,000+											9
Total		100	100	100	100	100	100	100	100	100	100

Sources: BMR 1972, 1976a, 1976b, 1976c, 1976d, 1976e, 1978a, 1979, 1980, 1981; RSA 1978.

*Data in columns 6–8 are not given in 1975 prices; prices rose by about 24 percent between 1975 and 1977 and by about 37 percent between 1975 and 1978. The distribution set out in these columns thus overstates the proportions of households in higher income brackets.

†Data in column 9 are 1979 data deflated to 1975 prices; data in column 10 are data from 1971 inflated to 1975 prices.

off households . . . were those without pensions and with small and erratic re-mittances, if at all. Some of these were involved in the informal sector and were marginally better off than the very poorest group—the handful surviving only on agriculture."

Data about incomes on white farms are even weaker than those for incomes in the reserves. A set of studies conducted in the mid-1970s indicates that farm workers' wages and nonwage forms of income varied between districts and provinces (see SALDRU 1977, 10–15). Monthly cash wages varied from as low as R5 (in parts of the western and northern Transvaal) to as much as R100 (among skilled coloured farm workers in the Cape). Among African farm work-ers, especially, cash wages were supplemented with payments in kind and access to land for growing crops and keeping livestock, as well as housing. Once these noncash earnings are included, farm workers' wages reached between R300 and R600 per year in many parts of the country. It is difficult to move from data about individual earnings to estimates of household incomes, but these micro-level data seems to support McGrath's calculation that average household incomes were about R670 per year. In late 1971 the BMR (1972) conducted a survey of African households in two white farming districts, Bethal and Viljoen-skroon (see table 3.6). About 44 percent of the surveyed households had in-comes below R500 per month, putting them into the bottom two income deciles. Another 38 percent had incomes placing them in deciles 3 or 4. Fewer than one in five had incomes high enough to put them in or above decile 5. In-comes were low, despite low unemployment and an average of two earners per household, because employment opportunities were limited to unskilled agri-cultural and domestic work. The African population had little or no schooling.

The state provided a very weak social security net for poor Africans, primar-ily by means of the government old-age pension system. The pension was in-creased to a maximum of only R15 per month (R180 per year) in 1975 (Pollak 1981, 157); unless pensioners had access also to other sources of income (most obviously, migrants' remittances), they would have fallen into the lowest decile. Moreover, take-up rates were low because administrative obstacles resulted in only one in three African men and women of pensionable age actually receiving a pension. Younger people lacked even this flimsy net.

RACE AND CLASS UNDER APARTHEID

This collation of fragmented survey data suggests that Houghton's characteri-sation of South African society in terms of three basic strata was broadly valid in the 1970s. Almost all of the poor were rural in African households, dependent on the wages paid to farm workers or the remittances sent by migrants in the cities. Urban African, coloured, and Indian households were clearly better off than rural African households, and white households were richer still. Race was still important, and it mediated the effect of other factors on incomes. But the importance of other factors was becoming clearer. The structure of employment was changing at the same time as the premium attached to a better education was rising, so that the importance of education grew rapidly. In Venda, working African people with grade 11 or 12 schooling earned, on average, more than twice as much as people with grade 3 to 6 schooling only (BMR 1978b). In the cities, the premium attached to better schooling was somewhat reduced, but in Johannesburg, an African person with grade 9 or more earned on average slightly less than double what people with no schooling earned (BMR 1982).

The parts of the country with the worst schooling and the fewest opportunities for skilled or white-collar employment were the areas where incomes stagnated or declined. Interregional differentials increased as intraracial inequality grew. In 1970 the average disposable income per capita among Africans in the Transkei was one-quarter that of Africans in the Transvaal. By 1980 the ratio had fallen to one-fifth, and by 1985 it was less than one-sixth (BMR 1989). It is not surprising that, given the big and growing differences between opportunities and earnings in different parts of the country, there were high rates of migration from rural to urban areas. Migration also meant that the coloured population stagnated in many districts in the Karoo, in the Western and Northern Cape. Emigration from African reserves was, of course, restricted by the pass laws. But residents who could migrate legally did so in ever larger numbers. The number of officially registered migrants leaving the Transkei rose from fewer than 30,000 in 1968 to 425,000 in 1978 (Muller, cited in Leibbrandt and Woolard 1999, 18).

The continuation of these trends during the late 1970s and 1980s meant that the relation between race and inequality changed dramatically. By 1991, according to McGrath and Whiteford, the Gini coefficient for the distribution of income in South Africa as a whole had barely changed, but the Gini coefficients for the distribution of income among white and African people had risen sharply. Intraracial inequality had risen sharply. Whiteford and McGrath calculate that the Gini coefficient among African people rose from 0.47 in 1975 to 0.62 in 1991; that for white people rose from 0.36 to 0.46 (cited in Whiteford and van Seventer 2000, 16). Rising intraracial inequality meant that some white households were becoming relatively poorer, falling into lower deciles, while some African households were becoming relatively richer and rising into higher deciles (ibid.).

Rising inequality within the African population was driven in the late 1970s and 1980s, as in preceding years, by the combination of increased inequality of earnings for different sectors and occupations and upward mobility into better-paying occupations by some African people. Unskilled workers' wages stagnated with the demand for unskilled work, and wages for skilled and white-collar work rose as demand increased. In Johannesburg, according to a BMR survey, skilled African workers earned about 30 percent more than unskilled workers in 1975; by 1980 the premium had risen to more than 120 percent (BMR 1982). This trend continued: between 1980 and 1985 the real earnings of unskilled African men continued to stagnate while those of semiskilled and skilled male workers rose steadily. Education was increasingly necessary for access to these better-paying jobs. Earnings of African workers with at least a ninth-grade education rose at more than three times the rate of the real earnings of men who had reached grade 6 or lower (BMR 1986).

Increasing intraracial differentiation was evident within urban and rural areas as well as between them. In the major urban areas, the proportion of African households with high incomes rose steadily during the 1970s and 1980s, and average household incomes per person generally rose also (this is figured using real incomes, that is, taking inflation into account). But the proportion of households with incomes below fixed poverty lines either stagnated or actually rose. Average incomes may have been rising, but so was inequality. The declining importance of race and the rising importance of intraracial class inequalities at the end of the apartheid era are examined in more detail in Chapters 6–8, using data from South Africa's first countrywide household income and expenditure survey, conducted in 1993.

ALTERNATIVE TRAJECTORIES

The trajectory of social and economic change in South Africa entailed the steady elimination of the African peasantry and the banishment of a poor class of the landless unemployed within the boundaries of the reserves. A large factor in these changes was the expansion of capitalism, both in the countryside and in industry. But the state made choices and implemented policies that steered South African capitalism down a particular route. Different choices and different policies would have led down significantly different routes. At this time, in many other parts of the world, colonial administrations and their independent successors were implementing different varieties of development, generally meaning that states encouraged or forced people to produce more for the market (Cooper 2002, ch. 3). South Africa was unusual in that it already had a highly commercialised economy, with limited subsistence production. In addition, the landowning (settler) class was politically and economically important. These two factors were crucial in shaping the route that South Africa followed.

One alternative route would have entailed land reform. The redistribution of land from (white) owners of large holdings to (African) peasant farmers could have preserved or even expanded the peasantry. This route was partly followed in two other parts of Africa where large tracts of land had been seized by white settler farmers and African landownership had been largely confined to demarcated reserves. In Kenya, about one-fifth of the good land had been settled by white farmers; in Southern Rhodesia (later Zimbabwe), half of the land had been settled (Ranger 1985 138). In both cases, a portion of this land was later redistributed to African farmers.

In Kenya, colonial officials began to promote an African peasantry after World War II (Heyer 1981, 101–7). In the mid-1950s, colonial officials ended white farmers' monopoly on coffee farming, opening up lucrative opportunities for African peasants to grow for export markets; at the same time small parcels were consolidated, enclosed, and registered. In the early 1960s, the colonial state embarked on a resettlement scheme according to which some white farmers' land was resettled with a mix of African yeoman farmers and peasant smallholders. In 1962 this limited scheme was superseded by the ambitious Million Acre Settlement Scheme, according to which one-seventh of the white-owned land in the "White Highlands" was purchased, subdivided, and resold to about thirty-five thousand peasant families, with bridging finance from the British government, the World Bank, and other sources. An equal number of peasant households were resettled using other schemes (ibid., 108). The Million Acre Settlement Scheme was taken over by the new government of Kenya after independence was proclaimed in 1963 and followed by further "peasantisation" initiatives (Leo 1984). The result of changing policy inside and outside the reserves was an extraordinary explosion in smallholder production of cash crops, especially coffee. There is disagreement about the precise distribution of benefits. Kitching (1980) emphasises that only a minority of peasant households participated in this agrarian revolution, with inequalities between a nascent rural petite bourgeoisie and a growing class of landless or almost landless rural labourers growing. Cowen (1981), however, documents the growth of the "middle" peasantry. Whichever interpretation is correct, there was a significant shift in the rural class structure.

In Zimbabwe land reform had to await independence in 1980. The guerrilla war of the 1970s had been rooted in African peasants' aspirations to recover the lands lost to white settlers (Ranger 1985). In total, fifty-two thousand African families were resettled on three million hectares (more than six million acres, or 16 percent of white-owned farmland) in the decade following independence. The Zimbabwean state sought, via regulation, to promote a class of small but full-time farmers that were more productive than the peasantry in the communal areas (the former reserves). In 1990 the government adopted the National Land Policy, which called for the redistribution of another five million hectares (Alexander 1994). In Zimbabwe (as in Kenya), land was also acquired by the new black elite, but this had no effect on the class structure itself (Moyo 1995).

In Kenya and Zimbabwe, land reform was made possible by major political change. In Kenya, it was overt rebellion (with the Mau Mau rebellion of the early 1950s) and chronic simmering discord that pushed the colonial administration into addressing the problem of growing landlessness and overriding many of the objections of white settler farmers. As it happened, hard times and the prospect of independence caused many white farmers to want to sell. The resettlement scheme was thus a scheme whereby the British government in effect underwrote the sale of white farms to African peasants. International capital also favoured the expansion of peasant agriculture because it expanded the supply of export crops such as tea and coffee. In Zimbabwe, the guerrilla war and "independence" made land redistribution possible. Indeed, much of the land redistributed in the 1980s had been abandoned by its white owners and occupied by African squatters. In both cases, land reform had the clear objective of social stability.

In South Africa white farmers carried much more political clout, which resulted in government subsidies and grants to stay on the land and (after 1948) legislative controls to ensure a protected supply of cheap labour. Families evicted from the farms were not resettled on smallholdings but were shunted into the reserves. There, contrary to the visions of Paton and the Tomlinson Commission, the peasantry was destroyed. While African families were losing access to land in South Africa, their counterparts in Kenya and Zimbabwe were expanding theirs. To be sure, in the latter two peasantisation was partial, with a large farm sector remaining, and demographic growth led to growing landlessness, the deagrarianisation of society, and increased inequality in the distribution of incomes. But at least this was delayed for some time after it was evident in South Africa.

The land-owning elites that stand to lose from land reform typically wield considerable political power. Consequently, many (perhaps most) cases of land reform have followed major political change, as in Zimbabwe. In Korea and Taiwan (and Japan), land reform took place under American occupation following the military defeat of the Japanese in World War II. Land-owning elites were compromised by association with Japanese wartime administrations, and small tenant farmers needed to be pacified. Land reform in China, Cuba, and Nicaragua all followed revolutions. There are few examples of land reform legislated via democratic political processes. Several such cases in Latin America were strongly backed by the American government as part of its explicitly anti-Communist Alliance for Progress.

Without external intervention or revolutionary change, land-owning elites can generally block pressures for land reform. In Peru, landowners blocked land reform until left-wing army officers seized power in a coup. The case of Brazil is telling, especially given the wide range of similarities between its social and political structures and those of South Africa. The first time that land reform got onto the political agenda was the mid-1980s, when the Sarney government proposed to redistribute some of the country's landed estates (*latifundios*) to 1.4 million farm workers. It was probably only possible because urban capitalists and state officials had come to view the latifundio sector as a redoubt of backward, inefficient, and socially destabilising farming practices and thus were prepared to support land reform against the agrarian elites. But an alliance of traditional agrarian elites and modern ranchers was nonetheless able to block the initiative.

In Brazil and many other parts of Latin America, as in South Africa, land-owning elites retained considerable political power throughout the 1950s and 1960s and into the 1970s. But in Latin America, in contrast to South Africa, landlessness resulted in urbanisation in the major cities rather than displaced urbanisation on the economic periphery. (Indeed, many observers argued that it was better to address rural poverty by the expansion of off-farm employment than with land reform.) This, then, is another alternative route to that followed by South Africa: industrialisation, the slow substitution of capitalist agriculture for feudal land ownership, and unfettered urbanisation. This was perhaps the vision of Peter Abrahams in *Mine Boy*. In many respects Brazil and South Africa were very similar in the apartheid era: neither was democratic, both were highly unequal, and in both, the urban industrial working class was in the relatively privileged, better-off half of the population. But whereas most of the South African poor were kept out of the cities, the Brazilian poor were increasingly to be found in the cities. This was the broad developmental trajectory envisaged by Lewis. People would move from the low-productivity rural sector to higher-productivity urban employment, with the result that inequalities would widen.

The outcome of this alternative route is mapped in terms of class by Portes (1985). At the top of the basic class structure of Latin American societies are a tiny dominant capitalist class and a larger "bureaucratic-technical class"; together, these compose up to 10 percent of the economically active population. Below them is the "formal proletariat," overwhelmingly urban and characterised by contractual agreements and bureaucratic regulation. This class composes more than 20 percent of the economically active population (and much more than this in the Southern Cone countries of Chile, Argentina, and Uruguay). Portes identifies an "informal petty bourgeoisie" employing casual labour (often family labour) on a noncontractual basis and substantially unregulated. Finally, there is an "informal proletariat" or semiproletariat, often labelled "marginal" but in fact integrated, albeit in unregulated and informal ways, into the economy. Until the 1950s, as in South Africa, much of this class combined subsistence agricultural production with casual labour on commercial farms, in mines, or in the cities; cyclical migration from and back to the countryside was common. But, as Portes emphasises, the trend of the 1950s, 1960s, and 1970s was "the gradual displacement of the rural semiproletariat to the cities" (16). The two informal classes accounted for two-thirds of the economically active population. As the semiproletariat migrated to the cities, so it became increasingly pulled into informal entrepreneurial activity (the informal petty bourgeoisie in Portes's scheme).

Whereas poor and landless South Africans were confined to the reserves by the pass laws and excluded from informal-sector activity by other apartheid-era regulations, their Latin American counterparts were drawn to the cities, where they joined a large informal sector as well as a growing, protected formal sector. In Brazil, three-quarters of the population lived in rural area and only one-quarter in urban areas in 1925. By 1990 the proportions were reversed. The most rapid urbanisation took place during the 1950s, 1960s, and 1970s. In these three decades the population of Rio de Janeiro tripled, and the population of São Paulo grew fivefold. Between them, these two cities were home to 25 million people in 1990. In Latin America as a whole, the urban population rose from 59 million people in 1950 to 306 million in 1990 (Villa and Rodriguez 1996). Many of the urban poor lived in shack settlements. The *favelas* of Rio de Janeiro were home to 30 percent of the city's residents, or 1.3 million people, in 1970. In São Paulo, 3.2 million people, or 31 percent of the city's population, lived in favelas in 1980 (Gilbert 1996). Whereas the overall population grew steadily at about 2.5 percent per year, the rural population actually declined (Bernstein 1992, 44).

The first of the alternative routes discussed above differed from South Africa's in that many poor families retained or gained access to the land. The second differed in that many poor families had access to a vibrant urban informal sector. In both cases, therefore, unemployment remained low. In South Africa, however, deagrarianisation combined with regulation (especially urban influx control) to confine the poor to the reserves, with the consequence of high and rising levels of unemployment; apartheid-era regulations appear to have restricted severely the informal sector in the towns, and outside the towns there was little opportunity for any significant activity in that sector. The consequence of this was rising unemployment, which needs to be seen as an integral element in the South African route of social and economic change. Shifting patterns of inequality in South Africa were structured directly and indirectly by government policies. It is to this that we now turn.

Chapter 4 Apartheid as a Distributional Regime

The apartheid distributional regime was built on foundations laid in the first half of the twentieth century, but the 1948 election nonetheless represented an important watershed. The reforms of 1944–46 promised to take South Africa along the route followed by most forms of welfare capitalism in more fully developed democratic countries: racial restrictions would probably gradually loosen and, as the economy grew, a rising share of GDP would be spent by the state on education, health, and social security. Even if the bold vision of the Social Security Committee had been scaled down, the result would probably have been steady redistribution and diminution of inequality. Democracy was not in the cards, but a more inclusive distributional regime was a real possibility. This was not to happen. After 1948, racially discriminatory labour-market policies were extended and strengthened, and despite economic growth, the share of GDP spent on welfare declined in the 1950s and 1960s. There was no decline in overall income inequality, and poverty deepened.

This chapter focuses on the way that distribution in South Africa was shaped by labour-market and welfare policies in the context of the broader growth path. The apartheid distributional regime emerged under conditions of full employment and as a racist project to protect and increase white incomes while ensuring economic growth—albeit of a racially repressive and capital-intensive variety. The distributional regime was never stable. Three changes distinguished its late stage from its early apartheid predecessor. First, and most obviously, the steady removal of institutionalised racial discrimination from the 1970s onward resulted in improving occupational opportunities for black South Africans, as well as more generous welfare provision and other social expenditures. Second, racially discriminatory public education policies in the early apartheid period resulted, in the later period, in most white South Africans' enjoying class advantages in markets; they therefore no longer required direct state intervention to protect their earnings. Deracialisation allowed the growth of skilled black labour, addressing a constraint on growth while posing little direct threat to white South Africans' incomes. At the same time, however, the economy changed from one with a surplus of labour to one with fast-rising open unemployment (as we shall see further in Chapter 5): the labour market was unable to absorb the rise in the number of job-seekers. The result was that the African middle class and urban African working class prospered while a growing class of unemployed people remained poor or grew poorer. The racial divide between skilled, well-paid whites and unskilled, low-paid Africans was to evolve into a class divide between the skilled and well-paid, regardless of race, and the unemployed, almost all African.

WELFARE, EDUCATION, AND WAGES UNDER EARLY APARTHEID

The early apartheid distributional regime, which included the 1950s and 1960s, coincided with the long postwar economic boom. Rapid growth in international demand for South African output together with massive and sustained flows of investment gave the apartheid government the economic space to undertake its project of large-scale, racially repressive social engineering. Although most African colonies experienced decolonisation during these decades, South Africa's government tightened its grip on power, harnessing the economy's mineral and industrial power in the service of white South Africans' economic and political interests. Whereas most of Africa's colonial and postcolonial states practiced a fairly authoritarian form of developmentalism (Cooper 2002), the South African state had more in common with the bureaucratic authoritarianism of much of Latin America (Collier 1979). But, like its Latin American

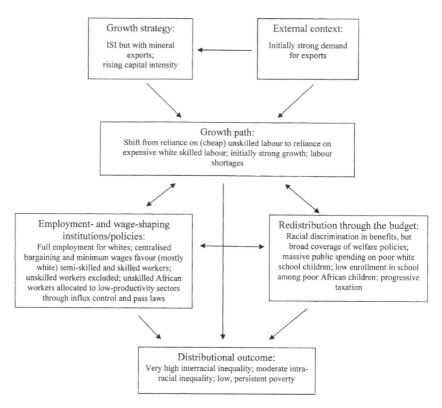

Figure 4.1. The early apartheid distributional regime

counterparts, the apartheid state could never fully control the economic forces it sought to regulate, and its political and economic project shifted with the process of class formation and economic development. The major features of the early apartheid distributional regime are shown in figure 4.1.

Welfare Policy

After its election in 1948, the National Party (NP) government reversed many but not all of the recent advances toward a more egalitarian welfare framework. Welfare expenditure (including health and education) fell as a proportion of government expenditure (Kruger 1992, 126–52). Actual cutbacks in spending on African people contributed to this trend in spending levels. The first policy reversal was the 1949 Unemployment Insurance Amendment Act, which required that African workers have a very high income in order to participate in the state-subsidised unemployment insurance system. This resulted in a near-total decline in UIF benefits paid out to African workers, whose average wages

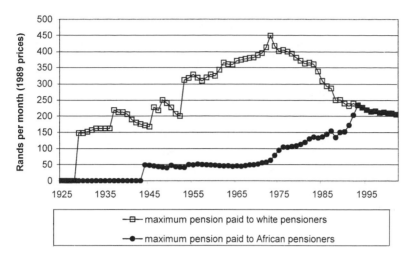

Figure 4.2. The real value of the maximum old-age pension paid to white and African pensioners, 1925–2002

would not rise above the minimum limit for inclusion in the UIF until 1967 (Meth and Piper 1984). Tellingly, the NP declined to set up parallel racially segregated funds, as it had demanded when it had been in opposition. The motivation for excluding African workers from the UIF was not to prevent cross-racial subsidisation, since the NP Minister of Labour acknowledged that there was no such subsidisation. Rather, it was to meet the criticism that unemployment insurance contributed to the labour shortage of the NP's important farming constituency.

Perhaps the most visible aspect of the attack on the embryonic universalistic welfare system was the widening gap between old-age pensions paid to the different race groups. Figure 4.2 shows the maximum value of the old-age pension paid to African and to white pensioners. The maximum value of the former remained steady in real terms from the mid-1940s until about 1970. At the same time the real value of the pension paid to white pensioners was increased, doubling in real terms during the 1950s and 1960s. The gap between the maximum pensions therefore widened steadily. The maximum value of an African pension fell from 25 percent of a white pension in 1947, to 18 percent in 1950, to 15 percent in 1960, and to its lowest point of 13 percent in the mid-1960s, when the payment was R3.70 per month. This sum, according to the government's own estimates, was insufficient to cover the minimum food budget for one person. Because African pensioners were paid less in small towns and rural areas than in the cities, many received pensions much lower than this. The maximum value of pensions paid to coloured and Indian people was several times higher than that paid to African people but also declined relative to white pensions, from 50 percent in 1947 to 47 percent (for coloured people) and 41 percent (for Indians) in 1966 (Pollak 1981, 157–59). Spending on education for African children was also cut back (as we shall see below), and government funding of black school feeding schemes was reduced and finally eliminated by 1960. Family allowances for Indians were ended in 1948.

This is a bleak but curious picture. Why did the NP government not abolish entirely the African pension or, alternatively, tie it to revenue raised from African taxpayers? The NP had opposed the extension of old-age pensions to African people in 1944, just as it opposed the inclusion of African workers in the UIF in 1946—yet it reversed one but not the other once it was in power. Further research is needed to answer this question fully, but several possible answers emerged in parliamentary debates. First was the cost of welfare, and especially the question of who paid. In opposition, prior to 1948, NP members of Parliament criticised the UIF on the grounds that white workers' contributions paid for benefits for the African unemployed. This was a wonderful issue for an election campaign, but it turned out to be unfounded. Old-age pensions were financed out of the general budget, but the cost was contained by allowing the real value of the pension to stagnate.

A second reason was the supposed connection between welfare provision and the willingness to work among African men and women. When African workers' participation in the UIF was abolished, it had more to do with the supposed effects of unemployment insurance on the availability of cheap labour for the farms and mines. The link between old-age pensions and the supply of cheap labour was more tenuous, and the incentive to exclude African people from the pension system was thus much weaker. As the economy shifted from labour shortage to labour surplus, so it became inconsequential whether welfare discouraged people from working.

Third, NP ministers spoke of the need to reform the system of old-age pensions for African people, but recognised that they could not simply abolish it. Some alternative was needed. In 1955 the minister of finance told Parliament that the present system would be continued for the time being, but his colleague, the minister of native affairs, intended to "introduce a method of social services which will be more in accordance with Native custom and tradition" (*Hansard,* 4 April 1955, 3831, quoted in SAIRR 1955, 221–22). The minister of native affairs told Parliament that old-age pensions were the "wrong way of dealing with the Native. We want to evolve a system whereby we reinstate the natural obligations of Bantu authorities and Bantu culture in regard to their old people" (*Hansard,* 13 June 1955, 7628, quoted in ibid.). Some money was allocated to the Bantu Authorities for social welfare, but little of it was actually disbursed. It is possible that a perceived incapacity among the Bantu Authorities contributed to the inertia on the government's part. It is also likely that the Bantu Authorities themselves felt that the political costs of ending pensions would be too high and opposed any such step. For whatever reason, the old-age pension system was not reformed. The value of the pensions for African people was reduced relative to the pensions paid to white people, but the pensions themselves were never abolished.

Education

Education was central to the state's project of ensuring that all white people enjoyed advantaged positions in society. Differential education was integral to the apartheid distributional regime. The contrast with public health provides an indication of the importance of education. Whereas health's share of total government spending declined by almost half between 1949–50 and 1975–76, education's share changed little (McGrath 1979b, 20). Spending on education in South Africa was low in comparison to that in many other developing countries (Moll 1990, 147), but it was highly concentrated. Both at the start of the apartheid period and at its height, the aggregate amount spent on health care for the African majority was larger than the aggregate amount spent on the white minority. But the aggregate amount spent on education for the African majority was much less than the aggregate amount spent on the white minority. The state assumed responsibility for almost all education in the country. In contrast, the state effectively rejected the Gluckman Report, which dealt with the reform of the public health system (see Chapter 2), and declined to take primary responsibility for health care (and increasingly devolved responsibility for old-age pensions to the private sector).

Education was important because it ensured that white South Africans were given huge advantages in the labour market, which in turn meant higher incomes and enhanced capacity to pay privately for health care and to save for retirement. Insofar as white South Africans were already privileged, differential education served to reproduce this privilege. Insofar as some white South Africans had few skills in the 1950s, the disadvantage of one generation was not passed onto the next. The improvement of public education was thus an important factor in the rising prosperity of Afrikaans-speaking white people. Verster and Prinsloo (1988) found that the differences between Afrikaans- and English-speaking children in aptitude and intelligence test scores narrowed dramatically. In the 1950s the gap was as wide as a half of a standard deviation; by the 1970s it had disappeared.

The early postwar apartheid period saw a great expansion of secondary education among white students. In the 1940s, only 50 percent of white pupils in grade 8 went on as far as grade 10, and only 30 percent reached grade 12. By the 1960s these proportions had reached 80 percent and 45 percent, respectively (Malherbe 1977, 287). By 1970 there were as many white pupils in grade 10 as in grade 1; only in grades 11 and 12 did the numbers drop off somewhat (ibid., 267). The expansion of secondary schooling was costly, with the real value of expenditure on white schools almost doubling between 1948 and 1960. Expenditure per white pupil rose steadily in real terms during the 1950s and 1960s, and the pupil-teacher ratio improved slightly (Fedderke et al. 2000).

Figure 4.3 shows the improvement in grade attainment by white men and women. The columns and the left-hand axis indicate the grade attained by the person at the top of the first quartile; this shows the improvement in education at the bottom end of the distribution, that is, among relatively poor white people. The line and the right-hand axis show the percentage of each age cohort that passed the matric examination at the end of grade 12. Under apartheid, the percentage of each age cohort passing matric rose from about 50 percent to more than 80 percent.

The story of education for African children was very different. Per-child expenditure on African schools rose in the first five years of the NP government. But in 1953, the expansion of state spending on schools for African children was tied once more to the level of African taxation; the grant from general revenue was kept at a constant R13 million (until 1972), and inflation eroded the real value of this figure. As Bromberger notes, this "effectively prevented redistribution of current income and future earning potential from rich to poor by making the poor pay for their own education" (1982, 174). In the course of the following decade government expenditure per African child fell in nominal terms. In 1953, such spending was 14 percent of that for each white pupil; by 1968, this figure had dropped to 6 percent (Auerbach and Welsh 1981, 79); this widening gap was in part due to the fact that white students were spending longer in secondary school, which was more expensive than primary school. Expenditure per black pupil stagnated and the pupil-teacher ratio rose dramatically (Fedderke et al. 2000).

White pupils started school at a younger age than their African counterparts,

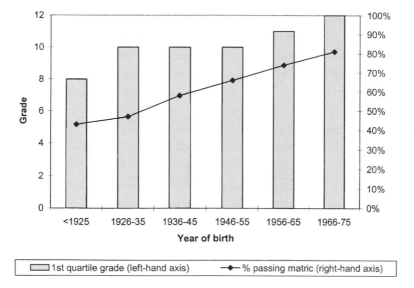

Figure 4.3. Educational attainment among white men and women under apartheid.
Source: Calculated from the 1995 October Household Survey.

repeated school years less often, dropped out less often, and thus progressed faster and further through the schooling system. By 1960, the number of white students passing matric was sixteen times the total number of coloured, Indian, and African students who passed (Malherbe 1977, 722). By 1970, the secondary school enrollment rate reached 90 percent among white children; among African children, it had risen to only 16 percent despite growing fourfold in the previous decade (Pillay 1990, 34).

The effects of public education on earnings are evident in Malherbe's analysis of the 1960 census. The census collected data about the earnings and education of white, coloured, and Indian workers. Malherbe (1977, 632) found a strong relation between education and median earnings for all racial groups. The median earnings of a white worker with primary schooling only was half that of a worker with matric and only one-third that of a worker with an undergraduate degree. (These differentials increased between 1960 and 1970, although fewer and fewer white workers were in the less well-schooled category.) Greater differentials existed among coloured workers. But most white workers with basic secondary schooling earned more than the median coloured worker with an undergraduate degree. Thus education raised earnings, but all white workers enjoyed massive benefits from wage or job discrimination; it is unlikely that much of the interracial difference can be explained by other factors such as experience. Men enjoyed higher earnings than women at all educational levels. Although race (and gender) strongly affected earnings, the government had learnt belatedly the lesson of the Carnegie Commission concerning white poverty in the pre-apartheid years: by changing the skill composition of the white labour force via public education, the state was able to give white people a large advantage in the labour market, with the result that interracial wage differentials widened.

The story of health care under apartheid stands in marked contrast to the story of education. The apartheid state did provide subsidised health care for poor white families, but a substantial private sector remained. The state also subsidised some health care for African families, perhaps out of concern with the general costs of disease. But the state never assumed the kind of role in health that it did in education. The state's share of total health care expenditure does not seem to have risen above about 60 percent during the apartheid era (McIntyre 1997, 135); it was much lower than its share of educational expenditure. In 1972, two of three doctors were employed in the private sector (ibid., 120). In South Africa, as elsewhere, the private provision of medical care resulted in marked inequalities, within the white population as well as in interracial terms.

The use of general government revenue to pay old-age pensions, to contribute to the funding of African education, and especially to finance limited health services for African people meant that there was a small amount of redistribution via taxation and social expenditures from white to African people throughout the apartheid period. White South Africans always enjoyed far higher expenditure per capita than African South Africans, by a factor of about eight at the start of the apartheid era. But they also paid a far higher proportion of tax revenue and, indeed, paid a higher share of their income in taxes. The data are not good, but McGrath estimates that white South Africans paid on average 22 percent of their income in tax, whereas African people paid only 9 percent of their income in tax (these figures encompass all taxes, including corporate and income taxes according to various assumptions about their incidence). Tax rates rose under apartheid for white and for African people, but the latter always received more in cash welfare payments and the in-kind benefits of health and education expenditures than they paid in taxes. McGrath's findings are sensitive to the assumptions he makes, but his middle estimates suggest that the average per capita incomes among African people were increased by 12 percent in 1949–50 and about 10 percent in both 1959–60 and 1969–70. In the same years the average per capita incomes of white people were reduced by about 5 percent. Redistribution from white to African people declined very slightly in the 1950s and 1960s (but redistribution from white to coloured and Indian people increased; McGrath 1979a, 31). Treating people as homogeneous racial groups probably disguises the significance of redistribution to particular beneficiaries. There appears to have been some bias toward city dwellers in the provision of welfare to African people, with better medical facilities and (until 1965) higher pensions for people in urban areas. Although living costs were higher, too the result was probably to increase the incomes of urban Africans by more than the average of 12 percent.

Wages

The apartheid distributional regime could accommodate minor redistribution from white taxpayers to African people via the budget because the budget was far from being the primary mechanism by which interracial distribution was shaped. Had the government not restricted expenditure on African schools and old-age pensions then the level of redistribution via the budget would have risen sharply, and in this sense the regime should be seen as a briefly successful system of limiting budgetary redistribution. More important, however, this regime was based on the policies inherited from the era of civilised labour, policies that structured labour markets in ways that boosted white workers' earnings. The gap between average wages for white workers and for African workers grew steadily between 1948 and 1970 in the core economic sectors (Nattrass 1990, 66). The consequence of this was that, despite the persistent demographic trend of African population growth relative to the white population, income shares by race changed little during the apartheid period. Using census data, McGrath (1979a, 1) estimates that the African population's share of total personal income in South Africa actually shrank from 22.2 percent in 1946–47 to 21.4 percent in 1960 and 19.3 percent in 1970. The ratio of per capita incomes of white and black South Africans rose from 10.6:1 in 1946–47 to 15:1 in 1970 (McGrath 1990, 92).

Some white people benefited more than others during this phase of apartheid. The share of total personal income of Afrikaans-speaking white South Africans rose from 27.9 percent in 1946 to 32.4 percent in 1960; the share of English-speaking South Africans declined during the same period (Steenekamp 1990, 57). (After 1960 the shares of both Afrikaans- and English-speaking white groups declined.) Inequality within the Afrikaans-speaking white population changed hardly at all, however; the Gini coefficient fell from 0.46 in 1946 to 0.44 in 1960—and these figures are almost certainly for income including transfers (Steenekamp, cited in Giliomee 1999, 89). Apartheid in the early post-war period benefited all Afrikaners, not only the poorer ones.

African workers' wages were held down by a battery of legislation as well as inferior education, which together confined them to low-wage jobs. Liberal critics have emphasised the legislation that denied the African population equality of opportunity, that is, the barriers to upward occupational mobility represented by low-quality education and the colour bar. Marxist critics have attached greater emphasis to the pass laws, which confined many African workers to low-wage sectors of the economy (especially farming and mining). Both sets of critics typically also pointed to the discriminatory effects of wage-setting institutions and restrictions on bargaining power brought about by a prohibition on unionisation. All of these were important.

The 1953 Industrial Conciliation Act excluded all African workers from the definition of "employee," barred them from officially recognised trade unions, and removed their right to strike. African workers were instead provided with a system of emasculated plant-level "works committees." At the same time, white workers were able to negotiate wages at industry level via industrial councils. The act provided for the reservation of certain classes of work for specified racial categories so as to "safeguard against inter-racial competition." In 1956 the act was revised to prohibit the registration of "mixed" unions (unions with both white and coloured or Indian members).

White workers had a strong hand in negotiations on industrial councils. Not only did they dominate skilled occupations and have the power to negotiate closed-shop agreements, but white unions could always threaten to apply to the government for job reservation when bargaining for wages and the racial division of labour. This increased their bargaining power substantially and enabled them to trade higher wages for limited encroachment by African workers in certain occupations. White unions also successfully prevented the training of African workers as artisans. Although the 1944 Apprenticeship Act contained a clause requiring that there be no discrimination on the grounds of race or colour, no African people were apprenticed outside the homelands until 1975. This exclusion resulted from the statutory sanction given to apprenticeship committees (on which white trade unions and employers' associations served) and industrial council agreements (Van der Horst 1981, 49).

During the war the Wage Board had intervened to raise wages for unskilled black workers, but in the early apartheid years the board's attitude toward unskilled work cooled noticeably. In 1950 the Wage Board observed: "If the unskilled worker strives to better his output of work and reaches the stage where more reliance can be placed on him by his employer, he will presumably be in a position to command a higher wage" (Union of S.A., 1950c, 50). The number of Wage Board determinations declined dramatically from an average of 8.1 per year between 1937 and 1947 to 3.4 per year for the next ten years. At the same time, the coverage shifted in favour of white workers.

With this range of legislation the state determined the institutional terrain whereby wages were set for particular occupations and industries. The pass laws served to constrain the supply of African labour in particular areas, thereby exerting upward or downward pressure on wages. Early radical analyses (for example, Wolpe 1972; Legassick 1972) argued that the pass laws provided employers with a general supply of cheap African labour. Later analyses (Hindson 1987; Posel 1987) argued that policies produced differentiated forms of African labour. This differentiation was based in the insider-outsider distinction inherent in the influx control system. The cornerstone of that system was section 10(1) of the Natives (Urban Areas) Act (as amended by the 1952 Native Laws Amendment Act). An African person was only permitted to stay in prescribed areas for longer than seventy-two hours (a) if he had resided continuously in the area since birth; (b) if he had worked continuously in the area for one employer for at least ten years or lived there continuously for at least fifteen years and had not been guilty of any major criminal offence; (c) if he or she was the wife, unmarried daughter, or nonadult son of a person qualifying under (a) or (b); or (d) if he or she had permission from a labour officer to be in the area (Posel 1991).

The Urban Areas Act created a major fault line through the African working class: those with section 10(1)(a), (b), or (c) rights comprised a group of urban "insiders" with protected access to urban jobs and facilities; those with section 10(1)(d) rights were migrants dependent on contract employment for their access to urban areas (although they were eligible for section 10(1)(b) rights if they satisfied the residential or employment criteria); those in urban areas illegally (that is, for longer than seventy-two hours) were vulnerable to arrest or exploitation by employers.

Workers with section 10(1)(a), (b), or (c) rights were permitted to remain in town if they lost or left their jobs. The result was high turnover in employment and a chronic labour surplus in the towns as urban workers searched for jobs with higher wages or better working conditions (see also Chapter 5). These insiders were able to avoid the less desirable occupations such as manual and domestic work and avoid dangerous and unpleasant employment down the mines. Because they had preferential access to manufacturing jobs, insiders were more likely to receive training and get access to more highly skilled employment (Simkins 1982a, 25–26). The incomes of these urban workers were thus somewhat protected under apartheid in that they did not face the downward pressures on wages that would have resulted from unfettered urbanisation and competition.

This was especially true in the 1950s, when the state adopted the urban labour preference policy. Urban employers were required to offer jobs, including unskilled work, to African people who were already resident in the towns—that is, they had section 10 (1)(a), (b), or (c) rights—in preference to employing migrants from the countryside (Posel 1993). This served further to raise urban wages and increase urban employers' preference for migrants!

Those without section 10 rights were heavily disadvantaged. They were supposed to find contract work through the labour bureaux.[1] The system comprised primarily district labour bureaux (attached to every magistrate's office) in white farming areas, urban local labour bureaux (in African townships), and territorial, district, and local labour bureaux in homeland areas (see RSA 1979).[2] In urban and peri-urban areas, employers had to register with a labour bureau, keep a record of all African employees, check that they had been authorised by the bureau, and inform it of all vacancies. In the rural areas, the labour bureaux channelled African labour into low-wage sectors that could not compete easily with the higher wages offered by urban employers. Because mining was able to recruit from neighbouring countries, the district labour bureaux in white rural areas concentrated on providing labour to commercial farms. Certain homeland areas were designated as suppliers of labour to agriculture, and once a person obtained a record of employment in agriculture, it was very difficult to shift sectors (Duncan 1977). The pass laws thus contributed to the perpetuation of low wages in the farming and mining sectors. This is what Simkins referred to as "administratively imposed disequilibrium in the African labour market" (1979, 14). In the mines, the real wages paid to African workers (including the value of food provided) were as low in 1969 as they had been in 1911 (Wilson 1972, 46), despite the tight labour market that prevailed in the 1950s. The mining companies colluded to set maximum average wages for African labour, thus preventing any competitive bidding up of wages when labour was in short supply.

In practice, many labour controls were less effective than they appeared on paper: the Native Affairs Department was too small to administer influx control when it was initially legislated (Posel 1987, 144), and many workers tried to bypass the labour bureau system and evade police enforcing the pass laws in order to obtain illegal employment in the towns (Hindson 1987, 65–66; Greenberg 1987, 41–43). Nevertheless, the labour controls clearly restricted rural-urban migration.

Most areas of public policy advantaged urban African people relative to rural ones. Uniform old-age pensions were not introduced until 1965. The distribution of hospitals, clinics, and doctors greatly favoured urban areas. In 1970 there were 109 people per hospital bed for African people in the principal urban areas but 191 per bed in the smaller towns and rural areas and as many as 233 per bed in the homelands. In the homeland of Kangwane, the ratio was 527 people per bed (McGrath 1979b, 134). Housing policy also favoured the urban areas (Pollak 1981, 21). The bantustans were privileged in terms of the construction of schools in the 1960s, but in the 1970s schools were built in urban areas at a very rapid rate.

Labour-market policies served to allocate different job opportunities to different people and to shape the ways in which wages were set for each occupation. The overall structure of employment in the economy, however, was driven by the growth path, which was itself shaped by a wider range of public policies.

THE APARTHEID GROWTH PATH DURING THE
POSTWAR BOOM

The apartheid growth path had many of the characteristics of a typical case of import substitution industrialisation (ISI). The state continued the promotion of secondary industrialisation with high tariffs, selective subsidisation of capital, and an overvalued exchange rate. As in other cases of ISI, especially in Latin America, these policies favoured politically powerful constituencies. The program enabled high wages to be paid to workers in capital-intensive, protected industries and in the "nontraded" sectors (sectors producing goods or services that cannot be traded internationally, including transport and most public works). White workers, in particular, benefited from the strategy because tariff protection was implicitly or explicitly contingent on the employment of white workers. Employers in protected industries also developed a vested short-term interest in the continuation of the strategy. In South Africa, white workers had great interest in a high-wage, capital-intensive growth path. A large (and growing) majority of white workers was employed in nontraded sectors. Devaluation would have shifted income from nontraded to traded sectors, hitting the incomes of politically powerful white employees (Moll 1990, 143). Given the political impossibility of reducing white labour costs or embarking on an extensive low-wage, labour-intensive growth path, capital also had an interest in high-productivity, capital-intensive growth.

As in most ISI situations, the state required the political support of rural elites. Politically powerful agricultural exporters also had to be compensated for the damage caused by an overvalued exchange rate. In most of Latin America the state facilitated rural elites' continued control of political power in the countryside, which in turn enabled them to maintain their economic privileges. In South Africa, "with the coming to power of the National Party all the restraints were removed on using the marketing boards as tools to keep weak farmers on the land" (Schirmer 2003, 3). White farmers were rewarded with cheap credit, high prices (raised by the marketing boards), and legislation that ensured abundant labour despite low wages. Between 1945 and 1955 soft government loans to agricultural cooperatives rose ninefold. In the 1960s the government facilitated mechanisation, primarily via cheap credit. As Schirmer (2003, 9) summarises, farmers "saw the tractor as a weapon to deal with 'troublesome' labour, and they called on the government to arm them." The government "armed" the farmers, then removed by force the one-third of the African population that was thereby rendered surplus. The state also, of course, prevented any land reform. The resources dedicated to white farmers reflected their political and ideological, not their economic, significance. In the late 1960s state aid contributed one-fifth of farmers' income (Nattrass 1988, 119), and this takes no account of the increase in farmers' incomes paid by consumers because of the increase in producer prices.

The South African growth path did have some features that marked it out from the standard ISI story. South Africa differed from most of Latin America in the strict controls on urbanisation and on entrepreneurial activity in the towns. The informal sector was severely repressed under apartheid. The state also restricted formal self-employment. The Group Areas Act not only provided the legislative basis for massive forced removals in urban areas but also (together with other legislation) restricted the location of African and Asian businesses and their access to white consumers. After 1963, restrictions on African traders in the townships were tightened further. A "one-man, one-shop" rule was imposed, the range of goods to be traded was severely limited, and black companies were banned from white areas (Bromberger 1982, 182). These restrictions served to divide still more sharply the privileged insiders from the marginalised outsiders.

An ISI-based growth path was perhaps not obviously irrational in the labour-scarce conditions of the early 1950s. Even mechanisation on the farms made some sense in the context of labour shortages. Moll (1990, 159 ff.) emphasises that there was an alternative model available: the export-oriented model of wartime industrialisation. But at the time, the limits to ISI were less evident than they are in hindsight. Support for ISI was pervasive and it had special appeal for nationalists.

The policies of the apartheid state steered the economy down a path that offered immediate gains for politically powerful constituencies but at a cost to the long-term growth rate and especially to groups that were dependent on growth for employment and hence an escape from poverty. Consider the pass laws. These were defended in parliamentary debates on the grounds that they allocated labour efficiently in a period of full or nearly full employment. But they confined a large proportion of African labour to two low-productivity, low-wage sectors of the economy: farming and mines. The result was high intersectoral wage differentials for African but not for white workers (Moll 1990, 150). Confining labour to these sectors was especially irrational given that the economy was characterised by labour shortages at the time. By preventing the higher-productivity sectors from absorbing more labour, the state not only restricted the earnings of many African workers but also slowed down the growth of the economy. (Labour policies also raised the cost of white and insider African labour for many urban employers, thus further constraining growth.) Later, when the state subsidised mechanisation in the mines, the main effect was not to release labour for use in higher productivity sectors but rather to sentence people to long periods of unemployment. The pass laws were used by the state to remove physically the surplus of unemployed people from farms rather than to promote labour-intensive production. Mechanisation in labour-intensive sectors was disastrous in distributional terms, once the economy had shifted from labour shortages to a massive labour surplus. By holding onto growth path policies that favoured capital-intensive production despite a growing labour surplus, the state both retarded growth and accentuated inequality.

The idea that the growth rate of the apartheid economy was constrained by public policy might seem implausible given the high growth rates of most of the 1950s and 1960s. Between 1960 and 1970, real manufacturing output expanded at an incredible 8.6 percent per year, investment expanded at 12.3 percent per year, and real net operating surplus at 5.2 percent per year. As can be seen in figure 4.4, the 1960s were a period of rapid sustained growth and rising per capita income. For early radical historians, this performance was proof that

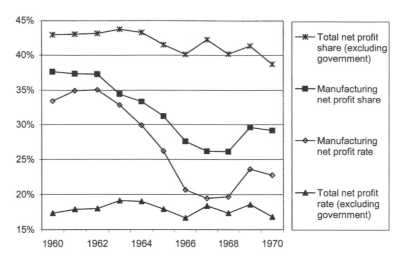

Figure 4.4. Trends in manufacturing and total profitability, 1960–70

apartheid was functional for capitalism. Given the coexistence of apartheid with rapid economic expansion, these writers suggested that there was "something highly functional and causally significant about the relationship between the economic system and the system of racial domination" (Johnstone 1976, 212). Wolpe made the point more bluntly, arguing that apartheid was instituted "for the purpose of reproducing and exercising control over a cheap African industrial labour force" (1972, 450). As Moll (1990) has shown, however, the performance of the South African economy was unimpressive in comparison with that of other developing countries. South Africa enjoyed fewer benefits from a booming global economy than did its immediate competitors. The country's share of global manufactured exports fell. The result was a falling rate of absorption of labour and growing skills shortages at the same time.

The cost of protecting white labour, in large part by failing to invest adequately in African education, came in the form of crippling skilled labour shortages. These eventually forced the government to *restrain* growth. During the capital-intensive boom years of the 1960s, skilled labour shortages were a constant source of complaint from businesses. Surveys conducted in 1969–71 reported skill shortages of 13 percent in construction and clothing, 8 percent in metals and engineering, 11 percent in motors, 12 percent in furniture, and an acute shortage of apprentices across many sectors (Lipton 1986, 145; RSA 1985, 103). As early as 1963, the governor of the South African Reserve Bank isolated such shortages as being the "only immediate limitations on the rate of economic growth" (de Kock 1963, 182). By the end of the 1960s, it was generally accepted that "the bottom of the barrel of skilled or usable Asians, coloureds and whites had been scraped [and] . . . the economy was checked at a labour barrier" (Dagut 1977, 75).

The apartheid distributional regime had costs and benefits to capital, but during the 1960s the costs rose sharply, especially for urban manufacturing. The profit share (that is, share of income going to capital) in manufacturing declined sharply (at more than 4 percent per annum) during the decade. This was largely a result of average wages' growing faster than productivity. These trends contributed to a similar decline in the net rate of profit (return on capital) (see figure 4.4). Such evidence is in clear contrast to claims of soaring profits in the 1960s that supposedly resulted when apartheid drove down the black wage bill (Saul and Gelb 1981, 70–74). Rather, there is little evidence of any stable "apartheid social structure of accumulation" (see Nattrass 1994b for a critique of this literature). Apartheid certainly repressed black trade unions and undermined the potential growth of black wage income, but this did not prevent tight labour market conditions from facilitating an increasing share of output going to labour as a whole.

Rapid economic growth unleashed economic pressures that drove up wages faster than productivity, thus eroding the share of income going to manufacturing capital. Average private-sector profitability was only able to remain broadly constant during the period as a result of countervailing trends in mining and commerce. It thus appears that cheap labour policies continued to benefit the mines but that the apartheid growth path was increasingly a problem for sustained development of the manufacturing sector. Subsidies and tariffs for manufacturing were not sufficient to prevent a decline in profitability. Given that the growth of manufacturing is essential to economic growth and development, these trends point to the limitations of the apartheid growth path for overall capitalist development in South Africa.

This raises some questions about the radical "cheap labour" theory of South African capitalist development. For example, when Lipton (1974) and Bromberger (1974, 1978) questioned the cheap labour hypothesis by pointing to the rapid growth of real wages paid to black people in the 1960s and early 1970s, Legassick replied that "institutions of racial discrimination and/or extra economic coercion may serve to 'cheapen' labour, to make it cheaper than it would have been in their absence, whether or not the absolute magnitude of the wage of employed persons is rising or falling" (1978, 73–74). Legassick is probably correct, but his position makes the cheap labour hypothesis impossible to test or disprove. (The same problem applies to such neoclassical economists as Dollery [1989], who, using a neoclassical general equilibrium approach, argued that profits were lower and wages were higher than they would have been in the absence of apartheid's restrictions on the labour market.)

Another way of approaching the "cheap labour" or labour exploitation hypothesis would be to see whether black labour was being paid less than its marginal productivity. This theoretical nicety is, however, impossible to test meaningfully because the assumptions that are required in any such modelling work drives the result. For example, Spandau (1973) compared estimated exponents of a production function with actual factor income shares and concluded that white workers were underpaid and black workers overpaid with respect to their marginal productivities. This approach ignored key structural features of the South African economy and utilised a very dubious methodology (see Archer and Maree [1975] for a critique). Ultimately, theoretical and measurement problems render this line of enquiry of little benefit to understanding either the nature or the history of South African capitalist development. Rather than endeavour to explain whether wages were "too high" or "too low," it is probably more useful to track the trend in wages and productivity and see how they affected profitability.

From the mid 1960s onward, the racial labour dispensation began to fray at the edges. Bottlenecks in the supply of skilled labour led to the colour bar's disintegrating, or "floating upwards," as white workers bargained wage increases for concessions concerning the racial division of labour. Social pensions for coloured people were increased (from 40 percent of white pensions in 1960 to 50 percent in 1965), and black pensions were increased marginally in the late 1960s. Real per capita spending on African education started to rise beginning in 1962—but, because spending on white pupils increased faster, the racial gap in per capita spending continued to grow (Bromberger 1982, 181).

While the racial segmentation of labour was slowly changing, the African labour force was increasingly becoming segmented along urban-rural lines. Controls on African urbanisation tightened, and pass law prosecutions increased during the 1960s. The 1967 Physical Planning and Utilisation of Resources Act attempted to reduce the demand for black workers in urban areas by refusing planning permission for certain industrial expansion in "controlled" areas (primarily the areas around Johannesburg and Port Elizabeth). It also encouraged South African manufacturing to become more capital- and skill-intensive. From 1968 onward, contract workers were required to break their contracts and return to the homelands so as to be ineligible for section 10(1)(b) rights.

LABOUR MARKET AND WELFARE POLICIES
UNDER THE LATE-APARTHEID
DISTRIBUTIONAL REGIME

By 1970 the apartheid project had shifted. In the tight labour markets of the early 1950s, apartheid had protected white workers from competition from cheaper African workers and had protected white farmers by providing them with cheap African labour. Later, amid a growing labour surplus, apartheid served a more political function, providing a refined form of indirect rule over the rural unemployed in terms of which white South Africans had limited or no responsibility for poverty in the bantustans. Influx control shifted from canalisation to, simply, restricted urbanisation.

The entire edifice of the labour bureaux, separate development, and independent homelands,[3] was constructed as part of this project to keep metropolitan areas white. Although this project did little more than stem an inevitable tide of social and economic transformation, it had the effect of firmly segmenting the African labour force between those with the right to be in the cities and those without. As job reservation was eroded and some African workers were allowed to "advance" up the occupational ladder, workers in the bantustans were denied opportunities for skill development and upward mobility. As African schools expanded during the late 1960s and 1970s, the children of urban workers were able to acquire skills that would stand them in good stead (at least relative to their rural counterparts) in the future labour market. Over time, the apartheid project shifted from fostering primarily racial segmentation for the benefit of the Afrikaans-speaking white population in particular to creating fault lines within the African labour force, which became ever more widely split between a relatively advantaged settled urban working class and a poverty-stricken rural labour force. The major features of the late apartheid distributional regime are set out in figure 4.5.

From the early 1970s onward the apartheid state began to deracialise many of its policies, reducing or removing explicit racial discrimination. New opportunities opened up for some African people to earn higher incomes. By the end of the 1970s, all statutory job reservations outside of mining had disappeared; the industrial conciliation machinery was about to be reformed to include the

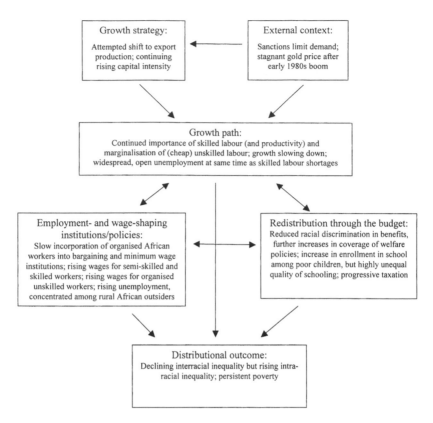

Figure 4.5. The late apartheid distributional regime

(now legalised) black trade unions. Shares of national income by race shifted drastically. Welfare payments to African pensioners were increased in real terms, as were expenditures on African schools. The budget became the vehicle for considerable redistribution. At the same time, unemployment grew. The result was that overall inequality did not diminish. Insofar as the capital-intensive growth path both increased the demand for skilled labour and limited the growth in demand for unskilled labour (leading to unemployment; see Chapter 5), so the pressures for deracialisation at the top end and the rise of unemployment at the bottom end of the income distribution were linked. They had a common cause: the particular growth path promoted by state policy.

Wages

By the early 1970s, the government had accepted that deracialisation was necessary to address South Africa's chronic skilled labour shortages and that measures should be taken to alleviate rising unemployment among unskilled African men and women (Bromberger 1982, 186–87). The restrictions of the colour bar were steadily phased out, and African workers' wages rose significantly. Upward occupational mobility and competition between mining and manufacturing for the available supplies of African labour resulted in rising wages for African workers. The racial wage gap narrowed significantly in all sectors in the early 1970s (Nattrass 1977). This shift was in large part market-driven, but it was also the result of militant action by factory workers. The 1973 Durban strikes, which marked the birth of the independent African trade union movement, helped boost the increase in wages substantially. Shortly after the strikes, the minister of labour instructed the Wage Board to revise key minimum wage determinations upward.

The Durban strikes also signalled the need for institutional change in the industrial bargaining machinery. If the disruptive power of African industrial muscle was to be contained, then it was clear that African trade unions had to be included in industrial conciliation. In 1979 the government-appointed Wiehahn Commission recommended that African workers be allowed to form registered trade unions and participate in industrial councils on an equal basis with white workers. The government accepted the recommendations, thus bringing about a crucial sea change in wage-bargaining and ultimately in the pattern of employment and wages for the following decades. In deracialising the wage-bargaining machinery, which had hitherto underpinned white incomes relative to African incomes, the apartheid government rebuilt a system that was to underpin the incomes of the employed relative to the unemployed.

The Wiehahn reforms made up one arm of a double-pronged labour reform strategy that sought to widen the rights of urban workers while tightening access to the urban labour market. In accordance with the recommendations of the Riekert Commission, the government attempted to impose further controls on the movement of African labour and introduced substantial fines for firms employing workers whose passes were not in order. This grand vision, however, failed to materialise, and in 1986 influx control was abolished. Similarly, attempts by the state to bar African migrants from membership in trade unions met with resistance and were quickly dropped. By the mid-1980s, the labour-relations machinery had effectively become deracialised.

Welfare and Other Social Spending

Government spending patterns also moved in more egalitarian directions. From the 1970s onward, spending on African people increased in the areas of education, public-sector wages, urban infrastructure, and development grants to the homelands (Bromberger 1982, 185–86). The value of the old-age pension paid to African people was increased from 13 percent of the value of a white pension in 1966 to 15 percent by 1971 and then to 30 percent by 1980. The real value of the African pension rose steadily, by an average of 7 percent per year between 1970 and 1993, such that it increased fivefold in this period; from the mid-1970s onward the real value of the maximum pension paid to white people was allowed to decline rapidly (see figure 4.2). Spending on pensions rose as a percentage of GDP from 0.6 percent to 1.8 percent during the same period (Van der Berg 1997, 488). Urban-rural differences in pensions were abolished in 1965, primarily in order to discourage urbanisation (Pollak 1981, 155) but with the effect of increasing redistribution. Racial discrimination in the old-age pension was finally abolished in 1993. Take-up rates also rose. Whereas in 1960, only 39 percent of the elderly received old-age pensions from the state, by 1993 this figure had risen to 79 percent (Van der Berg 1997, 489). By the end of the apartheid period pensions accounted for the bulk of welfare payments; in 1993, three of five grant recipients were old-age pensioners (ibid., 492–93). By equalising African and white pension levels, South Africa found itself with an "unusually comprehensive system compared with that found in other developing countries" (Lund 1993, 22), and the old-age pension became an important form of poverty relief for many African households (Ardington and Lund 1995; see also Chapter 6). Unemployment insurance also took an egalitarian direction. In 1979 the UIF's lower income limit was abolished, making unemployment insurance available to poorer workers. The UIF was extended in 1981 to include gold and coal miners and in 1993 to include farm workers.

Shifting patterns of expenditure were evident in education. Enrollment among African children rose steadily as more and more children spent longer and longer in the schooling system. Although the government formally retained its policy of limiting expenditure on African education to a subsidy fixed in nominal terms plus a share of taxes levied on African people, by the end of the 1960s it was compelled to subvent these sums with additional "loans." In 1972 the government abandoned its statutory limits on expenditure. Spending on African education rose very rapidly, and the interracial spending gap narrowed. Real expenditure on white pupils stabilised beginning in the mid-1970s, both in the aggregate and per pupil. Real expenditure on African pupils rose dramatically, increasing sixfold between the mid-1970s and the early 1990s; part of this was due to rising enrollment, but there was also a threefold increase in real spending per pupil (Fedderke et al. 2000; Hyslop 1999, 115, 144–45). Fig-

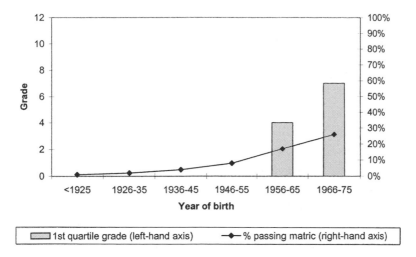

Figure 4.6. Educational attainment among African men and women under apartheid

ure 4.6 shows the consequences in terms of the steadily improving educational qualifications of successive cohorts of African people; as in figure 4.3, the columns and the left-hand axis indicate the grade level attained by the person at the top of the first quartile, and the line and the right-hand axis show the percentage of each age cohort that passed the matric examination. Attainment among African people was far below the levels attained by white men and women (see figure 4.3), but the increase at the end of apartheid was dramatic.

The effects of these shifts in the incidence of public expenditure are indicated in studies by Janisch, McGrath, and Van der Berg. Between 1949–50 and 1975–76 per capita public expenditure on education, health, welfare, and agriculture combined rose in real terms for all racial groups. There were marginal shifts in the incidence of taxation. The overall rate of redistribution from white to black South Africans remained more or less steady (McGrath 1979a). By 1993–94, however, the rate of redistribution had grown massively. Van der Berg writes that the ratio of social expenditure per capita on African and white people rose from about 12 percent up to 1975, to 21 percent by 1986, and to 69 percent by 1993 (Van der Berg 2001, 257). Of the total social spending, more than half went to white South Africans as late as 1975. Their share fell to about one-third in 1990 and to about one-sixth by 1993 (ibid., fig. 2). Analysis by Janisch, as reported and amended by Van der Berg (2001, 260), indicates that, by 1993, the net effect of income taxes and social spending was to reduce average white per capita income by almost one-sixth while increasing average African per capita income by more than one-third ("income" here including the value of in-kind benefits from public education and health care). The ratio of African to white per capita incomes rose from 10 percent to nearly 16 percent as a result of this redistribution. Its effects are larger still if all government spending is included.

Janisch's work also provides the basis for an analysis of redistribution not by race but by income quintile (McGrath, Janisch, and Horner 1997). Given uncertainty about the incidence of some taxes, Janisch and her co-authors provide two estimates of the tax burden, one placing the highest burden on the poor and the other, the lowest.[4] As can be seen in table 4.1, the lowest quintile (the poorest 20 percent of the population) bore a tax burden that was higher than its income share under both assumptions, thus indicating a degree of regressivity in the tax system. This was due to indirect taxes (especially value-added tax and excise duties). The top quintile bore a higher tax burden than its income share (because it paid almost the entire income tax bill), whereas the middle quintiles had higher income shares than tax burdens under both assumptions. By comparing Gini coefficients calculated on pre- and post-tax household income, McGrath, Janisch, and Horner concluded that central government taxation in 1993–94 served to widen inequality in South Africa (1997, 9). This is true even when social pensions are subtracted from household incomes in the pre-tax Gini calculation.

It is much harder to calculate the incidence of public expenditure because some items (such as education, health care, and social pensions) can be allocated directly,[5] whereas others (such as spending on roads and police) cannot. Expenditure that could not be allocated directly was attributed to households in two ways: first, on the assumption that benefits were distributed according to household income, and second, on the assumption that benefits were distributed on a per capita basis. These were then added to direct spending to arrive at two different estimates of total expenditure: one assuming a low benefit to the poor (that is, non-allocable expenditure distributed according to income shares) and the other a high benefit to the poor (that is, nonallocable expenditures distributed equally on a per capita basis).

McGrath, Janisch, and Horner (1997) combine their estimates into two scenarios: one based on assumptions that entail few benefits to the poor, the other based on assumptions that entail higher benefits to the poor. The gap between these estimates is quite large—much larger than the gap between the alternative estimates for the incidence of taxation. Nevertheless, as table 4.1 shows, both estimates indicate two key findings. First, the share of benefits rises as incomes rise, with the top quintile receiving the highest share; in this sense, public expendi-

Table 4.1. Redistribution via the budget, 1993–94

	Income Quintiles					
	1	2	3	4	5	Total
Income shares (%)	0.8	2.6	6.2	16.1	74.5	100
(1) Low estimate of tax incidence for the poor						
Total tax burden (%)	1.8	2.3	4.1	11.3	80.1	100
Taxes as a percentage of income (%)	30.1	15.3	15.3	22.6	36.2	
(2) High estimate of tax incidence for the poor						
Total tax burden (%)	2.3	3.6	5.5	12.5	75.7	100
Taxes as a percentage of income (%)	43.2	21.7	17.9	21.4	34.0	
(3) Low estimate of spending benefits for the poor						
Share of total expenditure (%)	6.7	10.8	13.1	18.0	51.4	100
Expenditure as a percentage of income	555.0	265.5	115.3	50.8	28.2	
(4) High estimate of spending benefits for the poor						
Share of total expenditure (%)	16.7	19.6	19.5	20.5	23.7	100
Expenditure as a percentage of income	1383.0	482.0	171.7	57.9	13.0	
Redistribution						
Best scenario for the poor, assuming (1) and (4)	6.1%	7.1%	6.1%	3.4%	−22.8%	0
Worst scenario for the poor, assuming (2) and (3)	1.8%	3.2%	3.1%	2.3%	−10.4%	0

Source: McGrath, Janisch, and Horner (1997).

ture is regressive. Second, all quintiles except the top quintile received shares of public expenditure that were greater than their shares of total income.

The Inter-American Development Bank (1998, 190–92) provides data for the incidence of public expenditure in Brazil and Chile with respect to social spending only. In Chile, social spending is highly progressive, with about 35 percent going to the bottom quintile and only 5 percent to the top quintile. In Brazil, each quintile receives approximately the same share. In South Africa, social spending was significantly regressive, with the top quintile receiving almost 30 percent of total social spending and the bottom quintile less than 13 percent. Castro-Leal et al. (1999) had similar findings with regard to the education and health components of social spending.

Combining estimates of the incidence of taxation and public expenditure raises an apparent paradox: redistribution can occur via the fiscus even when both are regressive. This is because we usually mean different things when we say that taxation and expenditure are regressive. With regressive taxation the poor pay a higher share of their income than the rich, that is, the share of taxation paid by the poor is higher than their share of income. With regressive expenditure the poor receive a smaller share of total expenditure than the rich. But the share of public expenditure given to the poor may be higher than their share of income or their share of taxation. This is the case in South Africa and probably in Chile but probably not in Brazil.

McGrath, Janisch, and Horner contrasted the actual tax burdens and spending benefits with a hypothetical neutral budget that allocated taxation and expenditure in accordance with income. As can be seen in table 4.1, redistribution occurred whether one assumed the worst-case scenario for the poor (high taxation and low benefits) or the best-case scenario (low taxation and high benefits). Thus the bottom quintile's share of post-redistribution income was between 1.8 and 6.1 percentage points higher than its share of pre-redistribution income, and the top quintile's share was between 10.4 and 22.8 percentage points lower.

In both scenarios, however, almost half of the redistribution away from the top quintile went to the third and fourth deciles, that is, to the relatively rich rather than the very poor. McGrath, Janisch, and Horner (1997, 15) write that these results "indicate that fiscal activities in 1993/4 were serving to redistribute income away from the richest quintile to the middle quintiles, and to a lesser extent to the poorest quintile. The lesson, which has been shown in studies of many other economies, is that the fiscal system in general is an extremely blunt instrument when used to redistribute incomes, and that the major benefits of the redistributed aspects of the fiscal system are captured by the 'middle class.'" Their figures suggest that taxation and social spending reduced the Gini coefficient in South Africa by about 7 or 8 points. The IADB calculates that the equivalent reduction in Chile is about half of this, at 3.4 points. The IADB provides no figures for Brazil, but it calculates that the equivalent reduction in Argentina is negligible at less than 1 point (IADB 1998 192). Even compared to Chile's budget, South Africa's was relatively progressive in redistributive terms before the first democratic elections in 1994—primarily because of its relatively progressive tax structure. McGrath, Janisch, and Horner were thus over-hasty in their conclusion that redistribution via the fiscus is a "blunt instrument." In comparative terms, the redistributive impact of South Africa's budget in 1993–94 was considerable.[6]

The findings of fiscal incidence studies such as these by Van der Berg and by McGrath, Janisch, and Horner need to be interpreted with care. There does not need to be much inequality of opportunity in the schooling system to ensure that inequalities are broadly reproduced, because differential education of children tends to mirror the differential income or class of their parents. Moreover, declining inequality in spending on education need not convert into declining inequality in the quality of schooling. A very high proportion of educational expenditure goes toward teachers' salaries. In an obvious sense, paying salaries entails a transfer to teachers (who are not the poor in South Africa today) at least as much as an in-kind transfer to the children, whether poor or not.

Redistribution via the budget may have increased dramatically, but shifts in interracial inequality were driven primarily by changes in the interracial division of labour as African workers advanced up the occupational hierarchy. As apartheid started fraying at the edges in the early 1970s and then disintegrating in the 1980s, the black share of income increased—from 20 percent in 1970 to 25 percent in 1980 and to almost 30 percent in 1993 (McGrath and Whiteford 1994, 4; Whiteford et al. 1995, 15). Racial discrimination declined dramatically (Moll 2000).

Yet despite declining discrimination and a rising African share in national income, overall inequality in the distribution of household income in South Africa did not change between 1975 and 1991 (McGrath and Whiteford 1994). This disturbing result reflects the fact that almost all the increased income accruing to the African population went to the richest 20 percent of households, with poorer households becoming worse off in real terms in 1991 than they had been in 1975 (Whiteford and McGrath 1998). In other words, intraracial inequality rose to such an extent that it overwhelmed the decline in interracial inequality, thus leaving overall inequality unchanged.

Deracialisation and increasing budgetary redistribution were politically feasible in part because white South Africans were no longer dependent on direct state controls or public spending to maintain their living standards. Privileged education resulted in greater skills and higher earnings, which in turn enabled white South Africans to provide for contingencies via the private rather than the public welfare system. It was thus not entirely a coincidence that deracialisation occurred alongside the privatisation of welfare.

The privatisation of welfare was striking with respect to healthcare services. A series of studies estimated that the public share of total healthcare expenditure in South Africa remained broadly stable at between 50 and 60 percent throughout the 1970s and early 1980s. By 1992–93, however, the public share had fallen to 30 percent (McIntyre 1997, 135, 148). Before 1948 and during the early apartheid period, private expenditure on health care took the form primarily of payments made directly to doctors, dentists, or nurses or to private hospitals (and to public hospitals for private care), as well as for medicines. By the early 1990s, medical aid schemes accounted for two-thirds of private-sector healthcare spending; direct payments by individuals accounted for less than one-fifth of private-sector spending (McIntyre 1997, 148). The rapidly rising share of private healthcare spending was partly due to rising costs but was also the result of rising coverage of the population by medical aid (and related) schemes. In 1970 about 2.5 million people were covered by registered medical aid schemes. This figure had risen to 4.3 million people by 1980 and to 6 million by 1990 (Dorrington and Zwarenstein 1988, 39; McIntyre 1997, 114). In 1970 only 59 percent of white people were covered; by 1980, 79 percent were covered. The proportion of the total population covered rose from 11 percent in 1970 to 16 percent in 1980 (ibid., 46). A further 3 million people were covered by unregistered medical aid schemes, medical insurance schemes, or employer-provided healthcare services such as that in the mines (McIntyre 1997, 117).

The growth of the private pension fund industry was even more dramatic than that of the medical insurance industry. Retirement funds were based on contributions paid by members during their working lives and were therefore limited to the employed (and self-employed). The proportion of the formally employed and self-employed population that contributed to retirement funds rose from about 17 percent in 1960 to 27 percent ten years later and 56 percent in 1980. By 1990 about six million people, or 73 percent of the formally employed population, were contributing to private retirement funds. Their contributions amounted to about 6 percent of GDP, or almost six times as much as the 1 percent of GDP spent by the state on its noncontributory old-age pension system. Retirement funds' assets had a value greater than one-half of GDP (RSA 1992, 2:394, 490, 595). Beginning in 1989 even mine workers were covered by a retirement fund, leaving only farm workers and domestics uncovered in the formal sector.

Growth in the number of pensions actually paid out obviously lagged behind the growth in the number of contributing members. By 1971 only 9 percent of elderly South Africans received pensions from contributory retirement funds (and two-thirds of these were pensioners in funds run by state or parastatal bodies). By 1990, 29 percent of the elderly were receiving pensions from such funds (ibid., 484–87). The number of pensioners receiving private retirement fund pensions was much smaller than the number of pensioners in the government's system, but the total sums paid out were many times larger. The proportion of elderly white people receiving government pensions declined from about 35 percent in 1960 to about 23 percent in 1991. The total value of government pensions paid out to white people peaked, in real terms, in 1981, whereas the total number of white pensioners receiving the government pension began to decline in the late 1980s (RSA 1994).

Education was the one area in which the apartheid state was slow to devolve responsibility to the private sector. The great expansion of schooling among African students did not coincide with any significant shift of white students into the private sector. Not until 1992, almost on the eve of democratisation, did the government adopt policies allowing some government schools (the "Model C" schools) to levy significant fees on parents of children.

THE GROWTH PATH UNDER THE
LATE-APARTHEID DISTRIBUTIONAL REGIME

During the 1970s and 1980s, just as white South Africans could dispense with state intervention via racial discrimination and rely instead on their advantages in the market, the apartheid growth path slowly ran out of steam. To some extent, South Africa's slowdown mirrored the end of the long postwar boom in advanced capitalist countries (Armstrong, Glyn, and Harrison 1991), although increases in the gold price provided some initial cushioning. The annual growth rate slowed from slightly less than 6 percent in the 1960s to 4 percent in the early 1970s to 2 percent in the late 1970s and then to 1 percent in the 1980s. Figure 4.7 shows that per capita income in South Africa peaked in 1980, at the height of a mini gold boom.

The manufacturing profit rate continued its downward slide into the 1970s (figure 4.8). Apart from a brief respite in the early 1980s, profitability remained lacklustre during the 1980s. The key factor behind the poor performance of manufacturing profitability was falling capital productivity. The sharp decline in capital productivity can be seen in figure 4.9, which shows a steady decline in the output-to-capital ratio, indicating that the growth in investment (particularly in the 1970s) was probably too rapid. It is possible that restrictions on black employment (emanating from the 1967 Physical Planning and Utilisation of Resources Act, which limited black employment in certain industries and urban areas), coupled with generous investment subsidies and negative real interest rates, resulted in an economically irrational degree of capital intensification. An additional factor might also have been the number of producers (en-

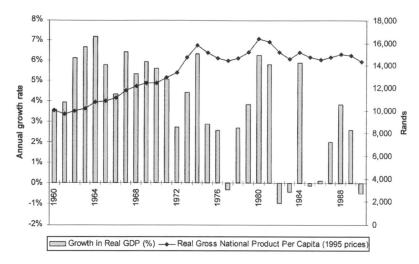

Figure 4.7. Growth in the South African economy, 1960–90

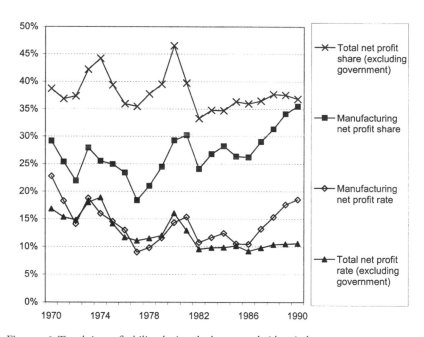

Figure 4.8. Trends in profitability during the later apartheid period, 1970–90

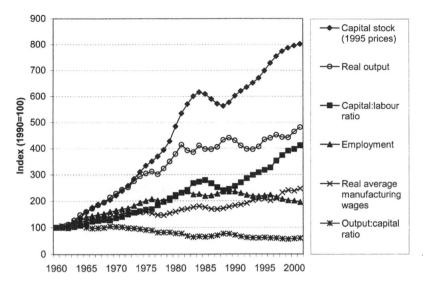

Figure 4.9. Key trends in South African manufacturing, 1960–2001. *Source:* Data are from the South African Reserve Bank.

couraged to enter certain markets by tariff protection) in relation to the limited size of the domestic market (RSA 1983).

Another factor behind the fall in manufacturing profitability in the 1970s was sharp increases in capital prices relative to value-added prices. The depreciation in the rand from 1985 onward contributed to the problem (Fedderke et al. 2001, 510). As firms were increasing their capital intensity (and lowering the productivity of capital as they did so) they were also experiencing a sharper increase in inflation on capital goods than they were experiencing for their output. Relative output-capital prices thus shifted sharply against capital, thereby undermining profitability. Although the manufacturing profit share recovered in the 1980s, these adverse trends in relative prices and declining capital productivity resulted in an overall decline in the net manufacturing profit rate for the period.

Why was there such a sharp increase in capital intensity in the 1970s? One of the reasons has to do with industrial strategy. As noted earlier, from the mid-1920s onward, South Africa had followed a Latin American—style inward-industrialisation strategy. This strategy initially supported strong employment growth in labour-intensive consumer goods industries, but by the late 1960s it had lost momentum. At that point, rather than opting for more outward-oriented export strategies (as in the East Asian economies), the South African gov-

ernment extended protection upstream into ever more capital-intensive industries (Levy 1992). This, together with large-scale strategic investments by the
state (in, for example, SASOL, which produced oil from coal) and negative real
interest rates and accelerated depreciation allowances, contributed to rising average capital intensity in the 1970s, especially in manufacturing (Kaplinsky
1995).

During the 1970s and early 1980s, the coincidence of rising wages and negative real interest rates meant that the cost of capital relative to labour fell to
about half the level it had been in the 1960s (Meintjies 1998, 11–12). Tax breaks
for capital investment further encouraged firms throughout the economy to
adopt more labour-saving techniques (see RSA 1985; Spies and Biggs 1983, 22–
24). The change to positive real interest policies reversed the downward trend
in the user cost of capital but failed to boost employment growth significantly.
Rising levels of industrial conflict may have contributed to this pattern.[7]

Hofmeyr (1994) shows that black trade unions successfully used the wage-
setting machinery to drive up the wages of less-skilled workers, thus resulting in
a new form of segmentation between unionised and nonunionised parts of the
formal sector. The wages of unskilled Africans fell in the late 1970s and early
1980s (as stagnant growth reduced the demand for such labour) but then rose
from the mid-1980s as African trade unions were able to use their new institutional muscle to push up these wages.

But the divide between union and nonunion workers was only one aspect of
the emerging segmentation within the African labour force. The incorporation
of African workers into the industrial council system created another: that between workers (unionised or not) who were covered by industrial council
agreements and those (such as farm workers, domestics, and most workers in
the service industries) who were not. As Moll (1996) puts it, the impact of deracialising the industrial council system was to "recycle" the old apartheid-era
wedge between white and black workers into a wedge between insiders and
outsiders (including the unemployed).

To the extent that such wage pressures encouraged firms to adopt labour-saving techniques, these trends would have contributed to the increase in capital
intensity.[8] The trend toward greater capital intensity worsened into the 1990s
and is one of the most important economic legacies of the apartheid growth
path for contemporary democratic South Africa.

This was a period of change for the mining industry also. For decades the
labour of migrants in the mines had been the major source of income for many
rural areas, despite the low wages paid. The benefits of migrant labour were

spread widely in part because few mine workers worked repeated contracts without break. In practice, there was "job-sharing" because many mine workers experienced periods of joblessness in between contracts. In the early 1970s the mines finally raised wages and starting in the late 1970s began to stabilise their workforce by employing a smaller pool of better-paid, more highly skilled workers for the long term rather than a larger number of less skilled workers who might work one year but not the next. By means of Valid Re-engagement Guarantee certificates, the mines locked privileged mine workers into repeated contracts. Although the number of South African men employed in the mines at any one time grew until the late 1980s, the total number employed during the entire year probably declined. The emergence of the "'career miner,' who had to work continuously on a particular mine or forfeit his job," meant higher wages (but perhaps poorer health) for a smaller total number of mine workers; the "stabilisation" of mine labour "shut out a whole generation of new work-seekers who could once have counted on a mine job, if nothing else" (Crush 1995, 25). The collapse of total employment in the late 1980s exacerbated the trend. "Mine work became a career for a smaller professional elite as opposed to a series of intermittent contracts for a mass of unskilled labourers" (Murray 1995, 8; see further Chapter 9).

Agriculture also became steadily less labour-demanding. With the rise of drastic labour shortages in agriculture in the late 1960s and early 1970s, government policy concerning agricultural labour shifted from assisting farmers via the old labour-repressive regime to helping them replace African labour with capital. White farmers continued to see "unreliable" labour as their most pressing problem. The Du Plessis Commission of Inquiry in Agriculture made this strategy clear: "White agriculture must . . . gradually be made less dependent on non-white labour and eventually be released from the need of it as far as possible" (quoted in Simbi and Aliber 2000, 4). As Simbi and Aliber note, "income tax provision to allow for the accelerated write-off of agricultural equipment, the encouragement of large-scale farming through the Subdivision of Agricultural Land Act 1970, negative real interest rates on agricultural loans were all measures designed to promote the development of a modern, labour-lean agricultural sector" (ibid., 4). Mechanisation in the 1970s included the introduction of combine harvesters into maize farming, as well as chemical weed killers and irrigation more generally. In the early 1980s the state shifted its policy regarding farming. The production of a massive maize surplus in 1981 (that had to be bought at inflated prices and then exported at a loss), followed by drought in 1982, required a large increase in state subsidies. The state made continued subsidies conditional on farmers' adopting more efficient and competitive methods. Between 1981 and 1987 approximately one-half of all white farmers received, on average, R1 million in subsidies—but were pushed to more competitive production (Schirmer 2000). This meant further capital intensification and reduced demand for unskilled labour.

Protection and subsidies also continued to undermine competitiveness. Vink and Kirsten (2000) compare the Chilean and South African experiences with respect to the production and export of apples. Chilean farmers were allowed to market their apples freely from the 1970s, but South African farmers were required to market their apples through a monopolistic agency until 1996. In the mid-1970s South Africa exported several times as many apples as Chile, but Chile caught up in the 1980s. By the early 1990s, Chilean exports were double South Africa's. During the two decades from 1975 to 1995, Chilean exports rose by 800 percent, whereas South Africa's rose by a mere 60 percent.

In short, employment growth was slowing down not only because the economy was slowing down but because growth itself became less labour-demanding in a range of sectors. According to Bowles (1995, 6), if only one-quarter of the capital stock invested in electricity generation, mining, and the beverage and paper-manufacturing sectors had instead been invested in the more labour-intensive clothing, furniture, construction, and fabricated metal sectors, then almost one million more jobs would have been created. Investment flowed into capital-intensive sectors in part because government policies kept the cost of capital low relative to the cost of labour despite rising unemployment.

CONCLUSION

Before and during the apartheid period, government policies ensured that white South Africans prospered in the short and medium terms. In the recessionary conditions of the early 1930s, policies had ensured that poor white people had jobs and hence income, whereas skilled white workers were protected from competition and declining wages. In the expanding economy of the postwar years, policies ensured that low-productivity sectors of the economy had cheap labour and that uncompetitive white workers had high incomes. It is crucial that the government invested heavily in the education of poor white South Africans so as to ensure that the uncompetitive position in the labour market of poor white parents was not passed on to their children. The government also encouraged greater capital intensity in order to lessen the depen-

Table 4.2. Managing supply of and demand for labour

		Depression 1930s	Early apartheid 1950s	Late apartheid 1970s/1980s
Supply (S) of and demand (D) for labour	Unskilled labour	S>D unemployment	S<D tight labour market	S>D rising unemployment
	Skilled labour		S<D skills shortages	S<D acute skills shortages
Management of racial labour "problems" via supply (S) and demand (D)	Managing the demand for unskilled (African) labour		ISI/mechanisation of agriculture reduces D	Continuing capital-intensification reduces D
	Managing the supply of African labour	Influx control: return unwanted labour to the reserves	Influx control: canalisation of scarce unskilled labour Restricted education means that African labour is unskilled	Influx control: removals/ displaced urbanisation into bantustans to control labour surplus; some deracialisa-tion to ease skilled labour shortages
	Managing the demand for white labour in the short run	Civilised labour policies in-creased D; wage-setting institutions increased wages; welfare safety net	Job reservation increased D; wage-setting institutions increased wages; de-clining need for welfare safety net	Problems solved! Leave it up to the markets
	Managing the supply of white labour in the medium term		Public education to produce a more skilled white labour force	
Implications for welfare policy		Welfare safety net required for white poor	Declining need for welfare safety net for white poor	Privatised welfare for the better off; in-creased redistribu-tion through bud-get to the poor

dence on African labour and to provide good jobs for white workers. In the later apartheid period, government policies sought to ensure that white South Africans' privileges, now based more on skills valued in the market, were protected against the social or political threat of the poor unemployed in the reserves via continued influx control. Employers' interests were provided for by the acceleration of public investment in black education, by the subsidisation of capital, and by the gradual floating upward of the colour bar.

The successes of government policies in the early apartheid period paved the way for the reform of the apartheid distributional regime thereafter. Education enabled white South Africans to prosper on the basis of skill rather than racial discrimination in the labour market. The mechanisation of agriculture and similarly capital-intensive industrialisation favoured land-owning or skilled people, albeit at immense cost to the unskilled, who were increasingly sentenced to chronic unemployment in the reserves. The later apartheid period saw steady redistribution and deracialisation in many areas of public policy, as well as the privatisation of welfare but saw continuing influx control as the state sought to manage the social costs of unemployment.

Table 4.2 summarises the key shifts during the apartheid era in terms of the labour market and their implications for welfare and education policies. The shift from unemployment to labour shortages and back again (as far as unskilled workers were concerned, but not for skilled workers) meant that the state, responsive to the interests of its white citizens, developed new mechanisms for managing the demand for white labour (and hence the wages received by white workers) and (under early apartheid) for unskilled African labour (because of shortages). But the overly successful management of demand for African labour led to a problem of managing the supply of unskilled African labour. Whereas earlier the state had sought to push labour out of the bantustans, under apartheid the state began to push labour back into the bantustans in order to gain political control of the growing labour surplus. Late in the apartheid era, deracialisation meant that the growing urban black population became the partial beneficiaries of a distributional regime premised on the social exclusion of large numbers of unemployed people in rural areas. Post-apartheid South Africa would battle with the contradictory legacies of this policy.

Chapter 5 The Rise of

Unemployment Under Apartheid

The most important change in the lives of many ordinary South Africans during the apartheid decades was the rise of widespread open unemployment. At the start of apartheid, unemployment had not been an issue. On the contrary, as we saw in Chapter 4, the South African economy then was plagued by chronic labour shortages, and employers and the state worried about securing sufficient labour. South Africa experienced the typical sub-Saharan problem of labour-constrained development. As Karshenas (2001) has argued, the Lewis model of development with "unlimited" supplies of labour did not apply in sub-Saharan Africa: either a labour supply had to be created by means of extraeconomic coercive mechanisms or higher wages had to be offered in the capitalist sector (see Chapter 1). The uniquely South African solution to this problem—initiated in the late nineteenth century, honed through the early twentieth century, and extended under apartheid—consisted of the use of coercion to undermine independent peasant production and channel labour to mines, commercial farms, and industry. The results were deagrarianisation, proletarianisation, and the transformation of South African society (see

Chapter 2). Food supplies were maintained via the growth of a large-scale, capital-intensive white commercial farming sector.

Economic growth slowed down sharply in the mid-1970s and performed poorly for most of the rest of the century. The growth that did occur resulted in little job creation. As the rising population swelled the labour force, so the economy became less and less able to absorb workers. By the end of the 1970s, unemployed men were crowding rural labour bureaux in unprecedented numbers and queuing outside urban factories. In striking contrast to the 1940s and 1950s, millions were sitting without work in denuded and overcrowded rural areas. The bitter tragedy for rural households was that by the time the demand for labour in the capitalist sector stagnated and then collapsed, peasant agriculture had been destroyed and the African labour force had become fully dependent on wage labour. There was sufficient work for people in neither the capitalist sector nor peasant agriculture. Two surveys conducted forty years apart in Keiskammahoek (a poverty-stricken part of the Ciskei) reveal the extent of this dramatic shift from labour shortage to surplus in African areas: in 1949, many poor households were unable to farm all of their land because they lacked labour (Houghton and Walton 1952); four decades later, up to 50 percent of the labour force in the area was unemployed (Sperber 1993, 19).

At the dawn of democracy in 1994, more than one-third of the African labour force indicated that they wanted work but could not find it. Unemployment had become a defining feature of the South African political economy, if not the most salient feature, yet our understanding of its contours and history is murky at best. This is in part a result of inadequate data and in part a reflection of conceptual and theoretical differences in the way that unemployment has been understood. Everyone agrees that by the mid-1980s, labour shortages had given way to open and visible unemployment. But the literature is confusing in its accounts of when and how the shift took place. One crucial question was, had there been significant unemployment in the early apartheid period, despite persistent and simultaneous labour shortages?

Part of the problem lies with rival understandings of "unemployment." The standard economic approach defines unemployment as a function of the wage: only those who are looking for work at prevailing wages but cannot find it should be counted as unemployed. This definition, however, is difficult to apply in practice, and most labour-force surveys instead classify people as unemployed if they do not have a job but want work and are actively seeking it. These differences yield rather different narratives about the rise of unemployment in South Africa.

To make matters more complicated, there was a third understanding of unemployment in the South African debate. The concept was understood by some scholars in terms of the underutilisation of labour. Using census and employment data, rather than data from labour-force surveys, Simkins and others estimated unemployment as the difference (or what we call the "gap") between actual and potential employment. By this measure, unemployment had been high even in the 1960s. Because this appeared to fly in the face of widespread evidence of labour shortages, neoclassical economists were especially critical of it. But as we argue below, gap estimates and economic interpretations of unemployment were highlighting different aspects of the apartheid labour market. If Simkins had instead referred to his measure as "underutilisation of labour" rather than "unemployment," more light and less heat might have resulted in the ensuing debate.

This chapter tells two stories. One story describes the rise of unemployment in South Africa. It draws on a range of secondary sources and shows how the labour shortage gave way to high and open unemployment in the mid- to late 1970s. The other story is about the historiography of unemployment. It shows how different conceptions of unemployment resulted in different narratives and in long-standing misunderstandings about what was meant by unemployment and how it was measured.

LABOUR SHORTAGES: FROM THE 1940S
TO THE MID-1970S

At the outset of apartheid, the Department of Native Affairs stated adamantly that there was no involuntary unemployment among African people (Union of S.A., 1950b, 33–38). Economists (for example, Van der Horst 1949), concurred. Workers who wanted employment could find it anywhere—especially during the war years, when influx control was relaxed. In this tight labour market, they opted for better-paying urban jobs rather than poorly paid, arduous, and unpleasant agricultural and mining employment. The mines struggled to retain their workforce in the face of relatively high manufacturing wages (Wilson 1972, 87), and even the manufacturing sector suffered shortages of labour in the 1950s and early 1960s in occupations considered obnoxious or poorly paid, such as hard manual labour (Posel 1991, 197–98; RSA 1962, 21–22; see also Chapters 2 and 3 above).

Commercial farmers, who had been complaining about labour shortages since the 1920s, became increasingly vocal. As young and middle-aged men flocked to the towns, attracted by manufacturing wages that were on average four times those of farm workers (including the in-kind value of food provided), it was said that "it is only the old crocks, the older women, and children who stay on the farms" (quoted in Posel 1991, 31). Commercial farmers were thus faced with a choice: either they competed with urban firms in this fast-unifying labour market or they lobbied the state to extend and tighten the system of controls that channelled labour to the mines and the farms—that is, to enforce the segmentation of the labour market by coercive means. Farmers favoured the latter strategy, but government officials in the immediate postwar period suggested instead that they pay higher wages (Duncan 1995, 144). The Department of Native Affairs reported that farms and mines in many areas were experiencing labour shortages simply because wages and working conditions were unattractive relative to urban areas (Union of S.A. 1950b, 33–38; 1951a, 40; 1953, 19).

Farming districts voted strongly for the National Party in the 1948 election, and fully one-half of the party's members of Parliament had backgrounds in farming. The result was that the new government was far more sympathetic to farmers' complaints. From 1952 onward a countrywide system of labour bureaux was introduced that was designed to channel African labour to the lower-paying commercial agriculture and mining sectors (see Chapter 4). This, together with influx control and the designation of certain parts of the country as supply areas for agriculture only, served to segment the labour market across sectoral lines. Prisoners were increasingly used on the farms; as many as two hundred thousand were working on farms by the late 1950s (Marcus 1989, 70–73). These coercive measures did not, however, eliminate the problem entirely. One survey conducted as late as 1969 reported shortages of 12.4 percent in white farming (cited in Knight 1977, 46).

Shortages of labour affected all sectors, including peasant agriculture. As noted above, poor households in Keiskammahoek in 1949 were reported to be labour-constrained (Houghton and Walton 1952). Delius (1996) reports that many households in Sekhukhuneland were unable to leave their cattle in remote cattle posts (where fodder was more plentiful) once the expansion of primary schooling reduced the availability of child labour. This suggests that labour constraints were affecting peasant agriculture in some areas right into the 1960s. This may have reflected, at least in part, a crisis of authority within African households. It is possible that heads of household were unable to control the labour of junior members as they had in the past. Thus there might have been surplus labour on white-owned farms or in reserves but no way of ensuring that it was available for use. Such a crisis of authority is evident in Van Onselen's biography of the sharecropper Kas Maine. As the years passed, Maine found it harder and harder to order his children to work in the landlords' fields or house or to work for him on the field he farmed. Joblessness could thus prevail at the same time as a labour shortage, if younger household members chose not to work (Van Onselen 1996).

Should someone who chooses not to work be counted as unemployed? According to conventional economic understandings of unemployment, the answer is an emphatic no. A person who chooses not to work at prevailing wages has effectively withdrawn from participation in the labour market. He or she will thus be jobless but not unemployed. Increasing the effective supply of labour thus becomes a problem of increasing participation in the labour force (rather than reducing unemployment).

During the 1950s, the problem of nonparticipation exercised the minds of government officials. They worried constantly about the problem of "idle" youth in the towns (Posel 1991, 86; Lodge 1983, 100; Sapire 1993, 264). The new secretary for native affairs, W. M. Eiselen, explicitly pointed out how "idleness" had spread to the towns: "Up to now these work-shy Natives have chiefly been those who were none too keen to part with the easy, idle life enjoyed especially by men in primitive Bantu society. During the past decade their ranks have been swelled by many young Natives who lead a parasitical existence in the cities because they are not prepared to do manual labour. These Natives will have to realise that if they are to share in the increased prosperity accompanying the rapid development of the country, they will have to do their share by doing an honest day's work" (Union of S.A. 1953, 6).

Eiselen continued, noting that it is difficult to improve "the mental attitude of the average Native . . . because so many of them are still slaves to primitive ideas and customs which clash with the demands of productive labour." Therefore, he concluded, what was needed was a system to ensure a more efficient distribution of labour—that is, the pass law system. This would solve the problem of "work-shy Natives who contribute nothing towards the development of the country" (ibid.). An interdepartmental committee found that 80 percent of young African men and women between the ages of fifteen and twenty were without gainful employment. The department addressed the problem by dispatching the older men to work colonies and the younger men to Bantu youth camps, where they provided cheap labour for farmers while being "rehabilitated" from idleness (Union of S.A. 1955b, 25; see also Union of S.A. 1959, 41–42). "Canalising" the workforce by means of influx control was thus represented as being in the interests of African workers as well as of commercial farmers.

Amid continuing concern with "unemployment" among urban youth (in the sense of nonparticipation in the labour force), another interdepartmental committee was appointed to examine the issue of "idle and non-working Bantu in the urban areas." The committee, chaired by deputy minister M. C. Botha, reported in 1962. Farming lobbies were still influential politically, but the pass laws had by now largely resolved the problem of shortages of (cheap) farm labour (Union of S.A. 1960); farmers in many districts were in fact evicting surplus labour. Rather, "idleness" represented a social—and prospectively political—problem because joblessness was seen as breeding delinquency and crime. As the Botha Committee put it, young African men, who "disappeared" from the school registers between the ages of seven and fifteen, began "a dissolute life of roguery on the streets, of gang-formation, gambling and petty-theft. Gradually they develop into the ubiquitous gangs of tsotsis that terrorise the townships. By the time they reach working age, they have either developed into a 'type' that refuses to work, or by virtue of their instability and untrustworthiness, have become unemployable" (RSA 1962, 3, author's translation).

This view was not held by officials alone. Urban African elites expressed concern about idle and wayward African youth (Glaser 1993, 297 ff). According to the Botha Committee, the problem of idleness was primarily applicable to young men under the age of twenty-five who chose not to work. The problem of unemployment was (correctly) seen as referring to the "great number of jobless Africans in urban areas who are making bona fide attempts to find work, but cannot obtain jobs because they are surplus to the requirements of the labour market" (RSA 1962, 3, author's translation). The committee went on to note that this form of unemployment was "complicated" by the fact that many work-seekers displayed a high level of "fastidiousness" or "pickiness" when it came to accepting work. This was particularly the case with regard to arduous manual jobs and jobs with long or irregular hours such those as in catering and domestic work. This undermined the government's urban labour preference policy as labour bureaux were forced to allow firms to bring in workers from outside the urban areas to fill vacancies, even though able-bodied manpower was already present (ibid., 3, 35). Some employers in fact preferred to employ migrants instead of "cheeky" and "difficult" urban workers (Posel 1991, 162–64, 178–79).

This suggests that the urban labour market in South Africa was itself segmented between low-paying jobs filled mainly by migrants and higher-paying jobs with better prospects favoured by city dwellers. If so, then it was clearly rational for some urban work-seekers to wait for the better jobs. Some open urban unemployment would thus occur as a result of queuing for better jobs. According to the Botha Committee, this was facilitated by the ability of such individuals to find support while waiting: "The Bantu apparently finds it not difficult, despite idleness, to subsist. In other words, the economic incentive to work at any job, and at any wage, is apparently not very strong. A contributing factor is the fact that unemployed and idle Bantu easily obtain meals and sleeping places amongst other members of their own race. In many cases, the sleeping place is in the servant's quarters in the back rooms of white residences, and the meal comes out of the white employer's kitchen" (RSA 1962, 22, author's translation).

This discourse of idleness was, on one level, profoundly racist. It assumed that the problem lay with a character flaw: natives were "work-shy," "unproductive," and "up to no good." This kind of demeaning analysis served to justify the barrage of labour legislation designed to force Africans into the labour force or boot them out of town. But, on another level, the discourse also indicated a deep frustration with African men and women for reacting as rational economic agents. They were not simply accepting any job: they were in some sense "choosing" to do nothing, that is, valuing their own time and freedom above the wages on offer or waiting to see if they could get work in the better-paying parts of the economy.

Official concern with idleness among the youth seems to have abated in the 1960s, probably because the problem itself was solved. It seems that three factors were important in this process. First, the rapid expansion of public schooling absorbed growing numbers of urban youth and kept them off the street. As Hyslop (1993) has argued, Bantu education was in part a response to the problem of governing the urban areas. Second, the rapid growth of employment and real wages in urban industry absorbed most of the unemployed who were waiting for better jobs. Third, we can speculate, the new townships were more easily and intensely policed, making it more difficult to earn a living informally (whether by honest trading or by crime). Revisions to the pass laws meant that many "idle" urban youth were arrested and sent to work on farms or to the reserves (Glaser 1993, 309).

The problem of labour shortage was managed fairly successfully in the 1960s (albeit at the cost of higher wages for industry)—but then exploded out of control in the early 1970s. Between 1972 and 1975, Africans' real wages increased dramatically; they rose by 30 percent per year in mining and by 9 percent per year in manufacturing (Hofmeyr 2000, 111). By the early 1970s, the labour-control machinery was no longer effective at allocating labour to low-wage sectors, and open wage competition between the sectors for the available supply of African labour had emerged (Hofmeyr 1994).

The upward trend in wages started in the manufacturing sector with increases in minimum wage determinations by the Wage Board and negotiated wage increases following the 1973 strikes. Mining wages started to increase at roughly the same time. The main motivation behind the mining wage increases appears to have been the desire to attract more South African nationals and to reduce the dependence of the gold-mining industry on foreign migrants. Prior to the 1970s, the mining industry had responded to shortages of South African labour by increasing the complement of southern African labour rather than increasing wages, which remained constant in real terms from 1911 to 1971 (Wilson, 1972). This had resulted in a decline in the proportion of South African workers in the mining workforce from 41 percent in 1946 to 22 percent in 1972 (Knight 1977, 44). But concern about the level of dependence on foreign labour had been growing for some time, and the fortuitous rise in the gold price starting in 1972 enabled the mines to finance a large increase in wages.

The mines were particularly dependent on labour from Malawi and Mozambique (which together supplied more than half of all mine workers). The suspension of recruitment in Malawi following an air crash that killed a planeload of migrants in 1974 was a major blow to the mining industry, as was the coup in Portugal, which raised questions about the reliability of future supplies from Mozambique. This reinforced the decision of the Chamber of Mines to increase its complement of South African miners, and it increased wages still further.

The Chamber of Mines had long believed that there was no significant pool of involuntarily unemployed African men in the homelands (ibid., 44). Therefore, after the government of Malawi suspended recruiting, the Chamber of Mines successfully lobbied the South African government to allow mining recruitment in some white farming districts that had previously been closed to them. This aroused expectations of growing competition with white agriculture for the available supplies of black labour.

This appears to have happened in some areas. Data from the Transvaal and the Orange Free State indicate that a real wage increase of 11 percent per year occurred between 1970–71 and 1974–75, "suggesting that an acceleration occurred in agriculture simultaneously with that in mining and manufacturing" (ibid., 46). Greater increases appear to have occurred in areas that competed with mining for migrant labour. This was the case with regard to the sugar-growing areas of Natal, which relied on migrant labour from the Transkei (because Zulu men apparently were not prepared to work as cane cutters). In 1969–70 the basic wage of a cane-cutter was 34 cents per day, and in 1975–76 it was R1.75 per day (ibid., 46–47). Such evidence indicates that competition from mining had a generalised impact on agriculture.

This evidence of labour shortages and rising wages is consistent with the existence of a tight labour market during this period. It suggests that labour shortage, and not unemployment, was the order of the day. But this situation was to change dramatically within a few years. By the mid-to-late 1970s, open unemployment had increased dramatically. This shift was captured by several labour-force surveys conducted at the time—and by the "gap" estimates of unemployment using (adjusted) labour force data from official sources.

UNEMPLOYMENT IN THE 1970S

Labour-force surveys set out to categorise people as employed, unemployed but seeking work (counted as being in the labour force), or "non–labour force participants." The unemployment rate is calculated as the number of unemployed work-seekers as a percentage of the labour force. In deciding who is unemployed (rather than not participating in the labour market), labour-force surveys typically ask jobless individuals of working age whether they (a) desire work and (b) are looking for work. They do not ask them whether they are looking for work "at the going wage," as is required by the conventional economic understanding of unemployment. The labour-force approach instead categorises people as unemployed or as nonparticipating according to an attitude (whether they desire employment) and an activity (whether they are actively seeking work). Broad or expanded definitions of unemployment simply require that a jobless person be available to work and desire employment to be classified as being in the labour force and unemployed. Strict definitions of unemployment require in addition that the jobless person be actively seeking work.

Table 5.1 shows how the labour-force approach categorises individuals. The dashed lines indicate that the size of the labour force and the number of people classified as unemployed will shrink if a strict definition of unemployment is used. A woman choosing to stay at home and look after children is not counted as part of the labour force. She probably works full-time at domestic duties, but because she is not offering herself for paid employment in the labour market

Table 5.1. Labour force and non-labour force participants

Total population					
Children (1–15 yrs)	Working age (15–65 yrs)				Elderly (65+ yrs)
			Labour force		
			Not employed but wanting work	Employed	
Pre-school children, school pupils	Older school students and students in university or other higher education	Other non-participants in the labour force; housewives, the disabled, people not wanting to work	Not looking for work / Looking for work	Formally employed / Self-employed	Retirees

174

she is classified as "not economically active" and hence as a non–labour force participant. The same applies to students in educational institutions, early retirees, and those too disabled to work, as well as people who, for whatever reason, do not want to work. In calculating the unemployment rate, such people appear neither in the numerator (the unemployed) nor the denominator (the labour force).

During the mid-1970s several localised household surveys were conducted, mainly by university-based academics, in response to the lack of good data about the emerging problem of unemployment. There were no good data because the parastatal statistics agency gave extraordinary instructions to the enumerators working on the official population census. For the 1970 census, enumerators were told to record as "employed" four classes of individuals who reported themselves as "unemployed." Men and women in rural areas who were without work but could indicate the occupation and industry in which they last worked were classified as employed (Loots 1978, 10). And, to make matters more complicated for those seeking to trace the rise of unemployment over time, census definitions of who counted as unemployed changed between successive censuses. In the 1960 South African census, "a male aged 16 or over in the homelands was classified as 'peasant farmer' unless another occupation was specified; a female in the same position was classified as 'housewife.' In the 1970 census, the homeland wives of household heads were classified as 'housewives' and thus 'not economically active,' but other females classified 16 or over were classified as 'peasant farmers.' Hence half the recorded increase in economically active female Africans between 1960 and 1970 is the result of a change in the definition" (Knight 1977, 32).

Faced with low-quality data from the census regarding unemployment and labour-force participation, scholars could either try to manipulate the official data to adjust for the problems (as in the "gap" estimation of unemployment by Simkins; see below) or conduct their own surveys. Such surveys were limited in their geographical coverage and were not strictly comparable in that they used different ways of classifying people as labour-force participants. They are, however, indicative of the broad shift from labour shortage to open unemployment in South Africa. All reported high rates of unemployment among Africans by the mid-to-late 1970s. Loots (1977) reported broad rates of unemployment of 19.5 percent in Crossroads in Cape Town, 23.8 percent in Pretoria's townships of Atteridgeville and Mamelodi, and 28.3 percent in the Pretoria-Witwatersrand-Vaal region as a whole. As regards the rural areas, Loots found unemployment to be 16.1 percent in Saulspoort, in Bophuthatswana (Loots, 1978), and Maree and de Vos (1975) estimated rural underemployment to range from 9.6 percent in Victoria East (in the Eastern Cape) to 28 percent in Bizana (in the Transkei). The highest unemployment rate was recorded in a resettlement area in Limehill (in KwaZulu), where Desmond (1978) found an unemployment rate (using a very broad definition) of 41.7 percent. Such resettlement villages were home to the most marginalised section of the population, removed from white farming areas and denied access to the towns (ibid., 14–25).

These findings were supported by more qualitative studies of growing desperation amongst work-seekers. In Sekhukhuneland in 1976, "labour bureau day at the magistrates offices was a chilling sight as crowds of desperate men crowded around the handful of recruiters hoping to be amongst the tiny minority who would secure work" (Delius 1996, 147). The labour bureau at Richards Bay reported having "a thousand people at the gate every day"; at Maluti the announcement of three hundred vacancies in 1978 attracted four thousand work-seekers; and in King William's Town, work-seekers flattened the fence around the labour bureaux when vacancies were announced (Greenberg and Giliomee 1985, 69–72).

Quantitative and qualitative studies suggest that these high rates of unemployment were of relatively recent origin. The first nationwide labour-force survey, conducted by the Department of Statistics in 1977, found that the unemployment rate (using a strict definition) among African men and women was more than double that suggested by the 1970 census—12.4 percent compared to 5.1 percent (Loots 1978, 12). Although there were serious problems with the way official unemployment was estimated (ibid., 10–12), the *trend* was nevertheless clear, not unexpected given that 1977 was the trough year of the worst postwar recession yet experienced by South Africa, and consistent with other studies indicating a sharp rise in unemployment in the first half of the 1970s (see, for example, Van der Merwe 1976).

Loots's 1977 surveys among Africans in the Mamelodi, Atteridgeville, and Saulspoort also support the notion that unemployment was a relatively new phenomenon. First, more than one-quarter of the unemployed men and more than half of the unemployed women were new entrants into the labour market. This suggests an increase in female participation compared to previous years, perhaps driven by the need to supplement family incomes in a time of hardship. Second, more than 70 percent of men and women in urban areas had been looking for work for three months or less, and more than 85 percent of those in rural areas had been looking for work for six months or less (see table 5.2). Long-term unemployment rates were thus significantly lower across the

Table 5.2. Unemployment in urban and rural areas in 1977

	Male		Female	
	Urban	Rural	Urban	Rural
Unemployed persons				
who had not held a job before (%)	26.9	25.0	50.5	47.8
looking for work for less than 3 months (%)	70.2	48.2	73.7	47.8
looking for work for 4–6 months (%)	12.5	38.9	14.5	47.8
looking for work for more than 6 months (%)	17.3	14	11.7	2.2
Unemployment rate	15.7	13.9	34.0	19.3
Long-term unemployment rates*	5.3	5.1	14.5	7.5

Source: Loots (1978).
*Long-term unemployment rates apply to those searching for three months or more in urban areas (as a percentage of the labour force) and for four months in rural areas (where job searches are more difficult).

board in 1977 than short-term unemployment rates. According to a survey of unemployed African men in Pietermaritzburg in 1982, 44 percent had been looking for work for six months or less (Hofmeyr 1985, 61). This suggests that the problem of long-term unemployment had grown significantly worse in the five years since 1977.

GAP ESTIMATES OF UNEMPLOYMENT AND UNDEREMPLOYMENT

The finding that high unemployment rates in the 1970s were of recent origin sits very uneasily with oft-cited data for unemployment rates over time, which seem to indicate that unemployment was high as far back as the 1960s and had simply become worse in the 1970s. This apparent contradiction, however, is a product of methodological differences between one-time survey measures of unemployment and estimates of *under*employment of labour over time from official data sources. Whereas the household surveys were able to ask precise questions about the length and nature of search activity in the 1970s, scholars estimating the trend in underemployment over time relied heavily on assumptions about labour-force participation and employment.

Until the late 1980s, there were only two official sources of time series unemployment statistics in South Africa. One was the official register of unemployed people, which excluded Africans and hence was of little value. The other was the census, which posed major problems for researchers because of the way employment and labour force participation were measured. In order to make any sense of the census data for African unemployment during the apartheid years, Knight and Simkins sought to adjust the data to correct for bias and to ensure consistency over time. They estimated trends in the labour force and employment, with the gap between the two serving as an indicator of underutilisation of labour. Until the 1990s, these gap estimates of under- or unemployment were the least flawed quantitative data available regarding unemployment (see Bromberger 1978).

Knight (1977) made the first attempt at estimating underemployment among Africans. He estimated three variables over time: the labour supply, employment outside of homeland agriculture, and employment in homeland agriculture. He called the difference between the labour supply and employment outside of homeland agriculture "residual labour" and the difference between residual labour and productive employment in homeland agriculture "underemployment." Knight produced various estimates (using different assumptions) for residual labour and found that it changed little in proportion to the labour supply between 1951 and 1970. In other words, employment outside of homeland agriculture grew broadly in proportion to the growing labour supply. His estimates for underemployment, however, showed a steady increase during the 1950s. On the basis of one set of assumptions, underemployment grew from 15 percent of the labour supply in 1951 to 23 percent in 1960, then remained at about this rate throughout the 1960s.

In calculating employment in the homelands, Knight relied on the Tomlinson Commission's estimate that 357,000 families could be supported in full-time farming in the reserves. Knight assumed that this amounted to the equivalent of full-time employment of either 357,000 or 714,000 peasant farmers depending on whether one assumed that one or two people were engaged in productive agricultural employment per family. He further assumed that the number of full-time job equivalents in homeland agriculture had not changed between 1951 and 1970. His fixed estimates of full-time productive agricultural employment in the homelands were then subtracted from residual labour for the various census years to get two measures of overall underemployment. The figures of 15 percent (in 1951) and 23 percent (in 1960) for underemployment, reported in table 5.3, result from the assumption that there were two full-time farmers per family in homeland agriculture. In Knight's calculations, underemployment rose because homeland agriculture failed to expand at the same rate as the labour supply countrywide.

There are two especially important features of Knight's study. The first is the direct linkage he posits between stagnation in homeland agriculture and the rise in underemployment. The second is that he estimates a series for *under*employment, not unemployment as it is understood in studies based on household surveys. Knight measures employment in terms of full-time equivalents. Thus two half-day jobs (for example, on white-owned farms) count as one full-time job equivalent. Homeland agriculture is converted into full-time equivalent employment without regard for how many people are actually involved in agriculture there.

Simkins (1978a) adopted an approach broadly similar to Knight's in estimating the underutilisation of manpower, although he did this for the population as a whole rather than only the African population. Simkins's methodology differed in two important respects from Knight's. First, he estimated employment on white farms differently, converting casual employment into full-time equivalents by dividing the casual worker wage bill by the average wage for regular farm workers. Second, he developed a better series for agricultural production and hence employment in the homelands.

Simkins took the Tomlinson Commission's estimate that an average gross annual income of R114 (in 1951–52 prices) was sufficient to keep an African worker in full-time peasant farming. Using activity rates from the 1960 census, he estimated that each family farming unit would be using the labour of 2.46 people and hence that as long as each was earning at least R46.3 per year (in 1951–52 prices), they could be said to be engaged full-time in peasant agriculture. He then converted gross homeland agricultural output to 1951–52 prices and divided it by R46.3 to get an estimate of full-time employment equivalents in homeland agriculture. Unlike Knight (whose estimates were static), Simkins estimated that employment in subsistence agriculture rose from 691,500 in 1965 to 889,700 in 1973 (1978a, 21). Kantor (1980) later implied that Simkins and others who believed that unemployment was high significantly underestimated incomes in subsistence agriculture. Simkins dismissed the claim as a "bizarre misunderstanding of the situation" (1981b, 38).

Like Knight, Simkins was generating gap estimates of the underutilisation of labour. In so doing, Simkins was following an established approach to labour-force underutilisation (ILO 1971, 43–63). But instead of referring to his results as "under-employment" he referred to them as "unemployment." He justified this on the basis that the unemployment problem was one of underutilisation rather than of distribution: "In countries where there is little in the way of social security, open unemployment is likely to be relatively rare, as workers are

Table 5.3. Trend estimates of underemployment and unemployment, 1951–82

	1951	1960	1965	1970	1973	1977	1980	1982
Africans only								
Residual labour as a percentage of the labour force (Knight 1977)*	34	38		34				
Underemployment as a percentage of the labour force (Knight 1977)†	15	23		22	24‡		22‡	
Nonwhites only								
Loots (1982)			15.2	12.8	12.2	13.7	16.2	20.9
All population groups								
Simkins (1978)			18.3	19.1	20.4	20.3	22.4	
Simkins in Bell (1984)			16.7	17.5	17.5	17.0	18.4	20.8	22.5
Van der Berg (1987)§	20.9	24.3	21.8	22.2	23.3	26.9	30.1	31.7

Sources: Knight (1977, 42–43), Simkins (1978a), Bell (1984, 5, 16), Loots (1982, 33; 1978, 18), Van der Berg, cited in RSA (1987, 11), Hofmeyr (1985, 40).
*Adjusted for census underenumeration and employment measured in full-time equivalents.
†Residual labour estimated as in the previous line and assuming two full-time farmers per family.
‡Projected.
§Percentage of the workforce without formal employment opportunities.

obliged to obtain some income in order to survive; people in this position share enough of the characteristics of the openly unemployed to make the open un-employment-underemployment dichotomy of dubious value. From the point of view of the origins of poverty and waste of labour time, the underutilisation problem *is* the unemployment problem in a society like ours" (1978a 43–44, emphasis in original).

Simkins provided several estimates of this unconventional use of the term "unemployment" (see table 5.3). According to his 1978 estimates, the unemployment rate rose from 18.3 percent in 1960 to 22.4 percent in 1977. (Simkins generated data for years in between censuses by means of extrapolation.) He subsequently revised his figures (Simkins 1982c, 1984b), the main adjustment being a reduction in the African labour-force participation rate to take into account the rising proportion of African people aged fifteen to twenty-four who were staying at school (see Bell 1984, 5). According to the 1984 figures, unemployment rose from 16.7 percent in 1960 to 18.4 percent in 1977 and to 22.5 percent in 1982. Even though Simkins used data allowing for rising employment in homeland agriculture, his estimates of unemployment still continued to rise because the slight increase in employment in homeland agriculture was nowhere near the rate of increase in the labour force.

Simkins's estimates were very much the product of his assumptions. Loots (1977) showed that estimates of underemployment or unemployment vary widely depending on what assumptions are made about the nature of employment in homeland agriculture (unemployment or low-productivity employment) and how one converts casual farming jobs to full-time equivalents. Loots came to more qualified conclusions about the level of unemployment (which he believed was somewhere between 10 percent and 15 percent in 1977) but agreed that there was indeed evidence for an upward trend. Bell (1984) came to a similar conclusion.

THE DEBATE ABOUT UNEMPLOYMENT

The gap estimates of high and rising unemployment proved highly controversial. For neoclassical critics, evidence of labour shortages and rising wages (particularly during the late 1960s and early 1970s) was indicative of a tight labour market rather than unemployment—and hence that the gap estimates were not providing a meaningful measure of unemployment in any economic sense of the term. Gerson (1981, 1982) took exception to the gap estimates and the results of labour-force surveys on the grounds that neither considered whether people were choosing to work at the going wage or not. He argued that a horizontal labour supply curve "is in fact implicit in Simkins' work and indeed in all surveys of unemployment which deny that workers choose between leisure and work . . . and therefore deny that the supply curve slopes upward" (1982, 147).

This is an important criticism because it points to the gulf in understanding of unemployment between neoclassical conceptions and the labour-force approach. According to neoclassical economic theory, labour supply is a positive function of the wage. This means that the higher the wage, the greater the number of people will enter the labour force (that is, look for work rather than opting for leisure). The labour-supply curve thus slopes upwards against the wage. Conversely, the demand for labour slopes downwards: the higher the wage, the fewer the number of jobs employers will be able to offer. In terms of this model, the equilibrium wage is determined by the intersection between the supply and the demand curves for labour (W_e in figure 5.1). If the "going wage" is below W_e then the demand for labour will be greater than supply and wages will rise. Rising wages such as those of the 1960s and especially in the 1970s were thus a sig-

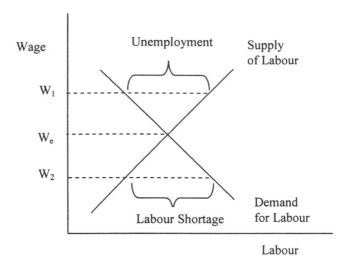

Figure 5.1. The conventional neoclassical model of the labour market

nal to neoclassical economists that labour shortage rather than unemployment characterised the labour market. They therefore rejected the gap estimates for the 1960s and 1970s and also the labour-survey results for the 1970s.

In essence, the neoclassical critique suggested that the gap estimates and the labour force surveys had overestimated unemployment because they had failed to ascertain whether labour force participants were looking for work at the going wage. According to the neoclassical model, jobless persons who wanted a job at a high wage (say, W_1) when the going wage was W_e should not count as unemployed because they were refusing to work at the going wage. Such individuals should at best be counted as "voluntarily unemployed"—that is, not really unemployed at all. Gerson's complaint was that labour force surveys and the gap estimates could not distinguish between voluntary and involuntary unemployment because the very notion of labour supply being a function of the wage was entirely absent.

There is some merit in this criticism, particularly given the evidence that labour supply in South Africa was indeed sensitive to wage increases. But the major problem with the neoclassical perspective was, as Simkins recognised, that it was poorly equipped to deal with South Africa's highly structured and coercive system of labour supply. It is thus difficult to untangle genuine market forces of supply and demand from what Simkins described as "administratively imposed disequilibrium" (1981b, 21). Given the barrage of interventions designed to channel African labour into low-wage mining and farming jobs, it seems bizarrely abstract to model labour supply as simply a function of the wage. By focusing on the individual's decision to supply labour in a given context (apartheid), the neoclassical framework deflected attention away from the way the system shaped and constrained the choices affecting labour supply. The radical critique of neoclassical and liberal approaches to apartheid was in large part a reaction to this limitation. In the context of a highly regulated and discriminatory system that displaced unemployment from urban to rural areas, it was argued that the individualist and ahistorical methodology used by neoclassical analysts was inappropriate and politically irresponsible. Maree, for example, devoted one sentence to the notion of voluntary unemployment, saying that it should be "dismissed with the contempt it deserves" (1978, 28).

Many neoclassical economists were, however, well aware that apartheid-era interventions distorted the labour market. Indeed, there are a range of neoclassical models based on the assumption that the labour market under apartheid was highly segmented, with the result that different wage levels were payable in different sectors—for example, low wages in commercial agriculture and mining and higher wages in urban industry (see Knight 1978; Porter 1976; Gerson 1981; Hofmeyr 1994). In terms of this perspective, a certain amount of unemployment could be explained with reference to "probabilistic" or "queuing" theories of unemployment: unemployed people were choosing to remain jobless and wait for better-paying urban jobs, rather than take low-paying jobs in mining and commercial agriculture. But whether such individuals were voluntarily or involuntarily unemployed remained moot. If it was assumed that jobless individuals should be taking low-wage jobs rather than wait for better jobs, then they would be classed as "voluntarily unemployed." If, however, it was assumed that it was rational and appropriate for workers not to participate in the low-wage labour market but instead wait for jobs in the higher-wage sectors, then they would be classified as "involuntarily unemployed" because they were prepared to work at the going wage, but no jobs were available. According to research conducted by Simkins in 1977, job-seekers in urban and rural areas had reservation wages (that is, the lowest wages they were prepared to accept) in line with those on offer locally (1978b, 56–59, 114). He thus concluded that unemployment was involuntary.

Bell approached the distinction between voluntary and involuntary unemployment from a different angle. He argued that it was arbitrary and shot through with social judgements, particularly in the South African context. He asked the reader to consider the case of a man refusing to accept a wage of R30 per week in a rural area when urban jobs for someone of his skill level were paying R100 a week: "Should we say that he is voluntarily unemployed and that his case at least is not part of a social problem of unemployment and should therefore not be included in the measure of unemployment? If we do regard this as 'voluntary' unemployment, would we take the same view if the wage available in the homeland area were R10 per forty hour week, or would society then say that his refusal of work at this rate was justified, and that his unemployment should be regarded as involuntary and thus as genuine unemployment?" (1984, 36).

The neoclassical and the gap approaches to unemployment were focusing on different dimensions of the labour situation under apartheid. The gap approaches highlighted the growing inability of the South African economy to create sufficient jobs for new entrants to the labour force; that is, they identified the emerging "structural" problem that was to be the core of the massive unemployment problem facing South Africa at the end of—and after—apartheid. They were, however, ill-equipped to deal with labour-market dynamics; as the neoclassical critics pointed out, rising wages in the 1970s raised questions as to how or whether surplus labour was affecting the labour market.

Even those sympathetic to the gap estimates of unemployment were concerned about the disconnection between the high gap estimates and the tight labour market. As Bromberger asks: "What is one to make of the fact that in 1975 and 1976, when according to our measurements unemployment and under-employment were rising, the gold mines in South Africa were recording the breaking of contracts by South African black workers and a consequent shortage of labour? It appears to have taken one to two years of slackening demand for labour from the secondary and tertiary sectors before the gold mines in 1977 found that they had all the labour they wanted" (1978, 18).

One answer to the conundrum might be that there was a shortage of the kind of labour needed in the mines, that is, young men between the ages of eighteen and forty years. But, as Knight's demographic analysis of the homelands showed, there was a considerable pool of such labour (1977, 45). Alternatively, one could argue that the labour supply to the mines was constrained by the fact that mining wages were so low that a worker would not "earn sufficient to make much difference to the level at which he and his family were living" (Wilson, 1975b, 528)—meaning that he would be unable to remit enough to his family to make the work worthwhile. This does not help resolve the unemployment debate because a neoclassical economist would immediately classify such workers as "voluntarily unemployed." A third way of reconciling the diminished supply of South Africans to the mines with high and rising unemployment refers to probabilistic theories of unemployment (Todaro 1969, 1971; Knight 1971; Simkins 1981a). When there is a gap between urban and rural incomes, migration to the cities occurs and urban unemployment increases until the expected value of an urban job equals rural income. The expected value is a positive function of the urban wage and a negative function of the unemployment rate (because the higher the unemployment rate, the lower the chances of obtaining a job). In South Africa's case, open unemployment in the towns was restricted by the pass laws, and hence such unemployment was transferred to the homelands. As Knight points out: "Insofar as Homeland men see a choice between employment in mining and the chance of employment in industry, then the greater the difference in wages, the more people are prepared, and the longer they are prepared, to wait in the Homelands for a job in manufacturing before accepting a contract of employment in mining. During the period 1958–71, in which the wage disparity between manufacturing and mining increased, the fall in the number of indigenous African miners need not be inconsistent with increasing Homeland underemployment" (1977, 46).

Simkins made a similar analysis, concluding that "much homeland unemployment, then, has to be regarded as urban unemployment displaced" (1981a, 68). Kantor (1980) and Gerson (1980), however, insisted that for theoretical reasons this was more of a problem of poverty than one of unemployment.

CONCLUSION

The shift from underemployment to open unemployment probably explains the inconsistency between the gap-derived estimates of unemployment and the other evidence about conditions in the labour market. In the 1940s and 1950s, the category of "underemployed" would have included idle African men and women in town looking for better-paying work, African families on white farms who were less than fully employed, and rising numbers of people in the ever more crowded bantustans. Brutally coercive apartheid policies pushed many of the "idle" African population out of the towns and surplus labour off white-owned farmlands. The underemployed were increasingly relocated into the bantustans, where the deepening crisis of subsistence agriculture meant that they were sentenced to complete unemployment. Some individuals—or families—might have exercises a degree of choice in choosing to be less than fully employed in the early apartheid decades, but in the late apartheid period, few, if any, people retained this option. A neoclassical economist might interpret this shift from underemployment to unemployment as an increase in the labour supply. The further collapse of subsistence agriculture, combined with rising wages from the early 1970s, certainly increased the labour supply.

The debate about unemployment during the late 1970s and early 1980s fizzled out as the economy slowed down and then stagnated. Whatever was happening to the labour supply, there was a significant slow-down in the growth of demand for labour starting in the late 1970s. This was especially marked for unskilled labour, as we saw in Chapters 3 and 4. In 1965, in the sectors covered by the government's Manpower Surveys (excluding agriculture and domestic service), unskilled manual jobs accounted for 28.5 percent of employment. By 1992 they accounted for only 18 percent of employment (see table 3.2).

In place after place, researchers documented unambiguously high unemployment. The worst areas were the resettlement areas in the bantustans. As we saw in Chapter 3, huge numbers of farm workers and their families were forcibly removed in the 1970s and 1980s from white-owned farms into the bantustans. By the time they were moved, there was no land left to farm, so they were typically dumped in essentially urban settlements located in supposedly rural areas. The population of Botshabelo in the Free State grew from almost nothing in 1979 to a half-million by 1986 (Murray 1992, 237). Moved at a time when the mines were cutting back on unskilled labour, and lacking contacts or rights in towns, these former farm workers faced lives of unemployment and poverty. According to one:

> Our burden is this. We are trapped. Our hands are tied. We have no right to seek work for ourselves wherever we like. We are supposed to stand around here maybe three months, five or six months or longer, waiting for work that never comes. When you go to Bloemfontein, you spend your own money on the busfare. You might get a job sometime, if you're lucky, but when you have to get fixed up at the pass office at Bloemfontein you are chased away. They say you've got no right to seek work for yourself: "Get back to Onverwacht [Botshabelo] and wait there!" We are men with families, we have children going to school. We need money for everything. We ask how can we manage to raise our families and feed them and keep the children in school when our hands are fastened like this? (quoted in ibid., 204).

Similar patterns of unemployment characterised the dumping grounds of QwaQwa, further south. "There's no work. We can't get jobs so that we can work for our children. . . . Work is the important thing," commented one of Murray's informants. "When we do get work around here we can't get anything like enough money to look after our children. When you want work and you go down to the office there [the labour bureau in Phuthaditjhaba] and hang

around but there's nothing at all, you could wait a year without picking anything up. And the children are being killed by hunger. That's our difficulty in
this place QwaQwa" (quoted in Murray 2000b, 7).

The former farm workers were worse off than people removed from urban
areas because the latter had histories of urban employment and thus "had built
up contacts there, and were often able to by-pass the official machinery of
labour recruitment in the Bantustan and find their own jobs," whereas the former farm workers "had few contacts in the rural areas, and few resources in the
form of savings or skills," and were therefore compelled "to rely on the official
labour bureaux" (Sharp and Spiegel 1990, 544). The authors describe the employment history of one of their informants in QwaQwa. He "had been without reliable wage employment for four of the five years since his arrival from an
Orange Free State farm." Much of these four "wasted years" (as he called them)
had been spent queuing fruitlessly at labour bureaus. Besides a couple of temporary jobs, he "had tried his hand at local retailing by hawking vegetables" but
lacked the capital to buy vegetables to sell and, as he put it, "all of us can't all sell
things all the time—someone's got to buy vegetables rather than sell them, and
there are just too many of us trying to sell and not enough able to buy" (Sharp
and Spiegel 1985, 144).

Even in the rural areas that had historically sent many men to the mines, the
stabilisation policies of the mining companies resulted in growing unemployment. With stabilisation, mining work was better paid but fewer men benefited. "Mine migrants have become a relatively privileged absentee rural elite in
the midst of abject poverty" (Crush and Jeeves 1995, 25). New—or retrenched—
workers were shut out of employment in the mines (James, 1992, 29).

Even neoclassical economists such as Hofmeyr conceded that involuntary
unemployment characterised the labour market. In 1982 he conducted a survey
of unemployed African men in Pietermaritzburg and found that 78 percent
were prepared to accept wages of R35 a week or less (Hofmeyr 1985). Because
this was below the going wage for labourers in construction, he concluded that
reservation wages of the unemployed were not generally out of line with market wages. When, in 1987, the President's Council concluded that unemployment was "unacceptably high" and rising (RSA 1987, 12), no one took exception
to this analysis. By that stage, the crisis in the South African labour market was
clear to all.

Chapter 6 Income Inequality

at Apartheid's End

Under apartheid, inequality in the distribution of incomes in South
Africa remained acute despite economic growth. At the top end of the
income scale, some South Africans lived lives of luxury, with swimming pools, holiday homes, and imported sports cars in the garage. At
the bottom end, many lived in deep poverty. The Gini coefficient for
the distribution of income has been estimated at between 0.58 and
0.68, depending on the precise data used (McGrath and Whiteford
1994; Whiteford, Posel, and Kelatwang 1995; Whiteford and van Seventer 2000; World Bank 1995b, 7; World Bank 1996, 56). This puts
South Africa among the most unequal societies in the world. Although most comparisons invoked in South African studies pay little
attention to the methodological difficulties involved (see Moll 1992;
Atkinson and Brandolini 1999), it is clear that inequality in South
Africa was higher at the end of the apartheid period than in, even,
most other middle-income countries.

   In previous chapters we showed that this unusually high level of inequality resulted, directly and indirectly, from the apartheid distributional regime. On one hand, a battery of racially discriminatory poli-

cies deepened inequality in the distribution of earnings. On the other, the state's policies pushed the economy into growing along a path that entailed rapidly rising unemployment at the same time as rising earnings for the skilled minority. Even as racial discrimination declined in the late apartheid era, inequality remained stubbornly high because the determinants of inequality had shifted. Whereas it was initially driven by the gap in racial incomes, this situation changed over time as some African workers advanced up the occupational ladder while unemployment increased. By the end of the apartheid period, inequality was being driven increasingly by the growing gap in incomes within the African population as some benefited from upward occupational mobility and rising wages while others found themselves unemployed and increasingly marginalised within the labour market.

Our analysis of the apartheid era has been constrained by the paucity of data about key issues. The apartheid state failed to collect reliable data about unemployment or incomes among its African subjects, and as soon as a bantustan achieved "independence," its citizens disappeared from *all* South African statistics, including those concerning population. Scholars therefore had to rely on their own local surveys, the manipulation of census or other official data, or qualitative research (all of which were used to powerful effect, as demonstrated in the papers presented at the 1984 Carnegie conference on poverty—see Wilson and Ramphele [1989]). Not until 1993 was South Africa's first countrywide household income and expenditure survey conducted—not by the state, but by the University of Cape Town together with the World Bank, with the strong support of the African National Congress as government-in-waiting (see Wilson 1996; PSLSD 1994). This chapter uses this unprecedented data set to analyse more precisely the pattern of inequality at the end of apartheid and on the eve of democratisation.

THE DISTRIBUTION OF INCOME

The Project for Statistics on Living Standards and Development (PSLSD) survey covered a representative sample of nearly nine thousand households across South Africa, including the nominally independent bantustans, in the second half of 1993. It collected data about incomes from a wide range of sources. These included the full range of cash income—wages from permanent and casual employment (after direct taxation), the government's old-age pensions and other government "transfers," rent, interest payments, profits from self-employment (whether small-scale hawking or large-scale business), remittances

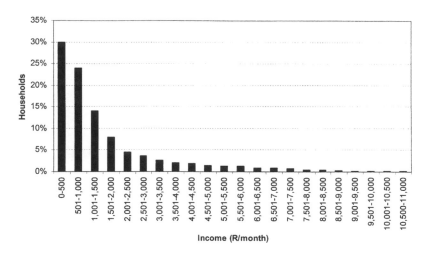

Figure 6.1. Distribution of household incomes, 1993

(that is, transfers between households, including from nonresident family members), and revenues from the sale of agricultural products. It also included income in other forms, such as remittances in kind, employers' subsidies of transport, housing, or food, the value of crops or livestock produced and consumed, and the imputed value of owner-occupied housing (PSLSD 1994, 312–13). No value was attached to unpaid domestic work done within the home by members of the household. No doubt, income from illegal activity also went largely unrecorded. The survey also collected detailed data about expenditure.

The survey found that the mean household income in late 1993 was about R1,960 per month (equivalent to R23,500 per year). The median household income was much lower at slightly more than R900 per month (or a little less than R11,000 per year). Figure 6.1 shows the distribution of income between households. Almost one in three had a mean annual income below R5,000.

The first two columns in table 6.1 present the minimum, maximum, and mean monthly incomes of each income decile. The final column shows the income share of each decile, that is, the share of total income earned by households in each decile. The bottom decile's share was less than 1 percent; the top decile's share was almost 50 percent. The top decile thus earned almost as much income as the other nine deciles put together. The mean income and income share of the top decile were approximately one hundred times those of the bottom decile. The poorest 40 percent of households, equivalent to 52 percent of the population, accounted for less than 10 percent of total income, whereas the

Table 6.1. Monthly household income and income shares by income decile, 1993

Decile	Range (R per month)	Mean (R per month)	Share (%)
1	0–199	92	0.5
2	200–369	293	1.5
3	371–499	433	2.2
4	500–679	590	3.0
5	680–899	788	4.0
6	900–1,199	1,050	5.4
7	1,200–1,669	1,415	7.2
8	1,700–2,599	2,074	10.6
9	2,600–4,699	3,491	17.8
10	4,700+	9,341	47.7
Mean		1,957	
Total			100

richest 10 percent of households, equivalent to 6 percent of the population, captured more than 40 percent of total income. As we saw in Chapter 1, this is an exceptionally skewed distribution of income.

The extreme level of inequality in South Africa was due in large part to the exceptionally high incomes of the richest decile relative to the rest of the population. This is the case in many countries in Latin America also. In the advanced industrialised countries the gaps between the income shares of successive deciles are not large. In South Africa and much of Latin America, there were (and remain) similarly small gaps between all of the deciles between the second and the ninth but large gaps between the first and second deciles and the ninth and tenth. It has been calculated that the Gini coefficient for highly unequal countries in Latin America is much the same as or lower than the Gini for the United States if the top income decile is excluded in each case (IADB 1999, 15–16). This was true in South Africa as well. A full examination of inequality must therefore pay attention to the reasons why the rich were super-rich. In South Africa, most of them were white. But they were no longer super-rich because they were the beneficiaries of explicit discriminatory labour market policies. Indeed, it is not clear that explicit discrimination boosted the incomes of the richest decile as much as it did the incomes of relatively poor white families, most of whom would have been in the eighth or ninth decile by the middle of the apartheid period. Nor, even if we take into account the underreporting of capital income, were families in the top decile because they owned the means of production and shared directly in the exploitation of cheap labour. Rather, the super-rich at the end of apartheid had especially high incomes primarily because they had benefited from privileged family backgrounds *and* public education and hence enjoyed huge advantages in terms of securing well-paid jobs. Having fewer children also meant that their incomes per capita were even higher. Weber is more useful than Marx in understanding not only differentiation among the middle deciles in society but also the particular position of the super-rich.

Measuring Inequality

Figure 6.1 and table 6.1 present income data for *households.* There are grave problems with using households rather than individuals as the basis for analysis in South Africa. However "household" is defined, the composition of many households varies over time as individuals move about (exhibiting what anthropologists have called "domestic fluidity"—see Spiegel [1996]), and the relations of individuals to the household differ. Given that many resources are shared, albeit unequally, we need to examine individuals in the appropriate collective categories, but we must acknowledge that studying the household is a crude way of doing so, and it obscures inequalities within households (by age and gender, for example) as well as relationships across households.

Many studies of poverty use data for per capita household income (or income per "adult equivalent," which means that different weights are attached to adults and children and sometimes according to the size of the household also). Because poorer households tend to be larger than wealthier ones, measuring inequality according to total household income thus probably understates the extent of inequality. For example, the Gini coefficient for total household income was 0.68 in 1991 as opposed to 0.71 for per capita household income (Whiteford and McGrath 1994). This chapter uses data for households as a whole for three reasons. First, the analysis leads to the mapping of social stratification in Chapters 7 and 8, using categories based primarily on occupation and source of income (for example, wage labour), not expenditure or consumption. The number of dependent household members may be important for understanding poverty but not stratification. Second, given our uncertainty about fluidity in household composition and interhousehold relationships, it makes sense to regard income sources as the independent variable. Third, we know so little about intrahousehold distribution that presenting data in terms of per capita income requires massive and dubious assumptions. These include judgments about the consumption weights given to different age groups, the economies of scale involved in living in large households, and the way income is distributed within households. Until we know more about such matters, we believe, presenting data in per capita terms adds little to the analysis we are attempting and may well serve to obscure rather than clarify issues of distribution.

Anthropologists rightly criticise household surveys for ignoring much of the complexity of the household. As Baber (1998, 97) summarises:

> Anthropological studies present a view of sub-Saharan households where the units of residence, consumption, production and investment often do not coincide, where membership is not stable, where the property of spouses if often not pooled, and where the authority of the household head is often limited. Instead, households are shown to be the site of overlapping interests and activities, with individual members drawing from and contributing to the resources of the collective group, while at the same time retaining control over their own individual resources, objectives and capital in social networks. Household membership is also shown to exist along spatially dispersed networks of support.

African households in South Africa are very different from the predominant form of household in northern (or "Western") societies. In the North, the model household comprises a family formed by a conjugal couple, including dependent offspring; children are born into one conjugal family household and later form their own on marriage. In practice, more and more households deviate from the model, but key features remain entrenched. Descent, for example, is understood as flowing equally through paternal and maternal lines, and the system in deeply individualistic in that men and women, once they leave their childhood families, live largely outside of kin groups. In African societies of southern Africa, in contrast, descent is patrilineal (even when mothers are unmarried) and kinship is agnatic; households often comprise extended families, including three generations and a wide variety of kin; children are often raised in households separate from those of their biological parents; and marriage is still generally less important than descent (Russell 2004). Living arrangements might have undergone considerable flux in the twentieth century, but they were not transformed into northern-style conjugal family households. As Russell concludes: "The implications for social scientists making household surveys are clear and dire. The assumption that those who at some surveyed moment are found living together constitute a persisting bounded interdependent unit, while valid for other parts of the world where conjugal kinship systems prevail, cannot be made in contemporary South Africa. . . . All data on the distribution of household incomes, especially that which compares rural with urban, must be viewed with scepticism. New research protocols are urgently required" (ibid.). The complexity of composition of households means that different members may have very different economic relationships outside of the household.

The PSLSD, like most surveys, used a primarily coresidential definition of the household. People were counted as members of a common household if "(i) they live under this 'roof' or within the same compound/homestead/stand for at least 15 days out of the past year *and* (ii) when they are together they share food from a common source *and* (iii) they contribute to or share in a common resource pool." This definition was rather more elastic than that used in most subsequent household surveys in that it includes absent migrants who live elsewhere for most of the year. But it assumed that coresidence, eating together, and sharing resources were generally coterminous, which was probably an erroneous assumption.

One of the most obvious problems with the PSLSD approach to households is that migrant workers living in hostels in town might be included twice: once as single-member households in towns, hostels, or compounds, separate from their dependents living in rural areas, a second time as absentee members of those rural households. This double-counting affects the distribution of income, inflating the numbers of better-off households including employed workers and the numbers of poorer households dependent on remittances. An alternative approach would view households as straddling the geographical divide. As Baber put it, there is "a division of labour between the migrant component, which generates the bulk of the household's income through wage employment, and the resident component, which maintains the household and contributes to the group's well-being through use-value production" (Baber 1998, 100–101). Baber proceeds to propose a complex typology of household types that could be used in survey design. These, too, would have their problems because they try to shoehorn a complex array of economic and social relations into replicable models, and it is yet to be demonstrated that any such reconceptualisation of the household could generate data that would improve our understanding of the key processes or issues involved.

One consequence of defining households in coresidential terms is that many rural African households are recorded as being headed by women because the men are absent for most of the year, working as migrants in towns or in the mines. Surveys find a high incidence of poverty among female-headed households in part because of their definition of the household. If respondents were allowed to identify the head of the household and could choose someone who was not usually resident, then there would be far fewer female-headed households and far more poor male-headed ones. The PSLSD allowed respondents to identify absentee as well as residential heads of household, but it is unclear how respondents understood the possible responses.

Taking the household, however defined, as the basic unit of analysis does obscure inequalities of gender and age. If some members have disadvantaged access to household resources, then a more nuanced analysis would find that poverty reaches into some nonpoor households (whereas some male members of poor households are individually nonpoor). Unfortunately, there has been too little analysis of the way South African households actually work to render inequality data adequately sensitive to gender and age. Given the complexities of relations between individuals across the boundaries of coresidential households and between individuals within the same household, it is unclear what per capita or "adult equivalent" measures of household income would actually mean. Haddad and Kanbur (1990) show that the neglect of intrahousehold inequality leads to an understatement of the overall *levels* of inequality and poverty but that the *patterns* of inequality and poverty might not be very different. In the South African case, much more work needs to be done to tease out the complexities of the relationships between and welfare of individuals, within and across households. Inequalities of gender and age need to be examined as part of a broader analysis of race and class. For the time being, however, we have little choice but to persevere with an analysis that assumes that households are much simpler than they really are.

The Location of Inequality

In South Africa, at the end of apartheid, the poorer deciles were overwhelmingly rural and were concentrated in provinces such as Limpopo (or what was previously called Northern Province) and the Eastern Cape. (Tables 6.2 and 6.3 indicate the provincial distribution and rural-urban distribution of households in the different deciles.) Households in metropolitan areas, by contrast, were concentrated in the higher deciles: three-quarters were in the top five deciles and more than half were in the top three. The top two deciles were predominantly metropolitan and were concentrated in provinces such as Gauteng and the Western Cape. Put another way, Gauteng and the Western Cape were relatively very rich (with almost three of every four households in the top five deciles), whereas Limpopo and the Eastern Cape were relatively very poor

Table 6.2. Income deciles by province, 1993

Province	S.A. Total (%)	1 (%)	2 (%)	3 (%)	4 (%)	5 (%)	6 (%)	7 (%)	8 (%)	9 (%)	10 (%)
						Income decile					
Western Cape	9	3	3	5	5	10	8	11	12	19	14
Northern Cape	1	2	1	1	1	1	1	2	2	2	2
Eastern Cape	15	30	14	23	14	13	10	13	13	9	7
KwaZulu-Natal	18	15	25	18	23	19	19	16	19	17	10
Free State	8	7	11	9	9	8	9	10	7	4	5
Mpumalanga	9	9	12	11	10	14	11	8	3	6	4
Limpopo	12	19	19	15	13	11	10	10	10	6	5
North-West	7	5	6	9	14	6	8	6	5	7	6
Gauteng	21	11	10	10	11	18	24	24	28	30	46
Total	100	100	100	100	100	100	100	100	100	100	100

(with almost two of every three households in the bottom five deciles). House-holds in the smaller urban areas were spread more evenly across the deciles.

The rural areas also accounted for more than three-quarters of the "poverty gap," that is the difference between actual household income and the poverty line such that very poor households contribute more to the poverty gap than do those that are just below the poverty line (May et al. 2000, 31). A simple assessment of the incidence of poverty suggests that it is less concentrated in rural areas in South Africa than it is in most parts of Africa and Asia, but it is more concentrated in rural areas than in most of Latin America—where, as we saw in Chapter 3, many rural poor migrated to the cities (Todaro 1994, 150).

At the dawn of democracy in South Africa, there was still a correlation between race and household income, although it was less close than it had been hitherto. About nine in ten households in the first six deciles were African; a small proportion was coloured, and a tiny proportion was white. The seventh and eighth deciles included mostly African households, but had a significant minority of white, coloured, and Indian households. The ninth decile comprised almost equal numbers of African and white households, with about one-quarter coloured and Indian. Three-quarters of the households in the top decile were white; African households comprised only 10 percent of this decile. The racial composition of the income deciles is indicated in table 6.4.

Many discussions of inequality stop at this point. The correlation between race and relative income in a society built on racial discrimination is often deemed sufficient as an explanation of inequality. But it needs to be examined further for at least two reasons. First, in the absence of explicit and systematic racial discrimination, race alone cannot be a sufficient explanation of inequality. Other factors must at least mediate the relation between race and house-hold income. For example, most black people might be poor because they are confined to poorly paid jobs or because of relatively high levels of unemployment. Such other factors need to be identified, especially if they assume an importance of their own once overt racial discrimination is ended. We discuss some of these determinants of inequality below. Second, by the end of apartheid vast inequalities existed in the distribution of income within racial groups. If we take African households only, the mean income in the top decile was more than sixty times that of the mean income in the bottom decile (Whiteford et al. 1995, 13).

There are different ways of estimating the relative contribution to inequality of interracial and intraracial inequality. As can be seen in table 6.5, the results vary depending on which statistical decomposition technique is used and to

Table 6.3. Income deciles by location, 1993

Areas	S.A. Total (%)	Income decile									
		1 (%)	2 (%)	3 (%)	4 (%)	5 (%)	6 (%)	7 (%)	8 (%)	9 (%)	10 (%)
Rural	50	73	73	72	68	59	52	42	30	18	11
Urban	22	15	17	16	17	20	24	29	29	30	22
Metro	28	12	10	12	15	21	24	29	41	52	67
Total	100	100	100	100	100	100	100	100	100	100	100

Table 6.4. Income deciles by racial or population group, 1993

Population or racial group	S.A. Total (%)	Income decile									
		1 (%)	2 (%)	3 (%)	4 (%)	5 (%)	6 (%)	7 (%)	8 (%)	9 (%)	10 (%)
African	75	95	97	93.5	94	89	87	80	66	37	11
Coloured	8	3	1.5	4	5	7	7	11	14	18	5
Indian	3	0	0.5	0.5	0.5	1	2	3	5	7	8
White	15	2	1	2	0.5	3	3	6	14	37	77
Total	100	100	100	100	100	100	100	100	100	100	100

Table 6.5. Measures of the contribution of "between-race" and "within-race" inequality to total inequality

	Theil-T (%)	Theil-L (%)	Atkinson ($\varepsilon = 0.5$) (%)
Between-race	48	41	50
Within-race	52	59	50
Total	100	100	100

Source: Leibbrandt, Bhorat, and Woolard (1999).

which data set it is applied. The most common measure is the Theil index. It can be decomposed into "between" and "within" group inequality (Theil-T) or weighted by the proportion of households in each group (Theil-L). The Atkinson measure allows additional weighting to be given to distributional objectives. The table shows that the contribution of intraracial inequality in South Africa is high by any measure, accounting for between 50 percent and 59 percent of overall inequality.

McGrath and Whiteford (1994, 20) calculate Theil indices for 1975 and 1991 data. Their figures for intraracial inequality are much higher than those of Leibbrandt et al. According to McGrath and Whiteford's estimates, the within-group or intraracial contribution to overall inequality rose from 57 percent in 1975 to 75 percent in 1991, and the contribution of the between-group or interracial component fell from 43 percent to 25 percent. Whiteford and van Seventer (2000, 17) subsequently revised their estimates, with the intraracial contribution rising from 38 percent to 58 percent (and on to 67 percent in 1996) and the interracial contribution falling from 62 percent to 42 percent (and further to 33 percent in 1996; see Chapter 9 below). It is unclear how much of the difference between estimates is the result of using different data sets (that is, whether census or survey data were used) and how much is due to different methodologies. But the overall trend is clear from all estimates: the contribution of intraracial inequality has risen sharply and exceeded the declining contribution of interracial inequality.

A comparison of the racial composition of income deciles in different years further illustrates rising intraracial differentiation. Estimates by McGrath and Whiteford (1994) and Whiteford and van Seventer (2000), using census data, show clearly that African people comprised a rapidly growing proportion of the top deciles, and white people comprised a more slowly growing proportion of deciles 6 and 7 in particular. In other words, some Africans were moving up the relative income scale while some white people were moving down, although most Africans remained at the bottom and most whites remained at the top. Overall levels of inequality changed little, but intraracial inequality grew. The PSLSD data for 1993 (shown in table 6.4) indicate far greater upward movement by African households than do the census data. White households comprised a majority of the top decile only. Of the households in decile 9, exactly the same proportion (37 percent) was African as white, with coloured and Indian households making up the balance. The effective ceiling for African households rose from around decile 7 in 1950 to around decile 8 by 1975 and around decile 9 by the end of apartheid.

THE HUMAN FACE OF INEQUALITY

Before examining the causes of this inequality it is instructive to consider what kinds of households fall into each of these deciles. In this section, we provide a profile of inequality in terms of actual households. This might help what Mills (1950) called the "sociological imagination," that is, the attempt to understand individuals' lives in their social context and to understand the social structure in terms of its ramifications for individuals within it. Put differently, we are trying to "people" the social structure. All of the examples below are drawn from the actual PSLSD survey, reporting income data for 1993 in 1993 prices.

The Poorest of the Poor: The Bottom Decile

Households in the bottom decile had a monthly income of less than R200 and a mean income of under R100. This means that almost nobody in this decile had either a permanent job or an old-age pension, because there were very few regular jobs paying less than R200 per month and the minimum pension payments were above this level. Almost all adult members of households in this decile were therefore not working but below pensionable age. These households were dependent on small and generally irregular remittances (R49 per month, on average), casual employment, or petty self-employment (such as small-scale hawking). Almost all lived in rural areas, in very simple houses or huts. Their expenditure was largely limited to food, and their diets were very limited.

The head of our first very poor household, Mrs. A, was forty-seven years old in 1993. She lived with one of her sons (age thirty), her only daughter (age twenty-eight), and her daughter's four children (ages one to nine) in a mud house in Thabamoopo, in Limpopo Province. Her house had a corrugated iron roof. There was no toilet, electricity, or water. Her daughter collected water from a nearly borehole. Although the borehole was only ten minutes' walk away, she had to make this journey six or so times per day. The family cooked with wood. Four times per week Mrs. A's daughter collected wood from a place one hour's walk away. Two of the small children walked to primary school, which took them about forty minutes each way. The family's only income consisted of the remittances sent by Mrs. A's second son, who was probably a worker on a large farm. In the month prior to the survey, he had sent about R50 and also brought back a small amount of food. The family had access to one hectare of communally owned land but did not farm it in 1992. None of the three resident adults in the family had paid jobs: Mrs. A and her daughter were busy with childcare; Mrs. A's son would have liked a job but said there were none available. The family said they spent about R70 each month on food—mielie meal, bread, potatoes (sometimes) and tomatoes (occasionally)—and almost nothing on anything else. They did not even have a radio in the house. It is unclear how they got by, because their claimed monthly expenditure exceeded their monthly income (they did say that they had a small debt to a friend). Proper sanitation and food aid were what Mrs. A wanted the government to help provide. Two of her grandchildren were sick at the time of the interview.

The household headed by Mrs. B also lived in Limpopo Province, but in the lowveld settlement of Mapulaneng. She was thirty-two years old in 1993 and had already been pregnant five times, although only three children were born alive. In 1993 she was again pregnant. Her oldest child, who was eight, went to a primary school twenty minutes' walk away. Her husband worked in Gauteng and sent home R200 three times each year. This was Mrs. B's only income. She had no land. She wanted a job but did not look for one because (she said) there were none. She and her children lived in a two-room cement-block house with a corrugated iron roof and a mud floor. They had electricity and an electric stove but could not afford to use it all of the time—so they also cooked with wood and used candles for lighting. They had no toilet, and they collected water from a public tap about quarter of a mile away. They spent about R80 per month more than their claimed income. Almost all of this went for food: mielie meal, potatoes, and tomatoes only, and Mrs. B. said the government's priorities should be jobs and piped water.

Most households in the bottom decile lived in rural areas; only a very small proportion lived in urban areas. An example of this latter group was Mrs. C. She lived in the township of Sebokeng in the Vaal Triangle (Gauteng). She was fifty years old in 1993 and widowed. Her three children lived with her in their four-room house. Her daughter, age twenty-six and with grade 9 schooling, had never had a permanent job. Her younger children were both at school. The family had a tap in the yard and a flush toilet. Electricity and water cost them nothing because they were boycotting their rent and service charge payments, which might explain why they also cooked and heated with gas and used candles for lighting: their electricity might have been disconnected at times. The family had several consumer durables: a radio, a television, an electric and gas stove, a refrigerator, and an electric kettle. This family had a much more varied diet than Mrs. A's or Mrs. B's, including rice, bread, meat, vegetables, fruit, and milk as well as the staples. They spent about R100 per month on food, as well as another R50 or so on food eaten outside the home. The house had a bond of R30,000. Their income came from casual employment, with Mrs. C spending two hours daily day washing clothes for about R60 per month. She walked to work, so she probably worked for someone else living in Sebokeng township. She and her daughter also ran a spaza shop (that is, an informal shop operating out of the house), which earned them a paltry R40 or so per month. Both Mrs. C and her daughter were actively looking for work. Although she suffered from high blood pressure, Mrs. C said she had no money to pay for transport to the hospital. The government's priorities should be food aid and jobs, she said.

Each of these three families spent more each month than they acknowledged earning. In Mrs. C's case, it is unclear how she could possibly be making repayments on a R30,000 bond. Perhaps she had been widowed recently; the family's income must have been much higher before 1993 in order for them to have been able to obtain a bond and to buy their various consumer durables. It is possible that Mrs. C's family had only recently dropped into the bottom decile. If she or her daughter—or either of her sons, still at school—found a job, they would have been lifted out of it. If not, it is difficult to see how they could continue to live the way they did. Perhaps they would take in lodgers. Although we do not have longitudinal data from the early 1990s, it is likely that the membership of this bottom decile was constantly changing: household incomes could plummet rapidly when the breadwinner died or lost a job but could rise equally fast if any unemployed household member found a job or if an elderly member reached pensionable age.

The Very Poor: Deciles 2 and 3

Households in deciles 2 and 3 had incomes in 1993 between R200 and R500 per month. They were also overwhelmingly rural. What distinguished them from households in the bottom decile was their access to old-age pensions, low-paid, mostly casual employment, or more regular remittances. More than one-quarter of these households were dependent on a member with an old-age pension (which was nominally set at R390 at the time of the survey). Pensions accounted for almost one-quarter of mean household income. Many households had members in very low-paid jobs. The two examples given below are of building labourers with little or no schooling. These households live in urban shacks or in mixed accommodation in rural areas. Most of their expenditure was on food; unlike households in decile 1, most of those in deciles 2 and 3 could afford to supplement basics (such as mielie meal, bread, and tomatoes) with some tinned fish and sugar. People in these deciles could not afford to smoke or drink very much.

Seventy-eight-year-old Mrs. D lived in Taung, in North-West Province. She had a government old-age pension. Two of her grandchildren, ages ten and sixteen, lived with her. Both attended school, which was about one hour's walk away. They lived in a two-room house with an outside pit latrine. Water had to be collected from a borehole. The two girls collected water twice each day; the round trip took about one hour (including the time spent waiting in line at the borehole). There was no electricity, so they cooked with wood and paraffin and lit their house with candles. The pension was their only income; they received nothing from the girls' parents. Their diet was basic, although they occasionally bought a chicken.

The family of Mr. E lived in a shack in Khayelitsha Site C, in Cape Town (in the Western Cape). He was forty-nine years old and earned R80 per week as a labourer on building sites. He had never gone to school. No money was deducted from his pay as a contribution to a pension scheme. He lived with his wife, three of their daughters (one aged seventeen, and the other two aged four), and one grandson. They had three other children living elsewhere (another five children had all died before the age of five). His wife and the older daughter looked after their home and minded the three younger children; the daughter dropped out of school after grade 5 in order to look after her child. Their shack was built out of wood, with an iron roof and a linoleum floor. They had an outside bucket toilet, collected their water from a public tap more than one hundred metres away, and used paraffin for cooking, heating, and lighting. The family had a radio and a bicycle but no other consumer durables. Except for Mr. E himself, the family spent much of each year elsewhere, probably in the former Ciskei or the Transkei. His wages were supplemented by money received from the father of his grandson, who lived in the Transvaal. Besides having made a one-time payment for the "damage" done when Mr. E's daughter became pregnant, the man also paid R70 every month as maintenance. The government, Mr. E said, should help with housing, electrification, and piped water.

Like Mr. E., Mr. F was a labourer on building sites; he had casual jobs rather than permanent employment. Nonetheless, he earned R500 monthly (more than did Mr. E). He, his wife, and their young daughter lived in Mapulaneng in a cement block two-room house, partially roofed with iron, with an outside pit latrine. The nearest tap was more than one hundred metres away. They had electricity, which cost them R10 per month, but generally cooked with wood (which Mrs. F collected for free once a week, taking three hours for the round trip). The family spent more than R100 per month on food and other groceries and repaid R120 each month for furniture they had bought on hire purchase. Whereas Mr. and Mrs. F had grade 3 schooling only, their thirteen-year-old daughter was already in grade 7. The family kept six chickens. Piped water was their most urgent demand, they said.

The family of Mr. and Mrs. G lived near Bolobedu in Limpopo Province. They and their two sons, their daughter-in-law, and her young daughter stayed in a plastered brickwork house with an iron roof and two thatch-roofed huts. They had a pit latrine but no tap or electricity; Mrs. G collected water from a borehole twice daily, each trip taking one hour. Three times a week Mr. and Mrs. G spent five hours collecting wood. They had a radio. Sixty-seven years of age, Mr. G received a pension of R390 monthly, but his wife was still too young to receive a pension. She and her daughter-in-law, who dropped out of grade 10 because she was pregnant, looked after the small child. The family's older son was unemployed and did not look for work because there were no jobs. The younger son was in grade 10 at school. Jobs and piped water were their priorities.

The Poor: Deciles 4 and 5

Households in deciles 4 and 5 had monthly incomes between about R500 and R900. About half of them had members working in low-paid employment: either the relatively better-paid farm work or unskilled work in urban areas (such as office cleaning and domestic work). Agriculture and domestic work together accounted for 42 percent of regular employment in the fifth decile. Households without employed members typically relied on a combination of incomes, such as a pension and a small remittance.

A farm worker near the mining town of Witbank, in Mpumalanga Province, Mr. H earned R400 per month, an annual bonus, and a share of the farm's profit but no pension. He lived with his wife and five children (ages three to seventeen) in a five-room cottage owned by his employer. They had an inside tap, an outdoor pit latrine, and electricity—although it had been disconnected, forcing them to cook with coal and wood. The family spent about half of Mr. H's wages on food. This family was in the fifth decile because their real income was boosted, nominally, by the imputed rent added to account for their free accommodation. They had a television and a radio. Neither Mr. nor Mrs. H had ever attended school, but their children did; their oldest was in grade 9.

In the heart of Sekhukhuneland (in Limpopo Province) lived Mrs. J and various members of her family. At any one time, one or more of her sons was working in what is now Gauteng, in Durban, or in Cape Town. In the previous year, two sons had remitted about R150 per month each. In addition, she received her old-age pension every month and earned a meagre income from selling the tomatoes and spinach they grew on their three-hectare plot, as well as some profit from petty hawking. The family lived in three buildings: one mud hut and two "flat-roofed" houses (that is, houses with corrugated iron roofing). They had no toilet. They collected water from a public tap some distance away. There was no electricity. Collecting wood took three hours, twice a week. None of the family smoked or drank, and almost all of their income was spent on food.

The twenty-eight-year-old Ms. K lived in Lehurutshe, formerly in the Bophuthatswana homeland and now part of North-West Province. She lived with her two younger sisters and one of her sister's children. She was studying for matric. She had a child living elsewhere with a relative. Her two sisters had both dropped out of school because, one of them said, it was too expensive. One worked as a cleaner in the local municipal offices for R600 per month (after tax); the other sister was unemployed and was not looking for work because there were not any jobs. They lived in a two-room cement block house with an asbestos roof that had a flush toilet inside and a tap in the yard but no electricity. They paid R18 per month in rent. They spent about one-third of their income on food and generally had a little left for "entertainment." They were very dissatisfied and said that the government must prioritise electrification, the provision of public telephones, and better transport.

Above Average: Deciles 6 and 7

Deciles 6 and 7 included many households in urban and metropolitan areas. Their net monthly incomes ranged from R900 to about R1,700. Unemployment rates were lower than in lower deciles. Only about one in five households had no member in regular employment. Far fewer jobs in these deciles were in agriculture than in lower deciles. In decile 6, agriculture, mining and manufacturing each accounted for about one-sixth of the total number of regular jobs. In decile 7, the proportion of people working in manufacturing was higher.

Many households relied on several different incomes, none of which was very large. For example, Mr. and Mrs. L were in their thirties and lived in St. Wendolin's, outside Pinetown in KwaZulu-Natal. They both had jobs paying about R600 per month (after tax). He worked as a petrol attendant in a garage; she worked as a cook in a takeaway restaurant. They rented one room in a house with a pit latrine and no tap. Their youngest child lived with them, but their three older children lived elsewhere, probably in a rural area with grandparents. They said that the government's priorities should be housing, jobs, and piped water.

Not far away, in Vulindlela, outside Pietermaritzburg, lived Mrs. M, a widow, together with seven of her children and two grandchildren. They lived in four huts with mud or wattle-and-daub walls and thatched or corrugated iron roofs. Water had to be collected from a borehole. They did not have electricity; wood had to be collected once per week from a long distance away (the round trip took them eight hours). The household's income comprised Mrs. M's pension, about R100 sent each month by a son working in Durban and the same by a son working in Pietermaritzburg, and about R400 earned each month by one of the sons living in Vulindlela and working as a small builder. One son and two daughters were unemployed; two of them said they were looking for work; the third was not, because there were no jobs available. None of these three had ever had a regular job. The two youngest children were still at school. Not one of the resident household members had a regular job. The family also grew maize and beans on their quarter-hectare plot, and they kept a few cows, goats, and chickens.

In these deciles were many single-member households consisting of workers living in compounds or hostels. For example, Mr. N worked for the South African Forestry Company (SAFCOL) near Barberton in Mpumalanga, earning R700 per month (after tax) but with heavily subsidised food and housing. He spent a lot of his income on clothing, shoes, and "holidays." A metalworker, Mr. P lived in a hostel in Tembisa (on the East Rand). He earned R1,000 per month after tax, R400 of which he sent to his wife in rural KwaZulu. Another hostel dweller was Mr. Q, a mine worker in Welkom. He also earned about R1,000 per month, and he remitted about R250 each month to his wife and mother in the Free State (in addition to paying off a hire purchase debt on furniture). Both Mr. P and Mr. Q had subsidised food and accommodation. Both were migrant workers (it is unclear whether Mr. N was also); they spent eleven months per year living in their hostel. But should they be considered as entirely separate households from their families, whom they supported?

The Relatively Rich: Decile 8

Households in decile 8 had monthly incomes of about R2,000. These households typically had one large income, sometimes supplemented by a small second income. Almost half of the adult population was regularly employed. Unemployment was below average. By far the largest sector of employment was manufacturing. There were large numbers of semiskilled and skilled workers, with a sizeable minority (15 percent of permanently employed people) in professional or managerial jobs. Forty percent of households in this decile lived in metropolitan areas, with 30 percent in rural and in urban areas. Very few lived in shacks or traditional huts.

The R family in Madadeni, in northern KwaZulu-Natal, had four sources of income. The parents, both retired, received an old-age pension each month. Their son was a teacher earning a salary of R1,000 per month after tax. Their daughter worked as a machinist in a garment factory, earning R150 per month. Getting to work to earn this meagre wage took her two hours. The fifth member of this household was the daughter's nine-year-old daughter, who went to school nearby. They all lived in a carpeted house built of cement blocks and a wattle-and-daub hut. They had a borehole and a pit latrine in the yard but no electricity. They spent more than R100 per month on coal and about R20 per month on paraffin for cooking, heating, and lighting. They had a battery-powered television. They had a varied diet, spending about R400 per month on groceries. They bought clothes and shoes regularly and managed to save as well. They had the use of about ten hectares of land, with a dam. In the previous year they had produced forty 80-kilogram bags of maize and one 80-kilogram bag of beans. They had six head of cattle and twenty or so chickens. According to Mr. R, the government should prioritise building clinics—his wife suffered from high blood pressure, and the nearest hospital was thirty minutes away and very overcrowded—as well as providing electricity and installing telephones.

In some respects, life was not very different in a shack settlement in the township of Duduza, in Gauteng, where Mr. S, who was fifty-one years old, lived with his much younger wife and their two small children. They paid R15 per month in rent for their four-room corrugated iron shack with a bucket toilet and a tap in the yard. Like the R family, they had no electricity. They cooked with coal (which cost R100 per month) and used candles for lighting (costing R35 per month). They had a varied diet including lots of meat, fish, eggs, and fresh milk. Their monthly grocery bill came to more than R600. They also bought clothes and shoes regularly and saved about R1,000 in the year before the survey. The S family had one source of income: Mr. S worked as a driver for a construction company, earning about R1,800 each month after tax as well as a small annual bonus (but no pension scheme). His wife would have liked to work but said there were no jobs available. They remitted R300 each month to his father, who lived somewhere in the Cape. According to Mr. S, the government should pay attention to jobs, housing, and electrification. One difference between the R family and the S family was that the latter had twice been victims of crime—assault and robbery—in the previous twelve months.

A widow, Mrs. T, lived with six children and one grandson in one of Witbank's townships. She earned R2,000 after tax per month as a teacher. Three of her children (between the ages of eleven and thirty-one) were still at school; one worked as a cleaner for R500 per month. The other two (aged twenty-six and twenty-eight) were unemployed; neither looked for work because, they said, there were no jobs. The family lived in a four-room brick house with tiled floors, inside taps, and flush toilet—for which they paid a mere R18 in rent per month. They had electricity but used wood and coal for cooking and heating. They collected wood once per week and bought the coal (Witbank being a coal-mining town). Because of Mrs. T's salary, the family had the financial leeway to spend R4,000 on furniture and to save more than R2,000 the previous year. They had a wide range of consumer durables including a television, two radios, a refrigerator, a stove, and a telephone. According to Mrs. T, the government should do something about housing.

The Rich: Decile 9

The ninth decile was the first in which African households did not predominate. African and white households accounted for a little more than one-third of the decile each, with coloured and Indian households accounting together for the rest. More than half of those in this decile lived in metropolitan areas; less than one-fifth lived in rural areas. Households in this decile had net monthly incomes between R2,500 and R4,700. More than half of the adult population was in regular employment in 1993, and the unemployment rate was low. Manufacturing was the largest employment sector. Almost 30 percent of permanently employed people were in professional or managerial jobs, with a further 23 percent in clerical and sales jobs.

One subject, Ms. U, was a "yuppie" living in Pretoria. She was thirty-one, lived on her own (and had never been pregnant), had most of the credits needed for a university degree, and worked in a professional occupation for the state (not full-time, however). She earned R5,400 before deductions but paid a lot of tax on this amount; after tax, she earned about R3,000 per month. She owned her four-room flat although it had a large bond (albeit with a housing subsidy). Her flat was, of course, electrified, and electricity was her only fuel. She smoked and drank (which together cost her almost R300 monthly) and had a part-time maid. She had a car, bought clothes regularly, went on holiday, and saved. The month before the survey she was sick for three days owing to stress. For one hour per day she worked as a sports instructor (perhaps in a gym) for R320 per month. She complained that taxes were too high and that petrol was too expensive.

At the opposite end of the country, Mr. V lived with his wife, four children, and six grandchildren in a semidetached brick house in Mitchell's Plain, Cape Town's largest coloured area. They had five rooms, inside taps, a flush toilet, a telephone, and all the basic electrical appliances. As a machine operator, Mr. V earned R1,000 per month. His wife earned R180 per month as a part-time domestic worker, and one of their daughters worked as a packing lady, earning about R625 monthly. All three of them commuted to work by train. In addition, Mr. V's son received a government disability grant of more than R300 per month. His two oldest daughters were both looking for work. With so many mouths to feed, the family's groceries bill came to more than R1,000 per month, but they still had enough to spend about R2,500 on clothing and shoes each year. Like many people living in urban areas, Mr. V had been the victim of an assault in the previous year.

A growing number of African households were in decile 9. Many had members in relatively well-paid, skilled working-class occupations like Mr. V's. For example, Mr. W was a truck driver in Dundee, in northern KwaZulu-Natal. He had grade 11 schooling and earned more than R2,000 monthly. He and his wife had six children, but only one lived with them in Dundee. They lived in a brick house with eight rooms, worth, he thought, about R75,000 (of which R15,000 was still outstanding on a bond). They had a car, a range of electrical appliances, and a telephone. The survey questionnaire was completed by the son, who said that the government should prioritise sports facilities, cinemas, and jobs (in that order).

The Very Rich: The Tenth Decile

Two in three households in the top decile were in metropolitan areas. Only one in ten was in a rural area. Net monthly incomes were above R4,700, with a mean income of more than R9,000. Almost three-quarters of the adult population was employed in 1993; unemployment was between 2 and 5 percent (according to the definition). Manufacturing was the largest sector, with education and finance not far behind. More than half of permanently employed people were in professional or managerial jobs, with almost another quarter in clerical and sales jobs.

Most of the households in this decile were white. A policeman, Mr. X lived with his wife and mother in what was often described as a white working-class area of Parow, in Cape Town's northern suburbs. He earned about R3,000 per month. His mother worked for the insurance giant Old Mutual, earning about R2,600 per month. His wife looked after the house, which had four rooms. The family had a large bond from the bank. They had three cars, and their payments for these cost them more than R1,000 per month. More than R200 per month went for cigarettes for Mr. X, and the family also ate out regularly.

Another family, Mr. and Mrs. Y, lived in Kempton Park, near Johannesburg International Airport. Thirty-nine-year-old Mr. Y worked as an airline technician, earning more than R5,000 per month after tax. His wife was a part-time nurse, earning about R1,000 per month after tax. They had four children aged three to ten. Their house was worth an estimated R160,000, and they had a bond of about R60,000. They had three cars and two televisions.

These households in decile 10 enjoyed lives that were very different from those of households in the lower deciles. They spent as much on groceries in a month as the poorest households spent in a year; they drove to work, whereas most poor people had neither jobs nor private transport; they lived in the city, not rural areas; they had televisions, refrigerators, and other indicators of high status.

SOURCES OF INCOME INEQUALITY

These examples of households in each of the income deciles point to the varying importance of different sources of income. Table 6.6 shows the composition of mean household income for each income decile—in other words, the sources from which the average household in each decile received its income. The bottom decile received most of its income (48.5 percent) from remittances (including monetary remittances and remittances in kind, for example, in the form of food). Old-age pensions were very important to deciles 2 through 4. For every decile from the fourth up, wages composed by far the most important source of household income.

The top five deciles were heavily dependent on wages from regular employment. The tenth decile supplemented its wage income (64.5 percent) with small but significant incomes from agriculture (6.8 percent), self-employment (9.0 percent) and income from capital (18.1 percent). Government old-age pensions were of minimal importance to the top decile (at less than 1 percent). The lower deciles relied more heavily on remittances and old-age pensions. Income from agricultural production was of little importance except to the top decile (which included high-income, capitalist farmers) and the bottom decile (where the incomes were so low that even R8 per month from smallholdings was an important contribution). Public transfer payments other than old-age pensions were of little importance.

Table 6.6 shows that remittances were *relatively* most important to the bottom decile and declined in importance as household incomes rose. The figures in table 6.6 were percentages of the mean household income of each decile. In *absolute* terms, however, there was little difference between the mean value of remittances received by households in each decile from decile 2 through decile 7—and this was higher than the mean value of remittances received by the bottom decile. In absolute terms, households in the top two deciles received, on average, almost as much in remittances as households in the bottom decile (R42 and R34 per month, respectively, compared to R45). Similarly, agriculture contributed 8.4 percent of decile 1's income, a higher proportion than for any other decile. But the absolute value of agricultural production for the average decile 1 household was a mere R8, less than the value for all but one of the other deciles, and a tiny fraction of the mean R632 received by households in the top decile (which includes commercial farmers). Table 6.7 shows the sources of household income by decile in absolute terms.

Patterns in the sources of income by race reflect the patterns by the deciles in which were located households in each racial category. Among African households, 68 percent of all income came from wages, 11 percent from pensions (and an additional 1 percent from other welfare grants), 8 percent from remittances, and 6 percent from self-employment. Only 2 percent came from agriculture. Among white households, 66 percent came from wages, 19 percent from capital, 6 percent from agriculture, and the same from self-employment. Neither welfare grants nor remittances were significant sources of income for white

Table 6.6. Composition of household income by income decile and source

	Income decile										Total S.A.
	1 (%)	2 (%)	3 (%)	4 (%)	5 (%)	6 (%)	7 (%)	8 (%)	9 (%)	10 (%)	(%)
Wage income	23.5	30.6	37.8	50.0	55.8	69.6	75.0	78.5	79.9	64.5	67.7
Remittances	48.5	30.0	18.4	15.0	10.0	6.8	5.1	2.9	1.2	0.4	3.4
Agriculture	8.4	4.4	3.0	3.3	2.5	0.7	1.3	1.0	0.7	6.8	4.0
Self-employment	13.0	6.1	5.1	4.0	5.5	3.9	3.8	4.8	4.6	9.0	6.7
Pension	0.0	23.2	27.9	21.8	18.8	12.1	7.6	4.3	1.9	0.5	4.6
Other transfers	1.0	3.2	4.8	3.7	3.5	3.0	2.0	1.6	1.1	0.3	1.2
Capital income	3.5	2.1	2.8	2.1	3.7	3.4	5.0	6.6	10.5	18.1	12.1
Total	100	100	100	100	100	100	100	100	100	100	100

Notes: Wage income includes regular wages (after tax), casual wages, and the value of employer subsidies of transport, food, and housing; "remittances" includes value of remittances in money and in kind; "agriculture" includes value of agricultural production whether consumed or sold; "self-employment" comprises the profits earned from self-employment; "pension" comprises government old-age pensions; "other transfers" comprise other public transfers; "capital income" includes income from capital, actual and imputed rent on land and property, interest on financial assets, and income from contributory pension schemes. Some column totals do not add up to 100 percent because of rounding errors and the omission of some very minor sources of income. $n = 8{,}567$.

213

Table 6.7. Composition of household income by income decile and source, in R/month

	Income decile										Mean
	1	2	3	4	5	6	7	8	9	10	
Wage income	22	90	164	295	440	731	1,062	1,629	2,791	6,023	1,325
Remittances	45	88	80	88	79	72	72	60	42	34	66
Agriculture	8	13	13	19	20	7	18	21	23	633	77
Self employment	12	18	22	24	43	41	54	99	159	841	131
Pension	0	68	121	128	148	126	108	90	65	43	90
Other transfers	1	10	21	22	28	31	29	33	38	25	24
Capital income	3	6	12	12	29	36	70	136	167	1,690	236
Total	93	293	433	588	787	1,044	1,413	2,068	3,285	9,289	1,949

Note: See table 6.6. The exclusion of very minor sources of income and rounding errors explains minor differences between the totals given here and the figures in table 6.1. *n* = 8,567.

households. Self-employment was particularly important among Indian households, and wages were particularly important for coloured households.

Remittances and Pensions

Tables 6.6 and 6.7 testify to the importance of both public and private transfers at the end of apartheid. Most of the private transfers entailed remittances sent to rural kin by migrant or urbanised workers. As many as one in three African rural households in 1993 reported having members who were migrant workers (Posel 2000, 9). Most of the public transfers were government old-age pensions. The scale of these public transfers reflects the remarkable expansion of the public welfare system in the last years of apartheid (as we saw in Chapter 4). As shown in table 6.6, about a quarter of household income in the second and third deciles came from state old-age pensions. Indeed, the presence of an old-age pensioner in a household was often the main factor lifting households out of abject poverty. Table 6.6 also shows that, in the aggregate, public transfers (that is, pensions and other grants) were about 60 percent more valuable than private transfers or remittances.

Although most recipients of private remittances were poor, nonpoor households accounted for a high proportion of the remittances received in society. Overall, a little more than one in four households (27 percent) received remittances, but the proportion was much higher in the lower income deciles. In the bottom two deciles, about 50 percent of households received remittances. In deciles 3 to 5 the proportion was about one-third. In deciles 6 and 7, only one in five households received remittances, and the proportion in the top three deciles was smaller still. There was a clear relation between income and the proportion of households receiving remittances. At the same time, the households in the richer deciles that did receive remittances received larger sums than their counterparts in poorer deciles.

Most remittances were sent by nonpoor households. Less than 15 percent of remitting households were in the poorest four deciles. This is because remittances were closely tied to wages. Although there are reported cases of pensioners sending a share of their pension to family members living elsewhere (Ardington and Lund 1995, 571; Baber 1998, 103, 163), the PSLSD data show that most remittances came from wage income. Overall, remittances represented a maximum of about 5 percent of total wage income.

Table 6.8 shows how the sending and receiving of remittances was distributed among the deciles. The first column shows the distribution of households

Table 6.8. Distribution of remitters, remittances sent, recipients, and remittances received, by income decile, 1993

Income decile	Remitters (%)	Remittances sent (%)	Recipients of remittances (%)	Remittances received (%)
1	4	2	19	7
2	5	2	17	13
3	7	4	14	12
4	12	10	11	12
5	12	10	11	12
6	17	19	8	11
7	15	17	8	11
8	12	12	6	9
9	9	10	4	6
10	6	17	2	5
Total S.A.	100	100	100	100

Note: These deciles are defined inclusive of remittances received but exclusive of remittances sent.

sending remittances (bearing in mind that migrant workers living in single quarters in a hostel were defined as separate households by the PSLSD survey). The second column shows the distribution of remittances sent by households in each income decile. These two columns show that remittances were distributed across all deciles (including the poorest) but the largest shares of remittances came from deciles 6, 7, and 10.

The third column in table 6.8 shows the distribution of recipient households, and the final column shows the distribution of the value of remittances received. One in every two households receiving remittances was in deciles 1, 2, or 3. Recipient households were thus concentrated among the poor. By contrast, only about one in four households receiving remittances were in the top five deciles. But because the average value of remittances to the poor households is so low, the bottom three deciles only account for one-third of the total value of remittances—less than the share of the top five deciles.

A comparison of the first two columns with the last two columns allows us to gauge the approximate extent of redistribution via remittances. We cannot link up remitters and recipients, but we can calculate the net transfer into or out of a decile via remittances. The figures should be treated with caution, not least because, in the PSLSD survey, the total value of remittances sent does not add up to the total value of remittances received. Tables 6.8 and 6.9 thus use the

Table 6.9. The redistributive effects of public and private transfers, 1993

Income decile	Net transfer via remittances (%)		Net transfer via taxes and public welfare (%)
1	+5	+16	+4 – +5
2	+11		
3	+8	+14	+22 – +23
4	+6		
5	+2	−6	+24 – +25
6	−8		
7	−6	−9	+10 – +12
8	−3		
9	−4	−16	−61 – −65
10	−12		
Total S.A.	0	0	0

Note: + indicates receipt, − indicates payment.

data for shares of total remittances rather than those for absolute amounts sent or received.

The first column of table 6.9 shows the net transfer of remittances by income decile (based on the figures in table 6.8). A figure less than zero indicates that the decile was a net recipient of remittances, receiving a larger share than it sent. Overall, remittances served in 1993 to transfer income from the top half of the income distribution (especially deciles 6, 7, and 10) to the bottom half (especially deciles 2 and 3). The second column of table 6.9 summarises the redistributive effect of public transfers, that is, the transfer of resources from taxpayers to old-age pensioners and the recipients of other noncontributory welfare payments (primarily disability and child maintenance grants). This column is calculated from the estimates of the incidence of taxation and public spending by McGrath, Janisch, and Horner (1997), as summarised in table 4.1 above. Because of uncertainty about the incidence of some taxes and some expenditures, their figures are presented as a range (see discussion in Chapter 4). Note that this assumes that welfare payments are funded in direct proportion to total taxation, and no adjustment is made for deficit financing.

Table 6.9 shows that the public welfare system redistributed massively from the top deciles to the poor in 1993. Note that the total value of redistribution via public transfers was about 1.7 times larger than the total value of redistribution via private transfers (remittances). Public transfers, and especially the government's old-age pension system, represented a major mechanism for redistribution to the poor (see also Ardington and Lund 1995; Case and Deaton 1998). The old-age pension was, paradoxically, an effective mechanism for getting resources into poor households where children lived, because so many children lived in three-generation households dependent on a grandparent's pension. Duflo (2003) found that children living in households where their maternal grandmother received a pension were significantly heavier and taller than other children of their age.

Even taking into account the fact that public transfers were, in total, 1.7 times more valuable than private remittances, table 6.9 shows that the poorest quintile benefited more in the aggregate from private redistribution than from public redistribution. (This is also clear in table 6.7). The second and third quintiles, however, benefited much more from public than private redistribution. This analysis is somewhat misleading, however. The quintiles in these tables are defined inclusive of transfers. Households in the bottom quintile were there largely because they were ineligible for public transfers; if they did include a pensioner, then the receipt of an old-age pension would have lifted them into the second quintile. It is not so much that public redistribution did not reach the poor as that it did not reach *all* of the poor: Most poor households were lifted out of deep poverty, but poor households without eligible members were not assisted.

In Chapter 4 we saw that the real value of public transfers via the old-age pension system rose dramatically in the last years of apartheid, as the National Party government reduced and finally removed racial discrimination in benefits. There are no equivalent data about trends in the total value of private transfers (via remittances) in the same period. But there are some hints that remittances stagnated or declined. Any such decline might have been related to the rise in value of government old-age pensions. Pensions appear to have had a crowding-out effect on remittances: as pensions rose, so remitters chose to send less money back to their families, presumably on the grounds that rural relatives were less in need than they had been before. Using data from surveys in Venda (the far northern part of Limpopo Province) in 1989 and 1992, Jensen found that a one-rand increase in the old-age pension led to a 0.25- to 0.3-rand reduction in private remittances received by a household (Jensen 2003). Posel (2001) found that the frequency and size of remittances depended on the income of the recipient household. A more curious effect of pensions has been detected by Bertrand et al. (2003). They find that the presence of an old-age pensioner in a three-generation household is accompanied by a drop in labour force participation by prime-age men. This is more marked when the pensioner is a woman. It appears to be the case that men work less if they can appropriate some of the income received by elderly women via the old-age pension. Jensen (2003) did not find this effect, however.

Posel (2001) found that remittances also depended on migrants' earnings (positively), the closeness of kin relationships (with larger sums sent to children and spouses than to less close kin), gender (women remitting more than men, other things being equal), and age (older migrants remitting more than younger ones). This helps illuminate further the decline in remittances received in poor areas. The rise in unemployment probably reduced remittance flows. In Mamone, in Limpopo Province, Baber (1998, 25) found that middle-aged men spent 90 percent of their economically active lives as migrants, but younger men had spent only 60 percent of theirs as migrants because of unemployment. Even if men had left the village in search of work, their chances of finding work were declining. Posel (2001, 169) reports that 20 percent of migrant workers failed to remit at all (see also Sharp and Spiegel 1985). In addition, migrants are more likely to have settled in towns and severed ties with relatives they left behind. Remittances may also have been discouraged by the collapse of agriculture in the reserves, itself due (as we have seen) to factors such as overcrowding, overstocking, and theft. Resources are invested in other forms of savings than cattle.

Subsistence Agriculture

The PSLSD data show emphatically how unimportant subsistence agriculture had become by the end of apartheid. Although South Africa might have still been a "rural" society in the sense that half of the population lived outside of the towns and cities (see table 6.3), it was far from being an agrarian society. As late as the 1920s, almost two-thirds of the labour force worked on the land (although even then agricultural production in the reserves was only adequate to provide for about one-half of the food subsistence requirements of the population there [Simkins 1981c]). On the eve of apartheid, as we saw in Chapter 2, there remained a significant number of African smallholding farmers, or peasants, and many other African families aspired to using their wage income to accumulate cattle and preserve an agrarian society. Land dispossession, forced removals, and the rising population of the bantustans resulted in the destruction of African smallholder agriculture in the 1950s and 1960s (see Chapter 3). By the end of the apartheid era, state policies combined with population growth ensured that almost all household income in rural areas had come from participation in the labour market (including remittance). Old-age pensions represent the only other major source of income. The PSLSD data for 1993 show that agricultural production provided only 4 percent of mean household income in South Africa (see table 6.6); if we exclude the commercial farmers in decile 10, agricultural production provided less than 1 percent of mean household income.

Shackleton et al. (2000) argue that the value of subsistence production and especially natural resource harvesting by poor rural households has been underestimated. They suggest that the value of natural resource harvesting—the collecting of wood, reeds, grass, wild food, clay, water, and so on—was, in the late 1990s, almost as high as the old-age pension per household per year (although Adams et al. [2000, 125] are more cautious). Insofar as these activities are significant, they are most likely to make a difference for the very poorest households.

Even if allowance is made for some underestimation of the value of subsistence agriculture and natural resource harvesting, the contrast between South Africa at the end of apartheid and a truly agrarian society is very stark. Tanzania, for example, remained a largely peasant society in the 1980s. The proportion of the labour force involved in agriculture in Tanzania was estimated to be 84 percent in 1990, compared to 14 percent in South Africa. Agriculture accounted for an estimated 58 percent of GDP in the former in 1995 but only 5 percent in the latter in the same year. By the end of apartheid, agriculture was less important in South Africa than in most other middle-income countries such as Brazil, Korea, Malaysia, and Poland (see World Bank 1996, 14–17). The differences between Tanzania and South Africa are reflected in terms of the sources of household income (see table 6.10). In Tanzania in 1980, agriculture (including both crops and livestock) provided almost three-quarters of the total income of the average village household. It provided an even higher proportion of the income of poor households, which were poor largely because they had very little access to any kind of nonfarm income.

In 1993 only one in five households in South Africa was engaged in any agricultural production (although others were involved in agriculture as paid farm workers). Even in the poorest deciles, barely more than one-quarter of the households were engaged in any independent agricultural production. The comparative figure for households in the upper deciles is very low. The value of agricultural production for households in the poorest three deciles was, on average, barely more than R10 per month (according to the PSLSD data). The mean value for those that engaged in this practice was below R50 per month. Agricultural production in South Africa is dominated by the large-scale commercial sector. According to the PSLSD data, only 3 percent of producers were

Table 6.10. Composition of household income in rural
Tanzania (1980) and rural South Africa (1993)

Source of income	Tanzania (%)	South Africa (%)	
Agriculture	73	14	
Remittances	4	9	
Wage income		53	
Transfers		14	
Self-employment	23	5	77
Capital income		5	
Total	100	100	

Sources: Tanzania: Collier et al. (1990, 76). South African data are calculated
from PSLSD data.
Note: Eighty-five percent of Tanzanians live in rural villages.

in the top income decile in 1993, but they accounted for 81 percent of the proceeds from production. More than two-thirds of households engaged in agricultural production were in the poorest five income deciles, but they accounted for less than 10 percent of production. By the end of apartheid, smallholder agricultural production was almost irrelevant in South Africa.

Given the low incomes of many poor households, as well as high rates of unemployment, it seems puzzling that some poor households left land uncultivated. An example of this was the first household profiled above: Mrs. A and her family in Limpopo Province. They had access to one hectare of land but did not cultivate it. In conditions of crushing poverty, why did this family (and families like it) not cultivate fully their land? They were far from unique; the same has been documented in Keiskammahoek in the Eastern Cape (Sperber 1993, 18), Nkandla in KwaZulu (Ardington 1995), and villages in Limpopo Province (Baber 1998; see also Bromberger and Antonie 1993).

The PSLSD survey provides some data about land use in 1993. Of respondents who said that they had access to communally owned land for growing crops, 26 percent said that they had cultivated none of it during the previous year. Another 17 percent said that they had cultivated half or less of "their" land. Only 56 percent said they had cultivated all of "their" land. There was little correlation between the size of the landholding and whether it had been used; families with small holdings were as likely to have left it fallow as families with medium-sized holdings, although families with large holdings farmed less of their land on average.

The most thorough study of reasons for noncultivation was done more than ten years earlier by Lenta (1981). Lenta conducted a survey of 110 households in three districts in what was then KwaZulu. He found that between 20 and 30 percent of arable land was not cultivated. The explanation given most often (by 58 percent of respondents) was a lack of capital in the form of oxen or tractors for ploughing but also of seed and fertiliser. Household capital was typically invested instead in education or used up for medical expenses. A shortage of labour was cited by 30 percent of respondents; household members were either too infirm or sick, at school or away (working as migrants). The remaining 11 percent said that the land was unsuitable, generally meaning that it was too rocky or steep, was not amenable to ploughing by tractor or oxen, and would require too much labour to hoe by hand. Households held onto land they were not farming for social reasons. They could not rent it out to other families to cultivate because of the insecurity of land tenure.

Lenta examined the amount of labour required to cultivate land and when the labour was needed. Many households did have the labour required to hoe the land by hand. He calculated that one hectare of maize required 360 hours of work per year, concentrated in three and a half months of almost full-time work. But people were unhappy to cultivate with hoes; if they could not use a plough, they left the land uncultivated. To some extent this reflected changing norms, Lenta suggests. But he also emphasises that the return on labour was very low. The average yield on one hectare was five bags of maize. Given the price of maize, the product of every three hours work was valued at merely the price of one loaf of bread. The picture painted by Lenta is not dissimilar to that painted of Keiskammahoek in 1949 by Houghton and Walton (1952): landholdings were small, and the land was often poor; a lack of capital meant that production was labour-intensive; intermittent constraints on labour supply exacerbated the problem of low productivity; the result was that the returns on effort were very low. "Under such conditions," Lenta wrote (1981, 41), "it seems more appropriate to ask why people cultivate at all, than why they do not make full use of their land." One possible answer comes from Lower Roza in the Transkei: "Mealies are often cultivated from habit or convention alone. A number of women felt that cultivation was entirely a waste of time, but grew mealies because their husbands and families expected it" (Moll 1994, 27).

More recently, Baber examined why households in two villages in Limpopo Province did not utilise their land fully. In one village, 20 percent of land was left fallow; in the second village the amount was 45 percent. As Lenta had found in KwaZulu, many families could not afford to pay for their fields to be ploughed by tractor. "Faced with the choice of either tilling a field by hand or leaving it fallow, households invariably choose the latter option. This suggests that even in the case of the poorest units the returns to manual tilling are so low as to be outweighed by the marginal utility of leisure" (Baber 1998, 39). Note that in the hands of a neoclassical labour economist this analysis could be seen as evidence of an absence of unemployment: if people are refusing to work at the going (very low) rate of return in agriculture, then they should be regarded as voluntarily unemployed (that is, choosing leisure), and hence outside of the labour force (see Chapter 5). Households' reluctance to farm fully their land reflects the equivalent of a reservation wage. To define people as not being unemployed, however, on the grounds that they are refusing to work for a pittance, that is, to be underemployed in agriculture, seems to be stretching the definition of unemployment into the realm of the absurd. The implicit reservation wage is very low indeed at less than one-third of a loaf of bread per hour of labour. One could argue about the nicety of the distinction, but the social problems of severe rural poverty and underemployment will remain.

Baber also points to the preference for maize (which, unlike sorghum and millet, cannot tolerate drought) and the cost of the fencing necessary to prevent damage by livestock (ibid., 239). This general picture accords with what we know to be the case elsewhere in Africa: successful small-scale production requires capital and hence access to off-farm income. Some households did blame a shortage of labour (ibid., 240–42). Why, then, did families not hire out unused land to others? They feared compromising their usufruct rights. There were two exceptions to this: a tractor owner could use an area of land for one season only in return for ploughing a similar area of land for the one allowing him to use it, and relatives could borrow land.

Although the PSLSD survey did not ask directly why land was left unused, the data do tend to corroborate the thesis that the reason was a shortage of capital and not of labour. Many households that were not using their land fully included unemployed members. Indeed, whether or not there was unemployed labour within a household seemed to make no difference to deciding how much of the land to cultivate. Lack of access to tractors or cattle for ploughing clearly remained a constraint. In 1993, according to the PSLSD data, 85 percent of rural African households had no cattle. About 4 percent had one or two cows, and another 8 percent had between three and eight cows. Only 3 percent had nine or more cows. The mean number of cattle per household was less than one. Baber (1998, 155) found that in Mamone, in Limpopo Province, migrants invested their earnings in housing, medical or life insurance, endowment policies, and savings plans rather than livestock. In the most rural areas, such as Nkandla, cattle holdings were both more common and larger (Ardington, 1995). Overall, however, rural households were dependent on tractors for ploughing, and the poorest households could not afford to hire a tractor. As Delius (1996) put it in his study of Sekhukhuneland, the cattle had indeed gone.

By the end of apartheid, crime had become an important deterrent to cattle ownership. Resettlement policies, the expansion of schooling, and the improvement of roads all facilitated sharp increases in stock theft in or around former reserves in Limpopo in the 1980s (Delius 1996), KwaZulu (Bonner and Ndima 1999), the Free State (Murray 2000), and the Eastern Cape (Peires 1994). A 1998 survey found that one in three households owning livestock said that they had been the victims of stock theft in the previous five years; 15 percent said that they had had stock stolen in the past year alone (RSA 1998b; see also Pelser et al. 2000, 16–19).

Access to Wage Income

In previous chapters we argued that, under apartheid, poverty and inequality in South Africa came to be rooted not in different levels of agricultural production but in the labour market: in part because of low wages and in part because of very high rates of unemployment. As Leibbrandt et al. point out, "access to wage income is central to determining which households are able to avoid poverty and, even, the depth to which poor households sink below the poverty line. This reasserts the importance of the labour market in understanding poverty" (1999, 12). Within the labour market, overt discrimination became less important. Wage differentials based on education and unemployment came to drive inequality. The 1993 PSLSD data provide strong evidence for these trends and their effects on inequality.

Participation and broad unemployment rates by decile are shown in figure 6.2. The participation rate (the proportion of adult household members participating in the labour force) rose steadily up the income deciles, from below 50 percent (in deciles 1 to 3) to 75 percent (in the top decile). The unemployment rate (the proportion of the labour force that is unemployed, using the expanded definition of unemployment that includes job seekers and those not actively seeking work) shows the opposite pattern: 71 percent for the bottom decile, declining to just 5 percent for the top decile. If the income deciles are defined in terms of household income per capita, then the correlation between unemployment rate and income decile is even sharper, with a 76 percent unemploy-

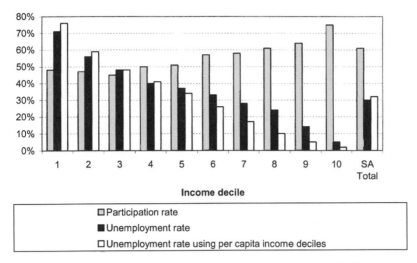

Figure 6.2. Participation rates and broad unemployment rates by income decile, 1993

ment rate in the bottom decile and a 2 percent unemployment rate in the top decile (Kingdon and Knight 1999, 7). Not only were poor households likely to have more unemployed adults than richer households, but they were also likely to have more adults who said they are not available for work (and hence are defined as outside the labour force). The dual correlation between unemployment and income and labour force participation and income suggests that low-income households were marginalised in the labour market.

The incidence of employment is shown in a different way in table 6.11. This table shows the proportion of households in each decile according to the number of members in employment. A majority of households in each of the bottom four deciles have no members in employment. At the opposite extreme, a majority in each of the top two deciles have two or more members in employment.

The link between lack of employment and poverty is particularly strong in South Africa. In the OECD also, the lack of access to wage income correlates closely with poverty: "households with no workers are often at the bottom of the income distribution and have the highest poverty rates" (OECD 1996, 151; see also OECD 1998b). In the OECD, the proportion of households in the bottom quintile without any members in employment is 42 percent, with figures ranging from 21 percent in Luxemburg to 65 percent in Ireland and 74 percent in Finland (OECD 1998a, 24). In South Africa, the corresponding figure was 83 percent. This contrast is all the more striking given that the OECD countries

Table 6.11. Employment per household by income decile, 1993

Number of persons employed per household	S.A. Total %	Income decile									
		1 (%)	2 (%)	3 (%)	4 (%)	5 (%)	6 (%)	7 (%)	8 (%)	9 (%)	10 (%)
0	39	92	75	66	51	41	25	16	12	8	9
1	40	8	23	29	42	49	63	66	54	41	26
2+	21	1	3	6	7	10	12	18	34	51	64
Total	100	100	100	100	100	100	100	100	100	100	100

have tax and transfer systems that alleviate the poverty associated with unemployment.

Although participation rates were low and unemployment rates high in the lower deciles at the end of apartheid, those deciles nonetheless included a significant number of low-paid workers. About 30 percent of the employed were in households in the bottom five deciles. They were predominantly farm workers and, to a lesser extent, domestic workers. The industrial working class, by contrast, was concentrated in the top five deciles. Only 13 percent of manufacturing workers were in households in the bottom five deciles. Fully 77 percent were in the top four deciles. Mine workers were distributed more widely, with the largest numbers in deciles 4 to 7. In terms of occupation, people in professional, technical, managerial, and administrative jobs were, not surprisingly, in households in the top two deciles. Most workers in clerical and sales occupations were in the top three deciles. Artisans were spread across the top four deciles. Most machine operators and similar semiskilled workers were in deciles 6 to 9. Unskilled labourers were found in deciles 4 to 8.

In short, access to the labour market was the major determinant of inequality by 1993. Whether an individual had a job, and what kind, played a crucial role in determining his or her position in the income distribution. According to calculations by Leibbrandt et al. (1999), access to the labour market accounted for 67 percent of overall inequality in 1995, of which 30 percent was driven by the gap between those with wage incomes and those without and 37 percent was driven by inequality within the distribution of wage income, to which we now turn.

Wage Inequality

During the apartheid era, racial discrimination was an important determinant of wage inequality. As the system slowly deracialised, the impact of racial discrimination declined accordingly. According to Moll (2000), the contribution of this factor to wage determination declined significantly between 1980 and 1993, dropping from 20 percent to 12 percent of the African wage (see table 6.12). Note, however, that this did not result in a one-to-one drop in the gap between white and African wages. It only resulted in a drop in that part of the wage gap that could be attributed to racial discrimination in terms of pay and access to well-paying jobs. The gap between white and black wages narrowed sharply from the 1970s onwards, but was still large in the 1990s. As can be seen in table 6.12, white wages were on average more than five times larger than those of Africans.

The racial wage gap at the end of apartheid is explained primarily by factors other than discrimination, such as differences in education and skill, location (urban or rural), and economic sector. As shown in table 6.12, African workers had the lowest educational qualifications, lived predominantly in rural areas, and had the highest concentration in low-paying sectors such as agriculture. Wage functions confirm the importance of such characteristics in explaining wage inequality (Schultz and Mwabu 1998a, 1998b; Moll 2000, Butcher and Rouse 2000). For example, Schultz and Mwabu show that African men working in agriculture earned substantially less than workers with similar characteristics working in manufacturing, and those in rural areas earned significantly less than those in urban areas (1998b, 690).

The PSLSD data show that education was particularly important. Schultz and Mwabu (1998a) show that one-half of the difference by race in earnings can be attributed to differences in educational qualifications. If it were possible to include a measure of the different quality of education received by white and African workers, then an even greater proportion of wage inequality could probably be explained by education. Africans workers with good educational qualifications were particularly well placed to obtain highly paid jobs. Schultz and Mwabu conclude that African men could command an extra 8 percent for every year of primary education, an extra 16 percent for every year of secondary education, and an extra 29 percent for every year of tertiary education. Such rates of return on education are higher than for all other racial groups (see table 6.12). The returns on secondary and tertiary education were even higher for African women.

Despite the decline in racial discrimination and in the wage gap between white and African workers, overall wage inequality had not declined by 1993. According to various measures, overall inequality in the distribution of wages remained unchanged between 1980 and 1993. The reason for this was that as racial wage inequality declined, intraracial wage inequality increased. Whereas racial inequality accounted for 65 percent of total wage inequality in 1980, it accounted for only 42 percent in 1993 (see table 6.13). The rise in intraracial wage inequality cancelled out the impact of falling racial inequality, thus leaving the overall measure of wage inequality unchanged. As can be seen in table 6.13, various measures of wage inequality report insignificant (if any) changes between 1980 and 1993 with regard to urban men.

The increase in wage inequality among Africans was in part the result of increased occupational mobility. There was a significant movement of Africans up the occupational ladder, with the proportion in the labourer and semiskilled

Table 6.12. Characteristics of the sample of wage earners, 1993

	African		Coloured		Indian		White	
	Men	Women	Men	Women	Men	Women	Men	Women
Years of education	6.8	7.6	8.5	8.5	11.0	10.7	12.2	11.2
Rates of return on education (%)								
primary	8.4	6.3	1.4	2.3	−9.5	−8.2	−1.2	−3.4
secondary	15.8	24.9	18.7	19.9	21.4	12.6	8.4	5.2
higher	29.4	39.6	18.6	30.7	21.4	30.4	15.1	13.9
Percent living in rural areas	56.1	47.2	10.3	9.9	1.8	0.9	6.6	6.8
Percent working in agriculture	20	11	14	11	0	0	4	1
Hourly wage in rands	R4.8	R3.3	R7.2	R5.1	R12.8	R8.2	R27.9	R15.8

Source: Schultz and Mwabu (1998b, 682, 687).

Table 6.13. Earnings inequality among urban men

	1980	1993
Measurement of earnings inequality from all employment sources		
Gini	0.52	0.51
L-statistic	0.49	0.50
Coefficient of variation	1.19	1.12
Ratio of mean African earnings to mean white earnings	0.18	0.24
Occupational distribution of Africans (%)		
Professional, technical, managerial, and administrative personnel	2.8	6.6
Clerical and sales workers	8.8	10.6
Transport workers	2.0	13.5
Artisans	9.0	11.1
Foremen and supervisors	3.0	5.1
Semiskilled workers	20.2	13.8
Labourers	37.0	24.4
Other	15.3	14.8
Total	100	100
Racial discrimination as a percentage of the mean (logarithm of the) African wage	20	12
Racial discrimination as a percentage of the mean (logarithm of the) white wage	16	10
Wage inequality accounted for by within-race inequality*	35%	58%
Wage inequality accounted for by between-race inequality*	65%	42%
Wage inequality among Africans within occupations†	0.12	0.18
Wage inequality among Africans within sectors‡	0.13	0.23

Source: Moll (2000) using 1980 census microdata and the 1993 PSLSD.
*Decomposition using the L-statistic.
†Using the L-statistic for selected occupations in the mining, manufacturing, construction, trade, and transport sectors.
‡Using the L-statistic for the following sectors: mining, manufacturing, construction, trade, transport, finance, domestic, and other services.

categories dropping from 57 percent in 1980 to 38 percent in 1993 (see table 6.13). As the number of Africans in higher-paying occupations increased, so the gap between highly paid and low-paid Africans increased, thus widening wage inequality. But this increased also as a result of widening inequality within occupational categories and within economic sectors. This reflected the trend toward greater wage inequality in other middle-income countries and in the advanced capitalist countries.

There was, however, a further force at work in the labour market affecting wage inequality: the trade union movement. New trade unions organising African workers were formed in the mid-1970s and grew rapidly in the 1980s. Union membership rose from 17 percent of nonagricultural employment in 1980 to 46 percent in 1990 and a peak of 59 percent in 1993 (Macun 2000, 60). With regard to the unionised part of the labour force, the trade unions narrowed both interracial and intraracial inequality. According to estimates by Schultz and Mwabu, an African unionised worker received a wage that was 60 percent higher than that of a nonunion worker with similar characteristics (1998b, 687). If industry is controlled for in the regression, then the union wage gap for Africans dropped to 19 percent. Using data for 1995, Butcher and Rouse find a union wage differential for Africans of 22 percent (2000, 16).

Union membership appears to have benefited those at the bottom end of the wage distribution the most. According to Schultz and Mwabu, being a member of a union increased the wages of African workers in the bottom 10 percent of the wage distribution by 145 percent and increased the wages of those in the top 10 percent by a mere 11 percent (1998b, 700). By boosting the incomes of low-paid workers relative to higher-paid workers, the trade union movement would thus have acted to narrow the wage distribution in the unionised sector (and hence encouraged further shifts towards capital-intensive production, making growth less likely to create jobs). Subsequent econometric work on the 1995 October Household Survey supports the conclusion that unions reduced wage inequality, albeit to a lesser degree (Butcher and Rouse 2000, 19).

Whether the trade union movement's efforts served to narrow the overall distribution of household income is another matter entirely. Higher union wages settlements would have encouraged firms to shed labour. According to Schultz and Mwabu (1998b), an increase of 10 percent in the union relative wage effect reduced employment by 5.6 percent. Workers who lost their jobs would have looked for work in firms and sectors not covered by wage agreements. If wages had fallen in response to this increased supply, then the result would have been a widening of the wage distribution measured across all firms and sectors (not only the unionised sector). If wages had not fallen, then the increased supply of workers would have translated into higher unemployment figures. Wage inequality would thus have remained unaltered, but overall inequality would have risen because the gap between those with jobs and those without would have grown. Schultz and Mwabu argue that if the union relative wage effect were cut in half, then African employment would increase by about 2 percent: "There would be a redistribution of wage payments from the upper-middle class African union workers to lower-wage non-union workers and the marginalised poor who are often now not actively participating in the labour market" (1998b, 701).

INCOME DYNAMICS AND SOCIAL STRATIFICATION

The PSLSD data show that, in the late apartheid period, some Africans were able to move into higher-paying occupations and the higher income deciles. The ceiling on prosperity for African people rose. The expansion of semiskilled and later skilled and white-collar employment under apartheid meant new opportunities for upward mobility for many Africans, as we saw in Chapter 3 (and as [Crankshaw 1997a] has documented). There was surely significant upward mobility between generations in *absolute* terms, such that in many families, perhaps most, children's occupations were very different from their parents'. By 1993 it was not unusual for a young office worker to have a father who was a semiskilled or skilled worker in manufacturing or a mother who was a domestic worker and grandparents who were farm workers or unskilled migrant mine workers (in the case of men) or who had never had formal employment and never left their homes in the reserves (in the case of women). Unfortunately, there are no quantitative data regarding this intergenerational mobility. Nor is there any evidence for *relative* mobility rates. What was the probability of a black person entering a highly paid occupation relative to the likelihood of a white person doing so or the probability of someone from a poor family doing so relative to someone from a nonpoor family? It was surely the case that, for Africans, absolute rates of mobility were high but relative rates were low: their opportunities to benefit from a changing economy were restricted by racial discrimination and educational disadvantage.

Changes in absolute or relative mobility rates need not have been spread evenly across all sections of the African population. As discussed in earlier chapters, there is selective evidence suggesting that public policy during the apartheid period not only stunted processes of class formation among the African population as a whole (via racial discrimination) but also shaped patterns of differentiation (and perhaps stratification) within it. Revisionist as well as liberal writers (for example, Hindson 1987, and Wilson 1975a) emphasised the segmentation of labour markets between urban insiders with section 10 residential rights and migrant workers without those rights. Schneier, using surveys among small samples of African workers in 1981, suggested that there were different inter- and intragenerational mobility rates among different sections of the African working class. Urban insiders and their children were in a better position to take advantage of the new opportunities opening up as a result of structural change in the economy and the erosion (or circumvention) of legal constraints (Schneier 1983; see Chapter 3 above). If the most advantaged section of the black population consisted of the urban insiders, then the most disadvantaged section consisted of the families of farm workers evicted from white-owned farms in the 1970s and dumped in remote bantustans at a time of high unemployment; resettled without any access to agricultural land and lacking education, nonagricultural skills, access to schools, or contacts in urban areas, they (and their children) were sentenced to enduring poverty.

Unfortunately, neither qualitative research conducted near the end of apartheid nor the PSLSD survey provides much evidence about income dynamics and changes over time. Qualitative research revealed the patterns of inequality and differentiation and some tantalising hints as to who filled which positions in the economic structure of society. For example, research conducted in the Free State and QwaQwa demonstrated that former farm workers removed to bantustans ended up in more disadvantaged positions than households removed from urban areas. But such insights were fragmentary.

The official population census adds a little to the picture. Thomas (1996), using data from censuses taken up to 1991, found that the improvement of educational opportunities for African men and women was distributed unevenly. For some, widening opportunities meant markedly greater grade attainment than had been possible previously, but for others, the new opportunities made little difference and grade attainment remained poor.

The PSLSD does not contribute much more to the picture. To see how people's lives are affected by new opportunities and old constraints, one really needs data from a study in which the same panel of respondents is reinterviewed over a long period of time. Since the late 1990s, researchers have been conducting panel studies in South Africa, but there are no panel data for the late apartheid era. A possible alternative is to ask retrospective questions about the past. By asking detailed questions about family background, schooling, and work history, a survey might shed some light on how and why people attained the positions they had at the time of the survey. The PSLSD data included only one semiretrospective question: What is the highest educational qualification of each household member? Unfortunately, data were collected only for adults and children who were coresident in the households in the sample.

This allows for two kinds of analysis of how inequalities are reproduced across generations. First, in the many cases in which schoolchildren live with one or both parents, the grade attained by age by the children can be compared to their parent's or parents' education, income, occupation, or class. Not surprisingly, in 1993 there was a strong correlation between parental income and children's progress through school. By the age of sixteen, children living in households in the richest quintile were generally several grades ahead of children living in households in the poorest quintile. Second, in the small number of cases in which *adults* live with their parents, the completed education or occupations or earnings of two generations can be compared. Hertz (2001) found a strong correlation between the earnings of coresidential mothers and daughters, adjusting for age, but a less strong correlation between the earnings of coresidential fathers and sons; he emphasised, however, that the confidence intervals on these estimates are very wide; that is, the results are far from certain. He also found that the respective education of fathers and sons and of mothers and daughters explains a relatively small share of the transmission of economic status.

After 1993, surveys collected more data that allow for a more detailed analysis of the reproduction of inequality over time. There are two categories of new data that are of use. First, surveys began to ask about the educational levels and past occupations of nonresidential parents, allowing for comparison of the education and employment of adults today with the previous generation in the past. Burns (2000, 11), using data concerning African people in KwaZulu-Natal, shows that there are strong correlations between the educational levels of adults and their parents, each relative to their respective generations. The correlations between people who went to school in the 1940s and their children who attended school in the 1960s were slightly weaker, and those between this second generation and their children who attended school in the late 1970s and early 1980s were slightly stronger. Second, data from panel studies or from more detailed retrospective questions allow us to track or reconstruct changes over time in the lives of specific individuals. In Chapter 9 we review the findings of a number of studies conducted since 1993 that show that, in the context of high rates of unemployment, there is considerable flux in incomes: household incomes rise and fall dramatically when a member secures or loses employment (or if an employed person joins or leaves the household). At the same time, disadvantage persists over time. Individuals with limited education and poor contacts are likely to spend more time unemployed, and when they do work, they are likely to be paid less than individuals with better education and contacts.

High rates of unemployment raise methodological problems for analysing the reproduction of inequality between generations (see Hertz 2001). When unemployment rates are high, current earnings or income will be more volatile than average lifetime earnings or income. Hertz addressed this problem by using, in his study of the intergenerational transmission of inequality, the average of the earnings and income of coresidential adults and their parents as recorded in 1993 by the PSLSD and in 1998 by a subsequent survey called KIDS (see Chapter 9). Using measured income at two points in time is preferable to relying on data from one point in time, but it is obviously still only a crude proxy for lifetime income.

In agrarian societies, poor people may be poor because they have too little land (in which case land reform may be an appropriate policy response) or because they have too little labour power to farm their land (in which case there is probably not much that the state can do to help). In South Africa at the end of apartheid, poor households did not for the most part lack labour power (although they lacked the kind for which there was strong demand in the economy—skilled labour). Poor households were poor largely because their members did not have jobs; when they did have jobs, they were low-paying ones. Poverty and inequality in the distribution of incomes were due to inequality in the distribution of jobs and skills. This brings us to social stratification, or the ways in which the distribution of opportunities is structured socially. Chapter 7 examines the class structure more fully. What classes exist in South Africa? How do they relate to each other? And how are they reproduced over time? How is social class related to the distribution of incomes? Do households fall in different deciles because of temporary factors or are there underlying causes? Chapter 8 takes the analysis further by exploring the extent to which the unemployed could be regarded as constituting a social class.

Chapter 7 Social Stratification

and Income Inequality at the

End of Apartheid

In previous chapters we have argued that the primary basis of inequality shifted from race to class under apartheid. Paradoxically, as apartheid drew to a close, most scholars retreated from class analysis. When class was discussed, it was generally without any empirical analysis of the class structure, despite the availability after 1993 of new sources of data. This chapter uses the 1993 PSLSD data to map the class structure of South Africa at the end of the apartheid era. Surveys such as the PSLSD provide the best available data, but the fact that these surveys were not designed for the purpose of analysing class means that they pose a series of methodological problems. Mapping class also entails theoretical problems. Our approaches to class are derived from the study of advanced industrialised societies of the North. How should they be modified to render them more appropriate for South African conditions?

This chapter provides both theoretical foundations for and empirical evidence about the South African class structure at the end of apartheid. But neither the theoretical foundations nor the data point to a unique map of the class structure: there is no single "correct" way of mapping it, and alternative approaches generate somewhat different class categories. We have discussed elsewhere (Seekings 2003a) some of the different ways in which the class structure can be mapped using the same PSLSD data. In this chapter we report the map, or schema, that we find most compelling.

In developing our analysis we seek to maintain a balance between theoretical foundations, on one hand, and observable consequences, on the other. The project of mapping the class structure can be conducted using categories predetermined by one or other theoretical framework. This might prove to illuminate the theory, but it seems to us to be nonsensical if we accept that real societies differ and our goal is to understand better one particular society. As the leading neo-Marxist scholar of class, Eric Ohlin Wright, has remarked, any such use of class is simply an "arbitrary convention." The major theoretical approaches to class have developed, at least in part, because of their utility to social scientists in understanding the patterns and dynamics of social and political life. The value of class categories depends in part on the observable correlation between the categories and other variables. In other words, the empirical value of class categories lies in part in their use in predicting other things, such as intergenerational mobility, lifestyles and health, attitudes and consciousness, and political behaviour. The analysis of class developed in this chapter is theoretically informed, considering power in terms of occupation, property ownership, and business activity. It seeks to take into account the differences between South African and advanced industrialised societies. And the classes so defined have promisingly demonstrable empirical consequences. But the analysis remains preliminary.

THEORETICAL FOUNDATIONS

Social stratification can be analysed in many different ways. First, societies can be analysed in terms of the categories that people themselves use, and the class structure can be mapped according to the categories in which people put themselves. There do not appear to be any studies of this kind of class imagery in South Africa. Second, class can be seen in simple gradational terms, according to income (or another material aspect of life). This approach cannot help us understand the relation between class and inequality in the distribution of income, of course, since class is defined by relative income. Third, class can be defined in terms of the productive assets (for example, land, human capital, or education) or entitlements (for example, the entitlement to an old-age pension) of individuals or households. The fourth method is to see class in terms of the relations between classes.

The most important analyses of class as a relational concept derive from the works of two great German scholars, Karl Marx and Max Weber. For Marxists, class is rooted in the patterns of ownership and control that determine relations involving production. The two great classes of capitalist society are the bourgeoisie, who own and control the material means of production, and the proletariat, who own only their labour power and therefore have to work for the bourgeoisie in order to survive. The relation between these classes is an exploitative one. This concept of exploitation is integral to Marxist class analysis. Weberians, in contrast, focus more on the different "life chances" determined in the market by factors such as skills and education as well as property. Whereas Marxists focus primarily on exploitation and the control of labour effort, Weberians emphasise the differential control of "market capacities" and hence of income. Both are concerned with aspects of economic power. For Marxists, economic power is defined in relation to production alone. For Weberians, it is also defined in relation to distribution.

Over time, the differences between Marxist and Weberian scholars of class have diminished. Weberians joke that "inside every neo-Marxist there seems to be a Weberian struggling to get out," and neo-Marxists retort that "inside every left-wing Weberian there is a Marxist struggling to stay hidden" (Wright 1997, 34–35). Weberians are now very much concerned with people's occupations, that is, their work as well as their market situations, whereas recent Marxists analyse contemporary capitalist society in terms of authority and skills or expertise as well as relation to the means of production. At the same time, as Westergaard (1995, 24) has written, the Marxist concern with who does what has blended with the supposedly Weberian concern with who gets what. Marxists have come to see capitalism as a system of distribution and not only as one of exploitation. Marxists and Weberians ask similar questions of the class structure: How permeable are boundaries between classes? How much mobility is there between classes, either within someone's lifetime or between generations? How are class, consciousness, and action related?

There is now considerable overlap between the empirical categories used by the preeminent Marxist and Weberian scholars in the world today, namely, the American Erik Olin Wright and the Briton John Goldthorpe. Wright says of his own work: "The empirical categories themselves can be interpreted in a Weberian or hybrid manner. Indeed, as a practical set of operational categories, the class structure matrix used in this book does not dramatically differ from the class typology used by Goldthorpe. . . . As is usually the case in sociology, the empirical categories of analysis are underdetermined by the theoretical frameworks within which they are generated or interpreted" (1997, 37).

One important factor driving this process of operational convergence between Marxist and Weberians is the need to analyse the growth of nonmanual occupations. Whereas at the beginning of the twentieth century most work in the advanced industrialised societies was manual, by the end of the century most work in these societies was nonmanual. Professionals and managers are easily separated out, but what about employees with limited skill or authority? Goldthorpe uses a seven-class scheme, in the middle of which are three "intermediate" classes: routine nonmanual workers, largely clerical workers, employees in administration and commerce, and rank-and-file employees in services; small proprietors and self-employed artisans; and lower-grade technicians and supervisors of manual workers (see further Goldthorpe 1997; Crompton 1993, 58–59). Wright, too, is concerned with the "problem of the middle class among employees." By distinguishing between occupations according to skills and authority, Wright's expanded typology of class separates out skilled supervisors, nonskilled supervisors, experts, and skilled workers (Wright 1997, 19–26).

Although there might be considerable similarities now between the approaches used by neo-Marxist and neo-Weberian analysts, there remain important differences in the ways in which these approaches are applied. The construction of class categories in practice requires an assessment of the alternative ways of operationalising class analysis. The critical evaluation of alternative schema requires the application of various criteria. The first key criterion relates to the theoretical foundations or derivation of a class schema. How explicitly and coherently is the classification or scale related to theoretical ideas? The terms used to describe the extent to which the measures used in a schema succeed in operationalising the underlying theoretical concept are "internal" or "criterion validity." Any schema is necessarily a proxy for other variables that are difficult to measure directly, but is it a good proxy? (See further O'Reilly and Rose 1997.) Wright's schema is often said to have strong theoretical foundations, whereas Goldthorpe's is said to involve a "retreat from theory." This has been challenged by supporters of Goldthorpe's schema, which, though perhaps not rooted in a theory of society comparable to the grandeur of Marxism, is conceptually well grounded in (a) the distinction among employers, employees, and the self-employed, and (b) that between employment relations based on a service relationship and those based on a labour contract (Marshall, Swift, and Roberts 1997, 202–4). Moreover, it has been demonstrated that Goldthorpe's schema displays criterion validity in Britain. The conceptual foundation of the schema should be reflected in variables such as forms of remuneration, promotion opportunities, and autonomy, especially as regards time. Classes defined in terms of Goldthorpe's schema do indeed display minor intraclass differences but evident interclass differences with respect to these kinds of variables (see Goldthorpe 1997, 42–48).

The second key criterion relates to the consequences of class. Does the schema have the capacity to display variation? How well does the classification or scale identify and display variation in dependent variables the relation of which to class or status is of interest? The satisfaction of this criterion is generally termed "external" or "construct validity." The measures relate to other variables of interest in ways predicted by the theory. Wright (1997) reports results for a range of countries that suggest that his schema has such construct validity, but Marshall et al. (1988; see also Marshall, Swift, and Roberts 1997) found that its performance was greatly inferior to that of Goldthorpe's schema when applied to Britain. In Britain at least, the construct validity of Goldthorpe's schema has been well established in studies ranging from intergenerational mobility to attitudes and from political behaviour to health.

Constructing Classes in Southern Societies

The ideal schema (or schemas) would have a clear theoretical basis, would be readily replicable, would be demonstrably consequential, and would be amenable to analysis linking the theoretical basis with the empirical consequences. But what does this mean in the context of societies in the South that are structured in ways so different from the advanced industrialised societies of the North? The problem in the South is both conceptual and operational: How should class be conceptualised? How should and can it be measured? This problem is most pronounced in societies that remain, at least in part, agrarian. The last major debate about class in southern Africa, which took place in the 1970s and early 1980s, revolved around the question of how to classify migrant workers who retained a foot in agrarian society. Murray (1981), for example, showed that, for Basotho men, a sustained period of wage labour as a migrant worker in South African mines was necessary for investment in land as late as the 1970s. At different points in their lives, these men were unambiguously wage workers and struggling peasants.

The decline of smallholder agriculture has not sufficed to bring the social structure of semi-industrialised southern countries into line with those of the industrialised north. The social structure of countries such as Brazil is different from that of, say, Germany or Britain. Portes (1985) delineated the class structure in Latin America. At the top, as in northern countries, are small capitalist and "bureaucratic-technical" classes. Below them is the "formal proletariat," composing about 20 percent of the economically active population. Portes identifies an "informal petty bourgeoisie" and finally a huge "informal proletariat" or semiproletariat, originally heavily rural (and with one foot in small-hold production) but increasingly urban (and involved instead in informal entrepreneurial activity). This class composes as much as two-thirds of the economically active population. It is certainly possible to apply class schemas that distinguish among manual, nonmanual, and agricultural employment. A series of studies have applied versions of Goldthorpe's schema (for example, Costa-Ribeiro and Scalon 2001; for an overview, see Aguiar 2002). But does the use of such class schemas exhibit the criterion and construct validity of those used in northern countries? Does Goldthorpe's foundational distinction between service relationships and labour contracts mean the same in Brazil's informal sector as in the more formal environment of (say) Britain? And showing that we can count the numbers of individuals in (or moving into and out of) these class categories does not mean that these categories "count," in the sense of being consequential.

Analyses of class in southern countries are constrained severely by the limits of available data. Data about occupations are typically collected for only one part of the working population or are collected in ways that are hard to translate into the conventional (northern) class schema. There are rarely any data about what class categories mean in the local context or about the consequences of class membership. All of these constraints hold for South Africa. The following analysis must be considered as exploratory; further research is required to "count" class in South Africa, to show that class counts, and most important, to count the classes that count.

Occupational Class in South Africa

Given the overwhelming dependence of South African households on wages as a source of income (as we saw in Chapter 6), occupations must be the starting point for analyses of class in South Africa. The leading study of occupational class in South Africa, by Crankshaw (1997a), employed an approach similar to Wright's and Goldthorpe's, although its ambition was very limited. Crankshaw's study focused on the changing relation between racial and class divisions during the apartheid period. He quantified and analysed the pattern of "African advancement" into occupations previously monopolised by white people: semiskilled and skilled employment, white-collar work (especially in the service sector), semiprofessional occupations (especially teaching and nursing), and, to a very limited extent, managerial and professional work. Crankshaw sought to identify the ways in which the dynamics of capitalist production and apartheid policy shaped the racial composition of different occupations. His study touched on issues of social mobility and the permeability of class boundaries, but he approached these in terms of aggregate occupational categories, not of individual or intergenerational mobility.

Crankshaw's ambition was limited in that, unlike Goldthorpe and Wright, he made no attempt to show that (or how) class counts; that is, he did not examine its consequences. He did not analyse it as an independent variable. To some extent he treated class (or rather the racial composition of occupational class categories) as a dependent variable, offering some explanation of changes in the occupational class structure and especially the racial composition of occupational class categories. But his concern was primarily to document the changing racial composition of occupational class categories, in much the same way that scholars elsewhere have examined the changing gender composition of occupational class categories.

Crankshaw's study was based on detailed data on occupations and other aspects of employment from the government's Manpower Survey. From the mid-1960s onward the Manpower Survey was conducted every year or second year, using a large sample of industrial and service-sector employers (including government institutions). Crankshaw combined the detailed categories into twelve composite categories, as set out in table 7.1 (using the 1992 survey data). These figures are estimates, since the results from the survey sample are inflated to reflect the total universe of employment in South Africa. In an appendix, Crankshaw (1997a, 123–40) lists the occupations he has combined into each of these composite categories. The category of "top managers" is limited to managing directors and general managers and is thus very small. "Middle managers" includes managers of departments within companies or government institutions and managers of shops, hotels, mines, and so on. "Professionals" includes, for example, engineers, architects and surveyors, doctors, academics, lawyers, and accountants—but excludes teachers, nurses, technicians, and priests, who are all categorised as "semiprofessional." The category "routine white-collar" includes bank and office clerks, cashiers, typists and telephonists, air hostesses, shop assistants, salesmen and agents, ticket inspectors, postmen, and chefs. "Routine policing" includes the military, police, and employees in the private security industry. "Supervisors" is self-explanatory. "Artisans/ap-

Table 7.1. Crankshaw's occupational classification, 1992

Occupational category	Number	Percentage
Top managers	54,947	1
Middle managers	201,054	3
Professionals	179,033	3
Semiprofessionals	706,522	12
Routine white-collar workers	963,594	17
Routine police officers	267,587	5
Supervisors	204,566	3
Artisans/apprentices	298,095	5
Semiskilled workers	1,423,361	24
Drivers	155,064	3
Unskilled manual workers	1,053,999	18
Unskilled menial workers	325,691	6
Total	5,833,513	100

Source: Table provided by Owen Crankshaw using data from the 1992 Manpower Survey.

prentices" includes bricklayers, plumbers, bakers, hairdressers, fitters, and turners. "Semiskilled" comprises machine operators. "Drivers" is also self-explanatory. "Unskilled manual" includes labourers, and "unskilled menial" comprises petrol pump attendants, cleaners, gardeners, and waiters—that is, unskilled jobs that do not entail heavy manual work.

These class categories are derived from what Crankshaw calls "an eclectic classification scheme which incorporated both workplace and labour market dynamics" (1997a, 6). He claims that Goldthorpe's schema is inadequate because "it does not provide any basis for understanding how the occupational structure is itself reproduced and changed" (ibid., 5). It therefore needs to be combined with elements from labour process theory, which allows for an analysis of the process of segmentation (and resegmentation) of the labour market, or rather labour markets. The logic of this critique of Goldthorpe is not clear, but it is of little import in that, as Crankshaw himself emphasises, the ensuing schema is not very different from a Goldthorpean one. His schema apparently takes into account the education and training required for different occupations, the authority involved, and the salary or wage. Crankshaw does not explain how, in practice, his schema differs from Goldthorpe's, nor does he demonstrate that it is superior by any specified criterion. Crankshaw was unable to test the internal or criterion validity of his class categories. There were no data, from the Manpower Survey or anywhere else, about the detailed character of employment relationships under apartheid.

The Manpower Survey did not collect data for some very important occupational categories, including farm managers and workers and domestic workers employed by individual households (Crankshaw 1997a, 8). In South Africa in the mid-1990s there were about one million farm workers in regular or casual employment and almost as many domestic workers (some of whom will have been included in the data given above because they work for companies or government departments rather than private households). As a survey of employment, the Manpower Survey also excluded the self-employed, whether shopkeepers or hawkers, doctors or herbalists.

For Crankshaw's purposes, the omission of domestic and agricultural work is of limited consequence. These categories were overwhelmingly dominated by black workers throughout the apartheid period. Although there might have been shifts in the racial composition of occupations in these sectors—with, for example, black workers moving up into semiskilled, skilled, and supervisory agricultural jobs and perhaps replacing coloured workers in some unskilled jobs—these shifts were probably not as substantial as the movement of black workers into semiskilled, skilled, white-collar, and semiprofessional occupations in industry and other parts of the service sector. For our purposes, however, it is necessary to reflect further on the occupations excluded from (and those relegated to the lowest class categories in) Crankshaw's schema. Below we argue that the employment relationship of workers in what we call the "marginal working class" was quite different from those in the "core working class," on theoretical grounds.

Mediated Class Locations

Even if we were to include farm managers and workers and all domestic workers, we would still only have occupational classifications for about eight million individuals in the early 1990s. These, together with the very small number of people who own factories and farms and employ other people to work for them, have what Wright (1997, 26) terms "direct class locations." Yet South Africa had a population of about forty million people. What do we do about the other thirty-two million? These were people who were not involved in employment (either as employers or as employees). They included children, "housewives" (or homemakers), retired people, people living on their assets, students, and the unemployed.

Many of these had what Wright (1997, 27) terms "mediated class locations."

They were the children, spouses, or other direct dependents of someone who had a job. The reasoning behind this takes us back to the underlying question of what we are trying to do by assigning class positions. Wright has this to say: "The central point of trying to assign a class location is to clarify the nature of the lived experiences and material interests the individual is likely to have. Being 'in' a class location means that you do certain things and certain things happen to you (lived experience) and you face certain strategic alternatives for pursuing your material well-being (class interests). Jobs embedded within social relations of production are one of the ways individuals are linked to such interests and experiences, but not the only way. Families provide another set of social relations which tie people to the class structure" (1997, 523–24).

The concept of a "mediated class location" requires that we treat the household as the unit of analysis. The jobless wife of a worker has a mediated class location by virtue of her membership of a household that includes a worker. Similarly, different members of a household may work in occupations that we would categorise in different classes. Wright prefers to treat individuals as having multiple, perhaps contradictory, class locations. This would introduce unmanageable complexity into our analysis of the social structure of post-apartheid South Africa, and instead we allocate a single class position to each household (that, is to each and every member of it). We apply the "dominance" approach, which entails assigning the class position of the dominant individual to the other members of the household (Runciman 1990, 382–83). Goldthorpe controversially advocates categorising the entire household according to the position of the breadwinner, who (in the advanced capitalist societies) is usually male. This approach has been widely criticised (see Marshall, Roberts, Burgoyne, Swift, and Routh 1997, 106–25; Wright 1997, 239–317), although Wright also concludes from his empirical analysis that the mediated class positions of women should be given higher priority than their own "independent" positions (Wright 1997, 538).

This is, in large part, an empirical issue. How, in South Africa, does cohabitation affect the behaviour and attitudes of dependent members of a household? There is little reason to believe that patterns of influence in a historically patrilineal society would be the same as in Western-style nuclear families. But many African households in South Africa are far removed from the historically predominant types (for the debate about this see Ziehl 2001, 2002; Russell 2002, 2004). Unfortunately, there appear to be no data about attitudes and behaviour within families or households in South Africa. In the absence of any data to the contrary, it is probably best to assume that the dominance approach holds in South Africa as elsewhere but not to assume that adult men are always the dominant individual in the household.

In South Africa, moreover, about 39 percent of households in 1993 had nobody in regular employment, and about 34 percent had nobody in either casual or regular employment. The members of these households did not have a mediated class location in the sense used by Wright. These were households that were dependent on government old-age pensions, remittances, and (to a very limited extent) agricultural production and minor informal sector activity. Some of these might be classifiable in terms of past occupation: pensioners and the unemployed might be classified in terms of the last job they had. Households dependent on remittances might be classified in terms of the occupational position of the person remitting money to them. But some cannot be classified even indirectly in occupational terms.

In summary, if we wish to map the social structure of South Africa as a whole, we have to confront a series of intractable methodological problems. Is the household or the individual the appropriate unit of analysis? How should we relate the social class position of jobless individuals in households to the occupational classification of household members who have jobs? How should we identify the social class position of individuals in households where nobody has a job and hence there is no clear-cut occupational classification? Below we identify a further problem: How do we allocate a class position to individuals or households that combine an occupation with income from property or business activities? There are no uniquely correct answers to these questions.

MAPPING CLASS IN SOUTH AFRICA IN 1993

We conduct the task of mapping the class position of South African households in three stages. First, we classify the occupations of individual people. Then we classify households on the basis of the occupations of working members. Finally, we modify this schema to take into account income from assets and entrepreneurial activity. The outcome is a nine-class schema.

Classifying Individuals' Occupations

The easiest place to start is to analyse households in terms of the occupations of working members. The PSLSD survey recorded data for each working person regarding occupation (using eleven categories), the kind of employer (private or public), and the economic sector. These data can be used to assign a crude or approximate class position to each employed individual. Ideally, we would use the PSLSD data to classify working people into categories similar to those suggested by Goldthorpe or Crankshaw. Unfortunately, there is insufficient detail in the PSLSD survey to do this. We are forced to identify five broader class categories that are, we hope, reasonable proxies for a more finely tuned schema:

- *upper class* (UC): managers and professionals;
- *semiprofessional class* (SPC): teachers and nurses;
- *intermediate class* (IC): routine white-collar, skilled, and supervisory workers;
- *core working class* (CWC): semiskilled and unskilled workers (except farm and domestic workers); and
- *marginal working class* (MWC): farm and domestic workers.

Does this five-class schema have any theoretical basis? The basis is, as for Goldthorpe and Crankshaw, the nature of the employment relationship. Each category, it is hoped, combines occupations with similar economic power in the sense that they have broadly similar employment relationships, that is, in terms of economic security, career prospects, and autonomy (see Marshall, Swift, and Roberts 1997, 22–24, 202–3). The upper and semiprofessional classes in our schema correspond theoretically to Goldthorpe's classes I and II, in which the employment relationship is one of service, characterised by the prospect of incremental advancement (whether salary increments or a career path), employment security, and a high degree of autonomy. Semiprofessional occupations are distinguished from professional occupations, as Crankshaw recommends, because the qualification required is lower (usually a diploma rather than a degree), there are limited prospects for upward occupational mobility, and there is little authority in the workplace (Crankshaw 1997a, 9–10). The core and marginal working classes correspond theoretically to Goldthorpe's classes VIIa and VIIb, in which the employment relationship is based on a labour contract and labour is provided under close supervision and within a closely regulated payment system. Our intermediate class encompasses Goldthorpe's classes III and V, in which the employment relationship combines elements of the service relationship and the labour contract. Thus the five classes in our proposed schema are intended to distinguish between occupations based on service relationships and those based on labour contracts.

There are two important respects, however, in which our proposed class schema differs from Goldthorpe's. First, we have also included in the intermediate class skilled manual workers (Goldthorpe's class VI). This is based on the supposition that, in the South African context, skilled manual workers often enjoy a degree of economic power comparable to that of supervisory and routine nonmanual employees, largely because of the high capital intensity of South African industry. Second, we suggest that there is a key distinction between the core and marginal working classes based on the nature of the labour contract. In the South African context, as in Brazil and many other southern societies, a large number of workers sell their labour for wages without any formal contract: their conditions of work are quite distinctive and they are especially vulnerable to employers. These clearly include many farm and domestic workers and arguably growing numbers of other workers as well (see below). In addition, we have at this stage not accommodated the self-employed, who fall into Goldthorpe's classes IVa, IVb, and IVc; we address this issue below.

Ideally, we would examine the internal or criterion validity of this schema. Do these five class categories in fact combine economic roles with similar degrees of economic power in the workplace? The PSLSD data do not allow us to answer this question, but a more recent data set could be used for this purpose. The Labour Force Surveys (LFSs) conducted since 2000 by the official statistics agency, Statistics South Africa, collect much more detailed data about work, including occupations and self-employment. The data for employees cover the permanency of employment, the ownership of tools used, whether the contract is written, whether the work is supervised, and whether payments are made to pension or retirement funds. Use of these data would allow both the testing of the internal validity of the crude PSLSD-based class categories (assuming that these could be re-created from the LFS data) and, if necessary, the development of more finely tuned class categories. Further research using the LFS data is clearly warranted. Unfortunately, however, the LFSs collect few data other than those concerning work, so they are of little value in examining whether class "counts," that is, has external or construct validity.

Using these categories, we allocate an individual occupational classification to every individual in regular or casual employment in the PSLSD survey. A small number of people, it turns out, had two jobs and two different occupational classifications. For example, the PSLSD sample included the case of a young woman living in Pretoria who had a full-time job working for the government in a professional occupation but also worked as a sports instructor for one hour a day. In such cases the individual was classified according to the highest class for which the jobs were eligible. Comparing Crankshaw's data from the Manpower Surveys with our classifications using the PSLSD data (excluding the farm and domestic workers omitted from Crankshaw's data) reveals several discrepancies. The PSLSD classifies a higher proportion of employed individuals as upper class, a smaller proportion as semiprofessional, a slightly higher proportion as intermediate, and fewer people as working-class (that is, core working-class).

One weakness of our classification is the delineation between the CWC and the MWC. Trade unions and social scientists alike have increasingly emphasised the growing distinctions between sections of the labour force according to the degree of protection provided by labour legislation and the opportunities for collective organisation in trade unions. The working class is said to be undergoing "resegmentation" (Kenny and Webster 1998). The more marginal sections of the working class include not only farm and domestic workers but also many casual workers as well as employees in some small firms, especially in sectors such as construction. Optimally, we would use a more nuanced set of criteria for distinguishing between the CWC and the MWC. These criteria might include other measures of precariousness in the labour market, such as some forms of casual employment. Separating out farm and domestic workers only is a manageable way of drawing distinctions, not the optimal way.

Classifying Households in Terms of Individual Occupational Classifications

Having given every individual in employment an occupational classification, we can begin to categorise the households of which they are members. The methodology for classification involves three stages. First, households with only one person in regular or casual employment are classified according to the individual class position of that person. Thus, a household that included a lawyer is classified as upper-class, and one that included a construction worker as working-class. Forty-two percent of the households in the PSLSD sample were in this position. Second, households with more than one person in regular or casual employment but in which all workers had the same individual class position are classified according to that uniform position. This accounted for another 11 percent of the sample. Some of these households had as many as six members with the same individual occupational classification. Finally, households whose multiple working members had different individual occupational classifications are classified according to the highest individual occupational classification of their members. Thus a household composed of a domestic worker and a semiskilled factory worker is classified as CWC, and one that comprised the managing director of a firm (UC) and a secretary (IC) is classified as UC. A total of 13 percent of the entire sample consisted of cross-class households in terms of employment. Most of them spanned a narrow range of individual occupational classifications, especially upper class—intermediate class and intermediate class—core working class. There were very few surprising combinations (such as upper class—marginal working class).

Another shortcut in the methodology is that, in allocating a class position to individuals and households, no distinction is made between permanent and casual employment. Thus, an individual with both a permanent and a casual job is categorised according to the higher classification of the two. More important, a multiclass household is categorised according to the higher classification of any of its members, even if that member had a casual job only and other members in lower class categories had permanent jobs. Although this shortcut is unlikely to make much difference, a more nuanced class categorisation might make allowance for such multiclass positions.

The classification of households in terms of the occupations of their members leaves 33 percent of households unclassified—and unclassifiable according to straightforward categories. This residual category is heterogeneous. It includes households in which people wanted to work but were unemployed, households in which people were self-employed, and households in which no one was in the labour force (because they had retired, they were disabled, they were children, or simply because they did not want to work). Some of these households were very affluent. For example, some had considerable incomes from self-employment (such as commercial farming) or from savings (retired people with substantial private savings). Most, however, were poor, dependent on government old-age pensions or remittances, or without any regular income whatsoever. It is clearly a problem to combine these disparate households into one category. It is revealing that the median household income in this residual category was very low but the mean household income was high, because there were both many very poor households and a few very rich ones in this category. This residual category can be classified in several different ways, none of which is the obviously "correct" way. Elsewhere (Seekings 2003a, 23–32) we report several alternative ways of classifying these remaining households: according to whether they included unemployed people, whether they received income from assets or entrepreneurial activity, and whether they received incomes from remittances or pensions.

Taking Account of Property and Business

No account has been taken yet of self-employment or activities other than employment, nor has any account been taken of the significance in monetary terms of employment relative to other sources. In Chapter 6 we saw that household incomes in South Africa in 1993 were dominated by wages and wage-related income. But there may have been households whose income came primarily from sources other than wages, even if they had wage income as well. For example, a rich household might have received more "unearned" income (from financial investments, rents, or profits) than income from salaries or wages, and a poor household might have received more from informal hawking or beer-brewing than from the casual or regular employment of its members.

In 1993, as many as 45 percent of South African households earned some income from wealth or from entrepreneurial activity. Ideally, we would classify these by some criterion independent of income, such as whether they employed other people or whether they themselves worked. But this is impossible with the PSLSD data. What we can do is categorise households according to the level of income earned from wealth or entrepreneurship, guessing that income was a crude proxy for the ideal criteria. To be more explicit, we might guess that the high-income entrepreneurs or property owners tended to employ other people and did not work fully themselves, middle-income entrepreneurs or property owners tended to employ others and work themselves, and low-income entrepreneurs tended to work themselves but not employ anyone else.

The PSLSD data indicate that in 1993 more than half of the households with income from entrepreneurship or wealth, 26 percent of all households, earned less than the value of an old-age pension from these activities. This tiny sum does not warrant any modification of the classificatory scheme. Thus, for example, households classified as CWC by occupation remain classified as such, whereas hitherto unclassified households remain unclassified. One-quarter of the households with some income from assets or entrepreneurship (which make up 11 percent of all households) earned more than the value of a pension but less than five times the value of a pension. Because this represents significant (albeit not massive) earnings, the household classification must take it into account. The choice of five times the value of a pension is not entirely arbitrary; it corresponds almost exactly to the mean household income in South Africa. Seven percent of households earned more than five times the value of a pension from wealth or entrepreneurial activity. More than half of these earned more than ten times the value of a pension, that is, more than R3,900 per month in 1993, which was a very substantial amount.

The household classification is modified, taking these earnings into account, as follows: all households (except those in the upper class already) with earnings from wealth and entrepreneurial activity higher than ten times the value of an old-age pension are classified as "WE1" (where WE stands for "wealth or entrepreneurship"). Households (except those in the upper class already) with earnings from these sources more than five times but less than ten times the value of a pension are classified as "WE2." Households in the core and marginal working classes and the unclassified categories that had earnings above the value of a pension but less than the five times this value are classified as "WE3." Of the households reclassified according to wealth and entrepreneurial activity, almost two-thirds were previously in the residual category, about one-sixth came from the semiprofessional and intermediate classes (and moved to WE1 and WE2), and one-sixth from the core and marginal working classes (and moved mostly to WE3).

This results in a classification of households based on two criteria: the occupation of household members in employment and the level of household earnings from wealth or entrepreneurial activity. The residual category therefore consists of households with no members in employment and negligible earnings from wealth or entrepreneurship. Most of these are dependent on remittances or old-age pensions. This residual category could be divided according to whether the households included unemployed members or according to the sources of household income. For simplicity, they are simply left as an undifferentiated "other" category in the tables that follow. In Chapter 8 we disaggregate this category further.

Household Classifications and Household Incomes

The distribution of households between these nine classifications based on occupation, wealth, and entrepreneurship, is set out in table 7.2. This approach allows us to see that important differences existed between the three classes based on wealth and entrepreneurship. Mean incomes among WE1 households were ten times the mean incomes of WE3 households. Put another way, the mean incomes of households in the WE1 and WE2 classes were above both the mean and the median incomes for society as a whole, whereas the mean household income in the WE3 class was below the mean but above the median. These differences were even bigger if one takes household size into account, because the WE1 and WE2 classes were smaller than average, whereas the WE3 households were larger than average.

Having classified every household, we can now turn to see how the class structure was reflected in material terms and how it fit into the picture of income distribution. Table 7.2 shows the mean income of households in each of the classes we have identified, together with the proportion of households in that class and the share of total income earned by that class as a whole. There is

Table 7.2. Class and household income, 1993

Class	Mean household income (R/month)	Median household income (R/month)	Households in class as a percentage of all households	Income of households in class as a percentage of income of all households	Average household size
WE1	15,732	8,520	1	11	4.5
UC	6,573	5,542	9	30	3.8
WE2	4,665	3,755	2	4	4.1
SPC	3,264	2,735	5	8	5.3
IC	2,257	1,700	19	22	4.7
WE3	1,442	1,115	5	4	5.7
CWC	1,187	1,008	19	11	4.7
MWC	618	518	12	4	4.5
Other	413	363	29	6	5.8
Total	1,957	907	100	100	5.0

very clearly a relation between class (as we have defined it) and household income. Mean household incomes in the WE1 class were twenty-five times the mean household income in the MWC and nearly forty times the mean household income of the residual class. Put another way, the three higher classes (WE1, UC, and WE2) together made up 12 percent of the households but accounted for 45 percent of the total income, whereas the bottom two classes made up 41 percent of all households but only 10 percent of total income. Figure 7.1 maps the class structure of South Africa using this schema, grouping classes together to illustrate its essentially three-part character.

There was a weak relation between class and household size. The upper class had the smallest average household size, at 3.8 members. The residual class had the highest average, at 5.8 members. The averages for the other classes all fell in between, in no apparent order. The core and marginal working classes had an average household size of 4.7 and 4.5 members, respectively (although both were pulled down by the inclusion of single-member households comprising migrant workers living in hostels). The semiprofessional class had an average household size above the overall mean, and the intermediate class an average household size just below the mean. The smaller size of the upper-class households and the large size of those in the residual class category mean that the average per capita household incomes of the different classes varied by more than the average household income.

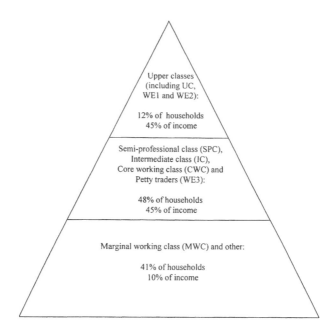

Figure 7.1. The class structure, 1993

If we compare the average household incomes given above with the overall mean (average) and median, we can see several interesting results. The mean household income, according to the PSLSD data, was about R1,960 per month, and the median household income was a little more than R900 per month. The average income of households in the upper, semiprofessional, intermediate, WE1, and WE2 classes were above both the mean and median incomes for society as a whole. The average income for households in the core working and WE3 classes were below the mean but above the median. Only in the marginal working and residual classes were the average household incomes below the median as well as the mean. Households in the core working class were not privileged in that they had average incomes below the mean for society as a whole, but they were privileged in that their incomes were nonetheless above the median.

The results shown in table 7.2 can be also be used to map the social structure in terms of how classes related to patterns of income distribution. Table 7.3 shows how each class was distributed in terms of income deciles, and table 7.4 shows the composition of each income decile in terms of classes. The three higher classes are combined in both tables. These higher classes were concen-

Table 7.3. Classes by income decile, 1993

Income decile	WE1, UC, and WE2 (%)	SPC (%)	IC (%)	WE3 (%)	CWC (%)	MCW (%)	Other (%)	Total (%)
	Household class							
1	0	0	1	0	2	11	29	10
2	0	0	2	0	4	19	23	10
3	0	0	3	11	8	19	18	10
4	0	0	5	10	14	17	13	10
5	0	1	8	18	16	17	9	10
6	1	5	13	17	20	11	5	10
7	4	13	18	18	19	4	2	10
8	9	25	22	14	15	1	1	10
9	26	35	19	10	5	1	0	10
10	59	20	9	3	1	0	0	10
Total	100	100	100	100	100	100	100	100

trated in the top two deciles, with more than half (59 percent) of their members in the top decile alone. Almost all (80 percent) semiprofessional households were in the top three deciles. Intermediate class households were more evenly distributed, but most (60 percent) were in deciles 7 to 9. The core working class was spread out between deciles 4 and 8, with the largest proportions in deciles 6 and 7. Most (72 percent) marginal working class households were in deciles 2 to 5. Only the marginal working class and the residual category were mostly in the poorer half of the population. The top deciles were dominated by the higher, semiprofessional, and intermediate classes, the middle deciles by the core working class, and the bottom three deciles by the marginal working class and the residual class. These bottom deciles consisted mostly of households without any employed members; the only employed members were generally in farm or domestic work (that is, in the marginal working class).

The relation between class and income distribution is also illustrated in figure 7.2. This figure shows that the class structure did not map onto income categories as clear strata but rather exhibited some overlap between classes. Some intermediate class households had higher incomes than some upper class households, many core working class households had higher incomes than some intermediate class households, and so on. But these maps do confirm clearly the general pattern. The upper-class and semiprofessional households were, in income terms, the most advantaged classes in society. Intermediate-

Table 7.4. Income deciles by class, 1993

| | Income decile | | | | | | | | | | |
Class	1 (%)	2 (%)	3 (%)	4 (%)	5 (%)	6 (%)	7 (%)	8 (%)	9 (%)	10 (%)	Total (%)
WE1, UC, and WE2	0	0	0	0	1	2	5	11	31	70	12
SPC	0	0	0	0	0	2	7	12	18	10	5
IC	1	4	5	10	14	25	34	42	36	17	19
WE3	0	0	6	5	9	8	9	7	5	1	4
CWC	3	7	14	26	29	36	35	26	9	1	19
MWC	13	23	23	20	21	13	5	1	1	0	12
other	83	66	52	39	26	14	6	2	0	0	29
Total	100	100	100	100	100	100	100	100	100	100	100

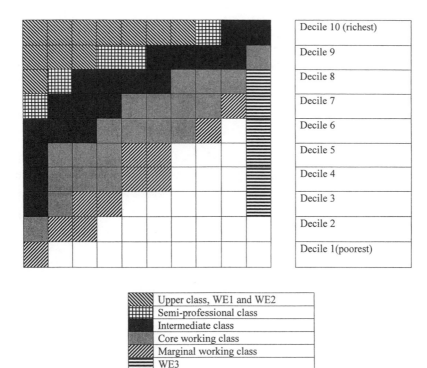

	Decile 10 (richest)
	Decile 9
	Decile 8
	Decile 7
	Decile 6
	Decile 5
	Decile 4
	Decile 3
	Decile 2
	Decile 1 (poorest)

	Upper class, WE1 and WE2
	Semi-professional class
	Intermediate class
	Core working class
	Marginal working class
	WE3
	Other

Figure 7.2. Distribution of classes across income deciles, 1993

class households were, in general, located below them in income terms, and core working class households were, in general, lower still. None of these classes, however, included very many households in the poorer half of the population, which comprised households in the marginal working class and the residual category.

In Chapter 6 we saw that there was by 1993 a clear and strong relation between inequality and unemployment. Almost two-thirds (62 percent) of the unemployed were in the poorer half of the population. This was in stark contrast with people in regular employment, fewer than one-quarter of whom were in the poorer half (and these were predominantly farm workers and, to a lesser extent, domestic workers, not members of the industrial working class). Given the scale of unemployment and its close relation to income, it is necessary to examine carefully how we map the class positions of the unemployed. In the analyses discussed above, we have treated the unemployed either (1) as members of households with mediated class locations according to the occupation of other members or the source of household income (including especially income from business or assets) or (2) as a residual category. In Chapter 8 we examine in detail whether we should identify all or some of the unemployed as a discrete class.

RACE, CLASS, AND GEOGRAPHY

Using the class categories set out in table 7.2, we can examine the relation between race and class as well as the provincial and urban-rural distribution and composition of the different classes. Figure 7.3 shows the composition of each class in terms of race. At the end of apartheid, the first three classes (WE1, UC, and WE2) were predominantly white, with white households making up between 55 and 70 percent of the total in each class. The semiprofessional, intermediate, and petty trader (WE3) classes were predominantly African, with African households making up between 62 and 71 percent of the total in each. The core and marginal working classes and the residual class were overwhelmingly African. There was therefore a clear relation between race and class, but it is far less neat or exact than it was in the early apartheid period. White households did not hold a monopoly of membership in the more privileged classes.

This relation is further exposed in figure 7.4, which shows the class composition of the different racial groups in South Africa. The proportion of African households in the first three classes was small (only about 10 percent), whereas the proportion of white households in them was very large (at almost 60 percent). Conversely, the proportion of African households in the last three classes was very large (more than 70 percent); the proportion of white households in these classes was small (less than 10 percent).

There is also a clear relation between the areas where people lived and the classes to which they belonged. Figure 7.5 shows the class composition of metropolitan, urban, and rural areas. It is not surprising that a majority of the marginal working class lived in rural areas, given that the category includes farm workers and their dependents, but it is perhaps surprising that almost half of the core working class also lived in rural areas. The large number of teachers in rural areas means that almost half of the semiprofessional class was also located in rural areas.

The distribution of classes between provinces and the class composition of each of the provinces in 1993 was much as one would expect, knowing that some provinces were predominantly metropolitan and others predominantly rural. Classes WE1, UC, and WE2 together made up 23 percent of households

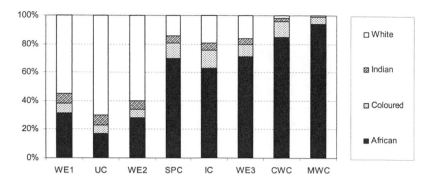

Figure 7.3. Class membership by race, 1993

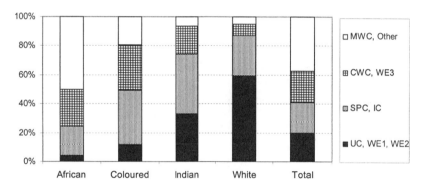

Figure 7.4. Racial distribution by aggregated class categories, 1993

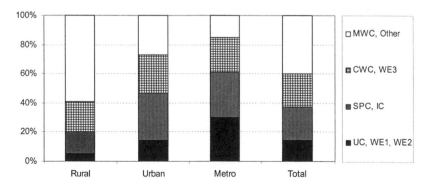

Figure 7.5. Rural or urban residence by aggregated class categories, 1993

in the Western Cape and 31 percent in Gauteng. But together they made up only 6 percent of households in the Eastern Cape and Limpopo Province. Looked at the other way around, 52 percent of the upper class was located in Gauteng alone, with another 12 percent in the Western Cape. About half of the WE1 and WE2 classes were in these two provinces. The semiprofessional class was distributed more evenly across the provinces. The intermediate class, however, was also concentrated in provinces with a large metropolitan population. About one in four households in the Western Cape and Gauteng were in the intermediate class, and these two provinces accounted for 43 percent of the class in South Africa as a whole. The core working class was concentrated in Gauteng, KwaZulu-Natal, the Western Cape, and North-West Province (which among them accounted for 63 percent of the class). The largest concentrations of the marginal working class were in KwaZulu-Natal and Mpumalanga. The residual class was, not surprisingly, concentrated in the Eastern Cape and Limpopo Provinces, with substantial numbers of households in KwaZulu-Natal as well. These three provinces accounted for about 70 percent of the class. In the Eastern Cape and Limpopo Provinces, more than 50 percent of households were in this class; the proportion in KwaZulu-Natal was a lot smaller. In Gauteng and the Western Cape it was less than 10 percent.

THE SIGNIFICANCE OF CLASS

At the outset we argued that the importance of class should be derived not from theory but from observable relations between class and other variables. Class is important, we suggested, if it is consequential. Unfortunately, the data from 1993 are insufficient to link class to behavioural or attitudinal variables, but there are data from PSLSD concerning the relations between class and some other variables. Ultimately, however, we do not have sufficient data to demonstrate that class was as important in South Africa in 1993 as it is in, say, the United States (see Wright 1997) or the United Kingdom (see Reid 1998).

Incomes and Living Standards

In the preceding empirical analysis of class in South Africa, we have already demonstrated the close relation between class and household income. Using the final set of class categories, the WE1 class has a mean household income that is more than ten times higher than that in the core working class, more than twenty times higher than that in the marginal working class, and more than thirty times higher than that in the residual category (see table 7.2 above). Both

Table 7.5. Living conditions and satisfaction by class, 1993

Class	Living in a house or part of a house (%)	Average number of rooms in the dwelling	Has piped water inside the dwelling (%)	Has toilet inside the dwelling (%)	Is very satisfied or satisfied with life, overall (%)
WE1	78	6.3	73	73	62
UC	76	6.3	90	89	67
WE2	80	6.2	81	81	67
SPC	76	5.2	52	51	40
IC	63	4.2	51	48	38
WE3	58	4.8	42	41	35
CWC	44	3.4	31	32	29
MWC	48	2.9	23	14	25
Other	39	3.8	9	12	20
Total	53	4.1	37	36	34

mean and median household incomes descend steadily as one moves from WE1 through all the categories to the residual class.

Given that household income determines or is correlated with many other variables concerning living conditions, it is unsurprising that PSLSD data also indicate a close correlation between class and living conditions and between class and general levels of satisfaction. Table 7.5 presents data for selected variables for the different classes. Living conditions worsened from one class to another. Thus upper-class households had an average of 6.3 rooms and almost all had piped water and toilets inside the dwelling, whereas core working class households had an average of only 3.4 rooms and only a minority had inside taps and a toilet. The higher classes were generally satisfied with life; the lower classes were not.

Class Mobility

The analysis in this chapter so far has looked at class using the "snapshot" picture of society provided by a one-time survey. But individuals' and households' class positions, like their incomes, can and do change over time. Mobility can take at least two forms. The first is mobility during the course of an individual's life, that is, "intragenerational mobility." Individuals can change occupations and hence their direct class position, or they can change their mediated class position by marrying or otherwise moving into a new household. The second is mobility between generations, that is, "intergenerational mobility."

The study of social and occupational mobility, that is, the ways people change social positions and occupations, is a major element in class analysis. It is not difficult to see why mobility is important in social and political attitudes and behaviour. As Erikson and Goldthorpe write:

> Most obviously, the degree of permanence or impermanence with which individuals are associated with different positions [in the social structure], and the rates and patterns of movement among them, may be expected to condition both the formation of identities and the recognition of interests and, in turn, to determine where, and with what degree of sharpness, lines of cultural, social, and political, as well as economic division are drawn. At the same time, the nature and extent of mobility can be expected to influence the evaluations that individuals make of the social order under which they live and, in particular, concerning the legitimacy or otherwise of the inequalities of both opportunity and condition that it entails. In short, mobility rates and patterns may be seen as a persisting and pervasive factor shaping the ways in which the members of a society define themselves, and in turn the goals they pursue and the beliefs and values that they seek to uphold or contest. (1992, 2)

Mobility is so important that Goldthorpe views the class structure not as a set of static positions but rather as a set of careerlike trajectories through positions.

We reported in earlier chapters that almost no work has been done on mobility in South Africa. We know that the economy was transformed so fast that in many families, children's occupations were very different from their parents' and grandparents'. This kind of mobility involves broad shifts over long periods of time. But we know that, in South Africa, by the end of the apartheid era there were also high rates of flux in individuals' labour-market status and earnings, and thus household incomes, over short periods of time. What are the implications of this for our analysis of class? It is certainly possible that individuals often shifted position in the class structure. For example, a young man might have gone to school in a rural area and lived with his grandparents in a household where no one worked. He would thus start life in a household we have categorised as residual. He might have then migrated to a town to look for work, perhaps living with one or both of his parents. Although unemployed himself, he would then have a mediated class position dependent on his working parents. If his father were a semiskilled factory worker, for example, the young man would then be in the core working class. Suppose he found employment as a security guard and moved out of his parents' house into a shack with a girlfriend and perhaps children of his own. He would then have been in the intermediate class. But if he were retrenched, and no one in his household was employed, he would drop back into the residual class (unless his girlfriend earned some money brewing beer or hawking food, in which case they might be in the WE3 class). If he spent much of his life oscillating between periods of employment and unemployment, he might have been forever shifting between classes. Eventually, when he retires on a government old-age pension, he is likely to return to the residual class in which he started out decades earlier.

In societies where unemployment is low and there is little structural change in the economy, it is likely that individuals will shift positions infrequently and in the same general direction. In a society like South Africa in 1993, where unemployment was high, there were high rates of turnover in the labour market, household composition was very fluid, and the economy was going through major structural changes, many individuals would jump around from one class position to another and back again. In Chapter 9 we examine some of the evidence gathered since 1993 regarding income and class mobility.

The Reproduction of Inequality

The study of class mobility is important for another reason as well. In most societies, people from different class backgrounds face unequal opportunities in life. It is almost certain that the social background of individuals shapes their participation in the educational system, with clear effects on future earnings, and it is surely also plausible that social background has effects on labour-market behaviour beyond those attributable to education alone.

Most of the work done on class mobility in the advanced industrialised societies examines the ways class backgrounds affect people's class positions in a situation where the overall class structure is changing slowly but steadily. The most important research concerning class mobility is that of Goldthorpe et al. (1980), extended into Europe by means of the CASMIN (Comparative Analysis of Social Mobility in Industrial Nations) Project (see Erikson and Goldthorpe 1992). These studies calculate absolute and relative rates of mobility. "Absolute rates" are the rates at which individuals from particular class backgrounds move into other classes; "relative rates" refers to mobility rates relative to those of individuals from other classes. Thus, in societies where the manual working class has been shrinking and the intermediate classes have been growing, there might be a high absolute rate of mobility from the former to the latter but a low relative rate of mobility because individuals from manual working class backgrounds are still much less likely to end up in the intermediate class than are individuals from intermediate-class backgrounds. Relative mobility rates make allowance for changes in the overall social or occupational structure.

Goldthorpe et al. found that, overall, there has been trendless fluctuation in absolute rates but considerable stability in relative rates. Cross-national variations were primarily due to the historical phasing of economic development. In the United Kingdom, the growth of the service class meant changing levels of absolute mobility but little change in relative mobility: "More 'room at the top' has not been accompanied by greater equality in the opportunities to get there," as Marshall puts it (1997b, 5). Erikson and Goldthorpe (1992) examined three cases of late industrialisation (Poland, Ireland, and Hungary) in which a majority of the labour force was engaged in agriculture until the mid-twentieth century (as late as perhaps 1960 in Poland). In Ireland and Poland, the decline of agricultural employment because of the breakup of peasant agriculture meant a sharp and more or less one-time increase in absolute mobility. Similar work concerning Brazil has shown that there have been high rates of absolute mobility with little change over time, whereas relative mobility rates have risen over time, in contrast to the general pattern observed by Erikson and Goldthorpe (Costa-Ribeiro and Scalon 2001).

Unfortunately, we have almost no data for absolute and relative mobility rates in South Africa. We know that public policy during the apartheid period not only stunted processes of class formation among the African population as a whole (via racial discrimination) but also shaped the patterns of differentiation (and perhaps stratification) that did emerge within the African population. As we saw in Chapters 1 and 4, a number of scholars emphasised the segmentation of labour markets between urban insiders and outsiders without urban residential rights, and Schneier (1983) found that urban insiders and their children were in a better position to take advantage of the new opportunities opening up as a result of the changing structure of employment. It is likely that the social and economic changes in the apartheid period resulted in sharp but perhaps unrepeated increases in absolute mobility (as in Ireland and Poland) but steady rates of relative mobility. In other words, opportunities may have expanded for all but remained unequal in more or less steady patterns. As we saw in Chapter 6, the PSLSD cannot shed much more light on this issue.

Further research should also help in more economistic enquiries. Analysis of class backgrounds might help explain some of the variance we find in occupations and earnings that cannot be explained in terms of education or experience. It might well be the case that people with identical educational qualifications have different prospects in the labour market today because of the different information, attitudes, and networks that they inherited or acquired through their contrasting social backgrounds. The children of migrant workers might be at a permanent disadvantage relative to the children of urban insiders. Such intergenerational effects will not be visible if studies simply use racial categories. Indeed, studies that fail to take into account the inherited effects of class can all too easily attribute to race differences in earnings that are really rooted in class. For example, Adler and O'Sullivan (1996) suggest that there remains a large element of racial discrimination in earnings because the difference between average earnings for African and white workers cannot be explained in terms of education and experience alone. But it might well be the case that the average earnings of African workers are an average of different classes, that the "unexplained" differences in earnings occur between these classes, and that the "unexplained" difference thus reflects not racial discrimination as much as class privilege.

Education and the Reproduction of the Class Structure

The PSLSD data do provide some powerful evidence that inequality is reproduced along class lines. Figure 7.6 shows the highest school grade completed, on average, by children of different ages in selected classes; no allowance is made for tertiary education, which would accentuate differences. If we take fifteen-year-olds, for example, children in upper-class, semiprofessional, and intermediate class households had, on average, completed grade 7. Children of the same age in core working-class households had, on average, completed grade 6 only, and children in marginal working-class households had only completed grade 5. By the age of nineteen, differences had widened. On average, children in upper-class households had almost completed grade 11, but children in marginal working-class households were still some way short of completing grade 8. Class made a difference of up to three grades at this age. Thereafter, differences widened further. Given the importance of education in determining earnings, children from marginal working class backgrounds were much more likely to end up in marginal working class occupations, and children from upper-class backgrounds were much more likely to end up in upper-class occupations. Inequality was thus being reproduced over time.

The relation between class and schooling shown in figure 7.6 is not dissimilar to the relation between race and schooling shown in, for example, Case and Deaton (1999, figure II), with Indian and white children completing, on average, three grades more than African children by the age of eighteen or nineteen.

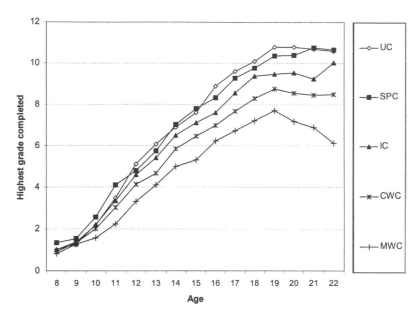

Figure 7.6. Highest school grade completed, by current age and class, all races, 1993

Lam (1999) shows clear differences by race in the mean years of schooling and the percentage of each age group that completed grade 7. Is it possible that the relation posited between class and schooling in figure 7.6 is simply a disguised reflection of the relation between race and schooling?

There remained in 1993 a close relation between race and class, as we saw above. But at the same time there were marked differences in schooling by class within racial groups. Figure 7.7 shows the relation between class and schooling for African children only. It shows that fifteen-year-old children in African upper-class and semiprofessional class households had completed at least two more grades, on average, than children of the same age in African marginal working-class households. By the age of nineteen, differences had widened slightly further. The differences between African households in the different classes were only very slightly smaller than those between all households in the various classes. Class affected education even when we look at African household only. There were some minor differences between the pattern for African households and that for all households. In African households, children in the semiprofessional class had gone the furthest in school, further, that is, than children in the upper class. Having a teacher or a nurse as a parent was crucial for African children.

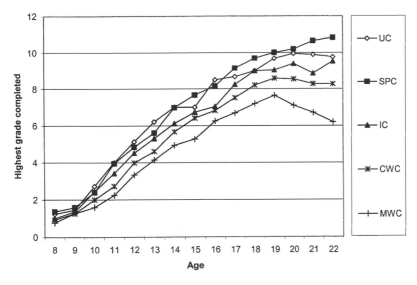

Figure 7.7. Highest school grade completed, by current age and class, African children only, 1993

Class, Health, and Mortality

In Britain and elsewhere, much of the impetus to the development of empirical class categories came from a concern with differential morbidity and mortality. In South Africa, health statistics are generally published in racial categories alone, with little or no regard for the inequalities that might exist within racial groups. The result is that we have very little idea as to how "class," however defined and measured, affects health. This is true even for the post-apartheid period because the 1998 Demographic and Health Survey (DHS), which is the main source of data about health and the use of healthcare services, asked inadequate questions about respondents' social and economic positions. The data can only point to some of the ways in which social and economic inequality may be reflected in unequal health outcomes; for example, there is a clear relation between mothers' education and infant and child mortality.

It is even harder to probe the relation between stratification and health at the end of the apartheid era. The PSLSD asked too few questions about health. It did ask whether the parents of household members were deceased, and the result might be viewed as a crude proxy for mortality rates. Elsewhere (Seekings 2003a) we have shown that the fathers and mothers of upper-class respondents were markedly less likely to have died than the fathers and mothers of respondents in the lower classes. It must be emphasised that parental mortality probabilities are crude proxies for mortality rates. In practice, however, the assumptions made in constructing them almost certainly result in *under*estimating the effects of class on mortality. First, no account is taken of the age at which the respondents' parents died. They might have been quite elderly when the respondent was born, raising the likelihood that they would have died at any time thereafter. Given that the age of first parenthood is probably higher for upperclass individuals, this serves to reduce the difference in probability rates by class. Second, the respondent's current class position (or destination, in the language of mobility studies) might not be in the same class occupied by his or her father or mother. Given that there is an overall pattern of upward occupational mobility, because of the changing occupational structure, this serves to classify many lower-class parents as members of the higher classes occupied by their children. Again, this serves to reduce differences in probability rates by class. Third, many respondents have a mediated class position, with the result that the parent's presumed class is in fact derived not from the child's individual class position but rather from the class of the dominant member of the child's household. Again, mediated class positions are generally raised, such that parents are allocated to a higher class than they should be, reducing interclass probability differences.

Other data from the PSLSD show little or no relation between class and health. Infant mortality rates do not seem to vary by class, which is very surprising given the subsequent DHS findings reported above. Anthropometric data do not appear to show that higher-class babies are taller or fatter than their lower-class counterparts. More research needs to be done with these findings.

Note that pointing to the importance of class in South Africa does not mean that people were located in the class structure independent of the country's racialised history. Nor does it mean that there were no cultural or social differences between people with different origins, traditions, and racial classifications. It is simply to suggest that people were rich or poor, enjoyed good or bad health, and had at least some attitudes that depended primarily on the work they did. Rich (and healthy) households in South Africa were rich because the people in them had well-paid work or had assets from which they derived an income (in the form of rent or interest or profit). Poor (and less healthy) households were poor because the people in them had no jobs or poorly paid ones and did not have the assets that generate an income. Ownership of assets and the ability to command high wages for their labour clearly reflected past practices of racial discrimination and dispossession. At the end of apartheid, inequality reflected the class structure, even if places in the class structure were filled primarily according to the racial structure of society even further in the past.

CONCLUSION

This chapter summarises exploratory research concerning the class structure in South Africa. Without more and better data, analysis of both the theoretical bases and the empirical consequences of class remains preliminary. But the basic social structure at the end of apartheid is apparent. Because of unemployment and the absence of smallholder agriculture, the classes in the middle of the social structure were actually working classes, and the so-called middle classes were actually a very privileged elite. A majority of core working class households (as we have classified them above) were actually in the richer half of the population, and most intermediate class households had incomes above the mean. The poorer half of the population comprised households that were dependent on very low-paid workers, mostly farm workers and domestic workers, or that were without working members and depend on remittances or pensions.

The analysis presented above can be interpreted in a range of ways as regards the positions in society of working-class households. Looked at one way, almost the whole of society could be considered working-class, in very broad terms: the category "working class" could be stretched to include households classified above as intermediate class as well as those classified as core and marginal working class. Households in the residual category might be considered working class if they were dependent on remittances sent by kin in the working class or if they comprised retired members of the working class. Only the top and bottom deciles would fall outside of the working class if such an elastic interpretation were used.

Looked at another way, however, the working class can be defined far more specifically to include only households that are dependent on wages from semiskilled and unskilled occupations and can be further divided into core and marginal working class categories. From this perspective, most households in the marginal working class lay below the median, whereas most of the core working class lay above it. The advantage of this approach is that it disaggregates wage-dependent households and enables us to analyse the differences. Looked at in this way, the membership of the Congress of South African Trade Unions extended across several classes in 1993: semiprofessionals (including teachers and nurses), the intermediate class (including office workers, skilled workers, and so on), and the core working class (including semiskilled and unskilled workers). Almost all of the households in these classes had incomes above the median income for South Africa as a whole.

The evidence considered in this chapter suggests that, subject to repeated methodological caveats, class was closely correlated with a range of other variables, including income, living conditions and satisfaction with life, children's education and health, and adult health. This is, of course, hardly surprising, but none of this has been explored adequately in the past, probably because of the understandable national obsession with race.

Chapter 8 Did the Unemployed Constitute an Underclass?

At the end of the apartheid era, approximately four million adults were unemployed and almost half of the population lived in households in which someone was unemployed. In previous chapters we argued that the growth in unemployment served to deepen inequality within the African population, contributing to the shift from race to class. But how should we make sense of the class position of the unemployed? Did they or some of their number constitute a separate class, or did they fall into the same classes as working people? In this chapter we argue that one segment of the unemployed constituted a discrete underclass, defined in terms of especially acute disadvantage in the labour market. In making this argument, we use research conducted since 1994. But we then return to the 1993 PSLSD data to explore the contours of this underclass at the end of apartheid.

People who are neither employed nor self-employed have long posed a problem for sociologists mapping the class structure of society. No class schema based on occupation or ownership of the means of production can easily accommodate retired pensioners, those engaged in unpaid domestic work, children, the disabled, single mothers living on welfare payments, or the unemployed. Some of these people can be accommodated within an orthodox class schema by means of mediated class positions, that is, they derive their class position from other individuals on whom (typically) they are directly dependent economically. Children and unpaid spouses thus have class positions mediated through the breadwinning household member. Pensioners, too, might be given a class position based on the position they were in prior to retirement (although, if life expectancy extends significantly longer than the age of retirement, this becomes less and less satisfactory). Thus class positions can be found for many people who are not in the economically active population. But what about the unemployed? In societies with very high unemployment such as South Africa, the unemployed constitute a huge challenge to analysts of the class structure.

The class schema developed in Chapter 7 entailed giving each household a uniform class location reflecting the occupation of the breadwinner, ownership of wealth, or self-employment. There were, therefore, many unemployed people in classes such as the intermediate, core working and marginal working classes, because they were dependent members of households in which someone else was working. But many other unemployed people lived in households with nobody working (or in lucrative self-employment) and thus fell into the residual category. Is it right to divide up unemployed people like this? And might households including unemployed people in the residual class be distinguished from households that did not include unemployed people (for example, that included only retired pensioners)?

Most recent work concerning South Africa adopts the approach that the unemployed are really displaced workers: workers and the unemployed are all parts of the "the working class as a whole" (to quote Gelb and Webster 1996, 74). An implication of this approach is that unemployed and employed African people have a common position in the social structure, are similarly disadvantaged, and share similar interests (see also Adler and O'Sullivan 1996; Adler and Webster 1999). This approach underestimates the importance of both actual employment and prospective access to employment in conferring advantage (or, if one prefers, mitigating disadvantage). The number of employed and unemployed members in a household has an important bearing on where the household is located in the income distribution. As we saw in Chapter 6, households with two or more working members were concentrated in the top income deciles, whereas those with no members in employment were poor. Precise gradations in access to the labour market clearly matter a great deal. It is correct that some workers, especially those in the marginal working class (farm workers, domestic workers, and their dependents), were not much better off in terms of income distribution than households without any working members. And, given that the marginal working class was predominantly African, the income gap between African households in workerless households and those in the marginal working class was not as great as that between the average unemployed household and the average employed household. But to categorise the entire African workforce, whether employed or unemployed, unionised or not, as uniformly "under-privileged" (as do Adler and O'Sullivan 1996, 181–82) is to miss crucial distinctions.

Unemployed people are disadvantaged relative to employed people. So when it comes to providing the unemployed with a class location, they need to be differentiated. There are good reasons for locating *many but not all* of the unemployed in a class of their own that we label the "underclass." The reasons for delineating an underclass comprising some of the unemployed (and their dependents) are related to the ways in which labour markets work in South Africa. Amidst a scarcity of jobs, access to employment opportunities can itself be a scarce resource. The unemployed are differentiated by uneven access to these opportunities. An underclass should be defined not simply as including people who lack employment but more specifically as including people who are excluded from access to opportunities to find it (or at least are very disadvantaged in terms of such access). By the end of apartheid, South Africa had a clear underclass of unemployed people in that economic and social conditions had created an especially disadvantaged class. The reasons for the acute disadvantages experienced by this class were rooted in the apartheid distributional regime, as analysed in previous chapters. The underclass was thus a legacy, perhaps the most terrible legacy, of apartheid.

THEORISING THE UNDERCLASS

In the 1980s, the concept of the "underclass" came to be used widely in the United Sates and Europe to refer to selected categories of people who were not working. The popular usage of the term was driven primarily by the writings of conservatives, especially Charles Murray (1984, 1990). Murray attributed the existence of an underclass to a distinctive subculture (entailing criminality and an aversion to paid work), which in turn he attributed to social disintegration and the provision of public welfare. This approach defined the class primarily in terms of a mix of attitudinal and behavioural characteristics that supposedly placed welfare dependents, the long-term unemployed, the ghetto poor, and criminals together and, in some sense, outside of the social, economic, or political institutions of "civilised" society.

This use of the concept of the underclass is echoed for South Africa by Adam, who writes of "the moral decay and the growing impoverishment of an unrepresented and marginalized underclass." This underclass is said to be responsible for crime and represents the "number one problem for long-term stability" in South Africa (1997, 2). South African society certainly exhibits many of the characteristics that underpin conservatives' use of the concept of the underclass: crime, unemployment, teenage pregnancies, and the disintegration of families and communities. The only obviously missing ingredient is welfare dependency, because South Africa's public welfare system only provides generous benefits to groups (the elderly and disabled especially) who are unable to work.

An alternative approach to the underclass starts not with supposed attitudes and behaviour but in class theory. If class is defined in terms of exploitation, where in the class structure do we locate people who are not exploited because they do not work? They certainly do not fit nearly into any of the orthodox class categories. The neo-Marxist scholar Wright (1997) suggests that the unemployed constitute an underclass that is oppressed but not exploited. But because his concern is with the working population only rather than society as a whole, he does not elaborate. The Weberian scholar Runciman (1990) similarly suggests that, if class is defined in terms of ownership, authority, or expertise, then there are good grounds for delineating an underclass in societies such as Britain.

The task of locating the unemployed in the class structure requires that we first reconsider the purposes of class analysis in general. Whereas economists are happy to understand inequality in terms of individuals' attributes (with, for example, the probability of being poor being related to geographical location, education, experience, race, and so on), sociologists seek to locate individuals in the social structure as members of identified social groups or classes. There are at least four reasons for this. First, class analysis might be of simply heuristic value. It is easier to conceptualise positions in society in terms of classes than of attributes. This kind of class analysis is primarily descriptive. Second, we can see that stratification in society is socially constructed, although the precise mechanisms by which people contribute to stratification might be unclear. Third, class analysis may be driven by theory, generally derived from the work of Marx. Finally, it may be driven by the consequential importance of class categories, that is, by the consequences of individuals' positions in the class structure for other social and political phenomena. Class analysis generally entails maintaining a balance between the two last concerns: class categories should be theoretically grounded but must also exhibit some consequentiality in order for class analysis to be anything more than a theological exercise.

Class may be consequential in two ways. First, classes may reproduce themselves over time, in that rates of mobility out of classes are low, whether across lifetimes or between generations. Of course, looking for the cause of low rates of interclass mobility leads to analyses of household decision-making about education, for example, as well as access to employment or other income-generating opportunities. Second, classes may be consequential in terms of specific phenomena, such as voting behaviour. Freed from the straitjackets of theoretical orthodoxy, sociologists and political scientists are showing that "class counts," as Wright proclaims in the title of his recent study of the United States (1997). The boundaries around classes remain relatively impermeable with respect to marriage and friendship patterns and to individual and intergenerational mobility; class also counts (albeit less consistently across national borders) with respect to attitudes (Wright 1997) and voting (Evans 1999).

Any class analysis requires some prior conceptualisation of the class structure. When Wright argues that class counts, he means that the class analysis he develops on broadly Marxist foundations generates class positions that help explain other social and political phenomena. His class categories are not, however, defined by their consequences. To do so would be to reduce class analysis to a set of tautologies. Fortunately, there has been a convergence between scholars of the practice of mapping classes in society. There is little difference between approaches of the neo-Marxist Wright and the neo-Weberian Goldthorpe. Both use broadly similar occupational categories to map the class structures of advanced capitalist societies. Both therefore also run into the problem of classifying people without occupations. As Wright puts it, "the empirical categories of analysis are *under*determined by the theoretical frameworks within which they are generated or interpreted" (1997, 37, emphasis in original).

The most influential studies of the underclass are those that have combined some theoretical foundation with an analysis of consequence. William Julius Wilson (1987, 1991, 1996) used the concept of the underclass to describe a distinctive group of people in the United States who suffer systematic and cumulative disadvantage in the labour and other markets. "What distinguishes members of the underclass from those of other economically disadvantaged groups is that their marginal economic position or weak attachment to the labour force is uniquely reinforced by the neighbourhood or social milieu" (1991, 474). Wilson is saying that *some* people on the edge of or outside the orthodox class structure are especially disadvantaged, such that disadvantage and marginality are reproduced over time. He emphasises the roots of disadvantage in changing labour markets, but other scholars emphasise the importance also of racial segregation (Massey and Denton 1993). Whatever the precise mix of racial and other factors, it is clear that growing up in a ghetto neighbourhood in many American cities raises considerably the chances of dropping out of school, failing to find work, having children while still a teenager, and thereafter being a single parent.

Disadvantage is cumulative in part because of the isolation of the underclass from the rest of society. As Massey and Denton put it, "residents of hypersegregated neighborhoods necessarily live within a very circumscribed and limited social world. . . . They rarely travel outside of the black enclave, and most have few friends outside of the ghetto. This lack of connection to the rest of society carries profound costs, because personal contacts and friendship networks are among the most important means by which people get jobs" (ibid., 161). In the United States, spatial and social isolation breed distinct speech patterns and language and an oppositional culture that in turn serve to reinforce isolation and disadvantage.

In Britain, discussion of an underclass has focused on the long-term unemployed. Detailed research concerning this group shows how disadvantage can be cumulative:

> As well as being deprived of work they were disadvantaged in health and housing. They became involved in local social networks consisting primarily of other people without work and employment. This ensured that they had lower levels of social support and tended to lock them into a position of labour market disadvantage. . . . [P]eople may be caught in a spiral of disadvantage in which small events may have large repercussions. Through an initial accident of job loss, a person may get trapped in a cycle of further unemployment. Unemployment frequently leads to depression, family break-up, and social isolation, which in turn makes the next job more difficult to find. (Gallie and Marsh 1994, 29–30)

According to this view, location in the underclass is consequential. Individuals are not simply temporarily displaced workers—that is, temporarily absent from other classes—but are locked into a class trajectory that leads away from rather than back to other classes. Research in Britain, however, suggests that long-term unemployment is not especially consequential in a range of other respects, in particular, attitudes about social, economic, and political issues (Devine 1997, 241–54; Gallie 1994; Marshall et al. 1996). Taking the long-term unemployed as a whole, the attitudinal differences between them and working people in Britain are not sufficient to consider them as a separate class; rather, they appear to be displaced members of the working class.

The factors that contribute to systematic disadvantage on the margins of or outside orthodox class categories vary between societies. In the advanced capitalist democracies of the North, states also vary in the ways they structure and address disadvantage, for example, via labour-market policies. The study of unorthodox class categories needs to be informed by the specific character of the society in question, rather than derived from some overarching theory.

UNEMPLOYMENT IN SOUTH AFRICA

By the end of the apartheid era, unemployment had been pushed to an extraordinarily high level. According to the broad measure of unemployment, which includes not only people who are actively looking for work but also "discouraged job-seekers," the unemployment rate was almost 30 percent in 1993, according to the PSLSD. The survey showed that almost one-half of the unemployed were in households with other members in employment, and almost one-tenth were in households with significant income from entrepreneurial activities or assets. But this leaves half of the unemployed living in households that cannot be categorised in orthodox terms. About one-half of the households in the "other," or residual, class category described in Chapter 7 included unemployed people. The other half had nobody in the labour force: their adult members were retired, sick or disabled, or working in the home and not wanting employment. Table 8.1 shows the composition of each class by working status, and figure 8.1 shows the participation and unemployment rates for each class.

Unemployment is not only widespread in South Africa, but it is also very often long-term. If it were a transitory phenomenon then it might make sense to ignore it when locating individuals and households in the class structure. The unemployed might instead be classified according to their past or prospective occupations, that is, by what Wright terms their "class trajectory" (1997, ch. 16). Thus a temporarily unemployed teacher might be considered as a displaced teacher, not a member of an underclass. All available evidence in South Africa suggests, however, that unemployment in the early 1990s was of unusually long duration (Bhorat and Leibbrandt 1996; Møller 1992; Riordan 1992, 79–80; CASE 1993). Eighty-three percent of the unemployed in South Africa had been unemployed for more than six months, compared to 66 percent of the unem-

Table 8.1. Working status by class, 1993

Share of the adult population (aged 16 years or older)	Class									
	WE1 (%)	UC (%)	WE2 (%)	SPC (%)	IC (%)	WE3 (%)	CPC (%)	MWC (%)	Other (%)	Total (%)
Employed	17	66	28	49	52	13	46	50	0	34
Self-employed	25	3	18	3	3	19	3	2	6	5
Unemployed	8	6	8	12	12	19	16	18	27	17
Not in the labour force	50	24	45	36	33	48	36	30	67	42
Total	100	100	100	100	100	100	100	100	100	100

Note: See Chapter 7 for an explanation of the class categories.

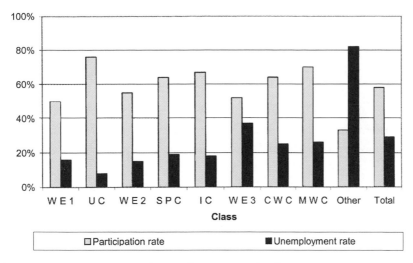

Figure 8.1. Participation rates and unemployment rates, by class, 1993

ployed in European countries that are part of the OECD. In those countries, about 48 percent of the unemployed have been unemployed for more than one year, compared to about 68 percent in South Africa. Only a few countries (including Italy and Ireland) have long-term unemployment rates similar to South Africa's, and in these countries the overall unemployment rate is much lower and the long-term unemployed have access to welfare benefits, which is not the case in South Africa (OECD 1999, 224, 242).

In South Africa in 1993, not only had most unemployed people been without work for a long time, but most reported that they had *never* worked. Bhorat and Leibbrandt (1996, 150) report that 65 percent said they had no previous occupation. This was because many of them had gone straight from school into unemployment (ibid., 147–48). Standing et al. are sceptical about these data:

> When one finds large numbers of people aged in their 20s and 30s reporting that they have never had a job, one wonders what they have been doing for the past five or ten years. Perhaps what they mean by a job is not the same as what the survey designers mean by it. . . . [M]any of the job-seekers may perceive that the work they had been doing did not constitute a "proper job" and therefore report to the enumerator that they had never held a job or that they had been out of employment for a longer time than if their unemployment was measured from the time when they last worked for pay, profit or family gain. (1996, 124–25)

Some people in marginal forms of income-earning activity probably do not regard the work they do as a proper job. This does not mean, however, that measured unemployment rates are substantially incorrect: those who report themselves as unemployed but who then admit to any other forms of income-earning activity are typically reclassified as employed (see Chapter 5). Moreover, even if the scepticism were valid, the implication for class categorisation is hardly clear. It is unlikely that many could be placed in occupational class categories on the basis of former casual or part-time employment. Most, we imagine, would have to be classified as former members of the WE3 class, that, is petty hawkers or traders, and then only if their income were sufficiently high.

WHO GETS JOBS? IDENTIFYING THE TRULY DISADVANTAGED IN SOUTH AFRICA

"The unemployed are not a homogeneous group," as Bhorat and Leibbrandt (1996) remind us. Some experience more systematic disadvantage than others. At any one time, some of the unemployed have not been unemployed for long and some will not remain unemployed for long. They might well be considered temporarily displaced workers. Most, however, are unemployed for the long term. They are typically poorer, less well-educated, and less likely to live in urban areas (Kingdon 1999). The duration of unemployment itself might accentuate their disadvantage. The longer people remains unemployed, the less employable they might be (that is, they become less attractive to employers); or, they may lose the resources to seek and secure employment. But the duration of unemployment is also itself the product of other underlying causes of disadvantage.

Some people are more likely to experience long-term (or indefinite) unemployment in part because they are already in a much more marginal position in the labour market. One source of systematic disadvantage is the *human capital* of the unemployed. Bhorat (2000) has suggested that some in this group are "unemployable" because they lack the minimum skills demanded in the labour market today. Among the older ones are many people who lack any secondary education. Typically they used to work in the mines or on farms but were retrenched and now live in rural areas. The decline in demand for unskilled labour means, according to Bhorat, that these men and women are unlikely ever to find permanent employment.

A second source of systematic disadvantage is the *social capital* of the unemployed. If people get jobs primarily via connections and networks, then these connections constitute a specific kind of social capital. Again, the absence of panel data makes it difficult to assess the significance of networks, but there is considerable evidence from a range of sources suggesting that people find jobs and employers fill vacancies through informal networks. In a survey of two thousand unemployed people in six provinces, Erasmus (1999, 59) found that "most relied on their family and friends who were employed to inform them of vacancies and/or put in a good word for them with their employers." Standing et al. (1996, 323) report that only 26 percent of manufacturing firms fill vacancies by advertising. Only 7 percent employ people who had applied directly at the factory gate. Thirteen percent said that they hire former employees, and 41 percent said they hire the friends and relatives of existing workers. Employers rely on informal channels in part because they face huge numbers of equally qualified potential applicants: "The 'formal' qualifications (notably the matric school leaving certificate) cease to be of value in a context in which there are literally tens of thousands of applicants who all share these qualifications" (Wittenberg 1999). Indeed, as Wittenberg and Pearce (1996) show, education is a poor predictor of the probability of employment. Qualitative research in rural areas also suggested the importance of networks and contacts (see, for example, Sharp and Spiegel 1985; Murray 1995).

This level of internal recruitment does not have a long history in South Africa. Under apartheid, huge effort was put into the bureaucratic allocation of black labour by means of pass laws, the administrative institutions of labour bureaux, magistrates, and administration boards, and the coercive institutions of the police and the courts. Manufacturers appear to have been the first to circumvent this system in the 1980s. McCartan (1984) interviewed employers in the Eastern Cape and found widespread internal recruitment of skilled and semiskilled workers and supervisors. Mines, farms, and the state seem to have persisted with the administrative system for longer, especially for unskilled labour (Greenberg and Giliomee 1985). African people have long sought to circumvent controls—hence the large number of prosecutions for pass law offences—but some work-seekers found it easier to circumvent the labour control system than others, because they had better links to the right kind of employers (see Murray 1995), and it was only in the late 1980s that the system completely broke down, replaced by a "free" but profoundly inegalitarian labour market. Stratification by ownership of human, social, or other capital replaced stratification by pass law status and labour bureau diktat.

Survey data from the 1990s indicate how fast labour markets changed. If employers were using internal networks to fill vacancies, then we might expect that the employment status of other members of a household would be a powerful predictor of employment. Wittenberg found that this was the case. The unemployment rate was much higher, for example, among the wives of unemployed men than among the wives of employed men. Of people who lived with their parents, unemployment was much higher among those with unemployed parents than among those whose parents worked (Wittenberg 1999). Wittenberg came to the "uncomfortable conclusion" that "employment and unemployment do tend to cluster in households" (ibid., 37).

Further evidence of the importance of networks is supplied by Samson et al. (2000, 13), who found a strong correlation between living standards prior to finding a job and the prospect of finding a job. Unemployed people living in high-income households have a much better chance of securing employment than do unemployed people living in low-income households. Samson et al. suggest that the success rate in the top income quintile is four times as high as that in the bottom quintile.

Another aspect of the importance of networks was illustrated in a report in the union-based *South African Labour Bulletin*. A die-casting factory on the East Rand, like most employers, filled most vacancies by word of mouth, with existing workers telling family members about jobs. But unemployed people protested against this "nepotism," forcing the employer to recruit by open lot. Six thousand unemployed people gathered outside the factory gates to participate in a kind of lottery for about one hundred vacancies. Tragically, eight were shot dead in a "drive-by" shooting. The shooting, according to Harvey, was the result of rivalry between two unions within the factory, with each seeking to control the appointments (Harvey 1996). In an economy where jobs are scarce, access to employment is an important resource, and control over that access warrants fighting—and killing. Unions seek to control new appointments, and this undoubtedly serves to advantage unemployed people who are linked to those who are working and to disadvantage those who have no such links. Other employers, such as Toyota, operate a pool system whereby vacancies are filled by former employees or the family members of current employees. It is surely the case that the number of discouraged unemployed in South Africa is large in part because vacancies are so often filled using such channels. Thus it is likely that, among the unemployed, there are some with good prospects for employment and others with poor prospects and that the former are more likely to be members of households with working members.

Access to employment opportunities presumably reflects some combination of location and social capital. In some areas, there are so few job opportunities that social capital does not count for very much in terms of finding employment locally. But in the South African labour market, where an unemployed person is located is in part the product of other factors. Klasen and Woolard (1998, 21–22) point to the interconnectedness of factors in arguing that the unemployed comprise two groups:

> One [group]—with bleaker job prospects, better access to resources in rural areas (pensions, land, etc.), [few] connections in urban areas and deterred by the high costs of urban living, and possibly less motivation—remains in rural areas or goes to rural areas to attach [itself] to a household of parents and relatives. It then does not engage in search activities and thus ends up among the broad (expanded) unemployed. The second group—with better job prospects, less access to resources in rural areas, better connections in urban areas, and possibly more motivation—attaches [itself] to a household of parents or relatives in urban areas and then searches for employment.

Simkins (1978b) reported long ago that migrant workers returned to the rural areas because they lacked contacts in the towns. After apartheid ended, unemployed people in Phuthaditjhaba (the old QwaQwa bantustan) said that they did not move to the cities in search of work because they did not know anyone they could stay with (Nattrass 2000c). Unemployed people are likely to divide into two categories: poorly connected, discouraged job-seekers who remain in (or return to) the rural areas, and better connected, active job-seekers who are in the towns or move into them (see also Sharp and Spiegel 1985; Murray 1995).

Social capital is important in rural areas as well, with men and women securing employment via "homeboy networks." A high proportion of migrant workers from one village in the Ciskei were employed in two specific dairies in Cape Town and Port Elizabeth (Sperber 1993, 35–36). In Limpopo Province, "many of those who were resident in the rural settlements throughout the twelve-month study period were waiting for news from friends and relatives of new opportunities within the urban labour market" (Baber 1998, 204). Men from one village were more successful in securing semiskilled employment than men in another, despite being less well-educated, in part because they were "able to draw on well developed migrant networks" that were largely absent in the other village (ibid., 216). Baber concludes that the South African labour market comprises "a protected group of 'insiders' and a considerably worse-off group of residual 'outsiders,'" trapped in unemployment or in low-paid unskilled jobs with high rates of turnover (ibid., 219–20). At any one time there are some insiders who are unemployed, but their experiences are likely to be very different than those of the more chronically unemployed outsiders.

Social capital thus comes in different forms. In some parts of the country it might be found primarily within the household, if access to employment opportunities is dependent on other household members who have jobs. In other parts of the country it will take the form of links to friends and relatives who are not only outside the household but may well be in distant parts of the country. The unemployed people who remain in rural areas (especially rural areas in the Eastern Cape and Limpopo Provinces) where there are few job opportunities are probably those who lack the social capital to escape the constraints of location.

The only detailed recent data about the importance of social capital in the labour market come from a survey conducted after the end of apartheid in Khayelitsha and Mitchell's Plain (the major African and coloured areas of Cape Town). Table 8.2 shows that almost two-thirds of the people who had had a job said that they got their first job via friends or family. Almost as high a proportion of people got their current job or their "previous" job (the job preceding their current one, or their most recent job if currently unemployed) the same way. Table 8.2 suggests that, for people working in Cape Town, friends or relatives in different households are more important than members of the same household. In the same survey, respondents were asked whether they agreed with the statement "Employers employ the friends and relatives of their existing workforce rather than other people." Thirty-eight percent agreed, and 43 percent agreed strongly; hardly anyone disagreed.

Unemployed respondents were asked whether they had "employed friends or family members who say that they may be able to find you work at their workplaces." Almost equal proportions said yes and no (47 percent versus 53 percent), indicating that even in this urban area the unemployed do not report equal social capital. Unemployed people with this social capital report a slightly longer duration of unemployment, on average, but this means little in the absence of controls for age, date of entry into the labour market, and so on. Much more revealing is that unemployed people with social capital were much more optimistic about finding employment than were those without social capital (see table 8.3). The proportion of unemployed people with social capital who thought that there was a realistic possibility of finding a job within the next month was twice as high as the proportion of those without social capital. Not surprisingly, those with social capital were much more likely than those without to have used networks to try to find work. More interestingly, unemployed people with social capital were also more likely to have looked in newspapers.

Table 8.2. Ways people obtained jobs in Cape Town, 2000

	First job (%)	Most recent job (%)	Current job (%)
Social capital			
A household member told me about the job.	15	9	10
A household member got me the job at his or her workplace.	4	4	4
A friend or relative (in a different household) told me about the job.	35	33	35
A friend or relative (in a different household) got me the job at his or her workplace.	10	12	10
Subtotal	64	58	59
Individual action			
I responded to a newspaper advertisement.	4	6	9
I went to a factory and waited outside until I got the job.	12	13	10
I knocked on factory gates and visited private homes and shops until I got the job.	10	10	8
I got the job through an employment agency.	3	3	3
I waited on the side of the road until I got a job.	1	1	0
I found the job on a notice board in a community centre or shopping centre.	0	0	1
Subtotal	30	33	31
Other	6	7	12
Total	100	100	100

Not only do people get jobs primarily via networks, but they also perceive the labour market as favouring people with previous work experience as well as contacts. Asked whether "people who have had jobs before have a better chance of getting a job than someone who has never had a job before," 44 percent of respondents agreed and 36 percent agreed strongly.

A final factor contributing to systematic disadvantage is a lack of *financial capital*. Financial capital can assist a person in escaping unemployment by facilitating a job search (including movement to locations where there are more job opportunities) or by making it possible to set up a small business, whether formal or informal. Unemployed people say that they do not become self-employed because they lack the money to start a business.

Table 8.3. Expected chances of finding employment by availability of social capital, Cape Town, 2000

		Unemployed persons with social capital responding yes (%)	Unemployed persons without social capital saying yes (%)
Do you think	. . . the next month?	43	22
there is a realistic	. . . the next three months?	58	37
possibility that you	. . . the next six months?	64	47
will get a job in . . .	. . . the next year?	71	56

MEASURING DISADVANTAGE AMONG THE UNEMPLOYED

There are theoretical and empirical grounds for identifying six possible factors underpinning or associated with special disadvantage in the South African labour market. These are not mutually exclusive: some might apply to one segment of the unemployed, others to a different section; alternatively, different factors might combine for any one group of unemployed people. The factors are:

- unemployability, in terms of a lack of the skills demanded by employers;
- a lack of social capital, in terms of living in a household where no one has the connections to help secure a job;
- a lack of social capital, in terms of having no friends or relatives in other households (perhaps some distance away) who help to access employment opportunities;
- a lack of financial capital, preventing the unemployed from becoming self-employed;
- location, in terms of the availability of local jobs in relation to job-seekers and the distance from other locations where the prospects of securing employment are better; and
- the duration of unemployment, insofar as it contributes to unemployability in ways other than the above.

Optimally, we would be able to measure these different criteria and assess the extent to which they overlap (using a single data set), and then examine the relations between them and panel data about who does and does not get jobs over time. Having established a good measure of disadvantage, we would then compare this with some of the other possible consequences of class—such as attitudes, political behaviour, living conditions, social relationships, health, and so on—to assess the utility of a class category defined in terms of these forms of disadvantage.

This ideal cannot be achieved in the early twenty-first century, and the data from the early 1990s are even more inadequate. The PSLSD did not ask about social capital or the duration of unemployment. As with the study of class more broadly, as we saw in Chapter 7, we are forced to take shortcuts. The PSLSD data do include one possible proxy for social capital: the employment status of other members of the household. We can divide the unemployed in the PSLSD sample into two separate categories: unemployed people living in households where another household member is working (that is, one with social capital) and those living in households where no one is working (that is, without social capital). Because the PSLSD defines the "household" as including people who lived in the homestead or stand for as little as fifteen days in the previous year, this definition of social capital covers many connections to family members who are migrant workers elsewhere in the country. This measure does not capture links to family and friends living permanently in other households, including family members who live elsewhere and remit income but never return to the homestead. Treating this variable as a proxy for social capital assumes that living in households without networks has a similar effect in South Africa as living in segregated impoverished urban neighbourhoods in some American cities (according to Wilson or Massey and Denton). Further research using primarily new surveys might reveal whether this measure is a good proxy for the kind of social capital that confers advantage in the labour market.

Using a crude proxy requires us to be tentative in our conclusions. But the PSLSD data do seem to suggest that we can identify an underclass of unemployed people at the end of apartheid. It comprised unemployed people (and the other members of their households) who lacked social capital as measured by the absence of working household members. Not all unemployed people were in the underclass. Many were less disadvantaged and can be considered more appropriately to be temporarily unemployed members of the working or other classes, because they do have access to social capital in the form of familial networks.

UNEMPLOYMENT, THE UNDERCLASS, AND
HOUSEHOLD INCOME

There was a strong relation between unemployment and inequality in 1993 in South Africa. Almost two-thirds (62 percent) of the unemployed were in the poorer half of the population (see table 8.4). This is in stark contrast to people

Table 8.4. Distribution of the unemployed by income decile, 1993

Income decile	All unemployed individuals (%)	Households with some employed and no unemployed members (%)	Households with employed and unemployed members (%)	Underclass households (no employed and some unemployed members) (%)
1	16	3	5	32
2	13	5	8	20
3	11	7	7	17
4	11	9	9	13
5	11	9	13	8
6	11	11	15	6
7	10	12	15	2
8	10	12	15	1
9	6	15	10	0
10	2	17	3	0
Total	100	100	100	100

in regular employment, fewer than one-quarter of whom were in the poorer half (these were predominantly farm workers and, to a lesser extent, domestic workers, not members of the industrial working class). The unemployment rate was inversely related to household income: it stood at 71 percent in the bottom income decile, falling to 48 percent in the third decile, 33 percent in the sixth decile, 24 percent in the eighth decile, and a mere 5 percent in the top decile. Participation rates were also positively related to income. A majority of households in the bottom four deciles had no members in employment, whereas fewer than 20 percent of households in deciles 7 and 8 and fewer than 10 percent of those in deciles 9 and 10 were in the same position. Wages rose as a proportion of household income as one moved from lower to higher deciles. These income deciles were composed of households ranked by level of disposable income, with no allowance for size or composition. The relation between unemployment rates and incomes was more pronounced if one used deciles defined in terms of income per capita (or per adult equivalent).

If we distinguish between households according to the mix of employed and unemployed people within them, we see a still more striking pattern (see table 8.4). There are clear differences between the distribution of households with only unemployed members, those with only employed members, and those with some of each. Two in three fully employed households in 1993 were in the top five deciles. Among the entirely unemployed households, in contrast, only 9 percent were in the top five deciles, with more than two-thirds in the bottom three deciles alone. Households with both types of members were less concentrated, but there was a bigger cluster in the middle deciles (with more than half, or 58 percent, in deciles 5 to 8). Put simply, if income is a measure of privilege, fully employed households were clearly privileged relative to entirely unemployed ones, and partly employed households were somewhere in between. If we define the underclass as comprising entirely unemployed households on the basis of their relative exclusion from employment opportunities, we can see that this class was especially poor. Bhorat and Leibbrandt (1996) come to similar conclusions using per capita rather than aggregate household incomes. It should be reiterated that this analysis does not consider the distribution of resources within households. It is quite possible that unemployed people in households with some working members have less of a claim on the household's resources and enjoy a lower standard of living than per capita data would suggest.

The superior quality of life of working people was also reflected in their living conditions in 1993. Consider some differences between households in which every economically active person was employed and those in which every economically active person was unemployed (or what we shall term South Africa's underclass). Fifty-one percent of the former had internal piped water, compared to only 10 percent of the latter households. Two out of three of the former had flush toilets, compared to only 18 percent of the latter. About one in three of the former had telephones, compared to one in thirty of the latter. Of the former, 54 percent said they were satisfied or very satisfied with life; only 22 percent of the latter said the same—with 71 percent saying they were dissatisfied or very dissatisfied. By such criteria, working people enjoyed a range of privileges relative to the unemployed.

Of course, the employed are themselves heterogeneous, falling into various class categories. Table 8.5 sets out some of the differences between the underclass and some of the other classes identified in Chapter 7. The residual category in Chapter 7 has now been split up into an underclass (that is, households with no employed members and thus no social capital) and a newly residual class of households comprising only nonparticipants in the labour force (that is, those not available for work), which we shall refer to by the ugly acronym of the NLF, or "no labour-force" class.

Table 8.5 shows that there were marked differences in 1993 between the indi-

Table 8.5. Selected social and economic indicators, selected classes, 1993

	UC	IC	CWC	MWC	Underclass	Other/NLF
Those with piped water inside dwelling (%)	90	51	31	23	10	n/a
Those with toilet inside dwelling (%)	89	48	32	14	18	n/a
Those very satisfied or satisfied with life (%)	66	38	29	25	16	23
Unemployment rate (%)	8	18	25	26	100	0
Mean household income (R/month)	6,573	2,257	1,187	618	377	442
Those saying that the government should increase employment to improve most the household's living conditions (%)	14	29	35	29	43	19
Mean educational attainment at age fifteen (grade)	7.6	7.1	6.5	5.3	6.1	6.2
Mean educational attainment at age nineteen (grade)	10.8	9.5	8.8	7.7	7.6	8.7

cators for the core working class (CWC) and the underclass. Underclass households were less likely to have piped water or a toilet inside the dwelling and less likely to be satisfied with life. The unemployment rate was much higher, of course, and household income was much lower. Underclass households saw jobs as a more pressing problem than did CWC households. And the educational attainment of their children was retarded relative to the children in CWC households. Underclass households also compared unfavourably with marginal working class (MWC) households according to some indicators but not others (such as education). The indicators for other or NLF households were also mixed. These data suggest that the quality of life of underclass households was worse than that of core working class households but not much worse than that of MWC households.

Income Support

The underclass, defined in terms of especially disadvantaged access to employment, was dependent primarily on public welfare (including old-age pensions and other transfers), which accounted for 57 percent of its income (see table 8.6). Private transfers (remittances) made up the second major source of in-

Table 8.6. Sources of income of the underclass compared to selected other classes, 1993

Source of income	IC (%)	CWC (%)	MWC (%)	Underclass (%)	Other (NLF) (%)
Wages	90	89	81	0	0
Remittances	1	3	6	36	41
Agriculture	0	0	2	5	5
Self-employment	1	1	0	1	6
Old-age pensions	2	5	9	46	43
Other public transfers	1	2	2	11	8
Capital income	5	1	1	4	1
Total	100	100	100	100	100

come at 36 percent, or about two-thirds the amount coming from public transfers. The underclass received nothing from wages (by definition), whereas wages provided the overwhelming share (between 80 and 90 percent) of income in the intermediate, core working, and marginal working classes.

Private transfers might have been less important than public ones, but social networks were clearly crucial to the survival of many underclass households. Some scholars have taken the argument one step further, pointing to remittances as evidence that working and unemployed people should be considered to be members of the same social group or class. Unions have claimed that "it is the employed workers who provide the social security net for the unemployed. . . . Given the absence of a publicly funded welfare net in South Africa, workers provide accommodation, food and other help to the unemployed family members" (quoted in Bhorat and Leibbrandt 1996, 144). Torres claims that "there is no doubt" that it is the working class that is "carrying the major burden of redistribution" (1996, 87).

Almost half (47 percent) of the unemployed lived in households with at least one formal-sector wage worker (Bhorat and Leibbrandt 1996, 154–55). These do not make up part of the underclass as we have defined it. Another 22 percent of the unemployed lived in households that received one-half or more of their total income in remittances. These do make up part of the underclass. In total, therefore, about 70 percent of the unemployed were dependent primarily on private inter- or intrahousehold transfers, almost all from wage-earners. Taking into account all unemployed individuals, therefore, in 1993 public welfare was of lesser importance than private transfers, even if this is not true of the underclass specifically.

Table 8.7. Persons receiving and sending remittances, by class, 1993

Class	Households in the class that received remittances as a percentage of all households doing so	Share of total remittances received (%)	Households in the class that sent remittances as a percentage of all households doing so	Share of total remittances sent (%)	Difference between shares of remittances received and sent
WE1	2	2	2	4	−3
Upper class	2	3	7	14	−11
WE2	1	1	2	4	−3
Semiprofessional class	3	4	6	6	−2
Intermediate class	7	8	25	24	−16
WE3	4	5	4	3	+2
Core working class	9	8	34	33	−25
Marginal working class	9	6	11	6	0
Underclass	25	22	4	2	20
Residual NLF class	37	41	6	3	38
Total	100	100	100	100	0

Data from the PSLSD allow us to identify broad patterns of redistribution in terms of class. Remittances entailed the redistribution of the equivalent of 5 percent of wage income (and 4 percent of total income) in South Africa as a whole. Table 8.7 shows that 25 percent of households receiving remittances were in the underclass, and they accounted for 22 percent of the total value of all remittances received. Not surprisingly, the underclass accounted for a negligible proportion of remittances sent. Most, but not all, remittances were sent by the core working class and intermediate class, which accounted for 33 percent and 24 percent of disbursements, respectively. One in three CWC households sent remittances, compared to 17 percent of all households. At the same time, the proportion of remittances sent by households in the WE1, upper, and WE2 classes is surprisingly large, at 22 percent. Of all the classes, the CWC remitted the largest share of its total income—6 percent (this is not shown in table 8.7).

The final column of table 8.7 confirms that the intermediate and core working classes were the major sources of redistribution: their share of remittances sent exceeded their share of remittances received by a combined 41 percentage points. The upper class was also a significant source of redistribution via private transfers. Indeed, the three "highest" classes combined were a larger source of redistribution than the intermediate class. The underclass and, especially, the residual NLF class were the major beneficiaries. Their shares of remittances received exceeded their shares of remittances sent by 20 and 38 percentage points, respectively. The residual NLF class benefited considerably more than the underclass.

Patterns of redistribution by means of public transfers are very different. McGrath et al. (1997) estimated that the top quintile (the ninth and tenth deciles) paid between 76 and 80 percent of all taxes in 1993–94. The fourth quintile (the seventh and eighth deciles) paid about 12 percent of all taxes. The poorest 60 percent of the population paid, in total, only about 10 percent of all taxes. McGrath et al. do not provide data broken down by class but, given the distribution of classes across deciles (see Chapter 7), we can safely assume that the share of taxes paid by the core and marginal working classes is small; even if we include the share paid by the intermediate class (which forms a significant minority of the top two deciles), the share is likely to be about one-third. More important, it is almost certain that these classes receive a larger share of public expenditure than they pay in taxes. Any redistribution to the poor, including the underclass, via the fiscus is redistribution from the higher classes. The value of this redistribution is probably about the same as, and may indeed be slightly higher than, the value of redistribution from the intermediate, core working, and marginal working classes to the underclass in remittances and in tax and welfare payments combined. If we took into account the value of publicly funded education, health care, housing, and so on, then the value of redistribution from the richer classes to the underclass would be significantly greater than the value of redistribution to the underclass from the intermediate, core working, and marginal working classes.

Divergent Interests? Wage Increases
Versus Job Creation

The fact that the underclass benefited from the transfer from other classes of a small proportion of their wage income does not preclude conflicts of interest between these classes in other respects. It is crucial to note that there may have been a conflict of interest between working people, who were seeking higher wages, and the unemployed, for whom job creation was more important. Although all classes shared an interest in economic growth, they had divergent interests with respect to the economic growth *path*. Given that the underclass comprised the people with the most disadvantaged positions in the labour market, the trade-off between wage growth and job creation was particularly important.

In previous chapters we argued that the economic growth path under apartheid encouraged capital-intensive growth, thereby boosting average wages while reducing the demand for unskilled low-wage labour. Labour-market institutions, including industrial-level bargaining, served to reduce the wage dispersion, further contributing to the reduction in demand for unskilled labour. The late apartheid state sought to address the ensuing problem of unemployment not by the creation of appropriate jobs but by political management, seeking to contain the surplus population in supposedly independent states. The economic growth path brought rising earnings to a large part of the population, cutting across racial lines. But the numbers of unemployed persons grew, and they remained confined to poverty. In Marxist terms, the growth path had the consequence of putting the unemployed, most of whom were unskilled and inexperienced, in an objectively different relation to the productive forces than the employed; and the relations of production served to reinforce and reproduce such divisions.

But we cannot show that the underclass experienced distinctive disadvantage over time relative to the unemployed in other classes or even members of other classes who were employed in 1993. Ideally, we would have longitudinal data for the persistence of disadvantage. As we have noted in previous chapters, there are no adequate data of this type for the apartheid period, a reflection primarily of the lack of interest of the apartheid state in the consequences of its policies. The only relevant data from the PSLSD concern the educational attainment of children. As we saw in Chapter 7, there were marked differences by class in the educational attainment of children, such that inequality was likely to be transmitted between generations. Table 8.4 above shows that the educational attainment of children in the underclass was significantly worse than that of children in the core working class. By the age of nineteen, children in CWC households had reached, on average, more than one grade more than children in underclass households. If we select only CWC households that have unemployed members, the differences were just as big. In other words, children in these households proceeded faster and further through the school system than children in underclass households with (by definition) unemployed members. Class made a difference to the education of children, even if we look only at households with some unemployed members.

THE ATTITUDES AND BEHAVIOUR
OF THE UNEMPLOYED

Is unemployment—and, in particular, the special disadvantage experienced by the underclass—consequential in terms of attitudes and perceptions? We have very little evidence concerning this. Some studies suggest that the unemployed see themselves as different from people with jobs. The most striking evidence comes from a study by Møller (1992) based on qualitative interviews and a quantitative survey among a total of thirteen hundred unemployed African people in 1987 and 1989 in Johannesburg, East London, and Durban. A little more than half were active job-seekers and the rest were discouraged job-seekers (ibid., 16–17).

Møller found that the unemployed not only had a far lower perceived quality of life than township dwellers as a whole but also experienced a range of psychological problems arising from unemployment. They were anxious, fearful, and depressed. According to one: "Everything is bad; friendship is bad, love is bad, even your own thinking is bad" (ibid., 51). Møller summarises: "Approximately one in two unemployed felt depressed, nervous, unable to concentrate, had difficulty falling asleep at night, or got angry and upset easily. Three to four in ten felt useless and without energy. There is some indication that the negative mood tone had been brought on by unemployment. Only one-third of the former job-holders reported that they felt depressed while they were still working in a job" (ibid., 54).

Unemployment disrupted relationships and produced boredom and low self-esteem. Møller reports that 59 percent of the unemployed said that they often or sometimes felt lonely, 46 percent felt that people avoided them, and 55 percent believed that employed people did not really care about their welfare (ibid., 84). Eighty-one percent in the pilot study agreed with the statement "People who lose their jobs, lose their friends." According to different unemployed informants: "Friends are people that you always share what you have with them. If you are unemployed you have nothing to share, then they walk away" from you. "The day I lost my job was the day I lost my friends." If you "keep asking your friends for cigarettes, beer and bus fare they get fed up and decide to keep away from you until you get a job." You become "a menace to your friends asking them for this and that, and finally you go without friends" (ibid, 50, 85).

Evidence of household formation adds to this picture. Klasen and Woolard (1998, 17) and Simkins (2001, 144–45) show that unemployment is associated with delays in marriage and independent household formation. Young unemployed people are typically resident in large households; young employed people live in separate and small households (Wittenberg and Pearce 1996). Simkins (2001, 145) suggests further that delays in marriage as a result of unemployment increase the risks of sexually transmitted diseases and HIV infections.

Many unemployed people express attitudes that seem to indicate that they think there is a trade-off between the immediate interests of people with jobs and those without. When Møller asked about the causes of unemployment, most unemployed people cited economic factors including labour issues. Some blamed immigration by foreign workers. Others blamed trade unions or "employed people . . . striking for better wages" because (as one unemployed person put it) "their protest blocks the chances for the unemployed" (1992, 137; see also Vlok 1998). Focus group research conducted among Africans in late 1994 found that expectations were generally modest because people saw that the government operated within tight economic constraints. In this unpromising economic climate, most people were very critical of strikes because they were seen as discouraging investors and jeopardising growth (Charney 1995, 29). Working and unemployed people seemed to differ with regard to the priority attached to job creation. Each of the focus groups was asked the following: "Some people say, 'Workers should get the highest possible wages they can, based on their skills and experience.' Others say, 'Workers should be willing to accept lower increases so that more people can get work.' What do you think?" Almost all of the groups favoured the second option. "Higher wages received preference over job creation only amongst the trade unionists and some formal township dwellers, particularly better-educated youth. They argued that the highest possible wages are the fairest, both to reward skill and experience and to reduce poverty. If wages are held down, it should be those of whites, not blacks" (ibid., 7–8).

Unionised African workers' views might be self-serving, but they may well be based in a moral perspective on justice and injustice. They may compare their positions and incomes with those of their bosses (mostly white), white workers, or white people in general and see the differences as unjust (which, of course, is not altogether unreasonable). The unemployed and the poor, however, presumably see their positions as underprivileged relative to working Africans. These different perspectives on the justice of rewards reflect the positions of most of the urban industrial working class, which is above the median but below the mean income, and of the poor and most of the unemployed, who are solidly below the median.

Opinion polls routinely show that the overwhelming majority of South Africans identify unemployment as the most important problem facing the country. In 1993, the PSLSD found that jobs were regarded as the most important problem in almost every income decile. How is this possible at the same time as marked differences in the priorities of working and unemployed people, as Charney found? Closer examination of the PSLSD data suggests an answer: the way respondents answer the question depends not only on their household income (and hence their decile) or on their class but also on their individual labour-market status and that of other members of their household. It is unusual for surveys to ask both attitudinal questions and questions about all household members. The PSLSD asked one household member attitudinal questions about the household's satisfaction with living conditions and priorities for government intervention. But because detailed data were collected for all members, we can examine how the responses to these attitudinal questions are affected by household composition.

Three patterns were clear (see further Seekings 2002b). First, both general satisfaction and the priority attached to job creation varied by class. There was a clear inverse relation between class and satisfaction, with the higher classes more satisfied than the lower ones. The picture was slightly more complex with respect to the importance of job creation, although the upper class attached least priority to it and the underclass the most. Second, there were important differences within each class according to the labour-market status of the respondent. Unemployed members of the intermediate class, for example, attached much more importance to job creation than did employed members of the same class. Third, even employed members of a class were more likely to prioritise job creation if other members of their households were unemployed than were employed members of the same class in fully employed households. The importance attached to job creation and general levels of satisfaction vary not only according to the respondent's class but also according to the respondent's labour-market status and that of other household members. Respondents in the underclass reported the lowest level of satisfaction of all classes (as we saw in table 8.5 above). They also attached more importance to job creation than any other class.

In other settings, the low self-esteem of the unemployed sometimes leads to heightened violence. In America, conservatives link the underclass to widespread moral deviancy and criminality. South Africa at the end of apartheid was clearly a violent and crime-ridden country (and remains so). Violence and crime are routinely linked to unemployment in the press and elsewhere (for example, Hirschowitz et al. 1994, 76). But there appears to be astonishingly little actual evidence concerning who is violent and why, and who engages in crime. There are two reasons why we should be cautious in linking unemployment to violence and crime. The first is the impression given by studies such as Møller's, conducted in the late 1980s. The unemployed, she emphasised, did not conform to the negative stereotype: "As far as one is able to tell, the unemployed in the main study show few of the typically negative characteristics of the unemployed. According to self-reports, they are not resorting to drink, thievery, idleness; they are neither dirty nor unkempt as the stereo-types suggest" (1992, 109).

Møller does note, however, that men responded to unemployment differently than did women: "Unemployed men tend to be more aggressive when it comes to airing their frustrations; women more retiring. Hence men are more inclined to act in socially unacceptable ways. The informal channels for gaining social support and an alternative income appear to serve women better than men. The person whose self-identity is possibly most at risk appears to be the mature man with little education, that is the retrenched unskilled labourer" (ibid., 147).

The second reason for being wary of linking unemployment with violence and crime is that research concerning the 1980s shows that a broad cross-section of people were involved then in politically linked violence, contrary to the widespread perception that unemployed youth were uniquely violent or anti-social (Seekings 1996). Further research is clearly needed, but we can conclude that there is little evidence at present that the unemployed engage in criminal behaviour or hold deviant morality to an extent that might distinguish them as a discrete underclass in the conservative sense of the term.

CONCLUSION

The concept of an underclass has unfortunate connotations. Its use may encourage the pejorative stereotyping of people whose only crime is to have suffered systematic disadvantage. We should therefore be cautious in using the concept. In South Africa, however, there are good theoretical and empirical grounds for recognising a section of the population that suffers especially acute disadvantage. This class comprises people who are not only unemployed in a society where unemployment means poverty but also lack the capital to give them a significant chance of securing employment in the future. The label "underclass" is an appropriate recognition of the systematic disadvantage that distinguishes this class from the bulk of the working population.

Moreover, the concept has certain demonstrable consequences. In South Africa unemployment clearly helps explain differences in income. Less clearly, unemployment shapes attitudes about labour-market issues, satisfaction, and self-esteem. The special disadvantages experienced by the underclass are reflected in very low incomes and poor living conditions. In some respects the unemployed have distinctive attitudes, but we have insufficient data to probe these attitudes specifically. There is no evidence, however, that the unemployed (or, specifically, those within the underclass as defined in this book) are any more likely to engage in acts of crime or violence than anyone else.

These findings remain tentative, given the inadequacy of the available data. There are many other issues that require further analysis. We have little evidence, for instance, about the crucial question of the ways disadvantage is reproduced over time. We know that unemployment and employment tend to cluster in different households but we do not know how long such effects last and how permanent they are. We have some evidence that the children of unemployed parents suffer lower levels of educational attainment than children of working parents. But does the underclass really reproduce itself over generations, with the children born into underclass households today predestined to long periods of unemployment in ten or twenty years' time? Do households or individuals escape the web of disadvantage, and if so, how?

In their study of the United States, Massey and Denton (1993) pay special attention to the "perpetuation" of the underclass. In their analysis, racial segregation plays a crucial role in reinforcing, again and again, the isolation of the underclass. In South Africa, with the passing of apartheid and the major changes in the demographic composition of society, racial segregation cannot play the same role. It is to be hoped that in the new South Africa opportunities for social mobility have improved across the whole of society. Even if prejudices and cleavages have emerged, it is surely unlikely that these can have the same force and effect as systematic racial segregation and discrimination. We begin to examine some of these issues in Chapter 9.

Chapter 9 Income Inequality

After Apartheid

By the end of the apartheid era, South African households were rich or poor according primarily to the number and earnings of wage earners, and earnings in turn depended overwhelmingly on education and skill. The affluence of white South Africans was based not on continuing racial discrimination but rather on the enduring legacy of past discrimination, especially in public education. White South Africans were reaping the benefits of the skills and credentials they had acquired in the past and that they could pass onto their children even when public education was deracialised. Privileges could be reproduced on the basis of class rather than race. A growing number of black South Africans had moved into the higher classes and income deciles, and they, too, could pass on their advantages to their children. At the same time, apartheid had ensured that many black households remained in deep poverty. In 1994 there were some working poor—especially workers in the agricultural and domestic sectors—but most people were poor because they or their prospective breadwinners were unemployed. Many of the unemployed were so disadvantaged in the labour market as to warrant identification as a discrete underclass.

They were as much the product of the apartheid distributional regime as were the increasingly multiracial upper classes. Apartheid-era policies had restricted formal- and informal-sector job creation, especially for the unskilled, and destroyed subsistence agriculture while denying many of the poorest South Africans the human or social capital needed to escape from poverty. The deracialisation of public old-age pensions in the last years of apartheid did lift many households out of the worst depths of poverty, but many poor households were not eligible for any government welfare payments.

What is striking about inequality in South Africa in the decade following the end of apartheid is the number of continuities from the preceding decade. The changes that took place were the continuations of changes that were evident before 1994. There continued to be rapid upward mobility into the upper classes and income deciles by black South Africans, and urban workers benefited from rising wages. But unemployment grew, the informal and smallholder agricultural sectors remained stagnant, and the ranks of the poor swelled. Inequality remained as high as ever, if not higher, even if interracial differentials declined. The expansion of opportunities at the top did not bring significant improvements for most of the people at the bottom. In this chapter we examine evidence for inequality after apartheid, before turning in Chapter 10 to an analysis of the post-apartheid distributional regime.

OVERALL LEVELS OF INEQUALITY
AFTER APARTHEID

The study of inequality since 1993 has been aided by an explosion in the availability and accessibility of survey data, including especially data about incomes (Seekings 2001). The first of these surveys was the 1993 PSLSD, run by the University of Cape Town. Thereafter the post-apartheid state invested considerable sums in the measurement of incomes by means of countrywide sample surveys, including especially the 1995 and 2000 Income and Expenditure Surveys (IESs) and the annual October Household Surveys (OHSs), conducted between 1994 and 1999. These data sets are in a completely different league than the data that scholars had to use prior to 1993. In previous chapters we cited the pioneering work using population census data by McGrath (1983) and Simkins (1979a) later extended by Whiteford and McGrath (1994, 1998) and then Whiteford and Van Seventer (2000). This work is immensely valuable, especially if combined with local studies, but (as the authors themselves were the first to emphasise) it was limited by the crudity of the measurement of income in the census. Combining data from the PSLSD and wage data with data from the population censuses, Simkins sought to improve on analyses that relied on census data alone (CDE 1995). Subsequent data from the IESs and OHSs, using representative countrywide samples much larger than the PSLSDs, should have made a major contribution to our understanding of changes in income distribution over time.

Unfortunately, the data from the IESs and OHSs are of uncertain value in the study of changes over time. The value of any survey data depends on the samples being representative of the general population. Achieving a representative sample is extraordinarily difficult in South Africa, primarily because of uneven response rates among different classes (with the rich, including most white people, being difficult to interview). If the IES sample comprised at least representative samples within each racial group, then the use of appropriate weights to scale up the results would provide an adequate representation of overall inequality. In practice, however, there remain significant doubts about the quality of both the racial samples and the interracial weights used in the IES. In particular, the weights estimated by Statistics South Africa (Stats SA) for racial groups in 2000 seem to underestimate the size of the white population, notwithstanding emigration. This is potentially consequential for the analysis of racial income shares and overall patterns of inequality. It also appears very likely that the 2000 IES undersampled higher-income African households, and no allowance was made for this in any of the weights used. This would have the effect of overestimating *inter*racial disparities and underestimating *intra*-African inequality and overall income inequality. Fedderke et al. (2003) report a series of other problems with using data from the OHSs: incomes are recorded in different ways and the samples vary, complicating the task of plotting trends over time.

The analysis in this section uses data from population censuses as well as from the 1995 and 2000 IESs. At the time of writing, income data from the 2001 population census were still unavailable, so the most recent census data were from 1996. The IES data are presented with two sets of figures for 2000: one set is derived using the implausible Stats SA weights, and the second uses a set of revised weights calculated by Simkins and Woolard. The figures derived using the revised weights are discussed in the text. The IES data should be treated with caution nonetheless. One of the reasons for this is that even the weights revised by Simkins and Woolard weight by race and province only and so make no adjustment for undercounting upper-income African households. Put another way, upper-income white households are taken into account be-

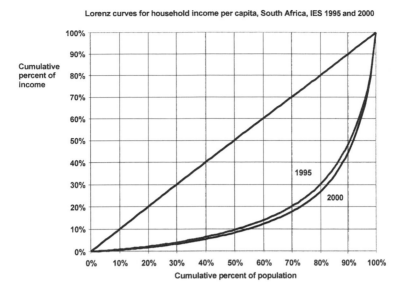

Figure 9.1. Lorenz curves for household income, 1995 and 2000

cause they are white and most white households are upper-income, but upper-income African households are not. The calculations using census data are by Whiteford and Van Seventer (2000); the calculations using IES data are unpublished work by Leibbrandt. We also report Simkins's estimates of racial income shares, based on his combination of PSLSD, wage, and census data.

Overall Trends in Inequality

The census data suggest that overall levels of inequality changed little during the second half of the twentieth century. The Gini coefficient for gross income inequality hovered closer to 0.7 than to 0.6. The IES data suggest that inequality worsened between 1995 and 2000, with the Gini coefficient for per capita incomes rising from 0.65 to 0.69 (using the Stats SA weights) or 0.70 (using revised weights). Fedderke et al. (2003, 20–22) show that the 1996–99 OHSs also show an upward trend in inequality. Figure 9.1 plots Lorenz curves for household income per capita using data from the 1995 and 2000 IESs.[1] The Gini coefficients suggest that the underweighting of white households in the 2000 IES resulted in a small underestimate of the extent of this post-1995 increase in inequality.

The IESs collected data about expenditures as well as incomes. The expenditure data need to be treated with as much caution as the income data. Although the IESs sought to ensure that income and expenditure data reconciled, there was a much weaker correlation between household income and household expenditure in 2000 than in 1995. Taken at face value, however, both types of data appear to indicate the same general trend. The Gini coefficient for expenditure per capita rose from 0.65 in 1995 to 0.68 in 2000 (using the revised weights). Inequality increased, although the increase is less than that measured using income data. One reason why the expenditure and income data suggest different rates of growth of inequality is these data diverged sharply among low-income workers in 2000. The IES income data indicated that, between 1995 and 2000, the incomes of low-income households dropped sharply in both real and nominal terms. Whereas the income and expenditure data correlate in 1995, in 2000 these households recorded incomes that were inexplicably lower than their expenditures. This serves as yet another salutary reminder that "findings" regarding trends may be sensitive to the ways in which data are collected and especially changes in the ways in which data are collected.

Interracial Inequality

Whereas overall levels of inequality might have changed little, there has been a steady shift in the income shares of the different "racial groups" (see table 9.1). Census data suggest that the white population's share of total income declined from about 71 percent in 1970 to 52 percent in 1996 and the African population's share rose from about 20 percent to 36 percent (Whiteford and Van Seventer 2000, 12). The estimates made by Simkins using census and other data for a shorter time period suggest that interracial disparities were lower than indicated by census data alone, but the trend was the same (CDE 1995, 16–17).

The IES data concerning incomes suggest that this trend continued to 2000, although the pace of change is very sensitive to the choice of weights. The white population's share of total income declined from 49 percent to 40 percent between 1995 and 2000, if you use the Stats SA weights for 2000—but only to 46 percent if you use the revised weights. The revised weights suggest that the African share was creeping rather than galloping up.

These trends were also reflected in the shifting racial composition of the higher income deciles. By 1996, Whiteford and Van Seventer found, African households made up 22 percent of the richest decile (see table 9.2). As interracial inequality declined, so intraracial inequality rose. Indeed, the rising share of income of the black population between 1991 and 1996 was due to the marked increase in the income share of the growing black elite (ibid.). A com-

Table 9.1. Racial income shares, 1970–2000

	Censuses				Censuses, wage data, and PSLSD				IESs		
	1970 (%)	1980 (%)	1991 (%)	1996 (%)	1985 (%)	1990 (%)	1991 (%)	1995 (%)	1995 (%)	2000 (revised weights) (%)	2000 (SSA weights) (%)
White	71	65	60	52	59	54	54	52	49	46	40
African	20	25	30	36	29	33	33	34	39	40	46
Coloured	7	7	7	8	8	9	9	9	7	9	9
Asian	2	3	4	4	4	5	5	5	5	5	5
Total	100	100	100	100	100	100	100	100	100	100	100

Sources: Census data are from Whiteford and Van Seventer (2000), 12; combined census, wage, and PSLSD data are from CDE (1995); IES data are from unpublished research by Murray Leibbrandt.

Table 9.2. Racial composition of the top two income deciles, 1975–2000

| | | Censuses | | | IESs | | |
		1975 (%)	1991 (%)	1996 (%)	1995 (%)	2000 (revised weights) (%)	2000 (SSA weights) (%)
Decile 10	White	95	83	65	73	61	55
	African	2	9	22	18	25	31
	Coloured	2	4	7	4	9	9
	Asian	1	3	5	5	5	5
	Total	100	100	100	100	100	100
Decile 9	White	83	61	42	38	22	17
	African	7	22	39	46	55	61
	Coloured	7	11	12	9	15	15
	Asian	3	6	7	7	8	7
	Total	100	100	100	100	100	100

Sources: Census data are from Whiteford and Van Seventer (2000), 15 (there was no census in 1975, so the 1975 data are actually estimates made by McGrath, extrapolating from 1970 census data); IES data (using per capita income deciles) are from unpublished research by Murray Leibbrandt.

parison of the income data in the 1995 and 2000 IESs suggests that these trends continued (although, as noted above, the 2000 IES probably included too few higher-income African households). Even across the short five-year period between the two surveys, the racial composition of the top two income deciles shifted dramatically. As shown in table 9.2, however, this finding is also sensitive to the weights used in the 2000 IES. The white proportion of the top decile was 73 percent in 1995 and either 61 percent or 55 percent in 2000, depending on the weights used. The white proportion of the top decile thus dropped by either 12 percentage points (a lot) or 18 percentage points (probably too much to be credible). The brain drain among white professionals and managers (and among graduating students aspiring to those occupations) is likely to have freed up some more "space at the top" for black professionals and managers, but precisely how much space is unclear because we have such unreliable data for emigration (see Brown et al. 2002) as well as for the remaining white population. Even using the more conservative revised weights, there were by 2000 about as many African households in the top income quintile as there were white households.

Table 9.3. Gini coefficients for the distribution of household income,
1975–2000

	Censuses			IESs		
	1975	1991	1996	1995	2000 (revised weights)	2000 (SSA weights)
African	0.47	0.62	0.66	0.56	0.61	0.61
White	0.36	0.46	0.50	0.44	0.46	0.46
Coloured	0.51	0.52	0.56	0.50	0.55	0.54
Asian	0.45	0.49	0.52	0.47	0.50	0.49
All South Africa	0.68	0.68	0.69	0.65	0.70	0.69

Sources: Census data are from Whiteford and Van Seventer (2000), 16; Income and Expenditure Survey (IES) data (using individual rather than household-level data, allocating per capita household income to all household members) are from unpublished research by Murray Leibbrandt.

Note: Ginis for household income will be lower than those for per capita household income in a society such as South Africa, where poorer households are larger than richer households.

Intraracial Inequality

Declining interracial inequality was accompanied by rising intraracial inequality. This is evident from changes in the Gini coefficients for the distribution of income for South Africa as a whole and the different racial populations within it. Table 9.3 reports the Gini coefficients calculated from census data (from Whiteford and Van Seventer 2000) and IES data. Not only are the post-1991 intraracial Ginis high (especially for the African population), but there is a clear upward trend. (There is little difference between the Stats SA and revised weights with respect to the Gini coefficients because the revised weights only took into account race and province; the choice of weights does, however, make a big difference whenever the aggregate distribution is being explained as the weighted composite of the separate racial distributions.)

The declining importance of interracial inequality and rising importance of intraracial inequality are also evident in decompositions using census data (conducted by Whiteford and van Seventer) and IES data. The Theil statistic is the most commonly used additively decomposable measure of inequality, as discussed in Chapter 6 (see further Bhorat, Leibbrandt et al. 2001, 24–28). The Theil statistic allows for decomposition into "within group" and "between group" components. The results of decomposing inequality using racial groups

Table 9.4. Decomposition of the Theil-T index for income inequality, 1975–2000

	Censuses			IESs		
	1975 (%)	1991 (%)	1996 (%)	1995 (%)	2000 (revised weights) (%)	2000 (SSA weights) (%)
Within-group inequality	38	58	67	56	59	54
Between-group inequality	62	42	33	44	41	46
Total	100	100	100	100	100	100

Sources: Census data are from Whiteford and Van Seventer (2000), 17; IES data (using individual rather than household-level data, allocating per capita household income to all household members) are from unpublished research by Murray Leibbrandt.

demonstrate the steadily declining importance of interracial inequality and rising importance of intraracial inequality (table 9.4). In 1975 the "between-group" (in this case, interracial) contribution to overall inequality was almost twice as important as the "within-group" (in this case, intraracial) contribution (see Chapter 6), but by the late 1990s this ratio was reversed.[2]

GETTING AHEAD: THE NEW AFRICAN ELITE
AND "MIDDLE" CLASSES

The accelerating growth of the African elite and "middle" classes was perhaps the most dramatic shift in the social landscape of post-apartheid South Africa. Whiteford and van Seventer's analysis of census data indicates the extent to which the benefits of changing incomes in the 1990s were concentrated in this group. Dividing each racial group into income deciles or quintiles, they calculate the growth in income between 1991 and 1996 that can be attributed to economic growth and add the aggregate income losses experienced by "loser groups" (that is, most white income quintiles). They then examine how this income was distributed among beneficiaries. About 12 percent of the benefit went to the white elite (the top white income decile in particular), whereas 52 percent went to the top African income quintile, with as much as 40 percent going to the top African income decile alone (Whiteford and van Seventer 2000, 20–22). Another way of indicating the rapid growth of the high-income African

Table 9.5. Sources of income of households in the top two income deciles, 1995 and 2000

	1995		2000	
Source of income	Decile 9 (%)	Decile 10 (%)	Decile 9 (%)	Decile 10 (%)
Wages and salaries	68	60	78	74
Profits	7	15	2	5
Rent, interest, and dividends	2	2	1	2
Private pension	9	7	4	6
Alimony and remittances	1	<1	3	1
Public pensions and grants	1	<1	2	1
Other income	12	15	10	10
Total	100	100	100	100

population is to look at the numbers of households in different income categories. Between 1991 and 1996, the number of households in South Africa grew by 26 percent. The number of households with incomes above R72,000 per annum in 1996 prices (which is how Whiteford and van Seventer define "middle-class" households) rose by only 15 percent. But the number of middle-class African households rose by 78 percent (ibid., 22–23).

This growing high-income African population was generally described in the media as an "elite" or "middle class." In terms of the classes defined in Chapter 7, these were members of the upper class, the clumsily labelled WE1 and WE2 classes, and perhaps also the semiprofessional class comprising households headed by teaches or nurses. In 1993, the first three of these classes were still predominantly white, whereas the semiprofessional class was predominantly African. As we saw in Chapter 6, these classes were in no way in the middle of the class structure: the application to them of the term "middle class" made little sense in the South African context, where the urban working class was really the middle class.

The new African middle class comprised people in salaried jobs (such as managers and teachers) and professionals whose income is generally treated as salary, as well as entrepreneurs and capitalists. The IES data indicate how much more important were salaried and quasi-salaried occupations than profit-generating activity in terms of the size distribution of income. Table 9.5 reports the sources of income of households in the top income quintile using IES data from 1995 and 2000. The discrepancies between the two surveys are striking:

the relative shares of the major categories of income vary by implausible amounts. The share of income of the top quintile from profits (which includes profits from commercial farming) plummeted between the 1995 and 2000 IESs. This is very unlikely to reflect a real trend (although profits in agriculture, for example, might have dropped). As ever, the IES data need to be treated with caution. What is clear is that the lion's share of the top quintile's total income came from wages and salaries, with relatively very small sums from profits, rents, or interest and private pensions. Even at the level of the 1995 IES, however, it is clear that black economic empowerment provided by business opportunities was much less important in the late 1990s in terms of changing patterns of income distribution than was upward occupational mobility, assisted by affirmative action and reflected in the distribution of salaries.

Analysis of these high-income classes is difficult because of the shortcomings of available data. In South Africa, response rates in surveys and censuses are closely and inversely correlated with income: response rates are low in high-income areas and high in low-income areas. This makes it difficult to plot the growth of the African high-income population. Table 9.6 reports the breakdown of top occupational categories by race from the 1996 and 2001 censuses. Overall, the number of people in these high-income occupations rose by 18 percent between the two censuses. But there were big variations between occupational categories and racial groups. The "legislators, senior officials, and managers" category grew strongly and the professional category shrank—but this decline was accounted for by declining numbers of African and coloured professionals, not white and Indian professionals. At the same time, the number of African and coloured technicians and associate professionals rose very rapidly. The number of African professionals declined by 43 percent whilst the number of African technicians and associate professionals rose by an incredible 173 percent. Shifts of this scale over this time period simply are not possible. What is possible is that coverage was different or that occupations were classified differently in the two censuses. Overall, the number of African men and women in these categories grew more strongly than the number of white men and women, with the result that the African share was, by 2001, almost equal to the white share. But it is also possible that the data are simply too unreliable for analysis of this sort.

The Labour Force Surveys, conducted by Stats SA twice per year since 2000, are another possible source of data about the racial composition of the top income deciles or high-income occupations. The state uses data from the LFSs to calculate the official unemployment rate, so it might be thought that the LFSs

Table 9.6. Racial composition of top occupational categories, 1996 and 2001

| | Legislators, senior officials, and managers | | | | Professionals | | | | Technicians and associate professionals | | | | All three categories | | | |
	1996 number (%)	2001 number (%)			1996 number (%)	2001 number (%)			1996 number (%)	2001 number (%)			1996 number (%)	2001 number (%)		
African	97,275 (27)	139,509 (27)			427,392 (49)	241,578 (36)			178,584 (33)	486,731 (53)			703,251 (40)	867,818 (41)		
Coloured	30,369 (8)	42,202 (8)			74,870 (9)	47,599 (7)			55,414 (10)	101,800 (11)			160,653 (9)	191,601 (9)		
Indian	27,418 (8)	46,591 (9)			41,800 (5)	48,192 (7)			36,338 (7)	48,762 (5)			105,556 (6)	143,545 (7)		
White	205,652 (56)	287,087 (56)			316,718 (36)	331,094 (50)			266,514 (49)	282,481 (31)			788,884 (44)	900,662 (43)		
Total	364,902 (100)	515,389 (100)			870,955 (100)	668,463 (100)			542,882 (100)	919,774 (100)			1,778,739 (100)	2,103,626 (100)		

Sources: Stats SA, 03-01-19 (1996), table 14.0, and 03-02-03 (2003), table 2.32.

Note: The small number of individuals whose racial group was unspecified or "other" in 1996 is included in the totals.

Table 9.7. Racial composition of top occupational categories, 2001

	Legislators, senior officials, and managers		Professionals		Technicians and associated professionals		All three categories
	LFS (%)	CEE (%)	LFS (%)	CEE (%)	LFS (%)	CEE (%)	LFS* (%)
African	25	14	35	42	52	29	41
Coloured	7	7	8	7	11	13	9
Indian	7	5	7	6	4	6	5
White	60	74	50	45	33	52	44
Total	100	100	100	100	100	100	100

Sources: Author's calculations from original LFS data; CEE data are from RSA (2003a).
*The CEE data cannot be aggregated because the CEE reports them in percentages only.

are more accurate than the population censuses. The results from the February 2001 LFS are shown in table 9.7, together with data from the Department of Labour's Commission on Employment Equity (from RSA 2003a). The LFS data are extraordinarily similar to the population census data. Moreover, a comparison of the February 2001 LFS with the other LFSs conducted between February 2000 and March 2003 shows that the LFSs data are very consistent with respect to the racial composition of these top occupational categories. By March 2003 the number of African men and women in the three categories combined was almost the same as the number of white men and women.

The statistics released by the Commission for Employment Equity indicated lower rates of African influx into these higher-paid occupations. But the coverage of these statistics is known to be very limited. The statistics were based on information filed by employers under the Employment Equity Act. But data were available for fewer than 3.5 million employees, which was a small fraction of the economically active population. Most small employers never filed the information.

Overall, there was clearly strong upward mobility by African men and women into higher-income occupations. This was especially pronounced in the public sector. Thompson and Woolard (2002) used public-sector payroll data from the Department of Public Service Administration to assess the changing racial composition of the upper ranks of the public sector between 1995 and 1999. Table 9.8 shows that the proportion of managers (at all levels)

Table 9.8. Racial composition of top occupational categories in the public sector, 1995 and 2001

	Public-sector managers (all levels)		Public-sector senior managers	
	1995 (%)	2001 (%)	1995 (%)	2001 (%)
African	30.0	51.1	33.3	42.7
Coloured	6.7	6.6	2.0	5.8
Indian	3.4	5.7	2.0	6.0
Total black	40.1	63.4	37.3	54.5
White	59.9	36.6	62.7	45.5
Total	100.0	100.0	100.0	100.0

Source: PERSAL data analysed in Thompson and Woolard (2002).

who were African rose from 30 percent in 1995 to more than 51 percent in 2001, with the total black proportion rising from 40 percent to more than 63 percent. The change in the composition of senior management was more muted, but nevertheless there were more black than white senior managers by 2001 and almost as many African as white senior managers. The racial composition of nonmanagerial staff in the public sector also shifted, with the African (and black) proportion rising and the white proportion falling.

Entry into these high-income occupations was in part a function of changing enrollment patterns in institutions of higher education. Between 1988 and 1998, student enrollment in higher education was transformed, with the proportion of African students rising from 29 percent (in 1988) to 45 percent (in 1993) to 56 percent (in 1998). In 1994 there were about equal numbers of white and African students in higher education; by 1999, there were almost twice as many African as white students (Cooper and Subotzky 2001, 14; Cloete and Bunting 2000, 18–19). But, as Cooper and Subotzky (2001) put it, this was a "skewed revolution." African students tended to complete fewer years of higher education, be enrolled in technikons rather than top universities, and be underrepresented in the more professional courses (such as engineering and accountancy). Institutions of higher education turned out very large numbers of African men and women with qualifications for middle class jobs but relatively fewer for the highest occupations (see also Bunting 2002).

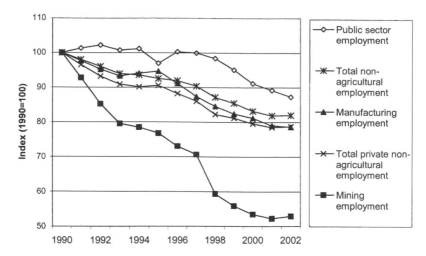

Figure 9.2. Trends in nonagricultural formal employment, 1990–2002. *Source:* Data are
from the South African Reserve Bank.

WAGES, EMPLOYMENT, AND UNEMPLOYMENT

The growth of the African upper (or so-called middle) classes was both dramatic and visible, but it was not the only change in the social landscape. Falling
formal employment is probably the key defining feature of economic growth in
the 1990s. As can be seen in figure 9.2, nonagricultural formal private employment and—to a lesser extent public employment—fell throughout the decade.
The magnitude of this fall was especially dramatic in the mining industry.
Coming on top of the "stabilisation" of mine labour in the 1980s, the consequences were dire in rural areas that had relied on migrant labour. Agricultural employment also fell, compounding the problem. These sectoral trends
affected unskilled labour especially hard.

Note, however, that there was some uncertainty about South African labour
statistics, and especially the extent to which economic growth was "jobless."
Table 9.9 shows how different sources generated very different pictures of the
South African labour market. Figure 9.2 is based on data from the South
African Reserve Bank, using surveys of firms. It shows a decline in employment
in the late 1990s. Data from household surveys (such as the OHSs), in contrast,
suggest that there was a rise in employment in the late 1990s that was due
largely to rising *informal*-sector employment. The LFS data from shortly after
2000 seem to indicate even higher levels of employment (at the same time as
higher unemployment rates).

Table 9.9. Employment according to different sources, 1996–2002
(in thousands)

	October Household Survey				Labour Force Survey		
	1996	1997	1998	1999	2000	2001	2002
Nonagricultural formal sector	5,242	5,139	4,945	4,840	6,678	6,678	7,036
Commercial agriculture	759	717	935	1,099	757	699	734
Subsistence or small-scale agriculture				1,508	653	792	
Informal sector	996	1,136	1,316	1,907	1,821	2,665	1,767
Domestic service	740	668	749	799	1,001	914	972
Total employed	9,287	9,247	9,390	10,369	11,880	11,837	11,393
	South African Reserve Bank						
	1996	1997	1998	1999	2000	2001	2002
Nonagricultural employment	5,233	5,144	4,965	4,864	4,734	4,658	4,663

Sources: Statistics South Africa PO210, September 2002; Statistics South Africa PO317, 31 July 2000; South African Quarterly Bulletin, June 2003, September 2002. SARB data draw on data from Statistics South Africa including the survey of employment and earnings in selected industries.

One of the problems with using data from firm-based surveys is that they typically underestimate employment because new firms and informal-sector firms are difficult to survey. Data from household surveys are better able to capture the number of people working. But the definition of "work" is rather different in household-level labour force surveys from that understood at the level of the firm. According to the standard labour force approach, anyone working for gain for as little as one hour a week is counted as employed even though this would not fit into most popular notions of what it means to have a job. By conflating employment and underemployment, household surveys typically overestimate employment. For example, Klasen and Woolard (1999) have shown that if employment in the 1995 OHS is reestimated in terms of "full-time equivalents" (that is, someone working only twenty hours per week will be counted as half employed rather than fully employed), then employment falls and the broad unemployment rate rises by three percentage points.

Taken together, the data shown in figure 9.2 and table 9.9 suggest that formal nonagricultural employment growth was probably strongly negative during the 1990s but that some of the job losses depicted in figure 9.2 may have been cushioned to some extent by a rise in informal employment. Given high levels of underemployment and low incomes in the informal sector, however, this type of "employment growth" must be treated with a great deal of circumspection.

Those who lost employment (or failed to find it) were the big losers in the 1990s. By contrast, most of the employed and owners of capital did relatively well (see Chapter 10). Fedderke and Mariotti (2002) show that the proportion of skilled workers in manufacturing rose sharply from 1990 onward and that this was associated with rising wages. Job loss at commercial mines and farms also contributed to the shift away from unskilled employment in South Africa over the decade (Edwards 2001; Simbi and Aliber 2000). Some of those who lost formal jobs may have been rehired as "casual" workers. Many, however, joined the ranks of the unemployed. Other studies point to the shift from un-skilled to skilled labour across a range of sectors (Bhorat and Hodge 1999; Bho-rat 2003; Oosthuizen 2003).

The 1990s saw continuing "resegmentation" of the labour market, with a deepening divide between workers in formal, regular employment and those in casual or contract employment (see, for example, Kenny and Webster 1998). The pace or extent of this resegmentation remained unclear, however. On the one hand, there were many reports of changing employment relationships (for example, ILO 1999; House and Williams 2000; Valodia 2000). On the other, surveys conducted by the International Labour Organisation in the mid-1990s suggested that flexible employment relationships in manufacturing were not as widespread as had been expected. As much as 93 percent of the manufacturing workforce was in regular, full-time employment (Crankshaw 1997b). The Labour Force Surveys of the early 2000s provide few indications of any signifi-cant casualisation of employment. About 80 percent of people working for someone else for pay said (in March 2003) that they were in permanent em-ployment, 4 percent were in fixed-period contracts, 10 percent were temporary, and only 6 percent were casual. Less than 2 percent said that their employment was seasonal. Very few workers said they were paid by a labour broker, contrac-tor, or agency. Between 2000 and 2003, the proportion of working people with-out a written contract actually declined slightly.

There is some evidence from surveys concerning the relative fortunes of different categories of workers. The advantages experienced by formally em-ployed workers (especially those with skills) have persisted in post-apartheid South Africa. Analysis of changes in individual earnings of African people in KwaZulu-Natal, using the 1993 PSLSD and 1998 KwaZulu-Natal Income Dy-namics Study (KIDS) data, shows that the real earnings of workers in regular employment rose by 30 percent between 1993 and 1998, compared to an overall average change in earnings of only 7 percent (Cichello et al. 2001, 130). The earnings of workers in regular employment grew faster than the average for everyone in the sample. Some of this spectacular increase occurred because new entrants into formal employment had higher wages than those who left. But even among workers who were in formal employment in both 1993 and 1998, earnings rose by 20 percent (ibid., 132).

This does not mean that all members of these classes prospered. The earnings of workers who lost or left their jobs plummeted. The aggregate gains of workers in regular employment should not obscure the fact that the composition of this group shifted. The data for KwaZulu-Natal from the PSLSD and KIDS have not been disaggregated into discrete occupational classes, but it is likely that white-collar and skilled occupations enjoyed positive real earnings growth during the late 1990s.

Unemployment

Unlike most employed workers and capitalists, the unemployed were unambiguous losers during the 1990s. Since 1993, unemployment rates have risen steadily. Table 9.10 presents data for unemployment rates from the PSLSD survey of 1993, the official OHSs of 1994–99, and their successors, the Labour Force Surveys (LFSs) of 2000–3. Unemployment rates rose in terms of both the official and expanded unemployment rates.

Despite some differences in survey and sampling design, post-1993 surveys showed a remarkably consistent pattern: unemployment was higher for Africans than for other population groups, higher for women than for men, and higher in rural than in urban areas. These patterns hold irrespective of whether unemployment was measured in strict or expanded ways. Table 9.11 shows that rural African women were the most disadvantaged with respect to access to the labour market: 35 percent of them wanted and were actively seeking work, and a further 20 percent wanted work but had given up actively seeking it. Unemployment rates were particularly high in the old homeland areas (Dinkelman and Piroux 2002, 879), illustrating one of the more pernicious legacies of apartheid.

The rise in unemployment contributed greatly to widening inequality in South Africa. Because there was no subsistence agricultural sector to fall back on, unemployment was closely associated with poverty. Unemployment rates were closely and inversely related to income, being lowest in the rich deciles and highest in the poor deciles (see Chapter 6). According to research by Meth

Table 9.10. Unemployment rates since 1993

| | PSLSD | OHS, 1994–99 | | | | | | LFS, 2000–3 | | | |
	1993	1994	1995	1996	1997	1998	1999	2000	2001	2002	2003
Unemployment (official)	12.7	20.0	16.9	19.3	21.0	25.2	23.3	26.7	26.4	29.4	28.2
Unemployment (expanded)	29.4	31.5	29.2	33.0	36.0	37.5	36.2	35.5	37.0	40.9	41.8

Sources: Klasen and Woolard (1999, 11); CSS, Statistical News Release P0317.10, 13 August 1998; Statistics South Africa, Statistical News Releases P0317 (18 May 2000), PO317 (31 July 2000), PO210 (September 2002), Po210 (25 March 2004).

Note: The PSLSD and OHS unemployment rates are not strictly comparable because of differences in survey design. For example, the OHS asked respondents whether they had looked for work in the past month (rather than in the preceding fortnight) and defined as broadly unemployed those who had not searched for work but who would accept a "suitable" job (rather than asking about why they had not searched for work). This probably explains why the rates of unemployment found in the PSLSD are lower than those in the OHS for the early 1990s. The LFS figures are for February in 2000, 2001, and 2002 and for September 2003. Note that the OHS figures for 1996 and 1997 have been reweighted to adjust for the lack of inclusion of mining hostels in the sample. The figures for OHS 1998 and 1999 include mining hostels in the sample.

Table 9.11. Unemployment rates by location and gender, 1999

	Urban		Nonurban		Total		
	Male (%)	Female (%)	Male (%)	Female (%)	Male (%)	Female (%)	All (%)
Official							
African	24.1	35.0	25.2	34.9	24.5	35.0	29.2
Total population	18.4	25.8	22.7	32.3	19.8	27.8	23.3
Expanded							
African	33.7	48.9	40.8	55.7	36.7	51.9	44.0
Total population	26.2	37.9	37.4	52.7	30.0	43.2	36.2

Source: OHS; Statistics South Africa, Statistical News Release P0317 (31 July 2000).

and Dias using expenditure data from the 1999 OHS and the September 2002 LFS, the number of people in poverty rose by between 3.7 and 4.2 million, and this was closely connected to the rise in the number of unemployed (about 2 million) in the same period (2003, 7–9).

During the late 1990s there was a debate about the extent and measurement of unemployment in South Africa (see Nattrass 2000a). The most substantive of these criticisms came from Standing et al. (1996), who argued that sampling and other measurement problems resulted in an overestimation of unemployment. But Klasen and Woolard (1999) found that adjusting the data to take these problems into account had an insignificant impact on measured unemployment.

A related debate concerned the size of South Africa's informal sector. Might the country's unemployment rate be overestimated because people working in the informal sector do not classify themselves as doing a "real job" and hence report themselves as unemployed to survey researchers? The problem with this suggestion is that labour-force statisticians classify people as "employed" if they report conducting *any* income-earning activities, irrespective of whether the respondent self-reports himself or herself as unemployed. They make careful use of selection procedures and "hurdle" questions to assign people a labour force status (Bhorat 1999). A person working in the informal sector would have to lie about all sources of labour income to be classified as unemployed. Schlemmer and Worthington (1996a, 1996b) and Schlemmer and Levitz (1998) adopted precisely such an argument, saying that differences between the personal income and expenditure of unemployed people probably represented undeclared informal earnings. Klasen and Woolard (1999) questioned the empirical basis of this claim, in part because it is difficult to draw distinctions between household and individual expenditure. Furthermore, the fact that income and expenditure figures from the 1995 IES correlated very well did not support the proposition that there were large amounts of unreported income emanating from unregistered microenterprises (ibid., 6).

The Informal Sector

The informal sector is notoriously hard to measure. The operating definition of the informal sector used by Stats SA in the LFS is that the business is registered neither as a company nor for paying value-added tax (VAT). Anyone who reported informal activity in the previous week (if only for an hour) was classified as being in the informal sector. Workers who reported that they were working for an informal-sector firm were also counted as being in the informal sector. This results in at least two sources of "noise" in the data that may account in part for the highly fluctuating measurement of informal activity in the LFS. The first is that people working irregularly in the informal sector may or may not be recorded as informally employed; it all depends on what they did in the previous week. If a high proportion of informally employed people work for only a few hours a week, then this kind of noise is likely. In a 2000 survey conducted in Cape Town (in Khayelitsha and Mitchell's Plain), 21 percent of those reporting self-employment worked for ten or fewer hours a week. The second source of noise arises from uncertainty among workers with regard to the status (formal or informal) of the firms for which they work.

According to the October Household Surveys, informal employment rose from 581,639 in 1997 to 743,179 in 1998 and to 1,207,366 in 1999. In 2000, according to the Labour Force Survey, it rose to more than 2 million (Simkins 2003, 6). Simkins argues that this growth was implausible and was probably the result of the OHS and the LFS getting better at measuring the informal sector (ibid.). He accordingly adjusts the estimates for informal sector employment upwards in earlier years. This results in an increase in estimated total employment (formal plus informal) in all years between 1997 and 2002 except for 2000 (see figure 9.3). What is potentially problematic about this, however, is that the 2001 LFS estimate for the informal sector is more than twice that estimated in the 2001 census (ibid.). Simkins assumes that the LFS covers the informal sector better than the census, but whether this can account for a difference of this order of magnitude remains an open question.

South Africa is unusual in that it is a middle-income developing country with high unemployment and a relatively small informal sector. In Latin Amer-

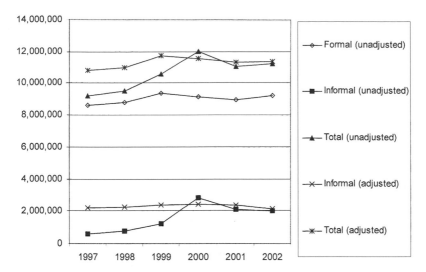

Figure 9.3. Estimates of formal, informal, and total employment, 1997–2002

ican countries, workers who lose their jobs (or cannot find work) in the formal
sector tend to find work in the informal sector (meaning less secure, poorly regulated, and low-paying jobs). In South Africa, those who lose formal-sector
jobs seem to end up in unemployment rather than the informal sector. Simkins
(2003) ran paired probit regressions to see what characteristics would predict
whether people were more likely to be actively searching for jobs (as opposed to
being unemployed and not searching) or informally employed (as opposed to
being unemployed and actively searching). He found that Africans were less
likely to be informally employed than searching for work and that women and
rural people were more likely to be informally employed. Increasing education
also made participation in the informal sector less likely (2003, 13). This is unsurprising given that those who did end up in the informal sector tended to
earn very low incomes.

This was confirmed by a survey conducted by Stats SA in March 2002 of
businesses in South Africa that were not registered for the payment of VAT
(Stats SA, 2002). The sample was based on a subsample of the LFS. Most (69
percent) of the enterprises were in wholesale or retail, most (76 percent) did not
add value during production (that is, did not use raw materials), and fewer than
10 percent were in manufacturing. About one-third operated without electricity and about one-third were without a toilet on site. Only 15 percent employed
anyone; that is, this sector was made up overwhelmingly of one-person trading

or hawking "businesses." Average turnover was about R1,150 per month and average profit almost R800 per month, barely more than the government old-age pension. In another survey, in Khayelitsha and Mitchell's Plain (in Cape Town) in 2000, average monthly profit for the self-employed was R580.

It was sometimes suggested that surveys were not capturing the full extent of the informal sector in South Africa. This claim became less and less credible as more and more household surveys looked for but did not find much evidence of a massive informal sector. Surveys such as the 2000 Khayelitsha and Mitchell's Plain survey probed the possible informal sector exhaustively and failed to reveal widespread activity.

The obvious question is, why was South Africa's informal sector not larger?" Put another way, what constrained prospective entrepreneurs from starting informal businesses, and what inhibited the accumulation of capital? One prime suspect was South Africa's regulation of the labour market. In a study of "small, medium and micro enterprises" (SMMEs), Berry et al. (2002) documented many of the grievances that small entrepreneurs had with labour regulations, particularly with regard to wage-setting and the costs of retrenchments. Anecdotal evidence suggests that social obligations (including the cost of funerals) and crime often wiped out working capital. Perhaps, also, there was a lack of an entrepreneurial culture and experience, which South Africa's public education system did little to redress. As Berry et al. concluded, however, "we are very far from having sufficient knowledge" of the factors affecting SMME growth (ibid., 57).

SHORT-TERM FLUX IN INCOMES

The data sets used above to assess how income distribution changed after the end of apartheid were all cross-sectional. Successive cross-sectional surveys (and censuses) can be compared over time if they have similar samples (or similar coverage, in the cases of censuses) and ask similar questions. Panel studies provide a different perspective on changes over time and have a different set of methodological weaknesses. In a panel study, the same panel of respondents is reinterviewed over a period of time. This means that changes over time can be linked to specific characteristics. For example, is poverty generally transitory or chronic? Do people drop in and out of poverty as incomes fall and rise or are they generally stuck in poverty for long periods of time? And, crucially in post-apartheid South Africa, were the new opportunities for getting rich distributed widely or were they limited to people who were already relatively better off?

Panel studies have two major drawbacks: the final sample is, at best, representative of the population at the time when the panel study was started and does not easily allow for births, deaths, and related demographic changes; and attrition, in the form of failure to reinterview members of the panel, may render the final sample even less representative.

The first major panel data set for South Africa that is relevant to the study of income dynamics was the PSLSD-KIDS data set from KwaZulu-Natal. African and Indian households interviewed in 1993 for the PSLSD were reinterviewed in 1998 by KIDS. The PSLSD-KIDS data have several major limitations for our purposes. First, the panel was not designed as a panel study in that the PSLSD was not intended to be the first of a series. Furthermore, the primary purpose of the 1998 study was to distinguish between chronic and transitory poverty (May and Roberts 2001), not to probe issues of general opportunity and mobility directly. The consequence of this is that neither the 1993 nor the 1998 survey asked many of the questions required for a thorough study of opportunities and mobility. Second, data about income, employment status, and so on were collected at only two points in time, five years apart. This interval is both short (in that we can only analyse short-term income dynamics) and too long (in that the data tell us nothing about changes that took place in between these two points in time). There were, unfortunately, no questions in the 1998 survey about employment history during the previous five years. Someone who was employed in both 1993 and 1998 might have been unemployed for most of the intervening period. Third, there are a number of aspects of the sample that require caution in interpreting the results.[3]

Nonetheless, the PSLSD-KIDS data do indicate clearly the importance of panel studies as opposed to series of cross-sectional studies. When analysed as two cross-sectional surveys, the 1993 and 1998 data suggest that the average real earnings of workers in formal employment rose by 30 percent, that is, that formally employed workers "got ahead." But analysed as a panel data set, a somewhat different picture emerges: the workers in formal employment in 1993 actually experienced on average a decline in real wages of 8 percent because some were no longer in formal employment in 1998 and thus suffered huge declines in earnings. For those who were in formal employment in 1993 and in 1998, real wages did indeed rise, by 20 percent. Conversely, some of the workers surveyed in 1998 had been unemployed or in informal employment five years previously and thus experienced big increases in earnings. Cichello et al. (2001) conclude that there was significant "churning" in the labour market as people's labour-market status changed.

Table 9.12. Income quintiles transition matrix, 1993 and 1998, African adults in KwaZulu-Natal

			1998 income quintiles					
			1 (%)	2 (%)	3 (%)	4 (%)	5 (%)	Total (%)
1993	1	(%)	37	26	17	15	5	100
income	2	(%)	32	28	23	11	6	100
quintiles	3	(%)	18	24	29	21	9	100
	4	(%)	9	20	23	31	18	100
	5	(%)	4	3	9	22	63	100
	Total	(%)	100	100	100	100	100	100

Source: Leibbrandt and Woolard (2001), table 6.

Income mobility needs to be analysed in terms of household incomes and not only individual earnings. Table 9.12 presents a transition matrix for household incomes showing the destination quintiles in 1998 of households according to their original quintiles from 1993 (see Leibbrandt and Woolard 2001). The table shows that 37 percent of households in the poorest income quintile in 1993 were still in the poorest income quintile in 1998, whereas 26 percent had moved up into the second quintile (and so on). A total of three in eight African households were in the same income quintile in each survey (see the shaded cells in table 9.12). Another three in households moved into an adjacent income quintile. One in four moved into nonadjacent quintiles. Most movement occurred in the middle of the distribution, with much less movement out of the bottom and (especially) top quintiles. Almost two-thirds of the households in the top quintile in 1993 were in the top quintile again in 1998 (and most of the new entrants to the top quintile came from the fourth quintile); put another way, one-third of the households in the top quintile in 1993 had dropped down into lower quintiles by 1997. More than two-thirds of the households in the bottom quintile in 1998 had been in one of the bottom two quintiles in 1993. Similar work has been done using expenditure data (see Maluccio et al. 2000; Roberts 2001, cited in Aliber 2003).

This flux was in part due to changes in individuals' earnings (Cichello et al. 2001). Among working people, the individuals who suffered the biggest drop in earnings were those with the highest earnings to begin with; the individuals who gained the most were those with no or low earnings in 1993. This is because the dominant factor behind rising and falling earnings was a change in an individual's labour-market status. Only 62 percent of the individuals in regular employment (or what they call "formal" employment) in 1993 were in regular employment in 1998. About 18 percent were in casual employment or informal-sector work, about 15 percent were unemployed, and 6 percent were not available for work. The shift from regular employment to nonemployment (whether unemployed or not available for work) was, of course, catastrophic in terms of earnings. The mean monthly earnings change among workers who were in regular employment on both dates was a gain of R189 (in 1993 prices), somewhat better than the mean for the sample as a whole of R139. But the mean for workers who changed from formal to informal employment was a loss of R152 per month, and the mean for workers who changed from formal employment to no employment at all was a loss of R797 per month. Viewed from the other end of the labour market, one in five individuals who had been unemployed in 1993 was in regular employment in 1998. Their mean monthly earnings rose by a massive R1,278. Slightly fewer had moved into informal employment (with much more modest earnings gains), while most remained unemployed (46 percent) or were no longer available for work (17 percent) and hence experienced no change in their earnings.

The overall picture is perhaps most easily grasped by comparing the fortunes of two groups of earners. The first group comprised the approximately 30 percent of working-age African men and women who had the same labour-market status in 1993 and 1998. They accounted for a very small part of the changes in earnings. The second group comprised the 23 percent of the sample who moved into or out of formal employment. They accounted for the lion's share, probably about two-thirds, of the total change in earnings. It is likely that a high proportion of the individuals who moved out of formal employment did so as a result of involuntary retrenchment. In a situation of very high unemployment, workers who are retrenched probably have advantages over the longer-term unemployed in terms of finding new jobs. But having better chances of reemployment does not mean that the chances are good. The result is that turnover in employment results in huge shifts in individual earnings.

Changes in household incomes can be divided into changes due to "income events," or changes in the household's money income, and changes due to "demographic events," or changes in the size or composition of the household (see Leibbrandt and Woolard 2001). Income events accounted for about three-quarters of the movements into or out of poverty (defined in terms of adult equivalent income), with demographic events accounting for the remaining quarter. The key income events were changes in the earnings from work of the household head or other household members. Not surprisingly, job losses and the acquisition of additional unemployed dependents both correlated with dropping behind. In sum, the PSLSD-KIDS data suggest that there was considerable income mobility in post-apartheid South Africa, due primarily to flux in the labour market as workers lost jobs and as unemployed people (or people working in the informal sector) secured employment.

LIFETIME PATTERNS IN INCOME DISTRIBUTION

In the context of high unemployment rates, flux in the labour market meant that there was flux in patterns of income distribution. But was this flux spread evenly across different sections of the population? What was the relation between short-term flux and lifetime earnings and hence household incomes in the long term? Were the currently poor (at any moment) more vulnerable to flux so that there was a correlation between current poverty and lifetime poverty, or was there so much flux across the board that lifetime earnings and household incomes tended to even out?

Long-term panel data (such as the Panel Study for Income Dynamics in the United States) can address these questions. In the absence of any similar data for South Africa, we have to resort to retrospective questions about employment histories. The 2000 Khayelitsha and Mitchell's Plain Survey (KMPS) asked retrospective questions about employment history as well as family background. The survey was conducted in parts of Cape Town with neither large "middle-class" or farm worker populations, but with a high unemployment rate (46 percent by the broad definition, 29 percent by the strict definition; see Nattrass 2003a, 77). All of the adults in the KMPS sample, including the unemployed and people not presently participating in the labour force, were asked questions about what proportion of their weekdays since leaving school had they spent in each of a list of activities, including "working as a regular wage earner"; "working as a casual worker"; "self-employed"; "working in the family business or farm"; "looking for work"; "domestic duties/child care"; "post-school education and training"; and "other" (which respondents were asked to define).

Tables 9.13 and 9.14 show that there were marked differences by occupational class (albeit using crude occupational classifications). Workers in higher occupations (managers, professionals, technicians, and clerks) spent a larger proportion of their lives in regular employment than those in intermediate occupations (service and sales workers, craftsmen, and machinists), who in turn

Table 9.13. Time spent working as a regular wage worker since leaving school, by occupation or employment status, Cape Town, 2000

| Proportion of time | In regular employment | | | Unemployed (African adults only) (%) |
	Higher occupations (%)	Medium occupations (%)	Elementary occupations (%)	
Almost all of the time	62	50	39	8
More than half of the time	21	25	25	10
About half of the time	5	8	12	9
Less than half of the time	7	11	14	15
None of the time	6	5	9	57
Total	100	100	100	100

Note: Higher occupations are defined here as Standard Occupational Classification codes 1000–5000; medium occupations are codes 5000–9000 excepting 5169 (security guards); elementary occupations are codes 9000–10000 plus 5169. Some respondents currently categorised as being in regular employment might say that they had spent none of the time in regular wage employment because respondents are given labour-market positions on the basis of their answers to a set of questions; many working people do not regard their work as "proper work" or do not see themselves as having "proper jobs."

Table 9.14. Time spent looking for work since leaving school, by occupation or employment status, Cape Town, 2000

| Proportion of time | In regular employment | | | Unemployed (African adults only) (%) |
	Higher occupations (%)	Medium occupations (%)	Elementary occupations (%)	
Almost all of the time	5	8	12	31
More than half of the time	6	6	11	18
About half of the time	5	8	10	11
Less than half of the time	23	24	23	17
None of the time	61	55	45	24
Total	100	100	100	100

Note: See table 9.13.

spent a larger proportion of their lives in regular employment than workers in elementary (unskilled) occupations. The proportions of time spent looking for work showed an inverse relation. Thus 62 percent of the workers in higher occupations had spent almost all of the time in regular employment, and 61 percent had spent none of the time looking for work, compared to 39 percent and

45 percent, respectively, of workers in elementary occupations. In short, the extent of churning in the work history of people seemed to be closely and inversely related to their occupational class. Given the close relation between race and class in Cape Town, these differences were reflected also in different patterns in the work histories of coloured and African workers.

The work histories of the unemployed were quite distinct, exhibiting chronic disadvantage compared with workers in regular employment. Only 8 percent of unemployed Africans said that they had worked regularly for almost all of their lives, and only 10 percent said they had done so for more than half of their lives (see the final column of table 9.13). These figures are very small compared with the figures for workers in elementary as well as medium or higher occupations (and are small even if African workers are considered separate from coloured workers). The comparable figures for African adults currently in casual employment were similar to those for the unemployed. Similarly, unemployed Africans have spent much more of their lives looking for work than have employed workers (see table 9.14).

Some of these differences might be related to age. Employed African adults had a very different age profile than that of self-employed African adults, for example. Analysis of employment histories by age cohort shows that each generation of African adults in Cape Town experienced a high level of churning, but there remained marked differences within each age cohort between employed and unemployed adults. The unemployed of all ages report higher levels of lifetime vulnerability.

The spectrum of vulnerability to unemployment thus seemed to run from people in the higher occupations at one end through skilled and semiskilled workers to unskilled workers in the middle, then on to casual workers and the unemployed at the other end. Some corroboration for this came from KMPS data on the duration of unemployment (to date for the unemployed, or prior to current job for the currently employed). Table 9.15 shows that the duration of unemployment was related to occupation and labour-market status. Currently unemployed African adults had been unemployed for, on average, nearly 33 months. The most recent period of unemployment for people working in elementary occupations had been 11.5 months, on average, and the equivalent duration of unemployment spells for adults in intermediate and higher occupations was shorter still.

The KMPS data suggested that there were real class differences within the coloured and African population in Cape Town, at the same time as some churning in terms of earnings and incomes. What is striking is not only that

Table 9.15. Duration of unemployment, Cape Town, 2000

Current labour market status	Mean duration of unemployment in months prior to current job, if working
In higher occupations	5.6
In intermediate occupations	9.8
In elementary occupations	11.5
Unemployed (African only)	32.8

some people got ahead but also that others clearly fell behind, dropping into a lifetime of intermittent unemployment and sporadic casual employment or, if they were lucky, occasional spells of regular wage employment in an unskilled occupation.

INTERGENERATIONAL MOBILITY AND THE REPRODUCTION OF INEQUALITY

Data from the PSLSD-KIDS panel and from the retrospective questions in the KMPS suggest that during the 1990s there was a high level of flux in income due to movements in and out of employment but that this flux was uneven across people's working lives, with higher levels among the poor than among the better-off. Disadvantage persisted across lifetimes. Was it also reproduced between generations? Were the children of poor parents destined to remain poor? Or was there a high rate of intergenerational mobility, with the children of poor parents becoming rich and, perhaps, the children of rich parents becoming poor?

In Chapter 3 we saw that there were high absolute rates of mobility in the later apartheid period as white, coloured, Indian, and finally African people advanced up the occupational hierarchy. White South Africans also enjoyed high relative mobility rates, because racially discriminatory policies reserved high-paying occupations for them while massive public investment in education meant that they secured preferential skills. For African people, absolute rates of mobility were high but relative rates were clearly low: their opportunities to benefit from a changing economy were restricted by racial discrimination and educational disadvantage. Within the African population, however, some groups were better placed than others to take advantage of new opportunities. As Schneier (1983) found, urban insiders were better placed than migrant outsiders. If the most advantaged segment of the black population consisted of the urban insiders (those with section 10 rights under the pass laws), then the most disadvantaged were the families of farm workers evicted from white-owned farms in the 1970s and dumped in remote bantustans at a time of high unemployment; resettled without any access to agricultural land and lacking education, nonagricultural skills, access to schools, or contacts in urban areas, they (and their children) were sentenced to enduring poverty. As argued in Chapters 7 and 8, by the mid-1990s the African population could be divided into discrete classes, including an underclass of households doubly disadvantaged in that they had neither any employed members nor the social capital necessary to secure employment.

Unfortunately, as we noted in Chapter 6, there is little quantitative evidence concerning intergenerational mobility at the end of apartheid. Education is the only aspect of this topic for which there are any data. By the 1990s, education served as a key mechanism by which inequality was transmitted from generation to generation. We have data about the importance of education in determining earnings and hence household incomes. Such data typically come from retrospective questions about the highest grade attained by working people together with questions about their current earnings. As we saw in Chapter 6, education is a major determinant of earnings (see further Moll 2000; Lam 1999; Case and Deaton 1999; Schultz and Mwabu 1998a; Anderson et al. 2001; Bhorat et al. 2001; Keswell and Poswell 2002). We also have some data about the relation between family background and a child's educational progress. Lam and colleagues (Lam 1999; Anderson et al. 2001, 46–47) use 1995 OHS data to show that children's schooling (measured in terms of grade attainment at specific ages) rises with mothers' and fathers' education. Children living with both parents also perform better than children living with one or neither parent (Anderson et al. 2001, 49–50). The combination of high returns to education with a wide dispersion in schooling explains a very large part of South Africa's very high level of inequality in the distribution of income (Lam 1999).

Most surveys only provide this latter type of data for coresidential generations, which means that it is generally limited to adolescents and their parents. The 1998 KIDS survey of African households in KwaZulu-Natal is unusual in that it also collected data about the educational achievement of *absent* parents, allowing analysis of intergenerational correlations for older generations. Burns (2000) uses these data to demonstrate a clear correlation between the educational attainment of household members and the education of their parents (see also Hertz 2001). Nimubona and Vencatachellum (2003) show that the correlation between successive generations' education is strongest among poor households, that is, that educational disadvantage is reproduced between generations especially strongly.

In Chapter 7 we examined the relation between family background and children's education in terms of class. Figure 7.6 showed the highest school grade completed, on average, by children of different ages in selected classes. It showed that by age fifteen, children in upper-class, semiprofessional, and intermediate-class households had completed grade 7, whereas children of the same age in core working-class households had completed grade 6 only and children in marginal working-class households had only completed grade 5. By the age of nineteen, differences had widened, with class making a difference of up to three grades. Given the importance of education in determining earnings, children from marginal working class backgrounds are much more likely to end up in marginal working class occupations, and children from upper-class backgrounds are much more likely to end up in upper-class occupations. Inequality thus tends to be reproduced over time. Although the relation between class and schooling shown in figure 7.6 is not dissimilar to the relation between race and schooling shown in other studies (for example, Case and Deaton 1999; Lam 1999), there are also marked differences in schooling by class within racial groups, as we showed in figure 7.7. It is clear that class affects educational attainment.

The reasons why inequality is reproduced via education are not difficult to identify. Under apartheid, resources were allocated unequally to schools attended by poor and rich children (see Van der Berg 2001a, 2002). Pupil-teacher ratios varied (although the importance of this remains unclear; see Case and Deaton 1999), and the quality of teachers probably varied (see Lemon and Stevens 1999, 223, 229). These factors must have some enduring effect. In schools in poor areas there might be no "culture of learning." Poor parents spend less than do richer parents on their children's education (Case and Deaton 1999), especially perhaps at the preschool level. They provide a less conducive home environment and probably are also less motivated. Within racial groups, educational achievement is also related to parental schooling (especially the mother's educational achievement), with the children of well-educated parents completing more grades than those with less well-educated parents (Anderson et al. 2001). All of these factors were recognised by the post-apartheid Department of Education (RSA 2000a).

Children enter the labour market with very different amounts of human capital, reflecting both the time they spent in school and the quality of that

Table 9.16. Education and vulnerability to Unemployment, Cape Town, 2000

Current labour-market status	Human capital: Mean highest grade attained	Mean highest grade attained by head of household during childhood	Mean highest grade attained by head of household's partner during childhood	Mean highest grade attained by father if not resident in the household during childhood
Higher occupations	10.6	7.4	7.1	7.0
Intermediate occupations	8.8	5.6	5.8	6.7
Elementary occupations	8.3	4.7	5.0	4.6
In casual employment	7.8	4.0	4.3	4.9
Unemployed (coloured)	8.6	6.6	6.3	n/a
Unemployed (African)	8.7 [8.3–9.0]	4.5 [4.0–4.8]	5.0 [4.3–5.5]	5.4 [4.6–5.5]

Note: The figures in square brackets in the final row give the range of means for the different types of unemployed persons defined by Nattrass (2003a): the higher figures are for actively searching unemployed, the lowest for passive unemployed, with network searchers in between; the exception is the final column, where these subcategories do not line up in the expected direction. Note that the final column refers almost entirely to Africans.

schooling, as well as the home environment. In the past, poor children often had left school early because of poverty: their parents could not afford to pay fees or buy uniforms, or children had been required to find employment to supplement household income. (Incentives to leave school declined in the 1990s amid very high levels of unemployment and reformed state policy regarding fees.) Using KMPS data for Cape Town, table 9.16 shows the mean grade attainment of adults in each occupational category, as well as the mean grade attainment of key adults in the households in which they were children and of nonresident fathers.

Social capital is also important in securing employment, as we saw in Chapter 8. It might well be the case that people with identical educational qualifications have different prospects in the labour market because of the different information, attitudes, and networks that they inherited or acquired from their contrasting social backgrounds. Employers fill vacancies primarily via word of mouth among their existing workforce. Almost two-thirds of the workers in the KMPS sample got their first job through either friends or family, and almost as high a proportion got their current or most recent job the same way (see table 8.2). South Africa is not alone in this, of course (see Granovetter 1974 on the

United States), but these tendencies may be more pronounced in South Africa. It appears that the bureaucratic allocation of black labour under apartheid (with advantage corresponding to pass law status) was replaced, by the end of the twentieth century, by a market allocation according to skill and social capital.

AIDS AND INEQUALITY

Studies of distribution often pay insufficient attention to demographic changes. In the previous chapters of this book we argued that population growth had important consequences for processes of social and economic change, including deagrarianisation. After the apartheid era, the major demographic factor affecting inequality was the mortality and morbidity resulting from the AIDS pandemic. According to the ASSA2002 demographic model,[4] an estimated 10.8 percent of South Africa's 45.9 million people were HIV-positive in 2004. This proportion rises to 18.7 percent for adults aged twenty to sixty-four. Of the 720,000 deaths expected in 2004, 46 percent were projected to be from AIDS. Despite South Africa's AIDS prevention interventions,[5] the model predicted that more than half a million new HIV infections would take place in 2004.

This was (and remains) a socioeconomic crisis of major proportions. It reduced the economic security of households by reducing the productivity of (and eventually killing) income earners while simultaneously diverting scarce household resources towards medical expenditure (Nattrass 2004). Women are especially hard-hit because they carry the burden of the disease and yet are expected to care for other HIV-positive members of the household (Walker and Gilbert 2002, 82).

There is a growing body of South African research which indicates that the impact of AIDS has been devastating at the household level (for example, Cross 2001; Desmond et al. 2000; Steinberg et al. 2002; Booysen 2002). In most of sub-Saharan Africa, where agriculture accounts for a significant portion of employment and output, there is evidence that HIV-AIDS is having an especially detrimental impact on rural households engaged in peasant agriculture and hence on food security (IFAD 2001; de Waal and Tumushabe 2003). By contrast, South Africa's experience of deagrarianisation and the destruction of peasant agriculture under apartheid meant that most food is produced by large, capital-intensive commercial farms. The impact of AIDS on the economic security of poor households in South Africa is thus felt primarily through declining employment and earnings rather than declining food production.

Survey data from the Free State province indicates that AIDS-affected households are in a particularly vulnerable position because they have higher rates of unemployment and are more dependent on nonemployment income like pensions (Booysen 2002). This suggests that one or more of the following is the case: people living in households with limited (if any) access to wage employment are more vulnerable to HIV-AIDS infection; affected households have experienced disproportional employment losses because of AIDS; and people living with AIDS migrate to households with pensioners in order to be taken care of.

What does this mean for overall inequality? All else being equal, households that lose a breadwinner to AIDS will fall further down the income distribution. If the job is taken by a previously unemployed person, then that new employee's household will move up the income distribution. The overall Gini coefficient will thus remain broadly unchanged. But if firms react to AIDS by shedding employment, then the number of households without any breadwinner will rise, thus worsening the Gini coefficient. If average wages rise at the same time (perhaps in response to increased pressure from workers to compensate them for the burden of higher medical insurance and health expenditure, or perhaps because the average worker is becoming more skilled as firms get rid of unskilled workers first) then inequality will worsen further.

Any discussion of the impact of AIDS on distribution requires information about the size of the pie (the GDP) and the number of people in need of a slice (the population). Different macroeconomic models come up with different predictions about the impact of AIDS on economic growth (Nattrass 2004). All predict that AIDS will slow growth but some predict a greater impact than others.

If the population falls faster than income, then per capita income will rise. Although this is theoretically possible, it is not common. Econometric research indicates that AIDS has either had an insignificant impact on the growth of per capita income in developing countries (Bloom and Mahal 1997) or has reduced it (Bonnel 2000). Bonnel's results indicate that "in the case of a typical sub-Saharan country with a prevalence rate of 20 percent," the growth rate of per capita income would be reduced by 1.2 percentage points per year because of AIDS (ibid., 846). Most international studies show a decline in per capita income as a result of the AIDS pandemic (see Barnett and Whiteside 2002, 286–87). But whether absolute per capita income is higher or lower as a result of AIDS in any particular country is ultimately an empirical question. Two of the three major South African models predict a rise in per capita income, whereas the third predicts a fall (see Nattrass 2004). Such results have to be treated with great caution, however, because the results of the modelling work are highly contingent on the underlying theoretical assumptions, data, and parameter estimates and guesstimates.

According to De Waal, AIDS is likely to increase inequality in Africa as, for example, some commercial farmers are able to buy up land cheaply from families stricken by AIDS and employ unskilled labour at low rates (De Waal 2003, 11). This practice is unlikely to be significant in South Africa, where there is little peasant or subsistence agriculture and it is access to jobs rather than to land that drives inequality. In South Africa, the impact of AIDS on inequality is mediated in large part by how government and private firms react to the pandemic by changing the level and type of employment and the benefits available.

If firms react by continuing to decrease their reliance on unskilled labour (a trend that started before the AIDS pandemic) and by moving out of economic sectors whose customer base comprises lower-income consumers, then poor households will find themselves doubly disadvantaged. Not only will their access to the labour market become ever more tenuous, but the products that they purchase may become scarcer (and more costly). Conversely, relatively skilled workers could benefit from greater employment opportunities (as production becomes more skill- and capital-intensive) and higher wages (as the relative demand for skilled labour increases). They will probably also live longer and more productive lives as firms provide them with greater access to antiretroviral treatment. They will probably also be the first in line to receive antiretroviral treatment from government hospitals because the treatment programme "rolls out" from urban hospitals first. As the cost of antiretrovirals decreases, more and more firms are likely to help extend the lives of their HIV-positive employees by providing them with access to life-prolonging medication. The size of the pie may shrink as a result of AIDS, but workers, especially skilled ones, will enjoy a growing share.

South Africa is increasingly divided along class lines, with the gap between the employed and unemployed being of major importance. The horrifying element that AIDS brings to the picture is that the divide will mean the difference between life and death for many people (Nattrass 2004). Those without access to jobs (especially good jobs) are bearing and will continue to bear the brunt of the AIDS pandemic. Whether inequality is lower or higher twenty years from now is a moot point. But over the next couple of decades, inequality will probably rise as AIDS lowers growth and slices its way through the poor and disadvantaged in South Africa.

CONCLUSION

Our analysis of post-apartheid trends in income distribution is bedevilled by the highly uneven quality of available data. But it seems clear that improved opportunities for some did not mean improved opportunities for all. Many households, especially African, coloured, and Indian households, got ahead, enjoying upward mobility into high-earning occupations. Workers in formal employment generally benefited from rising real wages. But there was considerable flux in incomes as some workers lost jobs, plunging their households into poverty, while some unemployed people found employment, greatly improving household welfare. Overall, inequality widened because of the deepening unemployment crisis. Moreover, rapidly changing patterns of mortality and morbidity due to AIDS meant many already poor households were pushed deeper into poverty, and many poor people experienced poor health and died young. People from disadvantaged backgrounds were more vulnerable to the shocks of unemployment and ill health and were poorly placed to take advantage of the opportunities that were opening at the top end of the income distribution.

South African society might be viewed in terms of a game of snakes and ladders. The "ladders" are the jobs that people find and the "snakes" are retrenchment, morbidity, and mortality of household members. There are a lot of snakes and ladders, but they are not distributed randomly. At the bottom end of society there are few ladders because people lack social and human capital and are more vulnerable to AIDS-related illness. The further up the board one proceeds, the more ladders there are: opportunities favour the already advantaged. En route there are many snakes, but the incidence of snakes declines just as the incidence of ladders rises.

In Chapter 7 we derived a figure representing the major lines of stratification in South African society. This is reproduced in figure 9.4. After apartheid, the top cluster of classes became more multiracial as African as well as coloured and Indian households moved into it. There are, therefore, ladders from the middle cluster of classes into the top cluster. At the bottom end, there are some snakes running down from the middle to the bottom cluster but few ladders leading up in the opposite direction. Children from households in the top cluster of classes generally start the game of snakes and ladders near the top, whereas most children from households in the bottom cluster start right at the bottom. Children from households in the middle cluster of classes tend to enter the game halfway up.

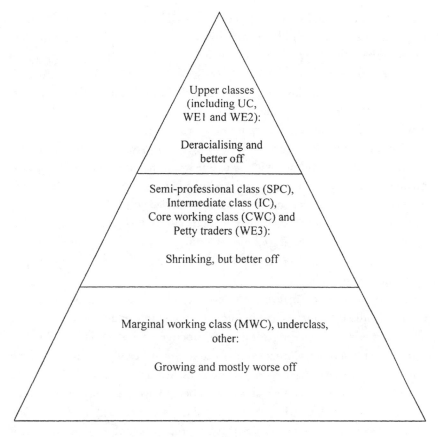

Figure 9.4. Stratification after apartheid. *Note:* See codes on p. 247.

Local studies allow us to describe in more detail the kinds of households at the bottom of the post-apartheid social structure. After apartheid, as at its end, the poor were overwhelmingly rural. Unemployment, which remained especially high in the former bantustans, underpinned poverty. A core group of the rural poor were former farm workers removed to quasi-urban settlements in the bantustans under apartheid. One such area was the QwaQwa bantustan, on the border between the (Orange) Free State and Lesotho. In the mid-1980s three distinct groups could be identified in QwaQwa. The richest of these comprised businessmen able to benefit from the dense population resulting from removals. The intermediate group comprised better-educated and -connected households in and around the town of Phuthaditjhaba, most of whom had been removed when entire Free State townships had been evicted. In the last years of apartheid this group enjoyed privileged access to the manufacturing jobs available in state-subsidised enterprises in the bantustans or as commuters to the nearer "white" towns (such as Harrismith in the case of QwaQwa). These jobs were poorly paid, but they were greatly preferable to unemployment. The mass of poorer households comprised primarily former farm workers settled in the remoter settlements outside Phuthaditjhaba; in this group, unemployment was high and poverty deep (Sharp 1994).

One reason why these former farm workers were so poor is that they were evicted from farms, without skills, at a time when the mines were cutting back on unskilled employment and only rehiring experienced and skilled mine workers. The former safety net provided by unskilled employment in the mines was pulled away. These former farm workers also lacked the connections that were so important in securing employment in manufacturing or services in the larger towns. Not only were they poor, but their children were disadvantaged by attending poor schools.

In 1998–99 researchers revisited QwaQwa. The closure of many of the formerly subsidised businesses had resulted in a rising tide of unemployment that affected everyone, including the formerly better-off households in Phuthaditjhaba. The value of remittances had also declined steadily. By the end of the 1990s, poverty was mitigated only when households had access to the meagre incomes earned in the informal sector or to old-age pensions (Slater 2001, 2002). A survey conducted in Phuthaditjhaba in 1998 revealed the desperation of households in the town. Three-quarters of the unemployed said that they would work for R63 per week, which was below the statutory minimum wage and about one-half the value of the old-age pension at the time (Nattrass 2000c).

The end of apartheid meant that farm workers were no longer forced into the former bantustans. Murray examined one group of ex-farm workers in the Free State who had moved into a shack settlement on the edge of the nearest town. Across the Free State as a whole, the "overwhelming majority" of the people in such shack settlements were evicted farm workers (Murray 2000a, 122). Without local employment, such households relied on remittances from migrants or old-age pensions. A survey conducted in the rural Western Cape in 2002 revealed the extent of poverty among households that moved from farms into shack settlements, generally because farms both reduced their permanent labour force and were anxious about the liability of housing workers on the farms. Unemployment was rife, and the jobs, already scarce, were often seasonal only (Du Toit 2003).

These kinds of households, whether in the Western Cape or the Free State, comprised the "underclass" (or the residual class). At best, they rose into the marginal working class, securing employment on farms, perhaps on a seasonal basis. Some—including especially the wives and children of migrant workers—received remittances, but the value of remittances sent to rural areas was probably declining (as rural kin with urban connections moved to town). Having a job meant that farm and domestic workers were better off then the underclass, but wages were generally so low as to leave many in poverty. When statutory minimum wages were gazetted for these sectors in 2000–3, the state was heedful of job losses and kept the minima low at R600 to R800 per month, depending on location.

Given the absence of opportunities in such rural areas, including small towns, why do these households not migrate to the bigger metropolitan or industrial areas? Most local studies of such households do not address this question. In Phuthaditjhaba, unemployed people interviewed in 1998 said that they remained there because they did not know anyone in the bigger towns and cities (Nattrass 2000c). People of working age who had contacts in the urban labour markets did move. Given that social—and human—capital were often spatially located, meaning that some communities had more of each than did others, some rural areas were much less vulnerable to poverty than were others. A case study of neighbouring areas on the Eastern Cape coast, in the far south of the former Transkei, illustrates this. In Dwesa (Willowvale), a history of mission education, entrepreneurial traditions, and migration linkages to Cape Town under apartheid resulted, after it ended, in Dwesa's being better off than Cwebe and Hobani (in Elliotdale, just across the river from Dwesa). As Fay and Palmer (2000) write, post-apartheid differentiation had historical origins.

Chapter 10 The Post-Apartheid
Distributional Regime

In the decade following the end of apartheid, there was little change in the overall level of income inequality; if anything, inequality increased after several decades of stability. At the same time, the general trends that characterised the late apartheid period continued. Interracial income inequality continued to decline but intraracial inequality continued to grow. Expanding opportunities in high-paying occupations meant that African people comprised a rising proportion of the highest income deciles. At the same time, growing unemployment underpinned persistent and perhaps deepening poverty, especially in rural areas. Households lacking social and human capital were effectively shut out of the labour market. This was especially true among former farm workers and their children.

Yet starting in 1994, South Africa was governed by a party rhetorically committed to, and with a clear political interest in, addressing poverty and reducing overall levels of inequality. This government inherited the set of policies affecting inequality that we termed in Chapter 4 the late apartheid distributional regime. Although this was less overtly discriminatory than the distributional regime of the early decades of apartheid, it nonetheless underpinned inequality by rewarding existing advantage and penalising the already disadvantaged. The persistence of inequality after apartheid reflected the continuities between the late apartheid distributional regime and the post-apartheid distributional regime. In short, after 1994, government policies did not ensure equal opportunities for all in the new, democratic South Africa.

In previous chapters we defined the "distributional regime" as encompassing the combination of economic, labour-market, and industrial policies that affect the economic growth path (and hence income distribution) as well as policies that redistribute more directly by means of the provision of public welfare and the benefits in kind of other forms of government spending, especially public education. In the latter part of Chapter 4 we showed how the late apartheid distributional regime was characterised by policies that promoted a capital-intensive growth path, despite high unemployment, but increasingly mitigated the ensuing inequality with redistributive social spending, including especially public welfare (with old-age pension benefits finally deracialised in 1993) and public education. Opportunities were concentrated in the urban areas, whereas the bantustans served as dumping grounds where the unemployed could be geographically isolated and thus more easily controlled politically.

In this chapter we examine changes in these policies in the decade following democratisation in 1994. The first section looks at the ANC-led governments' emphasis on deracialisation. Although deracialisation covered labour-market policies, public education, and social welfare policies, the major emphasis was on the promotion of a black economic elite and middle classes. As we suggested in Chapter 9, this helped change the racial composition of upper income deciles but was of little consequence for either poverty or overall inequality. The second section turns to the economic growth path, showing how policies continued to promote inequality. We then turn to redistribution via the budget. Overall, we show that key public policies were reformed rather than transformed after 1994, with the result that there was further deracialisation of opportunities at the top end of the income distribution but no or limited change in the position of people at the bottom end. It is crucial to realise that public policies exacerbated rather than mitigated the problem of unemployment. In the final section we analyse the politics of redistribution, explaining why there was not more political pressure to transform the distributional regime.

DERACIALISATION AND DISTRIBUTION

In the decade following its election into office in 1994, the ANC-led government consistently emphasised the priority of challenging the racially divided nature of South African society. Thabo Mbeki, then deputy president, famously expressed this in his "two nations" speech in Parliament in 1998. South Africa, he said, comprised "two nations, the one black and the other white":

> One of these nations is white, relatively prosperous, regardless of gender or geographical dispersal. It has ready access to a developed economic, physical, educational, communication and other infrastructure. This enables it to argue that, except for the persistence of gender discrimination against women, all members of this nation have the possibility of exercising their right to equal opportunity, and the development opportunities to which the Constitution of 1993 committed our country. The second and larger nation of South Africa is black and poor, with the worst-affected being women in the rural areas, the black rural population in general and the disabled. This nation lives under conditions of grossly underdeveloped economic, physical, educational, communication and other infrastructure. It has virtually no possibility of exercising what in reality amounts to a theoretical right to equal opportunity, that right being equal within this black nation only to the extent that it is equally incapable of realisation. (*Hansard,* 29 May 1998, col. 3378)

The notion of a society comprising two nations was not original. Benjamin Disraeli, who was later to become prime minister of Britain, first used this imagery in his 1845 novel *Sybil, or the Two Nations.* For Disraeli, the two nations were the rich and the poor of nineteenth-century England: "Two nations between whom there is no intercourse and no sympathy; who are as ignorant of each other's habits, thoughts and feelings, as if they were dwellers in different zones, or inhabitants of different planets; who are formed by a different breeding, are fed by different food, are ordered by different manners, and are not governed by the same laws" (1845/1930, 74). He contrasted the opulence of aristocratic life with the desperate squalor of industrial poverty, although his primary emphasis was on the social and cultural divide, rather than economic inequality per se. More recently, the imagery of two nations has been used in the United States with reference to interracial inequalities. Ghetto riots in the 1960s led to warnings from the National Advisory Commission on Civil Disorders that "our nation is moving toward two societies, one black, one white, separate and unequal." In 1992 a popular American political scientist, Andrew Hacker, used the imagery in a book on America titled *Two Nations, Black and White: Separate, Hostile, and Unequal.* Hacker surveyed the scope of interracial inequalities in late twentieth-century America across issues as varied as divorce rates, percentages of children born to unmarried parents, earnings and incomes, unemployment, educational achievement, and crime.

Mbeki's use of "two nations" imagery was like Disraeli's and Hacker's in that it was intended to draw attention to injustice. But, in contrast to Disraeli, Mbeki was not concerned with class but with race. Unlike Hacker, Mbeki reduced inequality to race: black equalled poor and white equalled rich. Indeed, Mbeki claimed, black South Africans were "equally incapable" of realising the right of equal opportunity. If Mbeki had attached more importance to social and cultural divides between white and black South Africans he would have been on stronger ground, but in emphasising interracial economic inequality he misunderstood the changing nature of inequality in South Africa, as we have described it in previous chapters. Race and class are no longer coterminous. A more appropriate use of the discourse of separate nations would mirror the image painted of the United States by America's Catholic bishops in 1995: "The US economy sometimes seems to be leading to three nations living side by side, one growing prosperous and powerful, one squeezed by stagnant incomes and rising economic pressures and one left behind in increasing poverty, dependency and hopelessness" (quoted in Fisher et al. 1996, 3). In South Africa, these descriptions fit the three categories identified in figure 7.1 and discussed further in Chapter 9. Of these, the prosperous category is increasingly multiracial, the middle one mostly African, and only the impoverished third one entirely African.

However ill-informed as an analysis of South African society, the "two nations" interpretation guided a wide range of policies under the Mandela and the Mbeki governments. Deracialisation was a dominant theme in public policy. With respect to distribution in particular, deracialisation had two major components. First, the government completed the process of removing racial discrimination from public policy. This is discussed below with reference to labour market and welfare policies. Second, it pursued policies designed to open up new economic opportunities for black—especially African—South Africans via policies of affirmative action and "black economic empowerment" (BEE). Affirmative action (or "employment equity") entailed expediting the promotion of designated groups—including African people and sometimes coloured and Indian people and even white women—in the labour market, and specifically moving them into higher-paid occupations. The policy of BEE entailed expediting the expansion of black entrepreneurial and business-owning classes.

The view that this kind of economic deracialisation would transform more than the top end of society was widely voiced as affirmative action and BEE were provided for in legislation. The 1998 Employment Equity Act raised the pressure on employers to implement affirmative action—supposedly not only to redress past discrimination but also to build the country's human capital more generally. The Black Economic Empowerment Act was passed in 2003 (following proposals made by the Black Economic Empowerment Commission, appointed in 1998). This act, according to the leading commentator Vuyo Jack, was "a turning-point, a historic moment which will have far-reaching consequences for the economy and the country as a whole. The country now has a legal framework for redressing the economic imbalances of the past." And, to underline the point, Jack added that "the ordinary man on the street now has a real chance to participate in the mainstream economy" (quoted in *Business Report*, 11 January 2004).

Affirmative action contributed to the fast-changing racial composition of higher-earning occupations identified in Chapter 9, especially in the public sector, and thus to the continuing shift in shares of income by race. The promotion of black business might also contribute to changing patterns of inequality. Using the 1993 PSLSD data, we can calculate that redistributing one-half of the income received by white households from *all* wealth and business activity to black households would have had the effect in 1993 of redistributing 6 percent of total income, that is, of reducing the white income share by about one-eighth and increasing the African income share by one-sixth. But redistributing income from business and wealth could only be of minor importance compared to shifts in the labour market. In 1993 the total income earned from business and wealth was less than one-third the total income earned from employment. Black economic empowerment could only make a limited difference to the overall distribution of earnings and incomes unless it increased the number of jobs or expanded significantly the small business sector so as to reduce unemployment.

Apologists for BEE suggested that it would increase skills in the economy and expand the consumerist middle class (the so-called missing middle), both of which will boost growth. The policy was presented as a growth or developmental strategy that would have a wide reach via "broad-based empowerment," including small- and medium-sized enterprises, pension fund investment, worker-owned cooperatives, and even rural trusts.[1] But in practice BEE focused on the very top: first, the transfer of equity, especially in the major corporations that dominate the high-profile sectors, and, second, procurement policies that reserve government and parastatal contracts for black-owned contractors. There is no reason to believe that these resulted (or could result) in increased employment or in a significantly increased small business sector. Indeed, the expense of complying with BEE requirements might have reduced investment in other perhaps more directly productive directions. It is unsurprising that critics, including President Thabo Mbeki's brother Moeletsi Mbeki, have charged that BEE entailed simply "enrichment of the few": "Black economic empowerment is an issue for the black middle class and big business." For big business it was a politically defensive strategy, not a growth-enhancing one, and for the black middle class it was a state-subsidised enrichment strategy. For "ordinary folks," Moeletsi Mbeki said, "it's really not an issue."[2]

In practice, BEE had a limited effect on business *ownership* in the first ten years of post-apartheid government. Measuring BEE is a notoriously difficult task. Studies typically focused on identifiable BEE "deals" and the ownership structure of companies listed on the Johannesburg Stock Exchange (JSE). In 2002, sixty-two deals were identified, with a value of R8 billion, whereas black-controlled firms accounted for only 3 percent of JSE market capitalisation, and black beneficial ownership (sharing in profit and risks but not necessarily in management) was estimated at between 12 and 15 percent of the JSE.[3] Although public procurement policies, which are harder still to measure, were probably more successful in terms of building black-owned business, the overall transfer of opportunities remained small.

This slow transformation of capitalist ownership is what drove the state in 2003 to a more interventionist approach, including the BEE Act. Assessing this shift, Southall concluded that the ANC government was "leaning towards construction of a pro-capitalist, Malaysian-style, interventionist state prepared to use its power, influence and divestment of assets to create a black bourgeoisie, expand the black middle class, and to generally produce a seismic transfer of wealth from white to black over a ten to twenty year period" (Southall 2003, 15–16). Even a "seismic" shift would, however, have a limited effect on overall patterns of income distribution. In any capitalist economy, ownership is in flux as new generations of entrepreneurs take over from or force out older generations. The main effects of BEE were (and would be) to accelerate this process while largely restricting the new opportunities to black South Africans, but it would not change significantly overall patterns of distribution. Those patterns depended, rather, on the broad growth path of the post-apartheid economy, changes in the labour market, and patterns of public social expenditure.

THE POST-APARTHEID GROWTH PATH

At the start of the negotiated transition in 1990, the ANC did not have a clearly formulated economic policy. The Freedom Charter, which had been adopted at the Congress of the People in 1955, was the ANC's closest approximation of a development strategy. It contained a commitment to redistribution and a strongly interventionist role for the state that included the regulation, control, and outright nationalisation of key sectors of the economy. Days after his release from prison in 1990, Nelson Mandela restated his support of nationalisation. But when this resulted in adverse market reactions and vocal criticism from business constituencies, the ANC embarked on a rapid process of policy reformulation. Over the next four years, economic policy statements evolved from an initial support for "growth through distribution" to more orthodox-sounding positions that eschewed nationalisation and committed the government not to embark on any inflationary or debt-driven expansion of demand (Nattrass 1994a).

This shift in policy stance from what appeared to be a form of socialism to more market-friendly strategies has been attributed by some analysts to the power of big business and the international financial institutions to impose their ideology on the prospective government (Bond 1996; Marais 1998; Terreblanche 2002). Whether this was the case or whether it was a function of genuine intellectual conversion or pragmatic adjustment to the realpolitik of the post-communist world, remains uncertain. What is clear is that in 1994 the ANC still seemed committed to a social democratic vision in which the needs of both organised labour and the poor would be addressed, but within a capitalist economic framework.

The new generation of policy makers had high hopes for transforming the economy in ways that brought further gains for organised labour but that also benefited capital, thereby promoting wages and growth (and thus jobs). Think tanks such as the Industrial Strategy Project argued that industrial and labour-market policies could propel the economy onto a new and better "high-wage, high value-added" growth path (Joffe et al. 1995). This strategy had several components. First, firms in "priority sectors" were to be provided with targeted support to help them to adopt new technologies and to develop export links. This idea was backed by comparative research that showed that a "developmental state" could support export-oriented industrialisation and help firms become competitive (Amsden 1980; Wade 1990; Weiss 1998).

Second, active labour-market policies were deemed necessary to promote skills development and training. It was hoped that training would facilitate higher wages without harming profitability because skilled workers are more productive than unskilled workers. Increased minimum wages were in fact seen as a lever to force firms to shift away from low-wage, low-value-added activities. The idea was simple: faced with higher wages for unskilled labour, firms would be compelled to upgrade their technologies and train their workers or face a profit squeeze. Supply-side measures (such as government support for training) would help firms make the necessary transition without shedding labour or going out of business. The firms that would go out of business despite government support for training were regarded as undesirable anyway, the general view being that South Africa could do without such sweatshops and "fly-by-night" producers. Proponents of this high-wage, high value-added strategy optimistically assumed that workers who lost their jobs would be reemployed once the economy shifted onto a higher and better growth path. In the meantime, they would be supported by public works programmes and other expanded welfare measures.

It was a commonly held assumption among ANC-aligned economists and policy strategists that the new government would pursue additional policies to promote job creation. They expected the government to embark on a major housing programme, thereby boosting the labour-intensive construction industry. This was one of the key proposals of the ANC's Macroeconomic Research Group (MERG 1993). They also expected an expanded national public works programme to provide some relief for the unemployed. The ANC's 1994 election manifesto, the Reconstruction and Development Programme (RDP), supported such expectations (ANC 1994). The RDP also referred to "basic welfare rights," which apparently embraced "the right to basic needs such as shelter, food, health care, work opportunities, income security and all those aspects that promote the physical, social and emotional wellbeing of all people in our country, with special provision made for those who are unable to provide for themselves because of special problems" (ibid., 52).

In short, this bold new social democratic vision saw the state providing a safety net for the poor while promoting major structural adjustment toward a high-wage, high-productivity economy. With their eyes fixed firmly on the long term, the new policy makers hoped that orthodox yet mildly redistributive macroeconomic policies would encourage private investment and that targeted industrial policies would provide further support for business while also increasing the number of new "good" jobs. Labour-market policies were seen as necessary for improving the supply of skilled labour and to help eliminate low-productivity (and hence low-wage) activities. Whereas the old apartheid growth model relied on cheap labour to drive accumulation, the proposed post-apartheid model saw higher wages as both a policy weapon to bring about, and an outcome of, a high-productivity growth path (MERG 1993; Joffe et al. 1995).

These ideas and arguments formed the intellectual basis for many of the post-apartheid government's industrial and labour policies, which we have described elsewhere as South Africa's "high productivity now" strategy (Nattrass 2001). This strategy entailed a mixture of incentives to encourage training and the development of high-value-added forms of economic activity and continued support for the aspects of labour market policy that hinder the creation of low-wage, labour-intensive jobs. One arm of the strategy was implemented by the Department of Trade and Industry (DTI) by means of its various supply-side policies to encourage South Africa's pattern of industrial production to move "up the value chain," that is, to shift the economic structure toward a more skill-intensive growth path. The other arm was implemented by the Ministry of Labour, which introduced various measures (including a skills levy on business to fund sectoral training initiatives) to promote a more highly skilled labour force earning higher wages and working under better conditions.

The post-apartheid government kept the old industrial conciliation machinery intact (including the extension of collectively bargained agreements to non-parties), thereby ensuring close continuity between the pre- and post-apartheid labour-welfare nexus. Trade unions and employers set minimum wages in bargaining councils that were then extended by the minister of labour to all firms in the industry. Given that bargaining councils were dominated by the relatively large (and better-paying) employers, the extension of the minimum wage to smaller, more labour-intensive firms may well have undermined the growth of labour-intensive firms and sectors, thus contributing to the growth of unemployment (Nattrass 2000b). This, however, was only one among many factors that contributed to the rise in unemployment during the 1990s.

With the benefit of hindsight, it is now clear that the High Productivity Now strategy was hopelessly overoptimistic on all fronts. As shown in Chapter 9, formal employment fell sharply and has been a major factor behind the increase in unemployment and poverty. Most disappointingly, employment fell in manufacturing, the very sector that was supposed to lead the South African economy on a new growth path. In 2003, Kaplan (who had been part of the old Industrial Strategy Project and then worked for the DTI) documented the poor score card for manufacturing and, by implication, for the DTI. Kaplan (2003) observed that South Africa's manufacturing sector performed poorly in comparison with those other countries and that output growth was only marginally higher in the 1990s than the 1980s. Even the country's most dynamic manufacturing products performed disappointingly. The DTI's own research revealed that firms that had been targeted for special support either did not know about the policies or thought they were of limited help. The ambitious vision of a DTI as the main arm of a developmental state providing supply-side support and direction to private industry was clearly not realistic. According to Kaplan, part of the problem was that the DTI had too many objectives in relation to available capacity to deliver.

To make matters worse, firms faced a very difficult macroeconomic environment in the 1990s. Instead of injecting demand into the economy, the new government was forced to deal with high levels of government debt and an explosive budget deficit, both legacies in large part of the profligate final years of the old apartheid government. Then, once the debt situation had been brought under control, this macroeconomic stance was codified into the so-called Growth, Employment, and Redistribution strategy (GEAR) of 1996. This strategy effectively sidelined the RDP and committed the government to more orthodox fiscal policies. The gamble taken by the Ministry of Finance was that this stance would encourage investment by sending a signal to investors that government finances would be "responsible" (Nattrass 1996). Historically high rates of investment in East Asia have been attributed to the absence of inflationary deficit financing (Birdsall and Jaspersen 1997). The GEAR modellers hoped to create precisely such a pro-investment environment.

The problem with this macroeconomic strategy was that one of the most important determinants of whether a firm invests is whether it expects to be able to sell its products. A high level of demand thus encourages higher investment (Chirinko 1993). If the government holds back on spending, and if private-sector incomes are growing slowly, then firms will worry about poor market conditions. They will lack confidence to invest, no matter what signals the minister of finance tries to send them about sound fiscal policy. Sluggish economic conditions in the 1990s may well have prevented investors from becoming the driving force for growth (as hoped for by the proponents of GEAR). Instead, private investment grew at about one-tenth the rate that the state had projected for the period 1996 to 1999 (Nattrass and Seekings 2001a).

Any assessment of GEAR is complicated by the fact that large parts of the strategy were never implemented. Only two of its four major components were implemented by 2004: the reduced budget deficit and trade liberalisation. The other two—labour market reforms and privatisation—were not. The pattern of labour market reforms certainly contributed to GEAR's not meeting its targets. Before the strategy was announced, the government had enacted the new Labour Relations Act, which entrenched and extended the system of wage determination by means of centralised bargaining. Following GEAR, the government enacted further legislation that contrasted with the vision of a more flexible labour market set out in GEAR. The 1997 Basic Conditions of Employment Act provided for longer annual and family leave (thus increasing the indirect cost of employing labour) and reduced hours of work (thus increasing hourly fixed costs). The overtime premium was also increased; the result was that "the total overtime premium in South Africa amount[ed] to up to two and a half times that of an employee working the same hours in a comparable upper middle-income country" (Barker 1999, 19). The government also extended minimum wage floors. Promised reforms to existing labour laws—such as amendments to the mandatory extension of collectively bargained agreements to nonparties—did not materialise.[4] The cost of retrenching workers rose in both administrative and directly financial terms.

According to evidence from the OECD (1999, 156–59), countries that have undergone macroeconomic stabilisation without addressing such labour market issues have paid the price of higher unemployment. Failure to coordinate fiscal, monetary, and labour-market policy is one of the many reasons for the decline in employment. The government has also failed to deliver jobs via short-term poverty-relief programmes. Although great plans for public works projects and the like were trumpeted (for example, RSA 1998a), the government had little success in deploying the few funds that were actually allocated for such purposes. State institutions lacked the capacity to implement policies (Nattrass and Seekings 1998). The Department of Welfare (later renamed Social Development) and the Department of Public Works were strongly criticised for their inability to spend funds allocated for job creation and poverty alleviation programmes.[5] The Department of Water Affairs, which ran the Working for Water public works programme, was an exception to this general pattern.

Some of the causes of South Africa's lacklustre growth performance were beyond the control of the government. The Asian crisis and the overzealous monetary policies of the independent reserve bank both acted as unexpected economic brakes. But it is nevertheless a moot point whether the government should have continued with its restrictive fiscal policies given the recessionary conditions of the time (Weeks 1999). There is mounting evidence that pursuing antiinflationary policies undermined growth in the developing world (Stiglitz 1998), and South Africa is unlikely to have been an exception to the rule. Furthermore, by continuing with trade liberalisation in the absence of labour-market reforms, the government probably contributed to employment losses. Industries that competed with imports (particularly the more labour-intensive industries, such as the clothing industry) were particularly hard-hit, with the result that South Africa's export industries became increasingly capital-intensive (Bell and Cattaneo 1997; ILO 1999).[6]

Under these conditions, it is not surprising that many manufacturing firms felt beleaguered rather than supported by government. As noted above, DTI surveys of firms reported complaints about labour regulations (particularly restrictions on firing) and the cost of labour (Kaplan 2003). Labour-intensive firms and sectors were particularly vulnerable. As these relatively low-wage, low-value-added activities died out, employment fell and average productivity rose. This was in line with the expectations of those who argued in favour of using a higher minimum wage as an instrument of industrial restructuring. The problem with this strategy, however, was that the supply-side policies behind rapid growth in high-value-added sectors did not work, and there was nowhere else for workers to find employment when they were retrenched.

By the early twenty-first century, South Africa had more of a high-wage, high-value-added economy, but the benefits were restricted mainly to (predominantly skilled) workers who had retained their jobs and to capitalists who had remained in business. By restructuring and "downsizing" their workforces, firms ensured that each remaining worker contributed more on average to output (that is, became more productive). They were also able to restore profitability.

One indication of profitability is the gross profit share (the share of gross output going to the owners of capital). If the growth in labour productivity is greater than the growth in real wages, then workers are contributing more to output growth than they are getting back in wages, and hence the share of output going to capitalists (the profit share) will rise. Figure 10.1 shows that the average rate of growth of productivity in South Africa exceeded that of real wages for most of the 1990s. As a result, the aggregate profit share was about 10 percent higher in 2001 than it was in 1990. Capitalists also benefited from rising rates of profit (the rate of return on capital) in most sectors. The High Productivity Now strategy appears to have resulted in rising real wages for workers with jobs. But it did little to improve the economy's capacity to create jobs. In the post-apartheid distributional regime, the unemployed were the biggest losers.

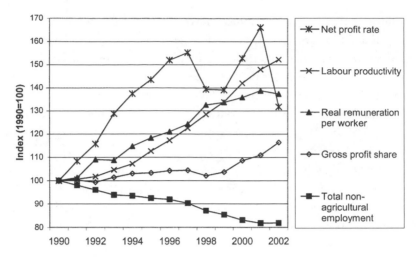

Figure 10.1. Labour productivity, employment, wages, and profitability, 1990–2002.
Source: South African Reserve Bank.

The South African government gambled that the shift to greater capital and skill intensity would provide a new engine for sustainable growth in the medium to long term. Unfortunately, skill shortages (which drove up the price of skilled labour relative to unskilled labour) continued to act as a constraint on growth—and this situation was exacerbated by the brain drain of young white professionals that was in part due to affirmative action policies.

One sector in which changes have particularly serious implications for the poor and hence for distribution is agriculture, despite its limited importance to the economy as a whole. At the end of apartheid, a high proportion of the marginal working class or the "working poor" were unskilled farm workers and their dependents, and commercial agriculture accounted for a considerable share of unskilled jobs in the country as a whole. Many households in the underclass comprised former farm workers who had been moved from farms to the resettlement areas in the former bantustans. The expansion of employment, including unskilled employment, on commercial farms would therefore have brought major benefits to the poor, as would improved access to land via land reform. But the post-apartheid distributional regime proved to be disastrous for the rural poor because policies contributed to continued deagrarianisation: farm workers continued to be evicted from commercial farms in large numbers and there was no major programme to resettle families onto smallholdings, so these largely unskilled families were pushed into the most disadvantaged positions in a labour market characterised by massive unemployment.

These evictions, unlike the ones carried out under apartheid, were the unintended consequences of policies intended to be pro-poor. The first set of policies was concerned with the liberalisation and deregulation of agricultural marketing. Under apartheid, as we saw in Chapter 4, white farmers benefited from massive state support, directly (in the form of government subsidies that invariably promoted capital-intensive production) and indirectly (in the form of marketing institutions that pushed up producer prices, to the disadvantage of consumers). Prices had been set on a generally "cost-plus" basis by monopolistic parastatal marketing institutions. In the early 1990s the state began to deregulate so as to eliminate subsidies to a tiny, privileged minority, thereby also reducing disincentives to labour-intensive production, and also to reduce consumer prices. This process was completed by the ANC government after 1994. The massive maize and wheat boards were abolished in 1997, and all other domestic marketing boards (except for sugar) followed in 1999. These shifts squeezed many smaller family farms, leading to further consolidation of commercial farmland into fewer, less labour-intensive farms.

As agricultural product markets were being deregulated, agricultural labour markets were regulated. Labour legislation was applied to the commercial farming sector, together with statutory minimum wages and social insurance (via the Unemployment Insurance Fund). Security of tenure, in terms of access to land and housing, was provided by the Extension of Tenure Security Act of 1997. All of these were intended to protect the working poor. The effect might have been the opposite. Landowners evicted farm workers in anticipation of the 1997 Act and thereafter continued to reduce the labour force resident on farms. Labour legislation also prompted employers to reduce their labour requirements, leading to rising capital intensity. This could be achieved in various ways, including changing crop patterns, shifting from crops to livestock, or converting agricultural land into game farming. Permanent employment was widely replaced by part-time or seasonal employment. Farmers even began to outsource labour-intensive activities. Growing agricultural production, in part a response to export opportunities, raised the demand for skilled labour, but the demand for unskilled labour continued to fall. Overall, as we saw in Chapter 9, agricultural employment declined dramatically. The rural poor were further impoverished by diminished access to on-farm housing and the other benefits of paternalism. The consequence was yet another generation of former farm workers, this one removed to shack settlements surrounding agricultural towns (see, for example, Du Toit 2003).

In the mid-1990s there emerged a vocal lobby advocating reagrarianisation by means of land reform. Some scholars as well as the World Bank argued that land reform could create a productive and sustainable class of smallholding farmers or peasants, reversing the process of deagrarianisation analysed in Chapter 3. Land reform could, it was argued, make a major contribution to reducing unemployment. Indeed, given the high level of prevailing wages when compared to international competitors', land reform was arguably the most promising strategy for reducing unemployment (Lipton et al. 1996; also Binswanger and Deininger 1993). Lipton et al. describe an imaginary nine-hundred-hectare farm using irrigation, tractors, combines, and centre pivots to grow maize but employing fewer than ten workers. "Alternatively," they suggest, "on the same land, three hundred farmers, each with three hectares, might mix maize with higher value beans on most of the land, growing intensive vegetables on the better soil, ploughing with stall-fed oxen, and irrigating with small scale manual methods, with mainly family labour plus seasonal employees. . . . If labour is plentiful, capital and irrigation scarce, and land becoming scarce, then the small farm system is more socially efficient. This is disguised if big farmers, or their political agents, succeed in biasing in their favour prices of (or institutions that allocate) water, research, credit, and other inputs" (ibid., vi).

This optimistic approach, based on an insufficiently critical reading of the Kenyan experience (see Chapter 3), initially found favour in the post-apartheid state. From 1994 to 2000, the state provided subsidies to enable African small farmers to buy land at market prices from white landowners. The government initially set itself the target of transferring about thirty million hectares, or 30 percent of the country's medium- to high-quality farmland, to six hundred thousand households by 1999. Some of this would be parceled out via land restitution—that is, the return of land to individuals or groups dispossessed under apartheid—but the lion's share would be transferred via a "willing buyer, willing seller" process. Poor people would be able to purchase land using a means-tested subsidy equal in value to the subsidy available in urban areas for housing (initially R15,000). Small farmers would have to join together, pool their subsidies and whatever other capital they could lay their hands on, and buy a farm from a landowner. After a very slow start, redistribution accelerated from 1996. By 2001, however, only 732,000 hectares had been transferred to about 87,000 poor households (Aliber and Mokoena 2003, 333).

Many of the beneficiaries were, in fact, not so poor. Murray (2000a) documents one example from the Free State. This family, headed by Qhesi Matsau, had made money in other small businesses before being granted a temporary lease on a five-hundred-acre farm, which they "shared" with the former farmer's workers—although only the family had much livestock. At the end of 1995 the farm was allocated to four applicants, each of whom qualified for a R15,000 subsidy. The applicants were Qhesi Matsau, his son-in-law, his sister's son, and his own son. The family then tried to squeeze the former farm workers off "their" land. As Murray summarises: "Matsau was typical of a stratum of local businessmen who were relatively well placed, on account of their established urban enterprises and corresponding ability to fund farming operations, to take advantage of the new opportunity" (ibid., 133).

Deininger and May (2000), in a study of the land reform experiment, concluded that, with minor reforms, it could make a major contribution to reducing poverty in rural areas. Schirmer (2000) was more sceptical. Land reform would not work, he argued, because smallholder productivity was low because smallholders lacked access to the necessary capital. Only if the state provided massive financial assistance could smallholders make the necessary investments and prosper. In addition, small farmers were especially vulnerable to price fluctuations, drought, and disease, struggled to mobilise family labour, and perhaps had lost their knowledge of farming. Just as many poor families left land unused or underused (see Schirmer 2000, 155–63), so land reform was more likely to result in land being used for residential than for productive purposes. Aliber and Mokoena (2003) suggest a different explanation for the poor performance of farmers on redistributed land: the Department of Land Affairs emphasised the continuation of the capital-intensive farming activities conducted by the former landowner and the generation of good livelihoods for a small number of people working full-time. The new farmers made little use of the one factor that most had in copious supply: labour.

In 1999 the new minister of land affairs and agriculture placed a moratorium on new redistribution projects pending a review of policy. The minister soon decided that the existing policy was neither fiscally nor administratively viable. In 2000 she announced a major policy shift, ending support for small farmers or peasants and shifting instead to an emphasis on black commercial farmers. Under the new policy, tellingly called Land Redistribution for Agricultural Development, government subsidies would be much larger for African farmers investing other funds of their own. In other words, the larger subsidies would be given to farmers with funds of their own already. The maximum grant would be a massive R100,000. The new minister of (both) land and agriculture explained the new policy in terms of BEE and the imperative of "deracialising" land ownership (Greenberg 2003; Mapadimeng 2003). The redistribution of land remained slow. In 2003 the government finally passed legislation allowing, under specific conditions, for the appropriation of land at market value; that is, it abolished the "willing seller" provision (but not the requirement that compensation be paid at market value). This was likely to expedite the redistribution of land to new commercial black farmers.

Overall, therefore, government policy has not succeeded in being pro-poor. Farm workers have experienced continued retrenchment and dispossession, despite supposedly protective legislation. Land reform has not benefited the poor significantly. The reforms that have been implemented have generally been to the benefit of a constituency that was already relatively advantaged. In this crucial sector, the post-apartheid distributional regime has not resulted in improved livelihoods for the poor.

REDISTRIBUTION VIA THE BUDGET

Budgetary redistribution is a core component of most distributional regimes in capitalist economies. Democratic states are typically subject to political demands to mitigate the inequalities generated in the market via redistributive patterns of taxation and public expenditure (see Chapter 1). The scope for increasing such redistribution in South Africa after 1994 was constrained predominantly by two factors. The first was the government's commitment to conservative macroeconomic policies, which precluded large increases in overall government spending without matching increases in taxation. The second was the fact that the ANC-led Government of National Unity inherited a budget that was already surprisingly redistributive. Despite these constraints, the value and effects of redistribution via the budget increased after 1994, according to standard measures, with the result that South Africa redistributed more extensively by this means than any other developing country for which data were readily available (Seekings 2002a).

Such redistribution entails the combination of taxation, cash transfers (such as the old-age pension) and benefits in kind (such as public education, health care, and housing). The redistributive character of the budget at the end of the apartheid period was discussed in Chapter 4. As we saw, the three pillars of redistribution were a progressive and efficient tax system, high enrollment rates among poor students, and an exceptional public welfare system based primarily on de facto universal and generous old-age pensions. McGrath et al. (1997) calculated that redistribution via taxes, cash transfers, and in-kind benefits reduced the Gini coefficient in 1993–94 from about 0.7 to about 0.6. Van der Berg recalculated the extent of redistribution, concluding that it was reduced to 0.6 after tax and cash transfers but to 0.51 if all social spending was taken into account.[7]

The budget became more redistributive after 1994. By 1997, according to Van der Berg (2001c), the Gini coefficient for the distribution of "income" was reduced by about eighteen percentage points (to about 0.50) if taxes and cash transfers were taken into account and by a further six percentage points (to perhaps 0.44) if the value of in-kind public social spending (primarily health care and education) was taken into account. Social spending on the poorest 40 percent of households (quintiles 1 and 2) rose by about 50 percent between 1993 and 1997. In 1993, 31 percent of public spending on education, health, social assistance, housing, and water was spent on households in the bottom quintile, compared to 21 percent on the second quintile and so on, up to only 12 percent on households in the top quintile (see table 10.1). By 1997 the proportion spent on the poorest quintile had risen to 33 percent, and the proportion on the top had fallen to 8 percent. During this period expenditure per capita rose, overall, by 24 percent. For the bottom three quintiles it rose faster than this overall average, whereas for the top two quintiles it actually fell. On the basis of these calculations, the Department of Finance (RSA 2000b, 145) claimed that "the first years after the political transition saw a large and significant shift of social spending from the affluent to the more disadvantaged members of society."

A small part of this was made possible by reduced spending on the rich, in that spending per capita on the top quintile actually declined. But the bulk of extra spending on the poor in the mid-1990s arose from increased and well-targeted spending by the government. Social spending, especially for public education, rose rapidly during this period. In the late 1990s, under the GEAR austerity program, real government spending declined by about one percent per year. Between fiscal years 1996–97 and 2000–1, social spending increased in real terms in the aggregate and rose as a proportion of total government spending—but at the same time it declined in real per capita terms and as a share of GDP (Van Zyl and Westhuizen 2003, 10). From 1999 onward, however, social spending increased in real terms at a very much faster rate. In the four financial years between 1999–2000 and 2003–4, total social spending was budgeted to increase in real terms by one-third again, outpacing the growth of the population or the GDP.[8]

Table 10.1. Social expenditure by income quintile, 1993 and 1997

| | Year | \multicolumn{6}{c}{Household income quintile} |
		1	2	3	4	5	Total
Primary and secondary education (%)	1993	23	23	19	18	17	100
[38%]	1997	29	28	20	14	9	100
Tertiary education (%)	1993	13	17	23	25	21	100
[8%]	1997	14	18	24	25	19	100
Health (%)	1993	26	25	24	18	7	100
[24%]	1997	28	26	24	16	7	100
Social assistance (%)	1993	59	18	13	8	2	100
[20%]	1997	58	18	14	8	2	100
Housing (%)	1993	9	12	19	28	32	100
[5%]	1997	33	47	5	7	8	100
Water (%)	1993	20	21	22	19	19	100
[4%]	1997	25	25	22	16	13	100
Total (%)	1993	31	21	22	19	19	100
[100%]	1997	33	25	19	14	8	100
Spending per capita	1993	1,969	1,246	1,364	1,686	1,569	1,555
(R)	1997	2,514	1,947	1,786	1,661	1,253	1,924
Increase or decrease in spending per capita (%)	1993–1997	+28	+56	+31	−2	−20	+24

Source: Van der Berg (2001c, 148). *Note:* Figures within square brackets in the stub are the shares of total social spending in each category in 1997.

The increased levels of social spending led the ANC government to claim, on the basis of extrapolating from the 1997 data, that it had further reduced "massively" the Gini coefficient (RSA 2003b, 17). But there is no thorough fiscal incidence analysis to support this. The only sector for which careful calculations have been done is social assistance, and that for only one year: 2000. Woolard (2003, 5) calculates that the share of social assistance going to households in the poorest quintile was almost the same in 2000 as Van der Berg had found in 1997; the proportion going to households in the top two quintiles was actually higher in 2000 than in 1997.

The increased and targeted expenditure entailed not *cash* income in the form of government welfare transfers but rather benefits *in kind*, especially in terms of public education (see table 10.1). Van der Berg (2001a) shows that the removal of indirect discrimination in teachers' salaries, together with the provision of some extra teachers and hence reduction in pupil-teacher ratios, entailed massive increases in spending in "African" schools, that is, schools with overwhelmingly African students, especially in poor rural areas. Under apartheid, teachers were paid on different salary scales. In 1996–97, all teachers were moved onto a single, consolidated salary scale, based on the scale of the former white education departments. Approximately 40 percent of teachers were moved into higher salary brackets, and average salaries rose by between 12 and 15 percent. This shift was probably driven by the need to deracialise salaries, especially given pressure from African teachers, rather than a concern with the poor. But if the value of public education is deemed equal to the cost of providing it, then the poor can be said to have benefited substantially from this increase (see further Seekings 2003c).

It is unlikely, however, that the quality of schooling improved dramatically, and the shift in spending toward the poor in this regard is probably somewhat misleading. Teachers in schools in poor areas remained inadequately qualified; many taught badly; some were often absent. In the short term, at least, the major beneficiaries of increased educational spending were teachers (who are not poor), not the students sitting in their classes. Unfortunately, there are no comprehensive indicators of the quality of education that can be matched with data concerning spending, because the only public examination was the school-leaving (matric) exam. But there is abundant evidence that the quality of education varied considerably and in many poorer areas was very low. Nationally, the pass rate for the matric examination (at the end of grade 12, or standard 10) was 58 percent in 2000 (with huge variations between provinces), but five hundred schools had a pass rate lower than 20 percent, and fifty-six schools failed to register a single pass. In 2001, 2002, and 2003, the matric pass *rate* improved rapidly, but the actual *number* of students passing matric rose only marginally, and the proportion of the total age cohort passing matric remained steady. Numeracy and literacy tests administered to samples of students in lower grades showed there were enormous variations within South Africa, but on average students' skills were lower than in any other country for which there are equivalent data (Seekings 2003c).

There are alternative ways of estimating the value of public expenditure on education. For example, the value of spending on an additional year of secondary schooling might be set at the estimated increase in earnings and income associated with that extra year of schooling. This would result in a much less egalitarian incidence, because the economic returns to education increase with each year of schooling. The value of schooling for children who later become professionals will be very high, but the value to children who spend their lives in unskilled employment or unemployed will be low.

In other areas besides education, apparently pro-poor public expenditure may not convert readily into sustained improvements in the lives of the poor. Considerable attention was paid after the year 2000 to the duration of benefit to the poor from public investments in municipal infrastructure, including especially the provision of water and electricity. Although government policy provided for free provision of limited water, an inability or unwillingness to pay for all water consumed led to a significant number of poor households having their water disconnected. McDonald (2002, 170), using data from a 2001 survey, claimed that ten million people had been affected by water cut-offs and a similar number by electricity disconnections; two million people had been evicted from their homes because they were unable to pay their water or electricity bills and a further 1.5 million people had had property seized. The government disputed these figures.[9] Although the precise numbers of households affected remained uncertain, it was clear that capital expenditure on the poor did not always lead to extended welfare benefits. Overall, therefore, there were substantial shifts in terms of where money was spent, but it is unclear how much the poor actually benefited in terms of the *quality* of the services provided.

One area in which government spending converts very closely into real and immediate gains for the poor is social assistance. The post-apartheid state inherited a very redistributive welfare system based around noncontributory old-age pensions and, to a much lesser extent, noncontributory disability and child maintenance grants. The total number of people receiving one or another of these grants rose from less than three million in the late 1990s to more than four million people—or one in ten South Africans—in May 2001 and almost six million by February 2003 (Woolard 2003, 2). The government's decision in 2003 to extend the cut-off age for child support grants was predicted to redistribute further tax revenues to the poor (see Van der Berg and Bredenkamp 2002).

The single most important instrument of redistribution via the budget is the old-age pension. As shown in Chapter 6, in 1993 pensions formed a major source of income for the poorest 40 percent of households. In the last years of apartheid the deracialisation of pension benefits was achieved with large increases in the real value of the pension paid to African people (see figure 4.2). Between 1993 and 2002 the real value of the old-age pension declined by an average of about 1.5 percent per year, or a total of about 20 percent, before rising

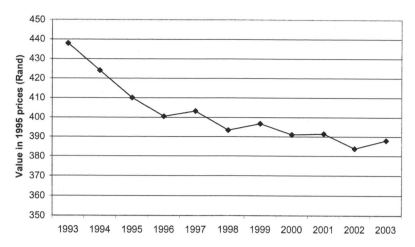

Figure 10.2. Real value of the old-age pension, 1993–2003

marginally in real terms in 2003 (see figure 10.2). This is perhaps because the new government believed that the dramatic increase in the African pension in the early 1990s was unwarranted and perhaps because of the government's commitment to restrain public spending. But the fact that the old-age pension declined faster than total government spending in the late 1990s indicates that the poor bore the brunt of the adjustment, while they also failed to benefit from expanded social spending after 2000.

Financial pressures on the Department of Welfare were certainly behind the far more drastic reduction in 1998 in the value of public financial support for low-income single parents. Until 1997, low-income single parents were eligible for State Maintenance Grants. The grant paid a basic R430 per month to the single parent plus R135 per child up to the age of eighteen years, subject to a limit of two children. Thus a single mother with two children could receive as much as R700 per month. In 1994, the combined value of State Maintenance Grants and foster care grants was almost R10 billion, paid out to about 400,000 beneficiaries (RSA 1994, 6.4). A little more than 200,000 children received the maintenance grants along with about 150,000 mothers (or, occasionally, other caregivers), suggesting that at least three in four recipient families were claiming benefits for one child only. The problem with the grants was that, even after the removal of racial restrictions on access, takeup rates among African parents were very low, especially in rural areas. In 1994, only one-fifth of the grants were paid to African recipients, whereas nearly 60 percent were paid to coloured recipients (ibid.). The grants absorbed 12 percent of the welfare budget. But if takeup rates had risen, the welfare budget would have skyrocketed (see, for example, IMF 1995).

Worried about the financial implications of increased takeup rates among the African poor, the national and provincial ministers of welfare were said to have considered terminating child support entirely. Instead, however, the minister appointed a Committee of Inquiry into Child and Family Support in February 1996. The committee, chaired by Francis Lund of the University of Natal, reported in late 1996. The committee proposed that the old State Maintenance Grants be replaced by new Child Support Grants at the much lower value of R75 per child, supposedly sufficient to cover food and clothing only, to the age of six years, and still for a maximum of two children. The grant would be subject to a maximum income of R800 per month. Applicants would also have to show that they had sought to secure financial support from the child's other parent, if appropriate, through the courts. The committee foresaw the new grant reaching as many as three million children by 2005 (IDASA 1997; Budlender 2000, 128–29). Obvious problems with the proposal were that the state lacked the capacity to deliver the grant in many poor areas, that the value of the grant was so low that many beneficiaries would still be living in deep poverty, and that a huge number of poor children over the age of six would receive no assistance whatsoever.

The cabinet accepted the Lund Committee's proposals in early 1997 and submitted them to Parliament. The proposals were met with public furor. Critics sympathetic to the financial constraints proposed instead that the grant be set at R135 per child per month, paid to the age of nine years. Haarmann and Haarmann calculated the total cost of the proposals on the basis of reasonable assumptions about the takeup rate (rising from 40 percent in the first year to 100 percent five years later) and administrative capacity. They showed that the total expenditure with the proposed changes would cost almost R3 billion less than the government spent on the existing State Maintenance Grants (IDASA 1997, 6–7). The compromise reached in Parliament was a grant of R100 per month up to age six, without the requirement that applicants try to secure support through the civil courts and with a phased withdrawal of the existing State Maintenance Grants. The result was that the Child Support Grant was introduced in April 1998 at a level of R100 a month. It was subsequently increased, reaching R160 per month in 2003.

The government defended this reform on the grounds that it freed resources for improved takeup rates in poorer parts of the country and was thus egalitarian. But initially takeup rates rose slowly. By June 2000 fewer than four hundred thousand applications had been made for the Child Support Grant, and takeup rates were highest in the richest province, Gauteng (Adams 2000, 3). Thereafter, however, takeup rates rose rapidly, passing two million in mid-2002 and nearly three million by July 2003 (Woolard 2003, 11). In 2003 the government began to extend the grant to older children, with the goal of covering children up to fourteen years of age.

Given that the value of the old-age pension declined in real terms and the reform of child support meant that much smaller amounts were dispensed in the short term, one might wonder what the Department of Welfare was doing to achieve the goals set out in the RDP and the Constitution. To be fair to the department, it faced considerable administrative challenges. In 1996 the minister of welfare appointed a Committee for the Restructuring of Social Security, chaired by Frank Chikane, to examine ways to integrate the segregated social security systems of the apartheid period, improve management, and combat fraud and corruption (which cost an estimated 10 percent of the budget, according to press estimates). The committee recommended that the welfare system be national rather than provincial in scope, with nationally determined norms and standards. The committee's work contributed to the drafting of the Social Welfare Action Plan in 1996 and the White Paper on Social Welfare, published in early 1997. It turned out, however, that the action taken by provinces to weed out fraudulent claims had actually denied pensions to many legitimate claimants, resulting in adverse publicity and litigation (see, for example, *Mail and Guardian,* 9 June 2000).

The Department of Welfare also sought to develop a clear strategy. The 1997 White Paper emphasised that social welfare should be "developmental" rather than simply dispensing "handouts." The minister explained what this meant at the height of the furor over child support: "In an ideal world, I too would wish to be able to spend more on social security in the immediate term. However, in a developing country such as ours, we have to balance competing demands and decide how to use scare resources in the most effective way. Ultimately, the most effective antidote to poverty is for all our people to have a meaningful stake in the economy. While administering cash transfers, the Department of Welfare, in collaboration with other ministries, has embarked on a number of projects aimed at giving a hand up to the many who remain excluded from the mainstream economy" (*Mail and Guardian,* 9 May 1997; see Budlender 2000, 125, 130–33). It was later revealed, however, that the department had failed to spend most of the funds earmarked for poverty relief programmes.

One important shift was the extension of unemployment insurance to cover workers in sectors that had previously been excluded. The Department of Labour extended the UIF to protect all workers in the private sector, including domestic, seasonal, and other informal workers. The benefit schedule was also revised to provide higher proportional benefits for low-income workers than for high-income workers. But these reforms did not bring public-sector workers into the UIF.

Although the fundamental shape of the welfare system remained unchanged, the ANC-led government faced growing pressures for major reform, focused on the proposal that a basic income grant be introduced. The grant would assist poor and especially unemployed people who were ineligible for the old-age pension because they were still young and who could not receive UIF because they had never contributed to it. The Congress of South African Trade Unions was at the forefront of demands for a basic income grant. In 1999 an interdepartmental task team was set up to investigate the issue, and in 2000 the Taylor Committee was appointed to report on the social security system as a whole (as we shall see further below).

One decade after the transition to democracy, therefore, the post-apartheid distributional regime remained much the same as its apartheid-era predecessor. Growth-path and labour-market policies buttressed the earnings of skilled workers while doing little to improve (if not actually reducing) the prospects that the largely unskilled unemployed would secure work. The welfare system provided generous assistance to old-age pensioners and limited assistance to single parents but none to the bulk of the poor—whose poverty was the result of unemployment. The children of the poor did benefit from redistribution via the budget, especially in the form of free public education and substantially free public health care, but the real value of these was muted by both the dire quality of much public schooling and the reality of high unemployment rates facing school-leavers (which reduced returns, measured in terms of income, to years spent in school).

The divide that existed between white and African households in the early apartheid period continued to shift, separating growing numbers of better-off African households from the African poor. The proportion of African households resorting to the private sector for the provision of welfare grew steadily. By 1997 almost one-fifth of the population was covered by private medical aid schemes, and coverage was closely related to income (South African Health Review 1997, 82). Most employees—including the core working and intermediate classes—were covered by private-sector retirement funds. Large numbers of

African people in urban areas paid fees to send their children to semiprivate schools. The provision of education, health, and retirement pensions had become increasingly linked to employment.

The AIDS pandemic was one challenge that the post-apartheid government failed to address in spectacular fashion, with the probable consequence of worsening inequalities (see Chapter 9). Despite the development of a comprehensive plan in the early 1990s and its adoption by the Government of National Unity in 1994, the government failed to implement a coherent or concerted effort to combat AIDS (Nattrass 2004). Instead, AIDS policy in the 1990s was characterised by scandal (the ANC's support for an "AIDS cure" that turned out to be a toxic industrial solvent), confusion, and hostility to using antiretrovirals for prevention and treatment. Even after it had been shown that it probably cost the government more to treat HIV-positive children for their AIDS-related opportunistic infections than it would have cost to save the children from HIV infection in the first place (by providing pregnant HIV-positive women with a short course of antiretrovirals), the government persisted in its refusal to implement a national mother-to-child transmission prevention programme. It took sustained legal action on the part of the Treatment Action Campaign to force the government to change its stance (ibid.). It was only in late 2003 that the government (again, in the face of an imminent legal challenge and mindful of the forthcoming election) agreed in principle to roll out a national treatment programme.

Analysis of redistribution via the budget generally focuses on the government's expenditure on social policies, including especially welfare, education, and health. But governments use other policies for distribution as well. Thus the appearance of what has been called a "hidden" welfare system comprising subsidies and tax breaks for special-interest groups, most of which include economically privileged members of society. Under apartheid, white farmers received massive support (as farmers do in most of the more advanced industrialised societies of the world). Some of these hidden programmes are very indirect. For example, racially discriminatory state procurement policies (one element of BEE) are difficult to cost, and it is hard to know how to assess the value of government investment of large sums in arms deals or port development that have a strong BEE component. If these were taken into account, then the state budget would appear far more redistributive in racial terms but far less redistributive in socioeconomic terms.

Nonetheless, post-apartheid South Africa did have an unusually generous and inclusive system of social assistance. It substantially reduced poverty among the elderly, the disabled, and poor families with young children (Woolard 2003). Its flaw was that the safety net nonetheless had a "loose weave," and many poor people fell through the holes (Samson 2002). As was the case with the apartheid distributional regime, the post-apartheid public welfare system made no provision for the many poor people who were not old enough to qualify for the old-age pension nor young enough to qualify for child support. There was no provision for the long-term unemployed, nor for people who had never been employed. Samson (2002) calculated that social assistance reduced the poverty gap by about 23 percent in 2001. Even with a 100 percent takeup of the grants then in place, the poverty gap would be reduced by 37 percent only. The extension of the child support grant to older children reduced further the poverty gap but came nowhere close to eliminating it. The apartheid distributional regime was premised on full employment; the post-apartheid distributional regime operated in the context of extremely high unemployment. The absence of any welfare net for the unemployed thus constituted a major problem.

The semiprivileged position of politically powerful African groups—including the urban industrial working class, sections of the intermediate class, and the semiprofessional class (especially teachers)—gave them good reasons to oppose a universal welfare system. If, as is likely, any radical welfare reform required increased taxation of these classes, they would become subsidisers of the poor rather than the beneficiaries of redistribution from the rich. Perversely, therefore, the legacy of apartheid included the formation of a politically powerful, cross-racial coalition of classes, some a lot more privileged than others, with an interest in opposing radical reforms to the distributional regime.

Tax reform in the decade following democratisation similarly failed to be markedly pro-poor. This is clearest with respect to trends in the incidence of income taxation. Figure 10.3 shows the income tax due on salaries at five different levels, kept constant in real terms. A farm worker with a monthly wage of R400 in 1993 prices would never have to pay income tax. An industrial worker with a monthly wage of R1,200 in 1993 prices should have paid a little more than 5 percent of his or her earnings in income tax in 1993–94. The effective income tax rate for an office worker (in the intermediate class) earning R2,500 per month in 1993 prices was about 16 percent, and junior professionals earning about R5,000 per month and executives earning about R10,000 per month paid income tax of about 28 percent and 35 percent of their earnings, respectively. Af-

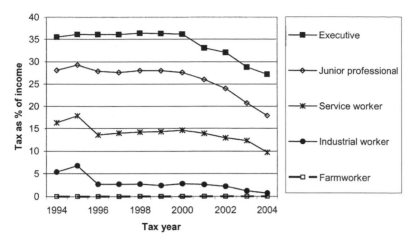

Figure 10.3. Income tax paid as a percentage of income for different occupations and earnings (set in constant real terms), 1994–2004. *Note:* Tax years are labeled according to the year in which they end, that is, the 1994 tax year is the 1993–1994 tax year.

ter 1994 tax rates rose briefly before declining steadily. By 2003–4, the executive was paying 27 percent of his earnings in income tax, the junior professional 18 percent, the office worker 10 percent, and the industrial worker almost nothing. What is clear is that income tax cuts across this decade benefited all earners who were paying any income tax, that is, anyone in the core working class and above. Figure 10.4 adds to the picture, showing the top marginal tax rate (on the left-hand axis) and the minimum income level at which any income tax was payable, that is, the tax threshold, presented in real terms (on the right-hand axis). The rich benefited from declining marginal tax rates, but the working class benefited from a rising tax threshold.

Overall, if we compare the late apartheid and post-apartheid distributional regimes, the continuities are at least as striking as the changes (compare figure 10.5 with figure 4.5). Deracialisation has continued, but the basic features of public policy affecting distribution and redistribution have changed little. The poor continued to be disadvantaged by industrial and labour-market policies that weaken the position of unskilled workers and contribute to unemployment. Although there is considerable redistribution via the budget, much of it is accounted for by education spending. Unfortunately, the quality of schooling does not match the sums spent on it. The post-apartheid system was not a pro-poor one.

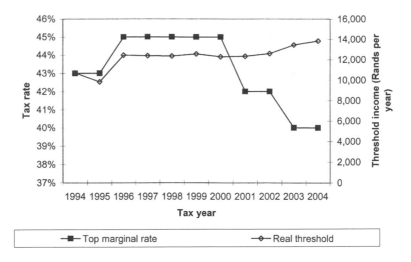

Figure 10.4. Income tax threshold (1993 prices) and top marginal income tax rates, 1994–2004. *Note:* Tax years are labeled according to the year in which they end, that is, the 1994 tax year is the 1993–1994 tax year.

THE POLITICS OF REDISTRIBUTION

The poor, overall, did not prosper in the decade following democratisation. As we saw in Chapter 9, inequality remained high, and perhaps grew, while poverty probably deepened. Moreover, trends in inter- and intragenerational mobility as well as in morbidity and mortality due to AIDS suggest that the poor suffered enduring disadvantage in a range of respects. Children growing up in poor households were likely to be disadvantaged in terms of both human capital (educational attainment) and social capital (connections in the labour market). They were (and are) much more likely to spend their lives moving between poorly paid, unskilled, and often casual work and long spells of unemployment. They were also more likely to fall sick and die, leaving dependents in an especially weak position. Churning in a labour market marked by high unemployment—and high rates of AIDS prevalence—meant that even people with regular, full-time employment could not be too confident of long-term income stability, but their prospects were much better than those of people from (and in) more disadvantaged settings. Some Africans enjoyed rapid real growth in earnings and income due to upward mobility. But the creation of more room for Africans at the top did not mean that all Africans had similar chances of getting to the top.

Why, then, were there not more pressures for a transformation of the distri-

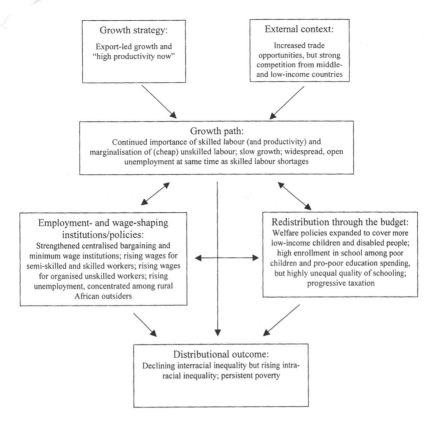

Figure 10.5. The post-apartheid distributional regime

butional regime, rendering it more effectively pro-poor? In short, new patterns of stratification (in terms of opportunities for mobility as well as current position) only slowly led to the emergence of social attitudes or political responses that were clearly differentiated along class rather than racial lines.

The first part of the explanation for this concerns identities and consciousness. It is very difficult to measure identities, not least because the salience of identity is often contextual and in surveys it is difficult to specify clearly any context. It is also difficult to link identities and attitudes to actual behaviour. Opinion polls suggest, however, that most South Africans continued to favour racial rather than class identities in the late 1990s. The 2000 Afrobarometer survey, for example, found that South Africans volunteered racial, ethnic, or linguistic identities five times more often than class identities (a higher ratio than in Nigeria). But the apparently limited salience of class consciousness does not mean that poorer people were content. South Africans identified job creation and crime as—by far—the most important problems facing the country and expressed strong discontent with the ANC-led government's performance with respect to both issues. But there were few signs of a distinct consciousness among the unemployed (Seekings 2002b). One reason for this is that state policies that might contribute to inequality were opaque. It was not easy for poor citizens to trace the links between the state's industrial and labour-market policies and unemployment and poverty, even if these policies contributed to rising capital intensity and productivity rather than job creation (Nattrass and Seekings 2001b).

Shortly after 2000 there were some indications of change in public attitudes. Mattes reports that surveys showed declining confidence in the economy and trust in government. Perceptions of "relative deprivation" also seemed to be increasing: "Even in 1995, despite one of the highest rates of income inequality in the world, only 32 percent of South Africans said they were worse off than others. This was largely due to the fact that black South Africans tended to compare themselves to other blacks rather than to whites. By mid-2000, however, this figure had increased sharply to 50 percent. In the same survey, 31 percent of blacks said their lives were worse now than under apartheid, up sharply from 13 percent in 1997" (Mattes 2002, 32).

In early 2003, the Institute for Justice and Reconciliation included in its "Reconciliation Barometer" a question about South Africans' perception of the "biggest division" in the country. The precise wording was: "People sometimes talk about the divisions between people in South Africa. Sometimes these divisions can cause people to feel left out or discriminated against. In other circumstances it can lead to anger and even violence between groups. What, in your experience, is the biggest division in South Africa today?" The options presented to the respondents were: (1) the division between different political parties such as the ANC and the IFP; (2) the division between poor and middle income or wealthy South Africans; (3) the division between those living with HIV-AIDS and other infectious diseases and the rest of the community; (4) the division between members of different religions; (5) the divisions between black, white, coloured and Indian South Africans; and (6) the divisions between South Africans of different language groups. The wording of the question might have led respondents to select either race (the fifth option, because of the reference to discrimination) or parties (the first option, because of the reference to violence). But only one in five of the respondents selected the fifth option, with a similar proportion selecting the first option. More—30 percent—selected the second option. The class option was selected by 29 percent of white and African respondents and a slightly higher proportion of coloured and Indian respondents. Within each racial group, it was the most popular option. Responses do not seem to have been related to household income.

Overall, the available evidence suggests that racial identities proved resilient, even if there was also a growing consciousness of class (although it is unclear how identities and perceptions were linked to each other or to electoral and other political behaviour). This resilience was in part due to constant reinforcement by the ANC, both as the government and as a competitive political party. As the governing party, the ANC took political advantage of its pro-poor policies and was adept at building new clinics and schools in areas where it was threatened electorally (such as the Eastern Cape in 1999). But it presented these achievements not so much as being pro-poor as undoing the discrimination of apartheid. Pro-poor policies were represented in terms of racial redress. The ANC played the race card effectively in elections (Davis 2003), preserving its cross-class racial coalition. The racialised discourse of two nations shored up racial identities and racialised allegiances.

At the same time, voters could see that some of these policies were pro-poor. In 1999 and 2000, the ANC proved adept at marshalling its resources—both symbolic, as in the charisma of the inimitable Madiba (Nelson Mandela), and material, as in the construction of new clinics and schools—in order to ward off electoral challenges. In local elections, critical independent candidates generally struggled to make headway against official ANC candidates even when the latter were regarded as having performed poorly. In provinces such as the Eastern Cape, where the record of service delivery has been appalling, the provincially based, predominantly black-led opposition, the United Democratic Movement, managed to secure only 15 percent of the vote in 1999. Anecdotal impressions suggest that discontent with the government about unemployment began to become more politically consequential after 2000, especially as the ANC elite came to be seen as feathering its own nest. But, again, the party responded astutely, raising social spending in preelection budgets and promising pro-poor policies (including massive job creation) in its election campaigning in 2003–4. Policies that disadvantaged the poor, including labour-market and growth-path policies, were typically opaque, meaning that their effects were not evident to poor voters.

For their part, poorer ANC supporters remained loyal to the party in part because they gave it credit for political as well as social and economic change, in part because of the lack of alternatives. Two features of the political system served to constrain change in the patterns of political activity. First, the ANC commanded sufficient patronage to keep most senior black politicians on board, denuding opposition parties of high-profile black leadership. The electoral system (at the national, provincial and, less completely, local levels) provided the party leadership with one important source of patronage: places on the ANC electoral lists. Control over appointments in the state and the parastatal sectors, and opportunities for both legitimate and illegitimate business activities, all served to keep aspiring black elites on board. Second, and in part in consequence, the major opposition parties were not attractive to disillusioned ANC supporters (Mattes and Piombo 2001). The result was that the party system remained racialised. As Friedman and Chipkin put it, there was no class-based party competing for power; insofar as struggles over class occurred, they were within, not between, racialised alliances (Friedman and Chipkin 2001, 11–12). And the outcome of discontent was lower voter turnout rather than intensified electoral competition.

There is another possible explanation of the acquiescence of poor voters. They might have been making decisions about political allegiance and protest based not so much on their social or economic position at the time as on their expected future positions. Citizens' perceptions of opportunities for upward mobility might be expected to have shaped their identities and allegiances as well as their judgment about the legitimacy of inequality. The perception that economic liberalisation might promote a more meritocratic society might explain why poor voters in a number of new democracies have endorsed market reforms when those reforms have heightened inequality (Birdsall and Graham 2000). In South Africa, there is evidence that expectations were important. Most poor voters remained loyal to the ANC in part because they were patient in waiting for their expectations of change to be fulfilled (Charney 1995; Nattrass and Seekings 1998). Perhaps this factor was more important than their experience of hardship—perhaps deepening hardship—at the time. There were, indeed, good reasons for expecting this. At its height, apartheid entailed an unprecedented combination of state interventions in markets (especially the labour market, via the industrial colour bar, pass laws, labour bureaux, administration boards, and magistrates' courts) with massively unequal public spending on education, with the intent and result that black South Africans faced very different opportunities than did their white counterparts. With the abolition of the pass laws and final vestiges of the colour bar and huge shifts in the incidence of public expenditure on education, the distribution of opportunities surely moved in a more meritocratic direction.

The most obvious site of struggle over class was thus *within* the ANC Alliance, between COSATU and the ANC itself. Some scholars (such as McKinley 2001; Bond 2000; and Marais 1998) viewed both as having "sold out" the more radical objectives of the anti-apartheid struggle. The ANC's "neoliberal" policies—especially trade liberalisation, privatisation, fiscal austerity, and cost recovery in urban services—were seen as being against the interests of the poor and the working class. Other scholars (such as Adler and Webster 1999) saw South Africa as moving instead toward a class compromise in which business did well but labour also secured gains, notably via labour-market policy. The ANC argued that the poor benefited from social policy. It claimed that the social wage (that is, the value of cash transfers together with public education, health care, and other services) helped make up for low (or no) wages earned in the labour market. In an earlier article (Nattrass and Seekings 2001b), we agreed with some of the ANC's claims and suggested that there was a "double class compromise" in South Africa in terms of which business secured broadly pro-business macroeconomic policies, the working class secured higher wages, and the poor secured pro-poor social policies. The poor were said to exert some power at the ballot box. The weakness of this argument is that some of the gains apparently made by the poor were actually gains won by other social groups. As mentioned above, the big increase in pro-poor social expenditure in the mid-1990s was in education, where increased spending on teachers' salaries certainly did not result in matching improvements in the quality of schooling enjoyed by poor children. Increased spending on the poor reflected in large part a transfer to teachers. This points us to a major issue in the politics of redistribution in South Africa: the social groups with the political power to extract concessions from the state or capital were nonpoor groups. Very few of COSATU's members were in the poorer half of the population. Most lived in households with incomes above the median but below the mean, meaning that they were disadvantaged relative to the rich (mostly white) minority but enjoyed a position that was privileged relative to the poor. Some COSATU-affiliated unions—including the teachers' union—had memberships that were mostly in households with incomes above the mean (see further Seekings 2004).

The limits to change in the politics of distribution in South Africa were evident in two political controversies early in the twenty-first century. The first related to the resurgence of so-called social movements, linked into antiglobalisation activists' networks and mobilising against evictions for nonpayment of rent or bond payments and disconnections of electricity and water supplies for nonpayment, among other things (see Desai 2003; Lodge 2003). These mobilisations were typically single-issue protests that involved very localised constituencies. More important, they entailed conflict over the symptoms of inequality (inability to pay for municipal services or for housing), not the causes of inequality (low-quality public schooling, high unemployment, and government policies that undermine labour-intensive growth). These localised and ephemeral conflicts failed to cohere into a mass movement of any consequence. Friedman and Chipkin (2001) suggested that retrenched workers might grow into a radical social constituency, but this potential development was always constrained by the fact that unemployed people lacked resources and did not necessarily share the same views about what changes were needed.

The second related to the debate—or rather, the nondebate—about the basic income grant (or BIG). In 2002 the government-appointed Committee of Enquiry into a Comprehensive System of Social Security for South Africa (the Taylor Committee) recommended that the government introduce a basic income grant once the administrative systems had been developed. The government initially delayed responding to the recommendation and sought to suppress debate (including that in ANC conferences). Only in mid-2003 did the government finally come out against the proposed BIG, opting instead for an extension of the child support grants and prospectively "massive" public works programmes. The "BIG Coalition" brought together a range of human rights and church groups, together with COSATU, but only the unions were capable of mobilising mass support. The unions supported the BIG in part out of self-interest, not because union members would benefit directly from the grant but rather because of the indirect benefits, in that the grant would reduce the pressures on workers to support dependent kin and might also deflect criticism of the unions' demand for high wages (which arguably undermine job creation). But these indirect benefits were probably insufficient for the unions to threaten their alliance with the ANC. In post-apartheid South Africa, unions did not organise the poorest of the poor but actually represented relatively privileged sections of society that had done quite well since 1994 (see Matisonn and Seekings 2003). A BIG would certainly move South Africa in a more social democratic direction (and for this reason is discussed in Chapter 11), but it did not enjoy the whole-hearted support of any sufficiently powerful political constituency.

As South Africa entered its second decade of democracy, electoral pressures might be expected to push the ANC-led government into pro-poor spending, but any such spending is likely to be discretionary (such as new schools, clinics, or public works programmes) rather than programmatic (such as a basic income grant). The uneasy balance of power between established white business, aspirant black business, and organised labour is unlikely to shift enough to allow for major reforms in government strategy. Without policies that encourage the growth of low-wage jobs for the unskilled unemployed and promote the more efficient use of public spending on education, inequality is unlikely to diminish significantly, if at all.

The post-apartheid distributional regime displays strong continuities from its predecessor, the late apartheid distributional regime, because the biggest losers under both have remained politically weak. The unemployed, and especially the rural poor without easy access to urban labour markets, were unable to use their electoral strength to secure pro-poor reforms, in part because it was unclear precisely what reforms would be pro-poor in the longer term. The powerful political constituencies in post-apartheid South Africa, on the other hand, were able to mobilise effectively and secure beneficial policies including lowered tax rates and raised wages and salaries for working people with skills. Deracialisation meant that African workers secured the benefits previously won by white workers, but it did not mean that the opportunities facing the unemployed and especially the rural poor improved. It is only by viewing the distributional regime as a whole that the contradictions between its different components become clear. Redistribution via the budget provided considerable relief to poor households, although not specifically for households that were poor because their members were unemployed. But unemployment was only such a crucial problem because of the government's policies affecting the growth path and the labour market.

Chapter 11 Transforming the Distributional Regime

The new South Africa was born in 1994 amid great hope for the future: the demise of apartheid would surely lead to policies that addressed the economic and social needs of the poor. Ten years later, the record was disappointing, with income inequality persisting and perhaps worsening. This was primarily due, we argue, to the strong continuities between the apartheid distributional regime and the post-apartheid distributional regime.

Policies changed in many important ways after the dark days of grand apartheid. Most important, South Africa's labour and welfare policies were deracialised beginning in the late apartheid period; the process was completed after 1994. The machinery of industrial relations was opened to workers on a nonracial basis starting at the end of the 1970s. The gap between old-age pensions paid to white people and to Africans narrowed, and parity was reached finally in 1993, on the eve of the democratic transition. The post-apartheid government completed the process of deracialising the welfare and labour systems by restructuring child grants and harmonising the labour regulations of the former bantustan areas with those of the rest of the country. Social expenditure was also deracialised, with radically increased spending on public education and health care for black people and reduced spending on these services for white people. Race ceased to be the explicit basis of structured income inequality in South Africa.

But inequality persisted because race had given way to class, with the advantages and disadvantages of class replacing racial discrimination as the motor driving stratification. The post-apartheid distributional regime underpinned and reproduced class advantage and disadvantage almost as emphatically as its predecessors had stratified society on the basis of racial discrimination and segregation.

By 1993 (as we saw in Chapter 8), South African society was marked by two class divides, and this continues to be the case early in the twenty-first century. The first divide was that between the rich, including the "middle classes" of professionals and managers as well as the owners of capital, and the working class (or classes). The second was between those who had jobs, or more precisely those who had jobs most of the time, and those who either did not have jobs or who had jobs in sectors (especially agriculture and domestic work) that were especially precarious. The post-apartheid distributional regime perpetuated these class divides in ways that displayed strong continuities from its predecessors. This is obvious in the case of welfare policy, with very different levels of provision for the different sections of society. The market-based welfare system provided for the increasingly multiracial middle classes and, increasingly, the working classes: private medical insurance and pension schemes ensured that workers continued to receive incomes when they were no longer working. At the same time, the provision of public welfare, though highly redistributive, continued to help only specified categories of deserving poor people: the elderly, the disabled, and children, as well as, in practice, anyone who lived with members of these groups who were recipients of grants. Public welfare policy after apartheid was thus organised around the same principle as its apartheid predecessor, albeit in a deracialised form: able-bodied adults of working age were expected to achieve income security via employment. The chronically unemployed and the less skilled poor, typically concentrated in low-employment rural areas, were covered by neither public nor market-based welfare systems; they were dependent on the other form of private welfare—kin or community—though this form of support was declining.

South Africa's days of full employment had clearly ended by the mid-1970s. By 1993, as we have shown in Chapter 6, unemployment drove income inequality. In the decade following 1994, inequality and poverty probably worsened as formal employment stagnated and unemployment rose further (see Chapter 9). The shift from shortage to surplus of unskilled labour was very much the result of the apartheid distributional regime. Labour-market and other economic policies served to promote capital intensification and secure prospects for skilled labour while reducing employers' need for (black) un-skilled labour. Tractors and forklift trucks (for example) replaced unskilled labour, and the now surplus labour was removed to the bantustans. The apartheid distributional regime was anti-poor not only because of its direct racial discrimination but also because it generated an economic growth path that systematically disadvantaged poor, less skilled people.

These kinds of policies remained unchanged after the end of apartheid. The deracialisation of labour-market and welfare policies was not accompanied by any fundamental change in the policies shaping the economic growth path. In Chapter 10 we showed how post-apartheid economic and labour-market poli-cies encouraged firms to employ fewer, more skilled, and more productive workers, with the result that average wages and profits rose—but at the cost of higher unemployment, especially among the less skilled. Indeed, the shedding of unskilled labour was especially pronounced in the mining and agricultural sectors, which had hitherto served as major employers of poorer, less skilled people in or from rural areas. The post-apartheid state did reform unemploy-ment insurance, extending temporary support to a wider range of workers in the event of retrenchment or ill health. But, overall, the post-apartheid distri-butional regime failed to provide income security for the overwhelming major-ity of the unemployed, who continued to fall through a large hole in the social safety net. At the same time, economic policies (including labour-market and industrial policies) did not succeed in creating the jobs to absorb new entrants into the labour market. In failing to address unemployment, the distributional regime was necessarily anti-poor, and it failed to reduce either poverty or in-equality.

Government expenditure in the post-apartheid period was not merely dera-cialised; it also become more redistributive in the sense that a larger share was spent on poorer households. But, as we saw in Chapter 10, this redistribution took the form of improved access to public services, especially education, rather than cash being put directly into the pockets of the poor.

Throughout the twentieth century, education repeatedly served as the mech-anism of class formation, intergenerational social mobility, and economic dif-ferentiation in South Africa. In the early apartheid period, education and skills development were crucial to intergenerational class mobility among poorer white people. Unskilled white workers were given advantaged positions in the labour market by means of direct racial discrimination in the form of the colour bar and other direct state interventions, but public education meant that their children did not suffer the same disadvantages and, when they entered the labour force, did not need the colour bar to earn higher incomes. By the 1980s, the vast majority of white people could rely on their skills. Racial discrimination could therefore be unravelled without undermining their privileged positions. For white South Africans, apartheid converted the state-imposed advantages of race into the market-rewarded advantages of class.

Similarly, the high absolute rate of occupational and intergenerational mobility of many African people since the 1970s was strongly linked to improved skills and education. Education again served as a mechanism for shaping class formation. But, again, the beneficiaries were *some* rather than *all* South Africans. Increases in public expenditure on schooling, especially in poor areas, has not resulted in improved opportunities, either during or after school, for many poor children. The value of educational expenditure to poor children depends on the actual quality of the education they receive, not simply the sums spent in the schools they attend. Unfortunately, there is little evidence that increases in teachers' salaries in the 1990s translated into improved educational services for the poor; pro-poor spending did not lead to significantly more egalitarian opportunities.

Although the post-apartheid state did implement various progressive policies, it did not confront the way in which the distributional regime served to reproduce the kind of inequality that emerged in the late apartheid period. There are three key dimensions to the problem. First, labour-market and economic policies combined to encourage a growth path that concentrated benefits on capitalists, the so-called middle classes and employed, generally skilled, workers, while excluding the growing numbers of unemployed people. Second, the quality of education was low, both undermining overall economic growth and limiting the ability of poor children to transcend their parents' class positions. Third, welfare policy was premised on full employment in that no real provision was made for income security for most unemployed people.

DEBATING ALTERNATIVES

Was—and is—there an alternative to the post-apartheid distributional regime, one that had—and has—a more egalitarian distributional outcome? If so, what would it entail? Most of the debate in post-apartheid South Africa about the links between public policy and poverty or inequality have focused on macroeconomic policy. A number of critics on the Left have accused the ANC of pursuing "neoliberal" policies, especially the GEAR strategy. Critics of the state claim that more expansionary fiscal and monetary policies would have boosted demand and fuelled growth. More radically, it is argued, a strategy of "growth through redistribution" would have ensured that the poor benefited. Against this, defenders of government policy emphasise the importance of attracting investment and ensuring that growth is sustainable.

In this debate, both the government and its critics tend to sidestep or ignore the challenge of unemployment. The post-apartheid distributional regime seemed premised on the possibility that the growth path of the East Asian tigers could be reproduced in South Africa. As Meth (2003) shows, even sustained economic growth offers few benefits to the poor if a country starts in a position of massive unemployment-based poverty. Critics of state policy tend to assume—or to assert explicitly—that South Africa could emulate the labour-market and welfare policies of the social democracies of northern Europe (especially Sweden; see, for example, Torres 1996). The working class could benefit from pro-labour legislation regarding employment, while the unemployed could be provided for by generous welfare assistance. In the South African context, however, the scale of unemployment and poverty makes it impossible to achieve even vaguely egalitarian outcomes with these policies alone.

What, then, would constitute a "social-democratic" or more egalitarian distributional regime in this context of massive unemployment? Our thinking about this issue has evolved during the first decade since the end of apartheid. Our first paper concerning this subject merely insisted on the need to take unemployment into account (Nattrass and Seekings 1996). In response to scholars who argued that increasing wages was the most important way of improving the position of the "working class as a whole" (Gelb and Webster 1995), we argued that the tension between maximising wages and creating jobs meant that the interests of the employed and of unemployed were not coterminous.

In a paper published in 1997, we suggested that the best way forward for a labour-surplus middle-income country such as South Africa might be to opt for a set of labour-market and welfare policies that encouraged the expansion of employment by the creation of low-wage jobs while providing limited, means-tested welfare for those who still failed to find work. This would result in greater wage inequality but lower inequality overall because the number of people without any work would fall (Nattrass and Seekings 1997). Expanding the ranks of the working poor would not be a progressive strategy in a low-unemployment economy (such as the United States in the 1990s), but it would be pro-poor in a high-unemployment one (such as South Africa); given fiscal constraints, it might be the most pro-poor alternative. But although such a strategy might be fiscally viable, it was not politically feasible (as we recognised at the time). There were simply too many vested interests (most notably organised labour) opposed to such an economic solution. Put differently, the corporatist institutions and tradition in South Africa were too strong for this to be a viable alternative path.

Of course, promoting the expansion of low-wage jobs could never be the sole component of an alternative distributional regime. In a paper written in 2001, we identified four necessary pillars of a "social democratic agenda" in South Africa, of which such job expansion was one. The other three pillars were, in different ways, as important. More equal educational opportunities for children would be inequality-reducing in the medium and long terms. Asset redistribution via worker ownership of firms and land reform in the countryside would facilitate more egalitarian distribution of incomes as well as helping to deepen democracy. And welfare reform would provide assistance to the poor, especially the unemployed poor, in the extended period before sufficient jobs were created (Seekings and Nattrass 2002).

Is this mix of responses politically viable? Or, to put it another way, how might such a package of policies be made politically attractive to a sufficiently powerful coalition of interests? In 2003 one of us was commissioned by the South African Department of Labour to write a discussion paper about social-democratic solutions to the employment crisis (Nattrass 2003b). The department requested an analysis of the lessons to be learned from countries that recently had been able to overcome a serious employment crisis by means of an accord negotiated among capital, labour, and the state. This was a very sensible request, because it took as given the power of organised labour and South Africa's corporatist institutions (notably the National Economic, Development, and Labour Advisory Council, or NEDLAC) and asked how these might form a basis for a new, more egalitarian distributional regime. It would not have been fruitful to seek lessons in the experience of the newly industrialising developing countries such as those in East Asia. These countries had grown rapidly in the 1960s and 1970s but under less-than-democratic circumstances. Instead, the task focused attention on countries with an institutional and hence political environment sufficiently similar to South Africa's and improved employment performance in the 1980s and 1990s. These countries might reasonably be seen as suggesting a politically viable alternative path for South Africa today. Two countries suggested themselves: the Netherlands and Ireland. They are quintessential examples of the "new social pacts" (Rhodes 2001) that arose in Europe in response to the adverse employment conditions of the 1980s.

In Chapter 1 we suggested that distributional regimes in the South need to be analysed in broader ways than is usual for the welfare and labour-market regimes of the North. Why, then, examine here the experiences of the Netherlands and Ireland? The answer is that in important respects South Africa sits in an uneasy position between the binary categories of "developed" and "developing" countries: it is a middle-income country that shares many developmental characteristics of poor countries (for example, high infant mortality and falling life expectancy) but also has an institutional and regulatory environment that is akin to that of developed countries (particularly with regard to the labour-market regulations, industrial policies, and the financial sector). South Africa's growth path is different from those of most other developing countries and from those of most other middle-income countries. This is particularly striking with regard to employment. As can be seen in figure 11.1, South Africa's employment trajectory has been dramatically worse than the middle-income average. Most important for our purposes, South Africa has a set of wage-setting institutions that empower organised labour and a peak-level tripartite institution (NEDLAC) that entrenches corporatist-style negotiations among labour, capital, and the state. No other developing country has this environment. The value of examining the Netherlands and Ireland lies primarily in these institutional and political conditions and what they mean in terms of formulating policies in response to an employment crisis.

EXPANDING EMPLOYMENT BY MEANS OF A
SOCIAL ACCORD: THE IRISH AND THE
DUTCH EXPERIENCES

Both the Netherlands and Ireland experienced employment crises in the early 1980s (see figure 11.1), and both addressed them with a process that entailed fashioning innovative links between labour-market policy, industrial policy, welfare policy, and taxation. In each case, organised labour made real concessions with regard to wage restraint and labour regulation in return for benefits such as lower taxation, enhanced representation, skills development, and other productivity-enhancing policies and measures. This negotiated route forward underpinned a dramatic improvement in employment.

What is particularly interesting about these two success stories is that they

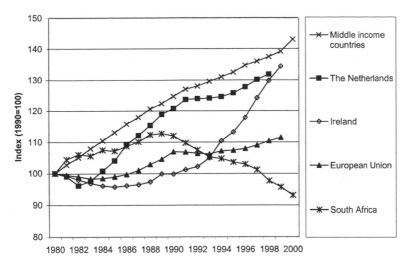

Figure 11.1. Employment trends in South Africa and elsewhere, 1980–2000. *Source:* World Development Indicators as reported in the WEFA data set.

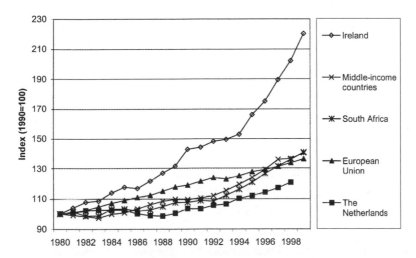

Figure 11.2. Trends in labour productivity in South Africa and elsewhere, 1980–99. *Source:* See figure 11.1.

achieved rapid employment growth via different routes. The Netherlands is variously considered as having a social democratic welfare state regime (according to Goodin et al. 1999) or an unusually egalitarian corporatist or conserva- tive regime (according to Esping-Andersen 1990 or Huber and Stephens 2001). Either way, it is very different from Ireland, which is categorised as a liberal market economy. But both were able to introduce and benefit from a social accord.

In addition to differences in their welfare regimes, there were also clear differences in economic policy. The Irish strategy was based on a high-productivity growth path (which saw output growing so rapidly that increases in employment were accompanied by increases in output per worker), whereas in the Dutch case, employment grew roughly in line with output until the 1990s, when output per worker started to increase (see figure 11.2). Average productivity actually *declined* in the mid- and late 1980s as part-time employment (and in particular, employment of women—see Garibaldi and Mauro 2003, 72) expanded rapidly. As discussed below, these different trends in average productivity are important for South Africa, which has to balance concerns about productivity with expanding the number of jobs in order to address poverty and inequality.

The Dutch Case

The social accord process in the Netherlands had its roots in the employment crisis of the late 1970s and early 1980s. Like the other advanced capitalist countries, the Netherlands suffered from the oil shocks. As Rhodes points out, however, "the negative consequences for the Netherlands were compounded by a breakdown in relations between the social partners that helped produce a vicious cycle in which real labour costs accelerated ahead of productivity gains, profits deteriorated, firms substituted capital for labour or relocated to low labour cost areas, and unemployment rose spectacularly" (Rhodes 2001, 181–82).

What was particularly impressive about the "Dutch Miracle" in the mid-1980s was the sharp turnaround in its employment performance. As can be seen in figure 11.1, Dutch employment performance far exceeded the average for the European Union. The Netherlands responded to the employment crisis by reviving corporatist forms of policy making. According to Rhodes, the Netherlands is now the "most advanced example of 'competitive corporatism' in Western Europe" (2001, 184). The key development was the 1982 Wassenaar Accord, a bipartite national social pact between employers and trade unions aimed at solving the problems caused by adversarial labour relations. It involved a considerable degree of decentralisation in wage bargaining (within a coordinated structure) and facilitated the increase in part-time and temporary employment contracts.

The accord was "consolidated" a decade later, in 1993, at a time when a new increase in unemployment was placing the consensus under pressure. The long period of wage moderation in the 1980s had resulted in an improvement in the Dutch competitive position. With German reunification, however, interest rates rose and growth slowed. This, together with the 5 percent real appreciation of the currency in 1992, prompted a new bipartite agreement ("A New Course") in which the social partners renewed their commitment to a "responsible wage policy": "Under this compromise, which reinforced the trend towards decentralisation of collective bargaining and greater involvement by sectoral and firm-level negotiators, employers gave up their blanket resistance to shorter working hours, while unions promised to beef up wage restraint. Both pledged to improve the unfavourable employment/population ratio and agreed on more flexible employment" (Hemerijck and Schludi 2000, 160).

In addition to facilitating wage moderation, the Dutch social accord process also produced agreements concerning social security reforms, work sharing, industrial policy, training, job enrichment, and minimum and "entry-level" wages. In the 1995–97 "flexicurity" accords the rights of temporary workers were strengthened, and in return unions agreed to loosen dismissal protection for core workers. As Rhodes observes, this "consolidates the general trend in Dutch reforms to build a distributional coalition by breaking down the traditional barriers between labour market insiders and outsiders" (2001, 182).

The Dutch government also came to the table with employment-friendly welfare reforms such as shifting the costs of social security contributions from employers to income-tax payers (Scharpf 2000, 112). It also subsidised a range of employment programmes that absorbed large number of less-skilled workers (Rhodes 2001, 183) and promoted employment flexibility by removing constraints on shops' opening hours, business licenses, temporary job agencies, and working time. Changes to labour-market regulation (for example, dismissal law) were legislated after labour and capital had agreed to them.

What did the trade unions gain in return? On the wage front, low-wage workers have been compensated for wage restraint by targeted tax breaks. Also, since 1993, Dutch unions and employers "have increasingly come to exchange shorter working hours, an expansion of leave arrangements, the warranty of income stability throughout the year and lower overtime rates against the annualisation of working hours and an expansion of working hours in the evenings or on Saturdays. The social partners are also in agreement that employers should honour workers' requests to work part-time unless there are compelling firm-related reasons for rejection" (Hemerijck and Schludi 2000, 160).

In a crucial move, the Dutch trade unions changed strategy with regard to part-time and temporary workers, organising them and championing their cause instead of opposing the creation of such jobs. This was in part a result of the recognition that part-time employment was popular among women. As a result of this shift, hourly wages for part-time workers were bargained to levels enjoyed by full-time workers, and part-time workers were guaranteed equal access to pension and social security benefits.

The Dutch case illustrates that a country can pursue productivity-enhancing strategies at the firm and industry levels while also expanding employment in ways that create a more inclusive growth path, albeit at the cost of lower average labour productivity. In other words, lower *average* labour productivity is to be expected (and welcomed) when employment growth involves by part-time employment (which amounts to a form of job-sharing) or government-sponsored job creation schemes. Productivity enhancement at the firm level is crucial for maintaining growth in profits and wages. But if raising productivity in this manner becomes the sole policy objective, then there is a danger that the growth path will exclude the many unemployed who wish to work. The Dutch solution to this problem was to ensure that productivity-enhancing measures (such as training) were accompanied by measures to boost employment—even though this implied lower average labour productivity in the short-to-medium term.

The Irish Case

The Irish social accord process started off as an attempt to restore profitability, investment, and growth and subsequently expanded in scope to include issues of education, health, and social welfare as well as incomes. The first neocorporatist accord was struck in the mid-1980s, when Ireland was mired in slow growth, rising public sector deficits, and high unemployment. Subsequent pacts negotiated in 1990, 1993, 1996–97, and 2000 linked incomes policies to wage restraint and reforms in taxation, education, health, and social welfare. Each agreement was preceded by the publication of a discussion document prepared by the National Economic and Social Council, an advisory body composed of representatives of the social partners and senior government officials. As the pacts developed, more emphasis was placed on supply-side measures to promote training and productivity growth. Over time, the accord process was expanded to include more representatives of civil society.

All five agreements emphasised the importance of macroeconomic stability, greater equity in the tax system, wage restraint, and labour market reforms (for example, in the areas of part-time work and unfair dismissals). Labour and capital agreed to a national framework for wage increases that would restore profitability and maintain macroeconomic stability. Government brought tax relief for low-paid workers to the table, along with improvements in social welfare, and labour promised industrial peace.

Partnership 2000 (negotiated in 1996–97) included a thirty-nine-month national wage agreement aimed at lowering inflationary expectations and creating stability in the investment environment. The agreement also introduced a local bargaining clause (which allowed management to tie negotiations to local labour-market conditions while maintaining wage moderation at the national level) and an appeals process for firms that could demonstrate an "inability to pay" the agreed wage increases. There is doubt, however, as to how much wage flexibility this actually produced. According to Haughton, it was "fortunate that the wage agreements have coincided with rapid economic growth, because the agreements create considerable rigidity in the labour market" (1998, 37).

The relatively limited labour-market reform is in part a result of the Irish commitment to improving productivity via industrial democracy and partnerships. Unlike the Netherlands (where efforts were made to boost employment via subsidised employment schemes and by expanding service sector jobs and part-time contracts), Ireland has a labour market and industrial strategies that are geared toward productivity enhancement (as in South Africa; see Chapter 10). Also, until 1996, the agreements were "largely tailored to the demands of the insider unionised sector and the main emphasis was on protecting the post-tax income of the employed 'insiders'" (Kavanagh et al. 1997). And, although Partnership 2000 was negotiated with a wider grouping of social partners, it concentrated mainly on improving industrial democracy and training in an effort to boost productivity by the adoption of best-practice techniques and via consensual labour relations.

The Irish experience seems to be an example of how a high-productivity strategy can succeed in lowering unemployment significantly. It required rapid rates of growth to achieve this aim, however. Rising average labour productivity meant that fewer additional jobs were created for each increase in output. But because output growth was so fast, employment shot up rapidly anyway and unemployment is now very low. Given that rapid growth is at the heart of the success of the Irish social accord, it is worth asking what accounts for this growth. The short answer to this question is investment, especially investment by transnational corporations (O'Hearn 2000; O'Donnell 2001). Given that investment (both domestic and foreign) drove growth, the question thus becomes, to what extent did the accord process facilitate investment?

Investors are interested in profitability and predictability in the business environment. The Irish accords delivered both. Wage restraint in the late 1980s and early 1990s helped ensure that profitability doubled between 1987 and 1996. As O'Donnell puts it, "the resulting environment of wage moderation and high profitability is almost certainly a key factor in Ireland's employment creation, attraction of inward investment and the unprecedented commercial success of indigenous companies" (2001, 11). In other words, it appears that wage moderation was a precondition for creating the investment boom that fuelled subsequent increases in growth, employment, and incomes.

ADDRESSING UNEMPLOYMENT BY MEANS OF A SOCIAL ACCORD IN SOUTH AFRICA

Social accords arise from a common sense of crisis and recognition of the need to restore profitability in order to ensure the sustainable growth of employment and income for all (Nattrass 2003b). As shown in Chapter 10, both the rate and the share of profit in South Africa rose for most of the 1990s—so it appears that profitability is being restored in the absence of a social accord. Rather than bargaining with labour about their strategy, South African firms are simply responding to the economic and policy environment by shedding unskilled labour and by ensuring that wage growth is matched by improvements in productivity. They have, in short, succeeded in recreating the conditions for renewed accumulation without an explicit commitment on the part of organised labour to wage restraint.

If the only objective of a social accord is to restore profitability, then South Africa does not need one. If, however, the objective is to facilitate a stronger, more labour-demanding, and less conflictual growth path, then a social accord could potentially be of value. An explicit agreement on the part of organised labour to restrain wage demands could help improve the investment climate (as was the case in the Netherlands and Ireland). Thus, there is certainly still room for a more cooperative growth path that could benefit both labour and capital. Such an accord could include the following:

1. A framework agreement (probably negotiated in NEDLAC) detailing agreed parameters for a wage increase. This could take the form of a blanket increase for all sectors (as in the Irish social accord) or it could be stratified by sector.
2. Industry-level wage bargains constrained by the framework agreement and procedures put in place (as in the Irish case) to accommodate firms that cannot afford the wage increases.

3. Continued government provision of support for training and skills development by means of various dedicated industrial and labour policies (as in Ireland and the Netherlands) and improvement of the quality of education (see below).

This kind of "insider" accord could help improve growth at the margin, but it is unlikely to have much impact in the short or medium term on employment. As shown by the Irish social accord process, the only way for a productivity-based accord to generate significant benefits to employment is if growth is extremely fast (and is fuelled by domestic and foreign investment). Such a scenario is unlikely in South Africa given the chronic problem of skills bottlenecks.

If South Africa is going to address the employment problem by means of a social accord, then it has to be inclusive of labour-market outsiders. Whether this means broadening the parties to the agreement to include the unemployed and civil society organisations (as in the Irish case) or simply mandating that government look after the interests of the unemployed with subsidised employment schemes and targeted employment reforms (as in the Netherlands) is an open question.

An inclusive social accord in South Africa would need to support high-productivity activities but not at the cost of slower employment growth overall. Training and skills development should continue in order to improve the competitiveness of high-productivity sectors. But at the same time employment needs to expand, perhaps in the form of job-sharing or lower-wage, labour-intensive activities or government-sponsored public works programmes. Most important, regulatory changes need to be considered so as to make it easier for lower-wage, labour-intensive activities to survive. Such developments will serve to reduce average labour productivity—but as the Dutch growth path shows, this can be an appropriate outcome if the objective is to address the problem of marginalised outsiders by creating jobs for them.

Note that average wages might fall as low-wage employment increases. Although this may well increase wage inequality, it will reduce overall inequality by reducing the number of unemployed people. Lower average wages are thus consistent with an egalitarian strategy. In an earlier debate, Gelb and Webster (1996) seemed to argue that the incomes of the "working class as a whole" would be maximised via wage increases, even if there is a trade-off between employment and wages. This argument makes no allowance for distribution within the "working class," by which Gelb and Webster clearly meant all of the noncapitalist classes in society. As we argue repeatedly, reduced inequality requires job creation. Gelb and Webster appear to hold to a utilitarian view of social justice: the wage bill should be maximised regardless of distribution. They also assume that higher wages will maximise the wage bill. Our approach is more of a Rawlsian one in that priority should be given to improving the incomes of the poorest members of society. At the very least, the wage bill should not grow in ways that benefit the semiprivileged (that is, people with jobs) at the expense of the poor. As low-wage employment rises, average wages will fall, even if no workers actually experience a decline in their wages. In practice, expanding employment and lowering average wages might lead to a larger total wage bill than a high-wage strategy. In any case, it would be more pro-poor.

The idea of employment subsidies as a means of boosting employment has been raised, most notably by Bowles (see, for example, Heintz and Bowles 1996). Employers would be paid a wage subsidy financed by a tax on capital assets, lowering the cost of employment without reducing workers' take-home pay or aggregate demand in the economy. This would benefit labour-intensive firms and penalise capital-intensive ones. But the potential benefits need to be weighed against the possible costs, which include subsidising inefficient use of labour, administration costs, and deadweight losses—that is, subsidising employment that would have been created without the subsidy (see Standing et al. 1996, 458–60). Taxing capital assets and subsiding employment should encourage labour-intensive production at the level of the firm; the economy-wide effects are unclear. More research is required concerning this issue.

An "outsider-friendly" social accord in South Africa could include the following as additional aspects of the accord outlined above:

1. Agreement by organised labour and business to labour-market reforms in order to encourage the growth of labour-intensive firms and sectors (for example, removing or lowering minimum wages for smaller, more labour-intensive firms and removing the extension of collective bargaining agreements to nonparties).
2. Where other labour legislation can be shown to be harmful to employment creation (for example, rules about retrenchment), consideration of additional labour reforms; and
3. Agreement by the government to increase the number of public works programmes, to remove all taxes on employment (for example, payroll taxes), or to extend the public welfare system to cover the unemployed (perhaps through the introduction of a basic income grant; see below).

South Africa cannot replicate social accords in the Netherlands and Ireland in providing tax concessions to workers in return for wage restraint. In South Africa, employed workers are relatively privileged. An inclusive social accord in a labour-surplus middle-income country like South Africa must tax privileged groups including employed workers if it is to redistribute to the poor via the budget. Indeed, a full-scale AIDS prevention and treatment programme together with expanded public works programmes or a basic income grant would require a substantial increase in taxation (Nattrass 2004). There are too many social demands in relation to the number of income earners for workers to be offered further tax cuts as a "sweetener."

One of the obstacles facing an inclusive social accord in South Africa is whether organised labour is prepared to accept the associated labour-market reforms and changes to welfare policies (which will probably require an increase in taxation). If the country is unable to make progress on the outsider-friendly points, then all that will remain is an insider accord that supports a growth path that has little, if any, chance of reducing unemployment in the foreseeable future. Such growth paths characterised late-industrialising societies such as South Africa and Brazil for much of the twentieth century and help explain why these societies remain so unequal.

Social accords in Ireland and the Netherlands entailed concessions by organised labour (in terms of wage restraint and labour-market reforms) in return for tax cuts and policies designed to promote skills development and training. In South Africa's case, organised labour has already achieved many of these policy gains. The situation was helped by COSATU's alliance with the ANC and by the dominance of labour-friendly policy-makers in the Department of Labour and the Department of Trade and Industry. More recently, the working class (like the richer classes) has been handed tax cuts by the minister of finance (see figures 10.3 and 10.4). Organised labour in South Africa has, in other words, achieved many of the direct benefits typically associated with the new social accords without having to make any concessions (other than to tone down its opposition to the government's macroeconomic policies). It is an ironic possibility that the South African government may have missed the opportunity to forge an inclusive social accord by handing over its bargaining chips for free.

Nevertheless, there is still potential for a social accord process to deliver meaningful changes to South Africa's policy environment and growth path. Simply bringing the social partners together to discuss problems has potential benefits. As O'Donnell remarks with regard to the Irish social accord process, the benefits extended far beyond bread-and-butter negotiations between labour and capital: "Bargaining describes a process in which each party comes with definite preferences and seeks to maximise their gains. While this is a definite part of Irish social partnership, the overall process (including various policy forums) would seem to involve something more. Partnership involves the players in a process of deliberation that has the potential to shape and re-shape their understanding, identity and preferences" (2001, 5).

South Africa is fortunate in having a strong tradition of social corporatism and a national-level institution (NEDLAC) that is capable of facilitating discussion and negotiation among the social partners. The main beneficiaries of NEDLAC have been labour and capital, but there is potential for drawing in a wider range of social interests and constituencies into an accord process. This could be done by expanding and empowering NEDLAC's "Development Chamber," which was set up to facilitate the inclusion of civil society (the "community sector") in certain negotiations. Negotiations in NEDLAC during late 2002 and early 2003 concerning an AIDS treatment programme illustrate that such broad-based discussion is possible (Nattrass 2004). But the reluctance of government officials to take the process seriously points to an important precondition for success: government must agree to abide by the decisions taken by the social partners. Without a political commitment to social democratic forms of consultation and bargaining, a social accord process will not succeed in being anything other than a talk shop.

ENHANCING THE VALUE OF REDISTRIBUTION VIA THE BUDGET

An egalitarian or pro-poor distributional regime in South Africa must include policies that reduce unemployment, even if the new jobs are low-paid, low-productivity jobs for less skilled workers. Reforms to labour-market policies might be negotiated by corporatist institutions if labour receives, in return, pro-labour policies concerning skills development and taxation. Reforms to social policy that enhance the value—to working people as well as to the poor—of social spending have the potential to strengthen a pro-poor political coalition as well as the pro-poor components of the distributional regime. In previous chapters we identified the three pillars of redistribution via the budget in South Africa: public education, the welfare system, and the progressive and efficient tax system. Each of these pillars can be reformed in ways that would make the distributional regime more effectively pro-poor.

South Africa's system of public welfare is exceptional in the South in terms of its support of the poor (primarily the elderly) with generous and noncontributory pensions and grants. But the social safety net has a loose weave, and there is no provision for people of working age who are poor because of unemployment. There are three main ways in which the unemployed might be supported: a means-tested system (or "dole"), a universal basic income grant, or public works programmes. The first of these has obvious disadvantages: the means test is administratively cumbersome and expensive, and it also creates disincentives to work. The opposition Democratic Alliance has called for means-tested grants to the unemployed. But the real choice in South Africa is between the other two options.

Support for a basic income grant (BIG) grew after 2000. Supporters converged on the proposal to pay R100 (or about US$12) per month to every South African, regardless of age or means (excepting people who are already receiving another grant or pension). Such a grant would contribute substantially to reducing poverty and inequality. The numbers of people living below the poverty line, and the overall poverty gap, would fall by about two-thirds (Samson 2002; Bhorat 2003b). The proposal was endorsed in 2002 by the government-appointed Committee of Enquiry into a Comprehensive System of Social Security for South Africa (the Taylor Committee), subject to the qualification that the introduction of a BIG depended on the development of cheaper administrative procedures than existed hitherto.

The introduction of a BIG is a very radical proposal. Not even in the rich democracies of the North do citizens enjoy guaranteed minimum incomes as a right (the partial exception being the American state of Alaska, where oil revenues finance grants to all citizens). It is on the agenda in South Africa for an unusual mix of reasons (Seekings 2002a; Matisonn and Seekings 2003). First, the country already has generous noncontributory old-age pensions and disability grants as well as (less generous) child grants; a BIG would simply extend the coverage of these grants to people of working age. The existing system of social assistance is not only often taken for granted by South Africans but also makes it easy to imagine a universal grant. Second, exceptionally high unemployment rates represent a special crisis. Third, the BIG enjoys the support of the labour movement, in part because trade unions want to shift support for the unemployed from their members (via remittances, that is, the familial welfare system) to the state. Fourth, the racialised character of income inequality in South Africa makes rich white people unusually anxious, resulting in widespread support for pro-poor policies. The Democratic Alliance, representing most higher-income white South Africans, supports one version of an income grant for the poor. And, finally, the country's high level of inequality also makes it easier to finance a BIG.

The cost is an obvious problem, but, ironically, it is easier to finance in a society in which incomes are distributed very unequally than in one in which the distribution is more equal. Le Roux (2002) demonstrates that a BIG could be financed by increasing indirect taxes by about 50 percent. The most important of the indirect taxes, Value-Added Tax (VAT), would need to be increased by about 7 percentage points from 14 percent (in 2004) to about 21 percent. Excise taxes (including "sin" taxes on alcohol and tobacco) and fuel taxes would need to be increased commensurately. The advantage of Le Roux's proposal is that it is broad-based. People who spend more than R1,000 per month end up paying more in consumption taxes than they benefit from the R100-per-month BIG and so are net contributors; those earning less than R1,000 per month receive more than they pay in additional taxes. In practice, households in the top quintile are net contributors and households in the bottom half of the income distribution are net beneficiaries. For households in the seventh and eighth deciles, direct benefits and contributions approximately balance each other out. It is precisely because incomes—and hence expenditures—are so unequally distributed in South Africa that indirect taxes serve to redistribute so effectively and neatly from the rich to the poor. Because everyone pays extra tax when they spend, the net cost of a BIG financed by indirect taxes is only about one-quarter to one-third of the total gross cost.

The alternative of financing a BIG with income taxes is less redistributive but also less feasible politically. Income tax financing is supported in the "People's Budget," which is a joint project of COSATU, the South African Council of Churches, and the South African NGO Coalition.[1] As COSATU has made clear, the cost of the BIG must fall on the rich. But whereas a financing system based on indirect taxes means that much of the grant is recouped, financing a BIG with income taxes allows very little of the grant to be recouped. The entire gross cost must be raised, which means a massive increase in income tax rates. Net benefits also accrue to the nonpoor in the seventh and eighth deciles (important support bases of the labour movement), as well as to the poor. It is likely that there is political and economic space for increased taxation of the rich (at least to reverse the trend illustrated in figures 10.3 and 10.4), but financing a BIG requires a broad-based tax strategy (using indirect taxes on expenditure) rather than a narrowly based one (using direct taxes on incomes).

Calls for a BIG have been resisted by the senior leadership of the ANC and the government (see Matisonn and Seekings 2003). Cost is one concern, especially given fears that political competition will result in increases in benefits. Another source of concern is that the grant amounts to a handout, which government ministers (among others) deem less desirable than providing people with the "dignity of work" by creating jobs.

Unwilling to introduce a BIG, the government responded to pressure by opting for the remaining alternative, public works programmes (PWPs). Providing low-wage jobs to the unemployed serves to "self-target" the poor, because only the poor will work for low wages without undermining the labour market. Well-designed PWPs have the potential to alleviate poverty (McCord 2002) and have the additional benefit of creating assets (including new roads or water catchment areas cleared of alien vegetation). The disadvantage of PWPs (relative to a BIG) is that a substantial proportion of resources (typically between 40 and 50 percent) is absorbed in administration, rather than being channelled more directly to the poor as wages. The more complex the PWP, the greater the proportion of resources absorbed by management and the greater the risk of inefficiency and failure. The more desirable PWPs are those that are complex because, for example, they attempt to provide some skills training as well as income.

Nevertheless, as the experience of Chile has shown, it is possible to absorb a high proportion of the unemployed in government-funded and -managed PWPs. In Chile, at one point, more than 8 percent of the labour force was employed on PWPs at wages equal to one-third of the minimum wage (Cortaza 1997, 237–39). In South Africa, according to McCord (2003), it would cost more than R22 billion per year to provide low-wage employment for 2.6 million unemployed people,[2] about one-third of the 7.7 million who report that they do not have a job and would like one. This is more than the *net* cost of a BIG, which Le Roux estimates at about R15 billion per year, and is about the same as the estimated cost of providing a full-scale AIDS prevention and treatment intervention (Nattrass 2004).

The larger the scale of a PWP, the larger the problem of capacity, the higher the administrative costs, and the smaller the proportion of funds reaching the poor. It is likely that a BIG would be better targeted than a national PWP in that it would reach more of the poor and less would be lost to administrative costs. A BIG has the added advantage of reaching those who are too ill with AIDS to participate in PWPs.

Unfortunately, a BIG and PWPs are not the only pressing claimants on the fiscus in a pro-poor distributional regime. The challenge of HIV-AIDS requires a large-scale treatment and prevention programme, which would itself require a significant increase in taxation. Such a programme, combined with a BIG, would require an increase in VAT of as much as 10 to 14 percentage points (Nattrass 2004). What are the economic costs of such large increases in taxation? Are such increases politically feasible? Different societies tolerate different levels of taxation under different circumstances. Welfare expenditure typically rises as a proportion of GDP as GDP itself rises. In times of crisis, including especially war, citizens often accept large increases in taxation as legitimate—and these increases are rarely reversed after the crisis has passed. The notion of what is and is not affordable varies according to the social and economic context. Given the scale of the unemployment problem, reasonable people might well agree to such an increase in taxation, as long as they are assured that the taxes will be spent efficiently. Such a decision requires deliberation and is more likely if the deliberation is broadly inclusive. In short, it should be part of a broad accord.

Much of the public expenditure on the poor is not efficient at present. This is most true of public expenditure on education. South Africa has high enrollment rates, with many poor children doggedly studying into their late teens or early twenties. A lot of money is spent on public education, and it is spent in surprisingly egalitarian ways. Yet skills tests suggest that students learn much less than they should, and this is especially true among poor children, who attend the worst schools. Improving the value of educational expenditure is crucial to forging a more truly egalitarian distributional regime. The quality of schooling must be improved, especially in poor rural areas.

The South African Department of Education has identified causes of poor performance. Some of these are outside of its control and cannot be changed in the short term: for example, the poor educational background of parents and poverty at home. Other factors are, in principle, the responsibility of the Department of Education: poor conditions for teaching and learning, inappropriate methods, lack of access to reading and other educational materials and libraries, poor school management, a lack of order and discipline among teachers and pupils (which often results in the loss of time for teaching and learning), and the low morale of principals and teachers (RSA 2000a, 40–44).

But what underlies these problems? Improving "value for money" in education spending requires, above all, holding teachers and schools to account. Successful teachers and schools should be rewarded. Chronically unsuccessful ones need to be provided with the opportunities to improve their performance; if they fail to take advantage of such opportunities, they should be penalised. Public education in South Africa has lacked any real system of accountability for more than a decade. During the political transition from apartheid to democracy, unionised teachers mounted a successful campaign to exclude the apartheid educational inspectorate from schools. But political change in the country as a whole did not lead to the reintroduction of a transformed inspectorate. Negotiations between teachers' unions and the state dragged. Only after 2000 was any progress made in reestablishing a system of appraisal of teachers, and this new system lacked any bite in that there was no provision for either reward or penalty.

The consequences have been predictable. Many teachers are industrious and conscientious, performing extraordinarily well in the face of great difficulties. But others have performed very poorly, to the chronic detriment of schoolchildren. Too many teachers arrive late for or miss classes. In class, they spend too much time on cell phones and too little time teaching. They are too often un- or underprepared and sometimes lack the basic competence to teach their subjects. Principals can rarely do much about this, and sometimes they, too, are incompetent or corrupt. The schooling system probably requires additional resources if it is to be improved radically; motivated and competent teachers require resources to do their jobs properly. But resources on their own achieve nothing.

The rich pay for this in that their taxes are soaked up in paying salaries to underperforming teachers. But the poor pay an even higher price: their children are denied the opportunity to get ahead, and the rich resist calls for more money to be spent on social policies. These are not problems that are easily addressed solely in negotiations between teachers and the state. Rather, they should be discussed in meetings that also include parents, rich and poor. Increases in resources for social programmes (including education) should be conditional on teachers' agreeing to reforms of the system of rewards and accountability. Above we identified six components of an "outsider-friendly" or pro-poor social accord in South Africa. Deliberation about the quality of public services might be considered the seventh component of such an accord.

An egalitarian distributional regime would be one that raises the welfare of the poor and ensures that poor children face improved opportunities in life. The first of these requires a growth path that produces more jobs, especially low-wage jobs for less skilled workers. It requires that some of the holes in the social safety net be repaired, whether via a BIG or PWPs. Improved opportunities for poor children require reforms to the schooling system that increase accountability as they equip teachers to perform better. But these interventions do not exhaust the range of appropriate components of an egalitarian distributional regime. Other, more radical strategies should also be considered. For example, worker ownership of firms could be promoted via the provision of de-velopmental support for worker-owned firms. If, for example, a clothing firm decided that it could no longer compete profitably on international markets, the government should consider offering the workers (who face retrenchment) the option of taking over the firm. This would enable them to earn less than the going wage—they would be drawing a share of profits rather than the old wage, which had put the firm under pressure in the first place. Such an arrangement would at least keep people employed, albeit at lower earnings. Moreover, worker-owned firms can be more efficient than capitalist ones (Bowles and Gintis 1998). With support (perhaps in the form of training or professional ad-vice), worker-owners might end up earning more than they did as wage-earn-ing employees.

The idea of promoting worker ownership in manufacturing and services is hardly on the public agenda at present and would probably provoke much knee-jerk opposition. Yet there is widespread public support for worker owner-ship in another sector of the economy: agriculture. Economic arguments for land reform typically combine concerns with efficiency and distribution: not only will income be more equitably distributed, in that there is no division be-tween profits for a few and wages for the many, but also there will be more re-sources for the poor because production on small farms will be more labour-in-tensive than production on large farms. Implicit in this argument are the views that small farms will save on supervision costs or will work at lower marginal returns than the prevailing wage for agricultural labour. There are, of course, other arguments for land reform: it provides security of tenure in accommoda-tion, perhaps has social or cultural significance, and certainly has symbolic po-litical importance.

Worker ownership and land reform are important in part because they allow for a proliferation of opportunities to make a livelihood, albeit not (usually) a generous one. The legacy of apartheid in South Africa was that livelihoods were largely restricted to a high-earning minority. What is needed is a wider range of opportunities, including the chance to earn income in low-productivity jobs or activities, whether these are on the land, in PWPs, or in manufacturing or ser-vice enterprises. A BIG would make a serious dent in poverty and therefore de-serves serious consideration. But in the longer term, it is the growth of employ-ment and other opportunities to earn a livelihood that will shape distribution in South Africa. Education reform would enable poor children to compete with richer children for these opportunities and improve people's ability to cre-ate their own opportunities.

Apartheid generated inequality in large part by limiting opportunities to earn a living. After its end, too many poor people continue to face severely limited opportunities. They leave school with few skills, enter a labour market with few opportunities for the unskilled, and have no access to agricultural land. Educational reform and the expansion of opportunities are required if the poor are to overcome the bitter legacy of apartheid.

Notes

CHAPTER 1. INTRODUCTION

1. Esping-Andersen uses the term "distribution regime" in a chapter heading but never elaborates on its meaning (1990, 105).

2. Castles and Mitchell (1990) point out that Esping-Andersen is more concerned with equality of status than income equality, i.e., with the status-conferring aspects of public policy rather than the distributional effects in terms of income. Esping-Andersen focuses on "decommodification," which renders citizens equal in terms of status but has more ambiguous effects on the distribution of income. As he himself writes: "We should not confuse the welfare state with equality" (1996, 261).

3. Longitudinal data from the United States and Britain initially seemed to indicate that there was a long period in which the relation between economic growth and distribution did indeed resemble an inverted U. According to Williamson, inequalities grew in the nineteenth century—giving rise to the horrors of Dickensian England (Disraeli's "two nations") and to Marx's anticipation of deepening class polarisation—before they began to decline in the early twentieth century (Williamson 1985, 1991). But subsequent work by Feinstein suggests that "the best conclusion one can draw from the very imperfect evidence is that the nineteenth century exhibited no marked fluctuations in inequality" in Britain (Feinstein 1988, 728).

4. A more recent body of discursive analytical work stresses the political nature of apartheid and aspects of governance (Norval 1996; Robinson 1996) but does not explore issues of distribution.

CHAPTER 3. SOCIAL CHANGE AND INCOME INEQUALITY UNDER APARTHEID

1. Some people, like Maine, may have moved twice, from a white-owned to a black-owned farm and then to a reserve. It is unclear whether they would be included in both figures.
2. It is difficult to know precisely what the figures provided in successive Department of Native Affairs reports mean. They are widely cited as a series giving the total number of registered labour tenants. But the figures up to and including 1964 appear to be a cumulative series, whereas subsequent figures (which are much smaller, after a massive drop between 1964 and 1965) are for new registrations only. It is also unknown what proportion of labour tenants was registered at any point.
3. These ranges are approximate. McGrath (1983) estimates that 24 percent of households had incomes below R500 per year, so the actual boundary between the second and the third decile would have been a little less than R500. Similarly, 44 percent had incomes of less than R1,000, so the boundary between the fourth and the fifth deciles would have been a little less than R1,000.
4. These BMR data are for multiple households only; that is, they exclude single-member households such as domestic workers living in employers' accommodation and hostel residents. Because single-member households typically are those of working individuals, household incomes were actually quite high (and per capita incomes very high).
5. These calculations are from the 1975 data published in BMR reports in post-1975 prices but here deflated to 1975 prices. Markinor surveys in metropolitan areas found a lower range of incomes in 1977. Approximately one in four African households was in decile 4 or below; at the other end of the range, one in five households was in decile 7 (including some in decile 8). Morris (1980) reported that the average household income in Soweto was slightly less than R2,400 (stated in 1977 but deflated to 1975 prices), which is very consistent with the BMR data.

CHAPTER 4. APARTHEID AS A DISTRIBUTIONAL REGIME

1. Not all the unemployed were eligible for jobs at the labour bureaux. Eligibility depended on having a *soekwerk* (workseeker's) stamp, and in far-flung apartheid dumping grounds like Botshabelo it was not easy or cheap to get one. Applicants were required to show that they were citizens of the relevant bantustan and that their reference books were valid. The (black) office staff often had to be bribed in order to get access to the more senior white officials who controlled the soekwerk stamp (Murray 1992, 227).
2. Prior to 1948, municipalities could determine the level of influx control, and hence the response to African urbanisation varied from area to area (Simkins 1982a). The 1945 Blacks (Urban Areas) Consolidation Act provided for areas to be "prescribed" (subject to influx control). During the war years, the government only prescribed areas at the request of the municipalities concerned. After 1948, the apartheid government required that all urban areas (and later many white rural areas) be prescribed. In 1952 local, district, and regional

labour bureau structures were created, and in 1968 this was extended to the homeland areas via tribal labour bureaux.

3. The 1970 Bantu Homelands Citizenship Act attached to all blacks citizenship of one homeland or another regardless of whether they had ever been there. The Bantu Homelands Constitution Act of 1971 enabled the state president to confer self-government on any homeland. The first homeland to become "independent" was the Transkei in 1976.

4. Personal income tax was apportioned according to income and the appropriate rate from official tax tables. Estates duty and donations taxes were allocated to the top 10 percent of income earners. Sales tax (i.e., value-added tax) and excise revenues were apportioned according to expenditure patterns, and the fuel levy was allocated to the consumers of transport services. Given uncertainty as to whether corporate taxes fell on shareholders (via a reduction in profits) or consumers (via compensatory price increases), McGrath et al. provided two alternative estimates of their incidence. Similarly, two estimates were provided for the incidence of customs and import taxes. This resulted in two scenarios for the incidence of taxation.

5. With regard to public expenditures that can be apportioned to individual households, McGrath et al. adjusted the survey data for pensions to fit actual spending on pensions, allocated educational spending to households with members in educational institutions, and allocated health spending according to supplementary information provided in the government's health expenditure review (1997, 10–11). Their estimates of the distribution of health and education spending across quintiles are similar to those of Castro-Leal et al. (1999), although Castro-Leal et al. allocate a larger share of health spending to the bottom quintile and a higher share of education spending to the top quintile than do McGrath et al.

6. In the United Kingdom, direct taxes and cash transfers reduce the Gini coefficient by about 15 points; taking indirect taxes into account would reduce this. Changes in tax and social security policy under the 1979–92 Conservative Party governments had the effect of cutting the redistributive effect by 5 points; this accounted for about one-half of the increase in inequality in post-transfer disposable incomes during this period.

7. The number of worker-days lost to strike action increased substantially during the 1970s and 1980s. Such disruption raises the costs of production and places further upward pressure on wages. A 1991 survey of manufacturing employers found that "labour problems" were cited as the most common cause of the continuing drift toward capital intensity (Welcher, cited in Meintjies 1998, 11).

8. Most calculations of employment elasticity in South Africa indicate that the labour demand curve is relatively elastic. Estimates range from −0.55 to −0.85, which suggests that a 10 percent increase in wages will result in a drop in employment of between 5.5 percent and 8.5 percent (EAGER Report, no. 10, Spring 1999: 7; Fedderke and Mariotti 2002, 860).

CHAPTER 9. INCOME INEQUALITY AFTER APARTHEID

1. These Lorenz curves were plotted by David Lam.

2. One caveat needs to be added to this general conclusion. The expenditure data from the 2000 IES tell a rather different story than do the income data, but this appears to be due to inconsistencies in the measurement of expenditure and income in poorer households. Because the 2000 IES recorded a substantial drop in household expenditure at the bot-

tom end, the Theil decomposition using expenditure data shows that the between-group share rises marginally.

3. Tracking reduced attrition, but data about household members were generally provided by a single respondent in each survey, with the possibility that different members answered in 1993 and 1998. The data sets also had to be pared down to exclude some unreliable fieldwork.

4. The ASSA2002 model was developed by Rob Dorrington and others for the Actuarial Society of South Africa. It is available at www.assa.org.za.

5. The ASSA2002 model takes into account South Africa's voluntary counselling and testing programme, its mother-to-child transmission prevention programme, and the nascent antiretroviral roll-out.

CHAPTER 10. THE POST-APARTHEID DISTRIBUTIONAL REGIME

1. Interview with Lionel September, official in charge of BEE in the Department of Trade and Industry, in *Mail and Guardian,* 4 April 2003.

2. Quoted in *Mail and Guardian,* 26 September 2003.

3. Estimates by BusinessMap, reported in *Mail and Guardian,* 5 September 2003.

4. Both the Ministry of Finance's GEAR strategy (RSA 1996) and the Ministry of Labour's Employment Strategy Framework (RSA 1998, 44) recommended that amendments be made to the extension of collectively bargained wage agreements to nonparties. Soon after the Labour Market Commission (LMC 1996) presented its report, the minister of labour announced that changes to the mandatory extension provision were imminent, yet nothing came of it. The state president made a similar announcement in early 2000 but it had no effect.

5. See "Now Public Works Betrays the Poor," *Sunday Independent,* 11 June 2000.

6. This is not to say that the net impact of trade liberalisation was to reduce jobs. Indeed, there is evidence that the overall impact has been marginally positive as export industries have helped boost labour-intensive downstream industries such as transport and services (Edwards 2001). The point is simply that a more flexible labour market probably would have reduced the negative impact of trade liberalisation.

7. Personal communication. Van der Berg's recalculations of the 1993–94 data in terms of income quintiles are explained in Van der Berg 2001b and 2001c.

8. Expenditure data are from the National Treasury's *Budget Review 2003,* p. 148, deflated using the consumer price index.

9. For examples, see Ronnie Kasrils (Minister of Water Affairs and Forestry), in *Sunday Independent,* 29 June 2003.

CHAPTER 11. TRANSFORMING THE DISTRIBUTIONAL REGIME

1. The "People's Budget" is available at www.cosatu.org.za.

2. This assumes that each person works ten days per month for R35 per day and that the wage bill absorbs 48 percent of the total resources required to run a national public works programme. The figure of 48 percent was based on the average for the National Economic Forum job creation programme between 1992 and 1998.

References

Abrahams, P. 1946. *Mine Boy.* London: Heinemann.

Adam, H. 1997. The Underclass vs the Liberation Aristocracy. Paper presented at the Centre for African Studies Seminar, University of Cape Town, 26 March.

Adams, J. 2000. Quarterly Sectoral Report: Welfare. *Budget Brief* no. 47. Cape Town: Institute for Democracy in South Africa.

Adams, M., B. Cousins, and S. Manona. 2000. Land Tenure and Economic Development in Rural South Africa: Constraints and Opportunities. In B. Cousins (ed.), *At the Crossroads: Land and Agrarian Reform in South Africa into the 21st Century.* Cape Town: National Land Committee and the Programme for Land and Agrarian Studies, University of the Western Cape.

Adelman, I., and C. Morris. 1973. *Economic Growth and Social Equity in Developing Countries.* Stanford: Stanford University Press.

Adler, G., and G. O'Sullivan. 1996. Rounding up the Usual Suspects: Recycling the Labour Aristocracy Thesis. In J. Baskin (ed.), *Against the Current: Labour and Economic Policy in South Africa.* Johannesburg: Ravan.

Adler, G., and E. Webster. 1999. Towards a Class Compromise in South Africa's "Double Transition": Bargained Liberalization and the Consolidation of Democracy. *Politics and Society* 27, no. 3:347–85.

Aguiar, N. 2002. What Are the Contributions of Quantitative Methods in the Social Sciences to the Knowledge of Social Stratification and Mobility Processes in Brazil? Paper presented at the Social Hubble workshop, Cape Town, February.

Akyuz, Y., and C. Gore. 2001. African Economic Development in a Comparative Perspective. *Cambridge Journal of Economics* 25, no. 3:265–88.

Alexander, J. 1994. State, Peasantry, and Resettlement in Zimbabwe. *Review of African Political Economy* 61: 25–45.

Aliber, M. 2003. Chronic Poverty in South Africa: Incidence, Causes, and Policies. *World Development* 31, no. 3: 73–90.

Aliber, M., and R. Mokoena. 2003. The Land Question in Contemporary South Africa. In J. Daniel, A. Habib and R. Southall (Eds). *State of the Nation: South Africa, 2003–2004.* Pretoria: HSRC Press.

Amsden, A. 1980. *Asia's Next Giant: South Korea and Late Industrialisation.* New York: Oxford University Press.

Anand, S., and R. Kanbur. 1993a. The Kuznets Process and the Inequality-Development Relationship. *Journal of Development Economics* 40, no. 1:25–52.

———. 1993b. Inequality and Development: A Critique. *Journal of Development Economics* 41, no. 1:19–43.

ANC (African National Congress). 1994. *The Reconstruction and Development Programme.* Johannesburg: African National Congress.

Anderson, K. G., A. Case, and D. Lam. 2001. Causes and Consequences of Schooling Outcomes in South Africa: Evidence from Survey Data. *Social Dynamics* 27, no. 1:37–59.

Archer, S. 1971. Inter-Racial Income Distribution in South Africa: Data and Comments. Discussion paper for seminar at the Abe Bailey Institute of Inter-Racial Studies, November.

———. 1973. Perverse Growth and Income Distribution in South Africa. Seminar paper, University of Sussex, February.

———. 1989. Industrial Protection and Employment Creation in South Africa During the Inter-War Years. *South African Journal of Economic History* 4, no. 2:5–24.

Archer, S., and J. Maree. 1975. Over and Underpayment in South African Industry: A Comment. *South African Journal of Economics* 43, no. 2:175–86.

Archer, S., and E. Meyer. 1984. Hanover: A Profile of Poverty on the Eiselen Line. *Carnegie Conference Paper* no. 34. Cape Town: SALDRU, University of Cape Town.

Ardington, E. 1984. Poverty and Development in a Rural Community in KwaZulu. Working Paper no. 9. Durban: Development Studies Unit, Centre for Applied Social Science, University of Natal.

———. 1995. Return to Nkandla: The Third Survey in a Longitudinal Study of a Rural Community in KwaZulu-Natal. Research Report no. 7. Durban: Centre for Social and Development Studies, University of Natal.

Ardington, E., and F. Lund. 1995. Pensions and Development: Social Security as Complementary to Programmes of Reconstruction and Development. *Development Southern Africa* 12, no. 4:557–77.

Armstrong, P., A. Glyn, and J. Harrison. 1991. *Capitalism Since 1945.* Oxford: Basil Blackwell.

Arndt, C., and J. Lewis. 2000. The Macro Implications of HIV/AIDS in South Africa: A Preliminary Assessment. *South African Journal of Economics* 68, no. 5:856–887.

Ashforth, A. 1990. *The Politics of Official Discourse in Twentieth Century South Africa.* Oxford: Clarendon.

Atkinson, A., and A. Brandolini. 1999. Promise and Pitfalls in the Use of "Secondary" Data Sets: Income Inequality in OECD Countries. Unpublished paper. Oxford: Nuffield College.

Auerbach, F., and D. Welsh. 1981. Education. In S. Van der Horst and J. Reid (eds.), *Race Discrimination in South Africa: A Review.* Cape Town: David Philip.

Baber, R. 1998. The Structure of Livelihoods in South Africa's Bantustans: Evidence from Two Settlements in Northern Province. Ph.D. diss., Oxford University.

Barker, F. 1999. On South Africa's Labour Policies. *South African Journal of Economics* 67, no. 1:1–33.

Barnett, T., and A. Whiteside. 2002. *AIDS in the Twenty-First Century.* New York: Palgrave Macmillan.

Beall, J., O. Crankshaw, and S. Parnell. 2002. *Uniting a Divided City: Governance and Social Exclusion in Johannesburg.* London: Earthscan.

Beinart, W. 1992. Transkeian Smallholders and Agrarian Reform. *Journal of Contemporary African Studies* 11, no. 2:178–199.

———. 1994. *Twentieth-Century South Africa.* Oxford: Oxford University Press.

Bell, C., S. Devarajan, and H. Gersbach. 2003. *The Long-Run Economic Costs of AIDS: Theory and Application to South Africa.* Washington, D.C.: World Bank.

Bell, T. 1984. Unemployment in South Africa. Occasional Paper no. 10. Durban: Institute for Social and Economic Research, University of Durban at Westville.

Bell, T., and N. Cattaneo. 1997. Foreign Trade and Employment in the South African Manufacturing Industry. Occasional Report no. 4. Geneva: Employment and Training Department, International Labour Office.

BER (Bureau for Economic Research). 2001. The Macro-Economic Impact of HIV/AIDS in South Africa. Paper no. 10. Stellenbosch: Bureau for Economic Research, University of Stellenbosch. Compiled by B. Smit, L. Visagie, and P. Laubscher.

Bernstein, H. 1992. Agrarian Structures and Change: Latin America. In H. Bernstein, B. Crow, and H. Johnson (eds.), *Rural Livelihoods: Crisis and Responses.* Oxford: Oxford University Press.

Berry, A., M. von Klottnitz, R. Cassim, A. Kesper, B. Rajaratnam, and D. Van Seventer. 2002. The Economics of Small, Medium, and Micro Enterprises in South Africa. Johannesburg: Trade and Industrial Policy Strategies.

Bertrand, M., D. Miller, and S. Mullainathan. 2003. Public Policy and Extended Families: Evidence from Pensions in South Africa. *World Bank Economic Review* 17, no. 1:27–50.

Bethell, L. 2000. Politics in Brazil: From Elections Without Democracy to Democracy Without Citizenship. *Daedalus* 129, no. 2:1–28.

Bhorat, H. 2000. Some People Are More Jobless Than Others. *Sunday Independent,* 5 November 2000.

———. 2003a. The Post-Apartheid Challenge: Labour Demand Trends in the South African Labour Market, 1995–1999. DPRU Working Paper 03/82. Cape Town: Development Policy Research Unit, University of Cape Town.

———. 2003b. A Universal Income Grant for South Africa: An Empirical Assessment. In M. Samson and G. Standing (eds.), *A Basic Income Grant for South Africa.* Cape Town: University of Cape Town Press.

Bhorat, H., and J. Hodge. 1999. Decomposing Shifts in Labour Demand in South Africa. *South African Journal of Economics* 67, no. 3:348–80.

Bhorat, H., and M. Leibbrandt. 1996. Understanding Unemployment: The Relationship Between the Employed and the Jobless. In J. Baskin (ed.), *Against the Current: Labour and Economic Policy in South Africa.* Johannesburg: Ravan.

Bhorat, H., M. Leibbrandt, M. Maziya, S. Van der Berg, and I. Woolard. 2001. *Fighting Poverty: Labour Markets and Inequality in South Africa.* Cape Town: University of Cape Town Press.

Bickford-Smith, V., E. Van Heyningen, and N. Worden. 1999. *Cape Town in the Twentieth Century: An Illustrated Social History.* Cape Town: David Philip.

Binswanger, H., and K. Deininger. 2003. South Africa's Land Policy: The Legacy of History and Current Options. *World Development* 21, no. 9:1451–75.

Birdsall, N., and C. Graham. 2000. *New Markets, New Opportunities: Economic and Social Mobility in a Changing World.* Washington, D.C.: Brookings Institution Press.

Birdsall, N., and F. Jaspersen, eds. 1997. *Pathways to Growth: Comparing East Asia and Latin America.* Washington, D.C.: Inter-American Development Bank.

Bloom, D., and A. Mahal. 1997. Does the AIDS Epidemic Threaten Economic Growth? *Journal of Econometrics* 77, no. 1:105–24.

BMR (Bureau of Market Research). 1972. Income and Expenditure Patterns of Multiple Bantu Households in White Rural Areas. BMR Research Report no. 31. Pretoria: Bureau for Market Research, UNISA.

———. 1976a. Income and Expenditure Patterns of Urban Black Households in Pretoria, 1976. BMR Research Report no. 50.2. Pretoria: Bureau for Market Research, UNISA.

———. 1976b. Income and Expenditure Patterns of Urban Black Households in Johannesburg, 1976. BMR Research Report no. 50.3. Pretoria: Bureau for Market Research, UNISA.

———. 1976c. Income and Expenditure Patterns of Urban Coloured Households in Cape Town, 1976. BMR Research Report no. 50.5. Pretoria: Bureau for Market Research, UNISA.

———. 1976d. Income and Expenditure Patterns of Urban Indian Households in Durban, 1976. BMR Research Report no. 50.7. Pretoria: Bureau for Market Research, UNISA.

———. 1976e. Income and Expenditure Patterns of Urban Black Households on the East and West Rand, 1976. BMR Research Report no. 50.15. Pretoria: Bureau for Market Research, UNISA.

———. 1977. A Regional Comparison of the Income and Expenditure Patterns of Urban Non-White Households in South Africa. BMR Research Report no. 58. Pretoria: Bureau for Market Research, UNISA.

———. 1978a. Income and Expenditure Patterns of Black Households in Bophuthatswana, 1977. BMR Research Report no. 66. Pretoria: Bureau for Market Research, UNISA.

———. 1978b. Income and Expenditure Patterns of Black Households in Venda, 1977. BMR Research Report no. 64. Pretoria: Bureau for Market Research, UNISA.

———. 1979. Household Expenditure in the Republics of South Africa, Transkei and Bophuthatswana by Population and Main Expenditure Group, 1975. BMR Research Report no. 76. Pretoria: Bureau for Market Research, UNISA.

————. 1980. Income and Expenditure Patterns of Black Households in Kangwane, 1978. BMR Research Report no. 82. Pretoria: Bureau for Market Research, UNISA.

————. 1981. Income and Expenditure Patterns of Black Households in Transkei, 1979. BMR Research Report no. 90. Pretoria: Bureau for Market Research, UNISA.

————. 1982. Income and Expenditure Patterns of Urban Black Multiple Households in Johannesburg, 1980. BMR Research Report no. 94.7. Pretoria: Bureau for Market Research, UNISA.

————. 1986. Income and Expenditure Patterns of Urban Black Multiple Households in Johannesburg, 1985. BMR Research Report no. 130.9. Pretoria: Bureau for Market Research, UNISA.

————. 1989. Personal Income of the RSATBVC Countries by Population Group and Magisterial District. BMR Research Report no. 163. Pretoria: Bureau for Market Research, UNISA.

Bond, P. 1996. The Making of South Africa's Macro-economic Compromise: Scenario Planning and the Narrowing of Development Strategies. In E. Maganya and R. Houghton (eds.), *Transformation in South Africa: Policy Debates in the 1990s.* Johannesburg: Institute for African Alternatives.

————. 2000. *Elite Transition: From Apartheid to Neo-Liberalism in South Africa.* Pietermaritzburg: University of Natal Press.

Bonnel, R. 2000. HIV/AIDS and Economic Growth: A Global Perspective. *South African Journal of Economics* 68, no. 5:820–55.

Bonner, P. 1995. African Urbanisation on the Rand Between the 1930s and 1960s: Its Social Character and Political Consequences. *Journal of Southern African Studies* 21, no. 1:115–29.

Bonner, P., and V. Ndima. 1999. The Roots of Violence on the East Rand. Paper presented at the Institute for Advanced Social Research Seminar. Johannesburg: University of the Witwatersrand.

Bonner, P., and L. Segal. 1998. *Soweto: A History* Cape Town: Maskew Miller Longman.

Booysen, F. 2002. Financial Responses of Households in the Free State Province to HIV/AIDS-Related Morbidity and Mortality. *South African Journal of Economics* 70, no. 7:1193–215.

Bottomley, J. 1990. Public Policy and White Rural Poverty in South Africa, 1881–1924. Ph.D. diss., Queen's University, Kingston, Ontario.

Bowles, S. 1995. Choice of Technology, Sectoral Priorities, and Employment: The Challenge of Job Creation in the South African Economy. Report to the Labour Market Commission, Cape Town.

Bowles, S., and H. Gintis. 1998. Efficient Redistribution: New Rules for Markets, States, and Communities. In S. Bowles and H. Gintis (eds.), *Recasting Egalitarianism.* London: Verso.

Bozzoli, B. 1991. *Women of Phokeng: Consciousness, Life Strategy, and Migrancy in South Africa, 1900–1983.* Johannesburg: Ravan.

Bradley, D., E. Huber, S. Moller, F. Nielsen, and J. Stephens. 2003. Distribution and Redistribution in Post-Industrial Democracies. *World Politics* 55, no. 2:193–228.

Bromberger, N. 1974. Economic Growth and Political Change in South Africa. In A. Leftwich (ed.), *South Africa: Economic Growth and Political Change.* London: Allen and Busby.

———. 1978. South African Unemployment: A Survey of Research. In C. Simkins and C. Desmond (eds.), *South African Unemployment: A Black Picture.* Pietermaritzburg: Development Studies Research Group, University of Natal.

———. 1982. Government Policies Affecting the Distribution of Income. In R. Schrire (ed.), *South Africa: Public Policy Perspectives.* Cape Town: Juta.

———. 1983. The Growth and Welfare Performance of South African Capitalism. *Perspectives in Economic History* no. 2:1–30.

Bromberger, N., and F. Antonie. 1993. Black Small Farmers in the Homelands: Economic Prospects and Policies. In M. Lipton and C. Simkins (eds.), *State and Market in Post-Apartheid South Africa.* Johannesburg: Witwatersrand University Press.

Brookes, E., and N. Hurwitz. 1957. *The Native Reserves of Natal.* Cape Town: Oxford University Press.

Brown, M., D. Kaplan, and J-B. Meyer. 2002. The Brain Drain: An Outline of Skilled Emigration from South Africa. In D. McDonald and J. Crush (eds.), *Destinations Unknown: Perspectives on the Brain Drain in Southern Africa.* Pretoria: Africa Institute of South Africa.

Bruno, M., M. Ravallion, and L. Squire. 1998. Equity and Growth in Developing Countries: Old and New Perspectives on the Policy Issues. In V. Tanzi and K. Chu (eds.), *Income Distribution and High Quality Growth.* Cambridge: MIT Press.

Budlender, D. 2000. Human Development. In J. May (ed.), *Poverty and Inequality in South Africa: Meeting the Challenge.* Cape Town: David Philip.

Bundy, C. 1987. Street Sociology and Pavement Politics: Some Aspects of Student/Youth Consciousness During the 1985 Schools Crisis in Greater Cape Town. *Journal of Southern African Studies* 13, no. 3:303–30.

Bunting, I. 2002. Students. In N. Cloete, R. Fehnel, P. Maassen, T. Moja, H. Perold, and T. Gibbon (eds.), *Transformation in Higher Education: Global Pressures and Local Realities in South Africa.* Cape Town and Pretoria: Juta and Centre for Higher Education Transformation.

Burns, J. 2000. Inheriting the Future from the Past: Intergenerational Persistence in Educational Status in South Africa. Paper presented to the Seminar on Theoretical Institutional Economics, University of Massachusetts, Amherst.

———. 2002. Inheriting the Future: The Role of Family Background and Neighbourhood Characteristics in Child Schooling Outcomes in South Africa. Paper Presented at the Development Policy Research Unit and Frederich Eberhardt Stigting Conference on Labour Markets and Poverty in South Africa, Johannesburg.

Burski, P. 1984. Poverty in Outshoorn: Some Impressions. Carnegie Conference Paper no. 37. Cape Town: SALDRU, University of Cape Town.

Butcher, K., and C. Rouse. 2000. A Study of Wage Impacts of Unions and Industrial Councils in South Africa. Working Paper no. 442. Princeton: Industrial Relations Section, Princeton University.

Camargo, J. M., and F. Ferreira. 2000. The Poverty Reduction Strategy of the Government of Brazil: A Rapid Appraisal. Discussion Paper no. 417. Rio de Janeiro: Department of Economics, Catholic University of Rio de Janeiro.

CASE (Community Agency for Social Enquiry). 1993. "Growing Up Tough": A National

Survey of South African Youth. Report for the National Youth Development Conference, Broederstroom, March.

Case, A., and A. Deaton. 1998. Large Cash Transfers to the Elderly in South Africa. *Economic Journal* 108, no. 450:1330–61.

———. 1999. School Inputs and Educational Outcomes in South Africa. *Quarterly Journal of Economics* 114, no. 458:1047–84.

Castles, F. 1985. *The Working Class and Welfare: Reflections on the Political Development of the Welfare State in Australia and New Zealand, 1890–1980.* Sydney: Allen and Unwin.

———. 1996. Needs-Based Strategies of Social Protection in Australia and New Zealand. In G. Esping-Andersen (ed.), *Welfare States in Transition: National Adaptations in Global Economies.* London: Sage Publications.

Castles, F., and D. Mitchell. 1990. Three Worlds of Welfare Capitalism or Four? Discussion Paper no. 21. Canberra: Australian National University Graduate Programme in Public Policy.

———. 1993. Worlds of Welfare and Families of Nations. In F. Castles (ed.), *Families of Nations.* Aldershot: Dartmouth.

Castro-Leal, F., J. Dayton, and K. Metra. 1999. Public Social Spending in Africa: Do the Poor Benefit? *World Bank Research Observer* 14, no. 1:49–72.

CDE (Centre for Development and Enterprise). 1995. Post-Apartheid Population and Income Trends: A New Analysis. *CDE Research* no. 1 (September).

Charney, C. 1995. Voices of a New Democracy: African Expectations in the New South Africa. Research Report no. 38. Johannesburg: Centre for Policy Studies.

Chaskalson, M. 1989. Punt Jansen and the Origins of Reform in Township Administration, 1972–1976. *African Studies* 48, no. 2:101–30.

Chenery, H., M. Ahluwalia, C. Bell, J. Duloy, and R. Jolly. 1974. *Redistribution Through Growth.* Oxford: Oxford University Press.

Chirinko, R. 1993. Business Fixed Investment Spending: Modeling Strategies, Empirical Results, and Policy Implications. *Journal of Economic Literature* 31, no. 4:1827–48.

Cichello, P., G. Fields, and M. Leibbrandt. 2001. Are African Workers Getting Ahead? Evidence from KwaZulu-Natal, 1993–1998. *Social Dynamics* 27, no. 1:120–39.

Cloete, N., and I. Bunting. 2000. *Higher Education Transformation: Assessing Performance in South Africa.* Pretoria: Centre for Higher Education Transformation.

Cock, J. 1980. *Maids and Madams: A Study in the Politics of Exploitation.* Johannesburg: Ravan.

Collier, D. (ed.) 1979. *The New Authoritarianism in Latin America.* Princeton: Princeton University Press.

Collier, P., and J. Gunning. 1999. The IMF's Role in Structural Adjustment. Working Paper WPS/99–18. Oxford: Centre for the Study of African Economies, Oxford University.

Collier, P., S. Radwan, and S. Wangwe. 1990. *Labour and Poverty in Tanzania.* Oxford: Clarendon.

Cooper, D., and G. Subotzky. 2001. *The Skewed Revolution: Trends in South African Higher Education, 1988–1998.* Cape Town: Education Policy Unit, University of the Western Cape.

Cooper, F. 2002. *Africa Since 1940.* Cambridge: Cambridge University Press.

Cortaza, R. 1997. Chile: The Evolution and Reform of the Labour Market. In S. Edwards and N. Lustig (eds.), *Labor Markets in Latin America: Combining Social Protection with Market Flexibility.* Washington, D.C.: Brookings Institution Press.

Costa-Ribeiro, C., and M. Scalan. 2001. Social Mobility Trends in Brazil. Paper presented at the Brazil Workshop, London.

Cowen, M. 1981. Commodity Production in Kenya's Central Province. In J. Heyer, P. Roberts, and G. Williams (eds.), *Rural Development in Tropical Africa.* London: Macmillan.

Crankshaw, O. 1996a. Changes in the Racial Division of Labour During the Apartheid Era. *Journal of Southern African Studies* 22, no. 4:633–56.

———. 1996b. Social Differentiation, Conflict, and Development in a South African Township, *Urban Forum* 7, no. 1:53–67.

———. 1997a. *Race, Class, and the Changing Division of Labour under Apartheid.* London: Routledge.

———. 1997b. External Labour Market Flexibility: Is There Employment Flexibility in South African Industry? Paper presented at the Workshop on Labour Markets and Enterprise Performance in South Africa, Johannesburg.

Crompton, R. 1993. *Class and Stratification: An Introduction to Current Debates.* Cambridge: Polity.

Cross, C. 2001. Sinking Deeper Down: HIV/AIDS as an Economic Shock to Rural Households. *Society in Transition* 32, no. 1:133–47.

Crush, J. 1995. Mine Migrancy in the Contemporary Era. In J. Crush and W. James (eds.), *Crossing Boundaries: Mine Migrancy in a Democratic South Africa.* Cape Town: Institute for Democracy in South Africa, and Ottawa: International Development Research Centre.

Crush, J., A. Jeeves, and D. Yudelman. 1991. *South Africa's Labor Empire: A History of Black Migrancy to the Gold Mines.* Boulder: Westview; Cape Town: David Philip.

Dagut, J. 1977. A Growing Economy: Land of Windfalls. In A. Wright (ed.), *South Africa: The Free World's Treasure House.* Sandton: Broadside.

Davies, R. 1973. The White Working Class in South Africa. *New Left Review* 8, no. 2:40–59.

———. 1979. *Capital, State, and White Labour in South Africa: 1900–1960; An Historical Materialist Analysis of Class Formation and Class Relations.* Brighton: Harvester.

Davies, R., D. Kaplan, M. Morris, and D. O Meara. 1976. Class Struggle and the Periodisation of the State in South Africa. *Review of Radical Political Economy* no. 7:4–30.

Davis, G. 2003. *Encouraging Exclusivity: The Electoral System and Campaigning in the 1999 South African Election.* Master's thesis, University of Cape Town.

De Beer, C. 1984. *The South African Disease: Apartheid Health and Health Services.* Johannesburg: South African Review.

De Gruchy, J. 1959. *The Cost of Living for Urban Africans.* Johannesburg: South African Institute of Race Relations.

Deininger, K., and J. May. 2000. Is There Scope for Growth with Equity? The Case of Land Reform in South Africa. Working Paper no. 29. Durban: Centre for Social and Development Studies, University of Natal.

De Klerk, M. 1984. "Seasons That Will Never Return": The Impact of Farm Mechanisation on Employment, Incomes, and Population Distribution in the Western Transvaal. *Journal of Southern African Studies* 11, no. 1:84–106.

De Kock, M. 1963. Review of the Financial and Economic Situation in South Africa. *South African Journal of Economics* 31, no. 3:175–208.

Delius, P. 1996. *A Lion Amongst the Cattle: Reconstruction and Resistance in the Northern Transvaal.* Johannesburg: Ravan; Portsmouth: Heineman.

Desai, A. 2003. Neoliberalism and Resistance in South Africa. *Monthly Review* 54, no. 8:16–28.

Desmond, C. 1978. Limehill Revisited: A Case Study of the Longer-Term Effects of African Resettlement. DSRG Working Paper no. 5. Pietermaritzburg: Development Studies Research Group, University of Natal.

Desmond, C., K. Michael, and J. Gow. 2000. The Hidden Battle: HIV/AIDS in the Household and Community. *South African Journal of International Affairs* 7, no. 2:39–58.

Devarjan, S., and S. I. Hossain. 1995. The Combined Incidence of Taxes and Public Expenditure in the Philippines. Policy Research Working Paper no. 1543. Washington, D.C.: World Bank.

Devereux, S. 1983. *South African Income Distribution, 1900–1980.* SALDRU Working Paper no. 51. Cape Town: SALDRU, University of Cape Town.

Devine, E. 1997. *Social Class in America and Britain.* Edinburgh: Edinburgh University Press.

De Waal, A. 2003. How Will HIV/AIDS Transform African Governance? *African Affairs* no. 102:1–23.

De Waal, A., and J. Tumushabe. 2003. HIV/AIDS and Food Security in Africa: A Report for DFID. London.

De Wet, C. 1995. *Moving Together, Drifting Apart: Betterment Planning and Villagisation in a South African Homeland.* Johannesburg: Witwatersrand University Press.

Dinkelman, T., and F. Pirouz. 2002. Individual, Household and Regional Determinants of Labour Force Attachment in South Africa: Evidence from the 1997 October Household Survey. *South African Journal of Economics* 70, no. 5:865–91.

Disraeli, B. 1845/1930. *Sybil, or The Two Nations.* London: Macmillan.

Dollar, D., and A. Kraay. 2000. Growth Is Good for the Poor. Washington, D.C.: Development Research Group, World Bank.

Dollery, B. 1989. Capital, Labour, and State: A General Equilibrium Perspective on Liberal and Revisionist Approaches to South African Political Economy. *South African Journal of Economics* 57, no. 2:124–36.

———. 2003. A History of Inequality in South Africa, 1652–2002: Review Note. *South African Journal of Economics* 71, no. 3:595–610.

Dornbusch, R., and S. Edwards. 1990. Macroeconomic Populism. *Journal of Development Economics* 32, no. 2:247–77.

Dorrington, R., and M. Zwarenstein. 1988. Some Trends in Health Care Expenditure (1970–1985). In C. Owen (ed.), *Towards a National Health Service: Proceedings of the 1987 NAMDA Annual Conference.* Cape Town: NAMDA.

Duflo, E. 2003. Grandmothers and Granddaughters: Old Age Pension and Intra-household Allocation in South Africa. *World Bank Economic Review* 17, no. 1:1–26.

Duncan, D. 1995. *The Mills of God: The State and African Labour in South Africa, 1918–1948.* Johannesburg: Witwatersrand University Press.

Duncan, S. 1977. The Central Institution of South African Labour Exploitation. *South African Labour Bulletin* 3, no. 9:5–17.

Du Toit, A. 2003. Hunger in the Valley of Fruitfulness: Globalisation, "Social Exclusion" and Chronic Poverty in Ceres, South Africa. Paper presented at the conference titled Staying Poor: Chronic Poverty and Development Policy at the University of Manchester, April.

Du Toit, M. 1996. Co-workers of State and Church: Female Afrikaner Nationalists and Gender Conflict in the Making of State Social Welfare Policy, 1929–1939. Paper presented at the Centre for African Studies seminar, University of Cape Town, 15 May.

EAGER (Equity and Growth Through Economic Research). 1999. EAGER *Report* 10. Arlington, Va.: n.p.

Eberstadt, N. 1992. *The Tyranny of Numbers: Mismeasurement and Misrule.* Lanham: AEI.

Edwards, I. 1996. Cato Manor, June 1959. In P. Maylam and I. Edwards (eds.), *The People's City: African Life in Twentieth-Century Durban.* Pietermaritzburg: University of Natal Press.

Edwards, L. 2001. Globalisation and the Skills Bias of Occupational Employment in South Africa. *South African Journal of Economics* 69, no. 1:40–71.

Engel, E., A. Galetovic, and C. Raddatz. 1999. Taxes and Income Distribution in Chile: Some Unpleasant Redistributive Arithmetic. *Journal of Development Economics* 59, no. 1: 155–92.

Erasmus, J. 1999. *Coping Strategies of the Unemployed.* Pretoria: Human Sciences Research Council.

Erikson, R., and J. H. Goldthorpe. 1992. *The Constant Flux: Class Mobility in Industrial Societies.* Oxford: Clarendon.

Escobal, J., A. Briceño, A. P. Font, and J. Rodríquez. 1993. Public Administration and Income Distribution in Peru. In R. Hausmann and R. Rigobón (eds.), *Government Spending and Income Distribution in Latin America.* Washngton: Inter-American Development Bank.

Esping-Andersen, G. 1990. *Three Worlds of Welfare Capitalism.* Princeton: Princeton University Press.

———. 1996. Positive-Sum Solutions in a World of Trade-offs? In G. Esping-Andersen (ed.), *Welfare States in Transition: National Adaptations in Global Economies.* London: Sage.

———. 1999. *Social Foundations of Post-Industrial Economies.* Oxford: Oxford University Press.

Evans, G. (ed.). 1999. *The End of Class Politics? Class Voting in Comparative Perspective.* Oxford: Oxford University Press.

Fay, D., and R. Palmer. 2000. Prospects for Redistribution of Wealth Through Land Reform in Dwesa-Cwebe. In B. Cousins (ed.), *At the Crossroads: Land and Agrarian Reform in South Africa into the 21st Century.* Cape Town: National Land Committee and the Programme for Land and Agrarian Studies, University of the Western Cape.

Fedderke, J., R. de Kadt, and J. Luiz. 1999. Uneducating South Africa: The Failure to Address the 1910–1993 Legacy. ERSA Working Paper no. 2. Johannesburg: University of the Witwatersrand.

———. 2001. Uneducating South Africa: The Failure to Address the 1910–1993 Legacy. *International View of Education* 46, nos. 3–4:257–81.

Fedderke, J., J. Manga, and F. Pirouz. 2003. Challenging Cassandra: Household and Per Capita Household Income Distribution in the October Household Surveys 1995–1999, Income and Expenditure Surveys 1995 and 2000, and the Labour Force Survey 2000. Paper delivered at the Development Policy Research Unit and Trade and Industrial Policy Secretariat Forum, Johannesburg.

Fedderke, J., and M. Mariotti. 2002. Changing Labour Market Conditions in South Africa: A Sectoral Analysis of the Period 1970–97. *South African Journal of Economics* 70, no. 5:830–64.

Feinstein, C. 1988. The Rise and Fall of the Williamson Curve. *Journal of Economic History* 48, no. 3:699–729.

Fischer, C., M. Hout, M. S. Jankowski, S. R. Lucus, A. Swidler, and K. Voss. 1996. *Inequality by Design: Cracking the Bell Curve Myth.* Princeton: Princeton University Press.

Foxley, A. 1979. *Redistributive Effects of Government: The Chilean Case.* Geneva: International Labor Office.

———, (ed.). 1976. *Income Distribution in Latin America.* Cambridge: Cambridge University Press.

Francis, E. 1999. Learning from the Local: Rural Livelihoods in Ditsobotla, North West Province, South Africa. *Journal of Contemporary African Studies* 17, no. 1:49–73.

Freund, B. 1984. *The Making of Contemporary Africa: The Development of African Society Since 1800.* London: Macmillan.

Friedman, S., and I. Chipkin. 2001. A Poor Voice? The Politics of Inequality in South Africa. Research Report 87. Johannesburg: Centre for Policy Studies.

Gaitskell, D., J. Kimble, M. Maconachie, and E. Unterhalter. 1984. Domestic Workers in South Africa. *Review of Radical Political Economy* nos. 27–28 (double issue): 86–108.

Gallie, D. 1994. Are the Unemployed an Underclass? Some Evidence from the Social Change and Economic Life Initiative. *Sociology* 28, no. 3:737–57.

Gallie, D., and C. Marsh. 1994. The Experience of Unemployment. In D. Gallie, C. Marsh, and C. Vogler (eds.), *Social Change and the Experience of Unemployment.* Oxford: Oxford University Press.

Garcia-Penalosa, C. 2000. Macroeconomic Determinants of Income Inequality: Theoretical Approaches. Paper presented at the conference on Growth and Inequality in Developing Countries, Marseilles.

Garibaldi, P., and P. Mauro. 2002. Anatomy of Employment Growth. *Economic Policy* 17, no. 34:7–65.

Gelb, S. 1987. Making Sense of the Crisis. *Transformation* no. 5:33–50.

Gelb, S., and E. Webster. 1996. Jobs and Equity: The Social Democratic Challenge. *South African Labour Bulletin* 20, no. 3:73–8.

Gerson, J. 1981. The Question of Structural Unemployment in South Africa. *South African Journal of Economics* 49, no. 1:10–25.

———. 1982. The Unemployment Issue. In B. Kantor and D. Rees (eds.), *South African Economic Issues.* Cape Town: Juta.

Gilbert, A. 1996. Land, Housing, and Infrastructure in Latin America's Mega-Cities. In A. Gilbert (ed.), *The Mega-City in Latin America.* Tokyo: United Nations University Press.

Giliomee, H. 1999. Afrikaner Entrepreneurship and the Afrikaner Economic Advance, 1900–1990: A Tale with a Puzzle and Some Twists. Paper prepared for the Centre for Development and Enterprise, Johannesburg.

Glaser, C. 1993. When Are They Going to Fight? Tsotsis, Youth Politics, and the PAC. In P. Bonner, P. Delius, and D. Posel (eds.), *Apartheid's Genesis, 1935–1962.* Johannesburg: Witwatersrand University Press.

———. 1994. Youth Culture and Politics in Soweto, 1958–1976. Ph.D. diss., Cambridge University.

Goldin, I. 1987. *Making Race: The Politics and Economics of Coloured Identity in South Africa.* Cape Town: Maskew Miller Longman.

Goldthorpe, J. 1997. The "Goldthorpe" Class Schema: Some Observations on Conceptual and Operational Issues in Relation to the ESRC Review of Government Social Classifications. In D. Rose and K. O'Reilly (eds.), *Constructing Classes: Towards a New Social Classification for the UK.* Swindon: Economic and Social Research Council and Office for National Statistics.

Goldthorpe, J., C. Llewellyn, and C. Payne. 1980. *Social Mobility and Class Structure in Modern Britain.* Oxford: Clarendon.

Goldthorpe, J., and G. Marshall. 1992. The Promising Future of Class Analysis: A Response to Recent Critiques. *Sociology* 26, no. 3:381–400.

Goodin, R., B. Headey, R. Muffels, and H. Dirven. 1999. *The Real Worlds of Welfare Capitalism.* Cambridge: Cambridge University Press.

Granovetter, M. 1974. *Getting a Job: A Study of Contacts and Careers.* Cambridge: Harvard University Press.

Greenberg, Stanley. 1980. *Race and State in Capitalist Development: South Africa in Comparative Perspective.* New Haven: Yale University Press.

———. 1987. *Legitimating the Illegitimate: State, Markets, and Resistence in South Africa.* Berkeley: University of California Press.

Greenberg, Stanley, and H. Giliomee. 1985. Managing Influx Control from the Rural End: The Black Homelands and the Underbelly of Privilege. In H. Giliomee and L. Schlemmer (eds.), *Up Against the Fences: Poverty, Passes, and Privilege in South Africa.* Cape Town: David Philip.

Greenberg, Stephen. 2003. Land Reform and Transition in South Africa. *Transformation* no. 52:42–67.

Griffin, K. 1989. *Alternative Strategies for Economic Development.* London: Macmillan.

Hacker, A. 1992. *Two Nations: Black and White, Separate, Hostile, Unequal.* New York: Charles Scribner's Sons.

Haddad, L., and R. Kanbur. 1990. How Serious Is the Neglect of Intra-Household Inequality? *Economic Journal* 100, no. 402:866–81.

Haggard, S. 1990. *Pathways from the Periphery: The Politics of Growth in Newly Industrialising Countries.* Ithaca: Cornell University Press.

Hall, P., and D. Soskice (eds.). 2001. *Varieties of Capitalism: The Institutional Foundations of Comparative Advantage.* Oxford: Oxford University Press.

Harris, J., and M. Todaro. 1970. Migration, Unemployment and Development: A Two-Sector Analysis. *American Economic Review* 60, no. 1:117–26.

Harvey, S. 1996. Labour Market Killing Fields. *South African Labour Bulletin* 20, no. 2:28–31.

Haughton, J. 1998. The Dynamics of Economic Change. In W. Crotty and D. Schmitt (eds.), *Ireland and the Politics of Change.* London: Longman.

Heintz, J., and S. Bowles. 1996. Subsidising Employment: Wage Subsidies and Job Creation. In J.Baskin (ed.), *Against the Current: Labour and Economic Policy in South Africa.* Johannesburg: Ravan.

Hemerijck, A., and M. Schludi. 2000. Sequences of Policy Failures and Effective Policy Responses. In F. Scharpf and V. Schmidt (eds.), *Welfare and Work in the Open Economy.* Oxford: Oxford University Press.

Hertz, T. 2001. Education, Inequality, and Economic Mobility in South Africa. Ph.D. diss., University of Massachusetts, Amherst.

Heyer, J. 1981. Agricultural Development Policy in Kenya from the Colonial Period to 1975. In J. Heyer, P. Roberts, and G. Williams (eds.), *Rural Development in Tropical Africa.* London: Macmillan.

Hindson, D. 1987. *Pass Controls and the Urban Proletariat.* Johannesburg: Raven.

Hirschowitz, R., S. Milner, and D. Everatt. 1994. Growing up in a Violent Society. In D. Everatt (ed.), *Creating a Future: Youth Policy for South Africa.* Johannesburg: Ravan.

Hofmeyr, J. 1985. *Labour Market Participation and Unemployment.* HSRC Investigation into Manpower Issues, Regional Development Study no. 1. Pretoria: Human Sciences Research Council.

———. 1994. An Analysis of African Wage Movements in South Africa. Research Monograph no. 9. Durban: Economic Research Unit, University of Natal.

———. 2000. The Changing Pattern of Segmentation in the South African Labour Market. *Studies in Economics and Econometrics* 24, no. 2:109–28.

Horner, D., and G. Van Wyk. 1984. Quiet Desperation: The Poverty of Calitzdorp. Carnegie Conference Paper no. 36. Cape Town: SALDRU, University of Cape Town.

Horwitz, R. 1967. *The Political Economy of South Africa.* London: Weidenfeld and Nicholson.

Houghton, D. H. 1964. *The South African Economy.* Oxford: Oxford University Press.

———. 1971. Economic Development, 1865–1965. In M. Wilson and L. Thompson (eds.), *The Oxford History of South Africa.* Vol. 2, *South Africa, 1870–1966.* Oxford: Clarendon.

———. 1976. *The South African Economy.* Cape Town: Oxford University Press.

Houghton, D. H., and E. Walton. 1952. *The Economy of a Native Reserve,* vol. 2 of the Keiskammahoek Rural Survey. Pietermaritzburg: Shuter and Shooter.

House, K., and A. Williams. 2000. The Status of Employment in the South African Clothing Sector: Diverting a Race to the Bottom. Paper presented at the TIPS Policy Forum, Muldersdrift, September.

Huber, E., and J. Stephens. 2001. *Development and Crisis of the Welfare State.* Chicago: University of Chicago Press.

Hyslop, J. 1993. A Destruction Coming In: Bantu Education as Response to Social Crisis. In P. Bonner, P. Delius, and D. Posel (eds.), *Apartheid's Genesis, 1935–1962.* Johannesburg: Witwatersrand University Press.

————. 1999. *The Classroom Struggle: Policy and Resistance in South Africa, 1940–1990.* Pietermaritzburg: University of Natal Press.

IADB (Inter-American Development Bank). 1998. *Facing up to Inequality in Latin America: Economic and Social Progress in Latin America, 1998–99 Report.* Washington, D.C.: Inter-American Development Bank, distributed by Johns Hopkins University Press.

IDASA (Institute for Democracy in South Africa). 1997. *Poverty Profile:* special issue on child maintenance grants. Cape Town: IDASA.

IFAD (International Fund for Agricultural Development). 2001. Strategy Paper on HIV/AIDS for East and Southern Africa, International Fund for Agricultural Development, October.

Iliffe, J. 1987. *The African Poor: A History.* Cambridge: Cambridge University Press.

ILO (International Labour Organisation). 1971. *Concepts of Labour Force Underutilisation.* Geneva: International Labour Office.

————. 1999. (Drafted by S. Hayter, G. Reinecke, and R. Torres). *South Africa: Studies on the Social Dimensions of Globalisation.* Geneva: International Labour Office.

IMF (International Monetary Fund). 1995. South Africa: Selected Issues. Washington, D.C.: IMF Africa Department.

ING-Barings. 2000. Economic Impact of AIDS in South Africa: A Dark Cloud on the Horizon. Research conducted by Kristina Quattek, Global Research.

Jeeves, A., and J. Crush. 1997. Introd. to *White Farms, Black Labor: The State and Agrarian Change in Southern Africa, 1910–1950,* ed. A. Jeeves and J. Crush. Pietermaritzburg: University of Natal Press.

Jensen, R. 2003. Do Private Transfers "Displace" the Benefits of Public Transfers? Evidence from South Africa. *Journal of Public Economics* 88, no. 1:89–112.

Joffe, A., D. Kaplan, R. Kaplinsky, and D. Lewis. 1995. *Improving Manufacturing Performance in South Africa: Report of the Industrial Strategy Project.* Cape Town: University of Cape Town Press.

Johnstone, F. 1970. White Prosperity and White Supremacy in South Africa Today. *African Affairs* 69, no. 274:124–40.

————. 1976. *Race, Class, and Gold.* London: Routledge and Kegan Paul.

Jolly, R. 1976. Redistribution with Growth. In A. Cairncross and M. Puri (eds.), *Employment, Income Distribution, and Development Strategy: Problems of the Developing Countries.* London: Macmillan.

Jones, J. D. R. 1949. Social Welfare. In E. Hellman (ed.), *Handbook of Race Relations in South Africa.* Cape Town: Oxford University Press, 413–41.

Kantor, B. 1980. Blacks: Is There Unemployment? *Businessmen's Law* 9, no. 4:104–7 and 9, no. 5:143–44.

Kaplan, D. 2003. Manufacturing Performance and Policy in South Africa. Paper presented to the Trade and Industrial Policy Secretariat/Development Policy Research Unit Forum, Johannesburg.

Kaplinsky, R. 1995. Capital Intensity in South African Manufacturing and Unemployment, 1972–90. *World Development* 23, no. 2:179–92.

Karshenas, M. 2001. Agriculture and Economic Development in Sub-Saharan Africa and Asia. *Cambridge Journal of Economics* 25, no. 3:315–42.

Kavanagh, E., J. Considine, E. Doyle, L. Gallagher, C. Kavanagh, and E. O'Leary. 1997. The Political Economy of EMU in Ireland. In E. Jones, J. Frieden, and F. Torres (eds.), *EMU and the Smaller Countries: Joining Europe's Monetary Club.* New York: St. Martin's.

Keegan, T. 1988. *Facing the Storm: Portraits of Black Lives in Rural South Africa.* London: Zed.

————. 1989. Mike Morris and the Social Historians: A Response and a Critique. *Africa Perspective,* n.s., 1, nos. 7–8:1–14.

Kenny, B., and E. Webster. 1998. Eroding the Core: Flexibility and the Resegmentation of the South African Labour Market. *Critical Sociology* 24, no. 3:216–43.

Keppel-Jones, A. 1949. Land and Agriculture Outside the Reserves. In E. Hellman (ed.), *Handbook of Race Relations in South Africa.* Cape Town: Oxford University Press.

Keswell, M., and L. Poswell. 2002. How Important Is Education for Getting Ahead in South Africa? Working Paper no. 22. Cape Town: Centre for Social Science Research, University of Cape Town.

Kingdon, G. 1999. Unpublished presentation at Workshop on Unemployment. Oxford: Institute for Economics and Statistics, Oxford University.

Kingdon, G., and J. Knight. 1999. Links Between Unemployment and Poverty in South Africa. Paper presented at the Conference of Poverty in Africa, Centre for the Study of African Economies, Oxford University, April.

Kitching, G. 1980. *Class and Economic Change in Kenya: The Making of an African Petite Bourgeoisie.* New Haven: Yale University Press.

Klasen, S., and I. Woolard. 1998. Unemployment, Household Formation, Poverty, and Nutrition in South Africa. Paper presented at a Workshop at the University of Pretoria, April.

————. 1999. Levels, Trends, and Consistency of Employment and Unemployment Figures in South Africa. *Development Southern Africa* 16, no. 1:3–36.

Knight, J. 1964. A Theory of Income Distribution in South Africa. *Oxford Bulletin of Economics and Statistics* 27, no. 4:289–310.

————. 1971. Wages and Employment in Developed and Underdeveloped Economies. *Oxford Economic Papers* 23, no. 1:42–58.

————. 1977. Labour Supply in the South African Economy and Its Implications for Agriculture. In F. Wilson, A. Kooy, and D. Hendrie (eds.), *Farm Labour in South Africa* Cape Town: David Philip.

————. 1978. Labour Allocation and Unemployment in South Africa. *Oxford Bulletin of Economics and Statistics* 40, no. 2:93–129.

Knight, J., and M. McGrath. 1977. An Analysis of Racial Wage Discrimination in South Africa. *Oxford Bulletin of Economics and Statistics* 39, no. 4:245–72.

Korpi, W., and J. Palme. 1998. The Paradox of Redistribution and Strategies of Equality: Welfare State Institutions, Inequality, and Poverty in the Western Countries. *American Sociological Review* 63, no. 5:661–87.

Kruger, J. 1992. *State Provision of Social Security: Some Theoretical, Comparative, and Historical Perspectives with Reference to South Africa.* Master's thesis, University of Stellenbosch.

Kuznets, S. 1955. Economic Growth and Income Inequality. *American Economic Review* 45, no. 1:1–28.

————. 1963. Quantitative Aspects of the Economic Growth of Nations. *Economic Development and Cultural Change* 11, no. 2:1–80.

Lacey, M. 1981. *Working for Boroko.* Johannesburg: Ravan.

Lam, D. 1999. Generating Extreme Inequality: Schooling, Earnings and Intergenerational Transmission of Human Capital in South Africa and Brazil. *Research Report* no. 99–439. Ann Arbor: Population Studies Center at the Institute for Social Research, University of Michigan.

Lecaillon, J., F. Paukert, C. Morrison, and D. Germidis. 1984. *Income Distribution and Economic Development.* Geneva: International Labor Organisaion.

Legassick, M. 1972. The Dynamics of Modernisation in South Africa. *Journal of African History* 13, no. 1:145–50.

———. 1974. Legislation, Ideology, and Economy in Post 1948 South Africa. *Journal of Southern African Studies* 1, no. 1:5–35.

———. 1978. Post-script to "Legislation, Ideology and Economy in Post 1948 South Africa." In L. Schlemmer and E. Webster (eds.), *Change, Reform, and Economic Growth in South Africa.* Johannesburg: Ravan.

Leibbrandt, M., H. Bhorat, and I. Woolard. 1999. Understanding Contemporary Household Inequality in South Africa. Working Paper no. 99/25. Cape Town: Development Policy Research Unit, University of Cape Town.

———. 2000. Understanding Contemporary Household Inequality in South Africa. *Studies in Economics and Econometrics* 24, no. 3:31–52.

Leibbrandt, M., and I. Woolard. 1999. *Rural Labour Markets, Migrant Labour and Rural Poverty in South Africa.* Report for the International Labour Organisation, Geneva.

———. 2001. The Labour Market and Household Income Inequality in South Africa: Existing Evidence and New Panel Data. *Journal of International Development* 13, no. 6:671–89.

Lemon, A., and L. Stevens. 1999. Reshaping Education in the New South Africa. *Geography* 84, no. 3:222–32.

Lenta, G. 1981. Land Shortage and Land Unused: The Paradoxical Patterns of KwaZulu. Occasional Paper no. 10. Durban: Economic Research Unit, University of Natal.

Leo, C. 1984. *Land and Class in Kenya.* Toronto: University of Toronto Press.

Le Roux, P. 2002. Financing a Universal Income Grant in South Africa. *Social Dynamics* 28, no. 2:98–121.

Levetan, L. 1984. Structural Shifts in the George Economy: Underemployment and Unskilled Labour as Conditions of Impoverishment. Carnegie Conference Paper no. 39. Cape Town: SALDRU, University of Cape Town.

Levy, B. 1992. How Can South African Manufacturing Efficiently Create Employment? An Analysis of the Impact of Trade and Industrial Policy. World Bank Informal Discussion Papers on Aspects of the South African Economy, Paper no. 1. Washington, D.C.: World Bank.

Lewis, W. A. 1954. Economic Development with Unlimited Supplies of Labour. *Manchester School* 20:139–91.

Lewis, W. A. 1976. Development and Distribution. In A. Cairncross and M. Puri (eds.), *Employment, Income Distribution, and Development Strategy: Problems of the Developing Countries.* London: Macmillan.

Lipton, Merle. 1977. South Africa: Two Agricultures? In F. Wilson, A. Kooy, and D. Hendrie (eds.), *Farm Labour in South Africa.* Cape Town: David Philip.

————. 1986. *Capitalism and Apartheid: South Africa, 1910–1986.* Aldershot: Wildwood House.

Lipton, M., F. Ellis, and M. Lipton, eds. 1996. *Land, Labour and Livelihoods in Rural South Africa.* Durban: Indicator Press.

Lipton, Merle, and C. Simkins. 1993. Introd. to *State and Market in Post-Apartheid South Africa,* ed. Merle Lipton and C. Simkins. Johannesburg: Witwatersrand University Press.

Lipton, Michael. 1977. *Why Poor People Stay Poor: A Study of Urban Bias in World Development.* London: Temple Smith.

LMC (Labour Market Commission). 1996. *Restructuring the South African Labour Market.* Report of the Presidential Commission of Inquiry into Labour Market Policy, Cape Town.

Lodge, T. 1983. *Black Politics in South Africa Since 1945.* Johannesburg: Ravan.

————. 2003. Politics, Poverty, and Policy in South Africa, 1994–2002. Paper presented at the nineteenth congress of the International Political Science Association, Durban, July.

Loots, L. 1977. Alternative Approaches to the Estimation of Unemployment. Paper presented at Workshop on Unemployment and Labour Reallocation, Pietermaritzburg.

————. 1978. A Profile of Black Unemployment in South Africa: Two Area Studies. Working Paper no. 19. Cape Town: SALDRU, University of Cape Town.

Lund, F. 1993. State Security Benefits in South Africa. *International Social Security Review* 46, no. 1:5–26.

Macun, I. 2000. Growth, Structure, and Power in the South African Union Movement. In G. Adler and E. Webster (eds.), *Trade Unions and Democratization in South Africa, 1985–1997.* London: Macmillan.

Mager, A. 1999. *Gender and the Making of a South African Bantustan: A Social History of the Ciskei, 1945–1959.* Portsmouth: Heinemann.

Malherbe, E. 1977. *Education in South Africa.* Vol. 2, *1923–1975.* Cape Town: Juta.

Maluccio, J., L. Haddad, and J. May. 2000. Social Capital and Household Welfare in South Africa, 1993–98. *Journal of Development Studies* 36, no. 6:54–81.

Maluccio, J., D. Thomas, and L. Haddad. 1999. The Mobility of Adults in Post-Apartheid South Africa: Levels, Determinants, and Consequences. Mimeo, International Food Policy Research Institute, Washington, D.C.

Mapadimeng, M. S. 2003. The Land Reform for Agricultural Development Sub-Programme: Opportunity for or Constraint to Land Reform, Rural Economic Development, and Poverty Alleviation. *Transformation* no. 52:20–41.

Marais, H. 1998. *South Africa: Limits to Change; The Political Economy of Transition.* Cape Town: University of Cape Town Press; London: Zed.

Marcus, T. 1989. *Modernising Super-exploitation: Restructuring South African Agriculture.* London: Zed.

Maree, J. 1978. Unemployment and the Labour Market. In C. Simkins and C. Desmond (eds.), *South African Unemployment: A Black Picture.* Pietermaritzburg: Development Studies Research Group, University of Natal.

Maree, J., and P. J. de Vos. 1975. *Underemployment, Poverty, and Migrant Labour in the Transkei and Ciskei.* Johannesburg: South African Institute for Race Relations.

Marks, S. 1994. *Divided Sisterhood.* New York: St. Martin's.

Marks, S., and N. Anderson. 1992. Industrialisation, Rural Health, and the 1944 National Health Service Commission in South Africa. In S. Feierman and K. Janzen (eds.), *The Social Basis of Health and Healing in Africa.* Berkeley: University of California Press.

Márquez, G., J. Mukherjee, J. C. Navarro, R. A. González, R. Palacios, and R. Rigobón. 1993. Fiscal Policy and Income Distribution in Venezuela. In R. Hausmann and R. Rigobón (eds.), *Government Spending and Income Distribution in Latin America.* Washington, D.C.: Inter-American Development Bank.

Marshall, G. 1997a. Classes in Britain: Marxist and Official. In G. Marshall. *Repositioning Class: Social Inequality in Industrial Societies.* London: Sage.

———. 1997b. Introduction: Class and Class Analysis in the 1990s. In G. Marshall. *Repositioning Class: Social Inequality in Industrial Societies.* London: Sage.

Marshall, G., S. Roberts, and C. Burgoyne. 1996. Social Class and the Underclass in Britain and the USA. *British Journal of Sociology* 47, no. 1:22–44.

———. 1997. Social Class and Underclass in Britain and the USA. In G. Marshall. *Repositioning Class: Social Inequality in Industrial Societies.* London: Sage.

Marshall, G., S. Roberts, C. Burgoyne, A. Swift, and D. Routh. 1997. Class, Gender, and the Asymmetry Hypothesis. In G. Marshall. *Repositioning Class: Social Inequality in Industrial Societies.* London: Sage. (Originally published in *European Sociological Review* 11, 1995.)

Marshall, G., D. Rose, H. Newby, and C. Vogler. 1988. *Social Class in Modern Britain.* London: Hutchinson.

Marshall, G., A. Swift, and S. Roberts. 1997. *Against the Odds: Social Class and Social Justice in Industrial Societies.* Oxford: Clarendon.

Marshall, T. 1949/1992. Citizenship and Social Class. In T. Marshall and T. Bottomore, *Citizenship and Social Class.* London: Pluto.

Massey, D., and N. Denton. 1993. *American Apartheid: Segregation and the Making of the Underclass.* Cambridge: Harvard University Press.

Masson, P. 2000. Aggregate Fluctuations and Inequality. Paper presented to the conference Poverty and Income Distribution in Developing Countries, Marseille, November.

Mather, C. 1997. Wage Workers and Labor Tenants in Barberton, 1920–1950. In A. Jeeves and J. Crush (eds.), *White Farms, Black Labor: The State and Agrarian Change in Southern Africa, 1910–1950.* Portsmouth: Heinemann.

Matisonn, H. and J. Seekings. 2003. The Politics of the Basic Income Grant in South Africa, 1996–2002. In G. Standing and M. Samson (eds.), *A Basic Income Grant for South Africa.* Cape Town: University of Cape Town Press.

Mattes, R. 2002. South Africa: Democracy Without the People? *Journal of Democracy* 13, no. 1:22–36.

Mattes, R., and J. Piombo. 2001. Opposition Parties and the Voters in South Africa's General Election of 1999. *Democratization* 8, no. 3:101–28.

May, J., and B. Roberts. 2001. Panel Data and Policy Analysis in South Africa: Taking a Long View. *Social Dynamics* 27, no. 1:96–119.

May, J., I. Woolard, and S. Klasen. 2000. The Nature and Measurement of Poverty and Inequality. In J. May (ed.), *Poverty and Inequality in South Africa: Meeting the Challenge.* Cape Town: David Philip.

Maylam, P. 1996. The Struggle for Space in Twentieth-Century Durban. In P. Maylam and I. Edwards (eds.), *The People's City: African Life in Twentieth Century Durban.* Pietermaritzburg: University of Natal Press.

McCartan, P. 1984. Recruitment and Wage Determination Procedures of Manufacturing Firms in the Eastern Cape. Carnegie Conference Paper no. 121. Cape Town: SALDRU, University of Cape Town.

McCord, A. 2002. Public Works as a Response to Labour Market Failure in South Africa. Working Paper no. 19. Cape Town: Centre for Social Science Research, University of Cape Town.

———. 2003. The Economics of Employment Generation. Paper presented at a Centre for Social Science Research seminar, University of Cape Town.

McDonald, D. 2002. The Bell Tolls for Thee: Cost Recovery, Cutoffs, and the Affordability of Municipal Services in South Africa. In D. McDonald and J. Pape (eds.), *Cost Recovery and the Crisis of Service Delivery.* Pretoria: Human Science Research Council.

McGrath, M. 1979a. The Racial Distribution of Taxes and State Expenditures. Black/White Income Gap Project Final Research Report no. 2. Durban: Department of Economics, University of Natal.

———. 1979b. Health Expenditure in South Africa. In G. Westcott and F. Wilson (eds.), *Perspectives on the Health System.* Johannesburg: Ravan; Cape Town: SALDRU, University of Cape Town.

———. 1983. The Distribution of Personal Income in South Africa in Selected Years over the Period from 1945 to 1980. Ph.D. diss., University of Natal, Durban.

———. 1984. The Determinants of Poverty: A Theoretical Analysis. Carnegie Conference Paper no. 269. Cape Town: SALDRU, University of Cape Town.

———. 1990. Economic Growth, Income Distribution, and Social Change. In N. Nattrass and E. Ardington (eds.), *The Political Economy of South Africa.* Cape Town: Oxford University Press.

McGrath, M., C. Janisch, and C. Horner. 1997. Redistribution Through the Fiscal System in the South African Economy. Paper presented to the Economics Society of South Africa Conference, Potchefstroom.

McGrath, M., and A. Whiteford. 1994. Inequality in the Size Distribution of Income in South Africa. Stellenbosch Economic Project Occasional Paper no. 10. Stellenbosch: University of Stellenbosch.

McIntyre, D. 1997. Health Care Financing and Expenditure in South Africa: Towards Equity and Efficiency in Policy Making. Ph.D. diss., University of Cape Town.

McKinley, D. 1997. *The ANC and the Liberation Struggle.* London: Pluto.

Meerman, J. 1979. *Public Expenditure in Malaysia.* Oxford: Oxford University Press.

Meintjes, C. 1998. Impediments on the Labour Absorption Capacity of the South African Economy. Discussion Paper no. 2. Halfway House: Development Bank of Southern Africa.

MERG (Macro-Economic Research Group). 1993. *Making Democracy Work: A Framework for Macro-Economic Policy in South Africa.* Bellville: University of the Western Cape.

Meth, C. 2003. Mass Poverty, Slow Economic Growth and Redistribution. *Social Dynamics* 29, no. 1:99–130.

Meth, C., and R. Dias. 2003. Increases in Poverty in South Africa: 1999–2002. Paper delivered at the Development Policy Research Unit and Trade and Industrial Policy Secretariat Forum, Johannesburg.

Meth, C., and S. Piper. 1984. *A History of the UIF in South Africa.* Mimeo, University of Natal, Durban.

Milanovic, B. 1999. Do More Unequal Countries Redistribute More? Does the Median Voter Hypothesis Hold? Mimeo.

Mills, C. W. 1950. *The Sociological Imagination.* New York: Oxford University Press.

Mkandawire, T. 2001. Thinking About Developmental States in Africa. *Cambridge Journal of Economics* 25, no. 3:289–313.

Moll, P. 1996. Compulsory Centralisation of Collective Bargaining in South Africa. *American Economic Review: Papers and Proceedings* 82, no. 2:326–29.

———. 2000. Discrimination Is Declining in South Africa but Inequality Is Not. *Studies in Economics and Econometrics* 24, no. 3:91–108.

Moll, T. 1984. A Mixed and Threadbare Bag: Employment, Incomes, and Poverty in Lower Roza, Qumbu, Transkei. Carnegie Conference Paper, no. 47. Cape Town: SALDRU, University of Cape Town.

———. 1990. Output and Productivity Trends in South Africa: Apartheid and Economic Growth. Ph.D. diss., Cambridge University.

———. 1991. Did the Apartheid Economy Fail? *Journal of Southern African Studies* 17, no. 2:271–91.

———. 1992. Mickey Mouse Numbers and Inequality Research. *Journal of Development Studies* 28, no. 4:689–705.

Møller, V. 1992. Quality of Life in Unemployment: A Survey Evaluation of Black Township Dwellers. Pretoria: Human Sciences Research Council.

Morifi, M. 1984. Life Among the Poor in Philipstown. Carnegie Conference Paper no. 33. Cape Town: SALDRU, University of Cape Town.

Morley, S. 1995. *Poverty and Inequality in Latin America: The Impact of Adjustment and Recovery in the 1980s.* Baltimore: Johns Hopkins University Press.

———. 2000. Distribution and Growth in Latin America in an Era of Structural Reform. Paper Presented to the Conference on Poverty and Income Inequality in Developing Countries: A Policy Dialogue on the Effects of Globalisation, hosted by the OECD Development Centre, Paris.

Morrell, R. 1987. The South African State in 1924. *Transformation,* no. 4:39–53.

Morris, M. 1976a. The Development of Capitalism in South Africa: Class Struggle in the Countryside. *Economy and Society* 5, no. 4:292–343.

———. 1976b. The Development of Capitalism in South Africa. *Journal of Development Studies* 12, no. 3:280–93.

———. 1987. Social History and the Transition to Capitalism in the South African Countryside. *Africa Perspective,* n.s., 1, nos. 5–6:7–24.

Morris, P. 1980. *Soweto: A Review of Existing Conditions and Some Guidelines for Change.* Johannesburg: Urban Foundation.

Moyo, Sam. 1995. *The Land Question in Zimbabwe.* Harare: SAPES Books.

Mujica, P., and O. Larrañaga. 1993. Social Policies and Income Distribution in Chile. In R. Hausmann and R. Rigobón (eds.), *Government Spending and Income Distribution in Latin America.* Washington, D.C.: Inter-American Development Bank.

Murray, Charles. 1984. *Losing Ground.* New York: Basic Books.

———. 1990. *The Emerging British Underclass.* London: Institute of Economic Affairs.

Murray, Colin. 1981. *Families Divided: The Impact of Migrant Labour in Lesotho.* Cambridge: Cambridge University Press.

———. 1992. *Black Mountain: Land, Class and Power in the Eastern Orange Free State, 1880s–1980s.* Johannesburg: Witwatersrand University Press.

———. 1995. Structural Unemployment, Small Towns, and Agrarian Change in South Africa. *African Affairs* 94, no. 374:5–22.

———. 2000a. Changing Livelihoods: The Free State, 1990s. *African Studies* 59, no. 1:115–142.

———. 2000b. Family Histories and "Household" Livelihoods: Qwaqwa, 1970s to 1990s. University of Manchester.

Nattrass, J. 1977. Narrowing Wage Differentials and Income Distribution in South Africa. *South African Journal of Economics* 45, no. 4:408–32.

———. 1979. The Impact of the Riekert Commission's Recommendations on the "Black States." *South African Labour Bulletin* 5, no. 4:75–86.

———. 1988. *The South African Economy: Its Growth and Change.* 2d ed. Cape Town: Oxford University Press.

Nattrass, N. 1990. Wages, Profits, and Apartheid. Ph.D. diss., Oxford University.

———. 1991. Controversies About Capitalism and Apartheid in South Africa: An Economic Perspective. *Journal of Southern African Studies* 17, no. 4:654–77.

———. 1992. Profitability: The Soft Underbelly of South African Regulation Analysis. *Review of Radical Political Economics* 24, no. 1:31–51.

———. 1994a. Politics and Economics in ANC Economic Policy. *African Affairs* 93, no. 372:343–59.

———. 1994b. Apartheid and Capitalism: Social Structure of Accumulation or Contradiction? In D. Kotz, T. McDonough, and M. Reich (eds.), *Social Structures of Accumulation: The Political Economy of Growth and Crisis.* New York: Cambridge University Press.

———. 1996. Gambling on Investment: Competing Economic Strategies in South Africa. *Transformation* no. 31:25–42.

———. 2000a. The Debate About Unemployment in the 1990s. *Studies in Economics and Econometrics* 4, no. 3:73–90.

———. 2000b. Inequality, Unemployment, and Wage-setting Institutions in South Africa. *Studies in Economics and Econometrics* 24, no. 3:129–42.

———. 2000c. Wage-Strategies and Minimum Wages in Decentralised Regions: The Case of the Clothing Industry in Phuthaditjhaba, South Africa. *International Journal of Urban and Regional Research* 24, no. 4:873–88.

———. 2001. High Productivity Now: A Critical Review of South Africa's Growth Strategy. *Transformation* no. 45:1–24.

———. 2003a. Unemployment and the Labour Force. In SALDRU, *Khayelitsha/Mitchell's*

Plain Survey 2000: Survey Report and Baseline Information. Cape Town: SALDRU, University of Cape Town.

———. 2003b. Social Accords and Employment: Lessons for South Africa? Discussion Paper prepared for the Department of Labour, 3 April, 2003.

———. 2004. *The Moral Economy of AIDS in South Africa.* Cape Town: Cambridge University Press.

Nattrass, N., and J. Seekings. 1996. The Challenge Ahead: Unemployment and Inequality in South Africa. *South African Labour Bulletin* 20, no. 1:66–72.

———. 1997. Citizenship and Welfare in South Africa: Deracialisation and Inequality in a Labour-Surplus Economy. *Canadian Journal of African Studies* 31, no. 3:452–81.

———. 1998. Democratic Institutions and Development in Post-Apartheid South Africa. In M. Robinson and G. White (eds.), *The Democratic Developmental State: Political and Institutional Design.* Oxford: Oxford University Press.

———. 2001a. Two Nations? Race and Economic Inequality in South Africa Today. *Daedalus* 130, no. 1:45–70.

———. 2001b. Democracy and Distribution in Highly Unequal Economies: The Case of South Africa. *Journal of Modern African Studies* 39, no. 3:471–98.

Nimubona, A., and D. Vencatachellum. 2003. Intergenerational Mobility in Education in South Africa. Paper presented to the Department of Economics, University of the Witwatersrand.

Norval, A. 1996. *Deconstructing Apartheid Discourse.* London: Verso.

Ntsebeza, L. 1993. *Youth in Urban African Townships, 1945–1992: A Case-Study of the East London Townships.* Master's thesis, University of Natal, Durban.

Nuttall, T. 1996. The Leaves in the Trees Are Proclaiming Our Slavery: African Trade Union Organisation, 1939–1949. In P. Maylam and I. Edwards (eds.), *The People's City: African Life in Twentieth Century Durban.* Pietermaritzburg: University of Natal Press.

O'Donnell, R. 2001. The Future of Social Partnership in Ireland. Discussion Paper Prepared for the National Competitiveness Council, May 2001.

OECD. 1996. *Income Distribution in OECD Countries.* Social Policy Studies No. 18. Prepared by A. Atkinson, L. Rainwater, and T. Smeeding. Paris: OECD.

———. 1998a. Recent Labour Market Developments and Prospects: Special Focus on the Patterns of Employment and Joblessness from a Household Perspective. *1998 Employment Outlook:* 1–30.

———. 1998b. Low-income Dynamics in Four OECD Countries. *OECD Economic Outlook* no. 64 (December): 171–86.

———. 1999. Labour Market Performance and the OECD jobs Strategy. *OECD Economic Outlook* no. 65 (June): 141–161.

O'Hearn, D. 2000. Globalisation, "New Tigers," and the End of the Developmental State. *Politics and Society* 28, no. 1:67–93.

O'Meara, D. 1975. The 1946 African Mineworkers Strike and the Political Economy of South Africa. *Journal of Commonwealth and Comparative Politics* 13, no. 2:146–73.

———. 1983. *Volkskapitalisme: Class, Capital, and Ideology in the Development of Afrikaner Nationalism, 1934–1948.* Cambridge: Cambridge University Press.

———. 1996. *Forty Lost Years: The Apartheid State and Politics of Afrikaner Nationalism.* Johannesburg: Ravan.

Oosthuizen, M. 2003. Expected Labour Demand in South Africa: 1998–2003. Working Paper 03/81. Cape Town: Development Policy Research Unit, University of Cape Town.

O'Reilly, K., and D. Rose. 1997. Criterion Validation of the Interim Revised Social Classification. In D. Rose and K. O'Reilly (eds.), *Constructing Classes: Towards a New Social Classification for the UK.* Swindon: Economic and Social Research Council and Office for National Statistics.

Parnell, S. 1989. Shaping a Racially Divided Society: State Housing Policy in South Africa, 1920–50. *Environment and Planning C: Government and Policy* 7: 261–72.

Parnell, S., and D. Hart. 1999. Self-help Housing as a Flexible Instrument of State Control in 20th-century South Africa. *Housing Studies* 14, no. 3:367–86.

Paton, A. 1948. *Cry, the Beloved Country.* London: Jonathan Cape.

Peires, J. 1994. Unsocial Bandits: The Stock Thieves of Qumbu and Their Enemies. Paper presented at the History Workshop conference, University of the Witwatersrand, Johannesburg.

Pillay, P. 1990. The Development and Underdevelopment of Education in South Africa. In W. Nassan and J. Samuel (eds.), *Education: From Poverty to Liberty.* Cape Town: David Philip.

Platzky, L., and C. Walker. 1985. *The Surplus People: Forced Removals in South Africa.* Johannesburg: Ravan.

Pollak, H. 1981. State Social Pensions, Grants, and Social Welfare. In S. Van der Horst and J. Reid (eds.), *Race Discrimination in South Africa: A Review.* Cape Town: David Philip.

Porter, R. 1976. A Model of a South African Type Economy. Discussion Paper. Ann Arbor: Center for Research on Economic Development, University of Michigan.

Portes, A. 1985. Latin American Class Structures: Their Composition and Change During the Last Decades. *Latin American Research Review* 20, no. 3:7–39.

Posel, Deborah. 1983. Rethinking the Race-Class Debate in South African Historiography. *Social Dynamics* 9, no. 1:50–66.

———. 1987. Influx Control and the Construction of Apartheid. Ph.D. diss., Oxford University.

———. 1991. *The Making of Apartheid: 1948–1961.* Oxford: Clarendon.

———. 1993. Influx Control and Urban Labour Markets in the 1950s. In P. Bonner, P. Delius, and D. Posel (eds.), *Apartheid's Genesis: 1935–1962.* Johannesburg: Ravan Press and Witwatersrand University Press.

Posel, Dorrit. 2000. Altruism, Kin Selection, and Intra-Family Transfers: Evidence from Remittance Behaviour in South Africa. Mimeo, Princeton University.

———. 2001. How Do Households Work? Migration, the Household, and Remittance Behaviour in South Africa. *Social Dynamics* 27, no. 1:165–89.

Przeworski, A., and J. Gandhi. 1999. Distribution and Redistribution of Income. Paper presented at the conference on Democracy and Redistribution, Yale University, November.

Psacharopoulos, G., S. Morley, A. Fiszbein, H. Lee, and B. Wood. 1997. Poverty and Income Distribution in Latin America: The Story of the 1980s. World Bank Technical Paper no. 351. Washington, D.C., World Bank.

PSLSD (Project for Statistics on Living Standards and Development). 1994. *South Africans Rich and Poor: Baseline Household Statistics.* Cape Town: SALDRU, University of Cape Town.

Ranger, T. 1985. *Peasant Consciousness and Guerrilla War in Zimbabwe.* London: James Currey.

Ravallion, M., and G. Datt. 2002. Why Has Economic Growth Been More Pro-Poor in Some States of India Than Others? *Journal of Development Economics* 68, no. 2:381–400.

Reader, D. 1961. *The Black Man's Portion: History, Demography, and Living Conditions in the Native Locations of East London, Cape Province.* Cape Town: Oxford University Press.

Reid, I. 1998. *Class in Britain.* Oxford: Polity.

Rhodes, M. 2001. The Political Economy of Social Pacts: "Competitive Corporatism" and European Welfare Reform. In P. Pierson (ed.), *The New Politics of the Welfare State.* New York: Oxford University Press.

Riordan, R. 1992. Marginalised Youth and Unemployment. In D. Everatt and S. Sisulu (eds.), *Black Youth in Crisis: Facing the Future.* Johannesburg: Ravan.

Roberts, M. 1958. *Labour in the Farm Economy.* Johannesburg: South African Institute of Race Relations.

Robinson, J. 1996. *The Power of Apartheid: State Power and Space in South African Cities.* Oxford: Butterworth-Heinemann.

Roiden, R. 1992. Marginalised Youth and Unemployment. In D. Everatt and E. Sisulu (eds.), *Black Youth in Crisis: Facing the Future.* Johannesburg: Ravan.

RSA (Republic of South Africa). 1962. Verslag van die Interdepartmentele Komitee insake Ledige en Nie-Werkende Bantoe in Stedelike Gebiede [Report of the Botha Committee, chair: M. C. Botha]. Pretoria: Department of Bantu Administration and Development.

———. 1966. Report of the Department of Bantu Affairs for 1964. UG 14/1966. Pretoria: Government Printer.

———. 1968. Report of the Department of Native Affairs for 1968. UG 17/1968. Pretoria: Government Printer.

———. 1971. Survey of Family Expenditure November 1966. Report 11–06–04, "Detailed expenditure of families according to occupational groups, income groups and family composition, 12 urban areas combined." Pretoria: Government Printer.

———. 1978. Survey of Household Expenditure, 1975. Report 11–06–01, "Detailed expenditure according to occupational group, household size and income group." Pretoria: Government Printer.

———. 1979. Report of the Commission of Inquiry into Legislation Affecting the Utilisation of Manpower (Excluding the Legislation Administered by the Department of Labour and Mines). RP32/1979 (Chair: Riekert). Pretoria: Government Printer.

———. 1985. Report of the Study Group on Industrial Development Strategy [Kleu Report]. Pretoria: Government Printer.

———. 1987. Report of the Committee for Economic Affairs on a Strategy for Employment Creation and Labour-Intensive Development. President's Council report no. 1/1987. Pretoria: Government Printer.

———. 1992. Report of the Committee of Investigation into a Retirement Provision System for South Africa. Vol.2. (Chair: W. Mouton). Pretoria: Government Printer.

———. 1994. South African Statistics: 1994. Pretoria; Government Printer.

————. 1996. Growth, Employment, and Redistribution: A Macroeconomic Strategy. Pretoria: Department of Finance.

————. 1998a. Creating Jobs, Fighting Poverty: An Employment Strategy Framework. Department of Labour, published in *Government Gazette* 397, no. 19040, 3 July.

————. 1998b. Victims of Crime. Pretoria: Statistics South Africa.

————. 2000a. Education for All: The South African Assessment Report. Pretoria: Department of Education.

————. 2000b. Budget Review 2000. Pretoria: Department of Finance.

————. 2003a. Annual Report of the Commission on Employment Equity. Pretoria: Department of Labour.

————. 2003b. Towards a Ten Year Review. Pretoria: The Presidency.

Runciman, W. G. 1990. How Many Classes Are There in Contemporary British Society? *Sociology* 24, no. 3:377–96.

Russell, M. 2002. Are Urban Black Families Nuclear? A Comparative Study of Black and White South Africans' Family Norms. Working Paper no. 17. Cape Town: Centre for Social Science Research, University of Cape Town.

————. 2004. Understanding Black Households: The Problem. Working Paper no. 67. Cape Town: Centre for Social Science Research, University of Cape Town.

SAIRR (South African Institute of Race Relations). 1955. *Race Relations Survey 1954–55*. Johannesburg: South African Institute of Race Relations.

————. 1961. *Race Relations Survey 1961*. Johannesburg: South African Institute of Race Relations.

————. 1962. *Race Relations Survey 1962*. Johannesburg: South African Institute of Race Relations.

————. 1971. *Race Relations Survey 1971*. Johannesburg: South African Institute of Race Relations.

————. 1983. *Race Relations Survey 1983*. Johannesburg: South African Institute of Race Relations.

SALDRU (South African Labour and Development Research Unit). 1977. Overview of Farm Labour in South Africa. In F. Wilson, A. Kooy, and D. Hendrie (eds.), *Farm Labour in South Africa*. Cape Town: David Philip.

Samson, M. 2002. The Social, Economic, and Fiscal Impact of Comprehensive Social Security Reform in South Africa. *Social Dynamics* 28, no. 2:69–97.

Samson, M., O. Babson, K. MacQuene, I. Van Niekerk, and R. van Niekerk. 2000. The Macroeconomic Implications of Poverty-Teducing Income Transfers. Paper presented to the conference on Towards a Sustainable and Comprehensive Social Security System, Institute for Social Development, University of the Western Cape.

Santana, I., and M. Rathe. 1993. The Distributive Impact of Fiscal Policy in the Dominican Republic. In R. Hausmann and R. Rigobón (eds.), *Government Spending and Income Distribution in Latin America*. Washington, D.C.: Inter-American Development Bank.

Sapire, H. 1987. The Stay-Away of the Brakplan Location, 1944. In B. Bozzoli (ed.), *Class, Community, and Conflict: South African Perspectives*. Johannesburg: Ravan.

————. 1993. African Political Organisations in Brakpan in the 1950s. In P. Bonner, P.

Delius, and D. Posel (eds.), *Apartheid's Genesis, 1935–1962*. Johannesburg: Witwatersrand University Press.

Saul, J., and S. Gelb. 1981. *The Crisis in South Africa*. London: Zed.

Schirmer, S. 1994. Reactions to the State: The Impact of Farm Labour Policies in the Mid-Eastern Transvaal, 1955–1960. *South African Historical Journal* no. 30:61–84.

———. 1995. African Strategies and Ideologies in a White Farming District: Lydenburg, 1930–1970. *Journal of Southern African Studies* 21, no. 3:509–27.

———. 2000. Policy Visions and Historical Realities: Land Reform in the Context of Recent Agricultural Developments. *African Studies* 59, no. 1:143–67.

———. 2003. Mechanisation Motives in South African Agriculture: c. 1940–1980. School of Economic and Business Sciences, University of the Witwatersrand, Johannesburg.

Schlemmer, L., and C. Levitz. 1998. Unemployment in South Africa: The Facts, the Prospects and an Exploration of Solutions. *Spotlight* series no. 1. Johannesburg: South African Institute of Race Relations.

Schlemmer, L., and K. Worthington. 1996a. Unemployment: How Bad is it? *Fast Facts*. April. Johannesburg: South African Institute of Race Relations.

Schlemmer, L., and K. Worthington. 1996b. New Evidence on Unemployment. *Fast Facts*, September. Johannesburg: South African Institute of Race Relations.

Schneier, S. 1983. Occupational Mobility Among Blacks in South Africa. Working Paper no. 58. Cape Town: SALDRU, University of Cape Town.

Schultz, T. P., and G. Mwabu. 1998a. Wage Premia for Education and Location, by Gender and Race in South Africa. Center Discussion Paper no. 785. New Haven: Economic Growth Center, Yale University.

———. 1998b. Labor Unions and the Distribution of Wages and Employment in South Africa. *Industrial and Labour Relations Review* 51, no. 4:680–703.

Seekings, J. 1989. Political Mobilisation in Tumahole: 1984–1985. *Africa Perspective,* new series, 1, nos. 7–8:105–44.

———. 1990. Quiescence and the Transition to Confrontation: South African Townships, 1978–1984. Ph.D. diss., Oxford University.

———. 1993. *Heroes or Villains? Youth Politics in the 1990s*. Johannesburg: Ravan.

———. 1996. The 'Lost Generation': South Africa's 'Youth Problem' in the Early 1990s. *Transformation* no. 29:103–25.

———. 2000. The Origins of Social Citizenship in South Africa. *South African Journal of Philosophy* 19, no. 4:386–404.

———. 2001. The Uneven Development of Quantitative Social Science in South Africa. *Social Dynamics* 27, no. 1:1–36.

———. 2002a. The Broader Importance of Welfare Reform in South Africa. *Social Dynamics* 28, no. 2:1–38.

———. 2002b. Unemployment and Distributive Justice in South Africa: Some Inconclusive Evidence from Cape Town. Working Paper no. 24. Cape Town: Centre for Social Science Research, University of Cape Town.

———. 2003a. Social Stratification and Inequality at the End of Apartheid. Working Paper no. 31. Cape Town: Centre for Social Science Research, University of Cape Town.

———. 2003b. Do the Unemployed Constitute an Underclass? Working Paper no. 32. Cape Town: Centre for Social Science Research, University of Cape Town.

———. 2003c. The Unmentioned Elephant in the Room: Teachers, Unions, and the Political Economy of Education in Post-Apartheid South Africa. University of Cape Town.

———. 2003d. Providing for the Poor: Welfare and Redistribution in South Africa. Inaugural Lecture, University of Cape Town, 23 April.

———. 2003e. Welfare Reform in the 1940s: South Africa in Comparative Perspective. Paper presented at the conference on South Africa in the 1940s, Queen's University, Kingston, Ontario.

———. 2004. Trade Unions, Social Policy, and Class Compromise in Post-Apartheid South Africa. *Review of African Political Economy* no. 100:299–312.   ⊃ UDF NOT LISTED

Seekings, J., and N. Nattrass. 2002. Class, Distribution and Redistribution in Post-Apartheid South Africa. *Transformation* no. 50:1–30.

Seekings, J., Nattrass, N., and M. Leibbrandt. 2003. Inequality in Post-Apartheid South Africa: Trends in the Distribution of Income and Opportunities and Their Social and Political Implications. Report for the Centre for Development and Enterprise, Johannesburg, September.

Selowsky, M. 1979. *Who Benefits from Public Expenditure?* Oxford: Oxford University Press.

Shackleton, S., C. Shackleton, and B. Cousins. 2000. The Economic Value of Land and Natural Resources to Rural Livelihoods: Case Studies from South Africa. In B. Cousins (ed.), *At the Crossroads: Land and Agrarian Reform in South Africa into the 21st Century.* Cape Town: National Land Committee and Programme for Land and Agrarian Studies, University of the Western Cape.

Sharp, J. 1994. A World Turned Upside Down: Households and Differentiation in a South African Bantustan in the 1980s. *African Studies* 53, no. 1:71–88.

Sharp, J., and A. Spiegel. 1985. Vulnerability to Impoverishment in South African Rural Areas: The Erosion of Kinship and Neighbourhood as Social Resources. *Africa* 55, no. 2:133–51.

———. 1990. Women and Wages: Gender and the Control of Income in Farm and Bantustan Households. *Journal of Southern African Studies* 16, no. 3:527–49.

Siebert, W. 1975. An Analysis of the Relative Pay of Whites and Non-whites in South Africa. Ph.D. diss., University of London.

Simbi, T., and M. Aliber. 2000. The Agricultural Employment Crisis in South Africa. Paper presented at the Development Policy Research Unit and Trade and Industrial Policy Secretariat Forum, Muldersdrift, September.

Simkins, C. 1976. The Distribution of Personal Income Among Income Recipients in South Africa, 1970 and 1976. Working Paper No.9. Pietermaritzburg: Development Studies Research Group, University of Natal.

———. 1978a. Measuring and Predicting Unemployment in South Africa, 1960–77. In C. Simkins and D. Clarke, *Structural Unemployment in Southern Africa.* Pietermaritzburg: University of Natal Press.

———. 1978b. African Unemployment in Urban and Rural South Africa. In C. Simkins and C. Desmond (eds.), *South African Unemployment: A Black Picture.* Pietermaritzburg: Development Studies Research Group, University of Natal.

———. 1979. The Distribution of Personal Income Among Income Recipients in South Africa, 1970 and 1976. Working Paper, no. 9. Pietermaritzburg: Development Studies Research Group, University of Natal.

———. 1981a. The Demographic Demand for Labour and Institutional Context of African Unemployment in South Africa. Working Paper no. 32. Cape Town: SALDRU, University of Cape Town.

———. 1981b. The "Mythical" Unemployment Problem? How Extensive Is Unemployment? *Businessman's Law* 10, no. 4:115–7.

———. 1981c. Agricultural Production in the African Reserves of South Africa, 1918–1969. *Journal of Southern African Studies* 7, no. 2:256–83.

———. 1982. Structural Unemployment Revisited: A Revision and Updating of Earlier Estimates Incorporating New Data from the Current Population Survey and the 1980 Population Census. Cape Town: Southern African Labour and Development Research Unit, University of Cape Town.

———. 1983. *Four Essays on the Past, Present, and Possible Future of the Distribution of the Black Population of South Africa.* Cape Town: Southern African Labour and Development Research Unit, University of Cape Town.

———. 1984a. African Population, Employment, and Incomes on Farms Outside the Reserves, 1923–1969. Carnegie Conference Paper no. 25. Cape Town: SALDRU, University of Cape Town.

———. 1984b. What Has Been Happening to Income Distribution and Poverty in the Homelands? Carnegie Conference Paper no. 7. Cape Town: SALDRU, University of Cape Town.

———. 1998. On the Durability of South African Inequality. Unpublished paper.

———. 2001. Can South Africa Avoid a Malthusian Positive Check? *Daedalus* 130, no. 1:123–50.

———. 2003. Employment and Unemployment in South Africa. Unpublished paper.

Simkins, C., and D. Hindson. 1979. The Division of Labour in South Africa. *Social Dynamics* 5, no. 2:1–12.

Skocpol, T. 1992. *Protecting Soldiers and Mothers: The Political Origins of Social Policy in the United States.* Cambridge: Harvard University Press, Belknap Press.

Slater, R. 2000. Tracking Livelihoods in Diappolo: Reflections on Longitudinal Study in QwaQwa. University of Manchester.

———. 2001. De-industrialisation, Multiple Livelihoods, and Identity: Tracking Social Change in Qwaqwa, South Africa. *Journal of Contemporary African Studies* 19, no. 1:81–92.

———. 2002. Differentiation and Diversification: Changing Livelihoods in Qwaqwa, South Africa, 1970–2000. *Journal of Southern African Studies* 28, no. 3:599–614.

Smith, R. H., and F. A. Byron. 1941. The Expansion of Industry and the Supply of Labour. *South African Journal of Economics* 9, no. 3:251–64.

South African Health Review. 1997. Durban: Health Systems Trust.

Southall, R. 2003. The ANC and Black Capitalism in South Africa. Paper presented at the Human Sciences Research Council/Review of African Political Economy Workshop, Johannesburg.

Spandau, A, 1973. Cross-Section Production Functions and Income Shares in South African Industry. *South African Journal of Economics* 41, no. 3:208–33.

Sperber, F. 1993. *Rural Income, Welfare, and Migration: A Study of Three Ciskeian Villages.* Master's thesis, University of Cape Town.

Spiegel, A. 1996. Introduction: Domestic Fluidity in South Africa. *Social Dynamics* 22, no. 1:5–6.

Spies, P., and F. Biggs. 1983. Issues in the Socio-Economic Environment in South Africa. In P. Spies (ed.), *Urban-Rural Interaction in South Africa.* Stellenbosch: Institute for Futures Research, University of Stellenbosch.

Stallings, B. 2000. Growth, Employment, and Equity: The Impact of Economic Reforms in Latin America and the Caribbean. Paper presented to the Conference on Poverty and Income Inequality in Developing Countries hosted by the OECD Development Centre, in Marseille, November.

Standing, G., J. Sender, and J. Weeks. 1996. *The South African Challenge: Restructuring the South African Labour Market.* Geneva: International Labour Organisation.

Stats SA (Statistics South Africa). 2002. *The Contribution of Small and Micro Enterprises to the Economy of the Country: A Survey of Non-VAT-Registered Businesses in South Africa.* Pretoria: Statistics South Africa.

Stats SA (Statistics South Africa). 2003. *Census 2001: Census in Brief.* Pretoria: Statistics South Africa.

Steenkamp, T. 1990. Discrimination and the Economic Position of the Afrikaner. *South African Journal of Economic History* 5, no. 1:49–66.

Steenkamp, W. 1962. Bantu Wages in South Africa. *South African Journal of Economics* 30, no. 2:93–118.

Steinberg, J., S. Johnson, G. Schierhout, and D. Ndegwa. 2002. Hitting Home: How Households Cope with the Impact of the HIV/AIDS Epidemic: A Survey of Households Affected by HIV/AIDS in South Africa. Kaiser Family Foundation and the Health Systems Trust.

Stiglitz, J. 1998. More Instruments and Broader Goals: Moving Towards the Post-Washington Consensus. WIDER Annual Lectures 2, UNU World Institute for Development Economics Research, Helsinki.

Terreblanche, S. 2002. *A History of Inequality in South Africa, 1652–2002.* Pietermaritzburg: University of Natal Press.

Thomas, D. 1996. Education Across Generations in South Africa. *AEA Papers and Proceedings* 86, no. 2:330–34.

Thompson, K., and I. Woolard. 2002. Achieving Employment Equity in the Public Service: A Study of Changes Between 1995 and 2001. Working Paper no. 02/61. Cape Town: Development Policy Research Unit, University of Cape Town.

Todaro, M. 1969. A Model of Labour Migration and Urban Unemployment in Less Developed Countries. *American Economic Review* 59, no. 1:138–49.

———. 1971. Income Expectations, Rural-Urban Migration, and Employment in Africa. *International Labour Review* 104, no. 5:387–414.

———. 1994. *Economic Development.* 5th ed. New York: Longman.

Torres, L. 1996. Welfare and Redistribution: Whose Responsibility Is It? *South African Labour Bulletin* 20, no. 2:85–89.

Union of S.A. (South Africa). 1941. Report of the Wage Board for 1940. UG 45–1941. Pretoria: Government Printer.

———. 1943a. Report of the Social Security Committee. Published in 1944 as part of UG 14–1944. Pretoria: Government Printer.

———. 1943b. Social Security, Social Services, and the National Income. Social and Economic Planning Council Report no. 2, published in 1944 as part of UG 14–1944. Pretoria: Government Printer.

———. 1944a. Report of the National Health Services Commission on the Provision of an Organised National Health Service for All Sections of the People of the Union of South Africa, 1942–1944. UG 30/1944 (Chair: H. Gluckman). Pretoria: Government Printer.

———. 1944b. The Future of Farming in South Africa. Social and Economic Planning Council Report no. 4. UG 10/1944, Pretoria: Government Printer.

———. 1944c. Report of the Witwatersrand Mine Natives' Wages Commission on Remuneration and Conditions of Employment of Natives on Witwatersrand Gold Mines. UG 21/1944 (Chair: C. Lansdown). Pretoria: Government Printer.

———. 1945. Memorandum on the Government's Proposals Regarding Some Aspects of Social Security. B6074/1/2/45. Pretoria: Government Printer.

———. 1946. The Native Reserves and Their Place in the Economy of the Union of South Africa. Social and Economic Planning Council Report no. 9. UG 32/1946. Pretoria: Government Printer.

———. 1948. The Economic and Social Conditions of the Racial Groups in South Africa. Social and Economic Planning Council Report no. 13. UG 53/1948. Pretoria: Government Printer.

———. 1950a. Official Year Book of the Union of South Africa: 1950. Pretoria: Government Printer.

———. 1950b. Report of the Department of Native Affairs for the Years 1948–49. UG 51–1950. Pretoria: Government Printer.

———. 1950c. Report of the Wage Board for the Year ended December 1948. UG 50–1950. Pretoria: Government Printer.

———. 1951a. Report of the Department of Native Affairs for the Years 1949–50. UG 61–1951. Pretoria: Government Printer.

———. 1951b. Report of the Industrial Legislation Commission of Enquiry. UG-62–1951 (Chair: Botha). Pretoria: Government Printer.

———. 1952a. Population on Farms of Whites. Bureau of Census and Statistics, Agricultural Census 1949–50, Report no. 6. Pretoria: Government Printer.

———. 1952b. Labour on Farms of Whites and Wages of Farm Labourers. Bureau of Census and Statistics, Agricultural Census 1949–50, Report no. 7. Pretoria: Government Printer.

———. 1953. Report of the Department of Native Affairs for the Years 1950–51. UG 30–1953. Pretoria: Government Printer.

———. 1955a. Summary of the Report of the Commission for the Socio-Economic Development of the Bantu Areas within the Union of South Africa. UG61/1955 (Chair: F. R. Tomlinson). Pretoria: Government Printer.

———. 1955b. Report of the Department of Native Affairs for the Years 1952–53. UG 48–1955. Pretoria: Government Printer.

———. 1958. Survey of Family Expenditure November 1955. Report no. 3, "Income." Pretoria: Government Printer.

———. 1959. Report of the Department of Native Affairs for the Years 1954–57, UG 14/1959. Pretoria: Government Printer.

———. 1960. Report of the Department of Bantu Affairs and Development for the Years 1958–59. UG 51/1960. Pretoria: Government Printer.

Valodia, I. 2000. Economic Policy and Women's Informal and Flexible Work in South Africa. Paper presented at the TIPS Policy Forum, Muldersdrift, September.

Van der Berg, S. 1997. South African Social Security Under Apartheid and Beyond. *Development Southern Africa* 14, no. 4:481–504.

———. 2001a. Resource Shifts in South African Schools After the Political Transition. *Development Southern Africa* 18, no. 4:405–417.

———. 2001b. Trends in Racial Fiscal Incidence in South Africa. *South African Journal of Economics* 69, no. 2:243–68.

———. 2001c. Redistribution Through the Budget: Public Expenditure Incidence in South Africa, 1993–1997. *Social Dynamics* 27, no. 1:140–64.

———. 2002. Education, Poverty, and Inequality in South Africa. Paper presented at the Conference of the Centre for the Study of African Economies, Oxford, March.

Van der Berg, S., and C. Bredenkamp. 2002. Devising Social Security Interventions for Maximum Policy Impact. *Social Dynamics* 28, no. 2:39–68.

Van der Horst, S. 1942/1971. *Native Labour in South Africa.* Cape Town: Oxford University Press.

———. 1949. Labour. In E. Hellmann (ed.), *Handbook of Race Relations in South Africa.* Cape Town: Oxford University Press.

———. 1981. Employment. In S. Van der Horst and J. Reid (eds.), *Race Discrimination in South Africa: A Review.* Cape Town: David Philip.

Van der Merwe, P. J. 1976. *Black Employment Problems in South Africa.* Bureau for Economic Planning and Analysis, Report no. 6, November.

Van Onselen, C. 1996. *The Seed Is Mine: The Life of Kas Maine.* Cape Town: David Philip.

Van Zyl, A., and C. Westhuizen. 2003. Deep Cuts? Social Service Delivery Under GEAR. Paper delivered at the Development Policy Research Unit conference, Johannesburg.

Verster, J., and R. Prinsloo. 1988. The Diminishing Test Performance Gap Between English Speakers and Afrikaans Speakers in South Africa. In S. Irvine and J. Berry (eds.), *Human Abilities in Cultural Context.* Cambridge: Cambridge University Press.

Villa, M., and Rodriguez, J. 1996. Demographic Trends in Latin America's Metropolises. In A. Gilbert (ed.), *The Mega-City in Latin America.* Tokyo: United Nations University Press.

Vink, N., and J. Kirsten. 2000. *Deregulation of Agricultural Marketing in South Africa.* Johannesburg: Free Market Foundation monograph no. 25.

Vlok. E. 1998. An Unholy Alliance? Organising the Unemployed. *South African Labour Bulletin* 22, no. 5:40–45.

Von Amsberg, J., P. Lanjouw, and K. Nead. 2000. The Poverty Targeting of Social Spending in Brazil. Background paper for the World Bank.

Wade, R. 1990. *Governing the Market: Economic Theory and the Role of Government in East Asian Industrialisation.* Princeton: Princeton University Press.

Walker, L., and L. Gilbert. 2002. HIV/AIDS: South African Women at Risk. *African Journal of AIDS Research* 1, no. 1:75–85.

Weeks, J. 1999. Stuck in Low GEAR? Macroeconomic Policy in South Africa, 1996–98. *Cambridge Journal of Economics* 23, no. 6:795–811.

Weiss, L. 1998. *The Myth of the Powerless State: Governing the Economy in a Global Era.* Cambridge: Polity.

Wentzel, W. 1984. Hard Times in the Karoo: Case Studies and Statistical Profiles from Five Peri-Urban Residential Areas. Carnegie Conference Paper no. 38. Cape Town: SALDRU, University of Cape Town.

Westergaard, J. 1995. *Who Gets What? The Hardening of Class Inequality in the Late Twentieth Century.* Cambridge: Cambridge University Press.

Whiteford, A., and M. McGrath. 1994. *The Distribution of Income in South Africa.* Pretoria: Human Sciences Research Council.

———. 1998. Income Inequality over the Apartheid Years. SANER Working Paper no. 6. Cape Town: South African Network for Economic Research.

Whiteford, A., D. Posel, and T. Kelatwang. 1995. *A Profile of Poverty, Inequality, and Human Development.* Pretoria: Human Sciences Research Council.

Whiteford, A., and Van Seventer, D. 2000. Understanding Contemporary Household Inequality in South Africa. *Studies in Economics and Econometrics* 24, no. 3:7–30.

Williams, G. 1996. Transforming Labour Tenants. In Michael Lipton, F. Ellis, and Merle Lipton (eds.), *Land, Labour, and Livelihoods in Rural South Africa.* Durban: Indicator Press, University of Natal.

Williamson, J. 1985. *Did British Capitalism Breed Inequality?* London: George Allen and Unwin.

———. 1991. British Inequality During the Industrial Revolution: Accounting for the Kuznets Curve. In Y. S. Brenner, H. Kaelble, and M. Thomas (eds.), *Income Distribution in Historical Perspective.* Cambridge: Cambridge University Press.

Wilson, F. 1971. Farming: 1866–1966. In M. Wilson and L. Thompson (eds.), *The Oxford History of South Africa.* Vol. 2, *South Africa, 1870–1966.* Oxford: Clarendon.

———. 1972. *Labour in the South African Gold Mines.* Cambridge: Cambridge University Press.

———. 1975a. The Political Implications for Blacks of Economic Changes Now Taking Place in South Africa. In L. Thompson and J. Butler (eds.), *Change in Contemporary South Africa.* Berkeley: University of California Press.

———. 1975b. Unresolved Issues in the South African Economy: Labour. *South African Journal of Economics* 43, no. 4:516–47.

———. 1996. South Africa: Poverty Under Duress. In E. Øyen, S. M. Miller, and S. A. Samad (eds.), *Poverty: A Global Review.* Oslo: Scandinavia University Press.

Wilson, F., and M. Ramphele. 1989. *Uprooting Poverty: The South African Challenge.* Cape Town: David Philip.

Wilson, W. J. 1987. *The Truly Disadvantaged: The Inner City, the Underclass, and Public Policy.* Chicago: University of Chicago Press.

———. 1991. Public Policy Research and the Truly Disadvantaged. In C. Jencks and P. Petersen (eds.), *The Urban Underclass.* Washington, D.C.: Brookings Institution.

————. 1997. *When Work Disappears: The World of the New Urban Poor.* New York: Vintage Books.

Wittenberg, M. 1999. Job Search and Household Structure in an Era of Mass Unemployment: A Semi-Parametric Analysis of the South African Labour Market. ERSA Working Paper no. 3. Johannesburg: University of the Witwatersrand, Economics Department.

Wittenberg, M., and C. Pearce. 1996. Youth and Unemployment: Some Perspectives from the South African Living Standards and Development Survey. In L. Chisholm et al. (eds.), *Out-of-School Youth Report: Policy and Provision for Out-of-School and Out-of-Work Youth.* Johannesburg: Education Policy Unit, University of the Witwatersrand.

Wix, E. 1951. *The Cost of Living: An Enquiry into the Cost of Essential Requirements for African Families Living in Johannesburg, Pretoria, and the Reef Towns, August—December 1950.* Johannesburg: South African Institute of Race Relations.

Wolpe, H. 1972. Capitalism and Cheap Labour Power in South Africa: From Segregation to Apartheid. *Economy and Society* 1, no. 4:425–56. (Reprinted in W. Beinart and S. Dubow [eds.], 1995. *Segregation and Apartheid in Twentieth Century South Africa.* London: Routledge.)

————. 1977. The Changing Class Structure of South Africa: The African Petit-Bourgeoisie. In P. Zarembka (ed.), *Research in Political Economy,* vol. 1. Greenwich, Conn.: JAI.

————. 1988. *Race, Class, and the Apartheid State.* London: James Currey.

Woolard, I. 2003. Social Assistance Grants, Poverty, and Economic Growth in South Africa. Paper presented at the Development Policy Research Unit Conference, Johannesburg, 8–10 September.

World Bank. 1995a. *World Development Report 1995: Workers in an Integrating World.* Washington, D.C.: World Bank.

————. 1995b. Key Indicators of Poverty in South Africa. Report for the South African Government's Office of the Reconstruction and Development Programme, by the World Bank.

————. 1996. *World Development Indicators 1996.* Washington, D.C.: World Bank.

————. 2001. *World Development Report 2000/2001: Attacking Poverty.* Washington, D.C.: World Bank.

Wright, E. O. 1997. *Class Counts: Comparative Studies in Class Analysis.* Cambridge: Cambridge University Press.

Yosslowitz, J. 1984. A Study of Poverty Among the "Coloured" Community: A General Analysis and a Case Study of Worcester. Carnegie Conference Paper no. 32. Cape Town: SALDRU, University of Cape Town.

Yudelman, D. 1983. *The Emergence of Modern South Africa: State, Capital, and the Incorporation of Organized Labor on the South African Gold Fields, 1902–1939.* Westport, Conn.: Greenwood.

Ziehl, S. 2001. Documenting Changing Family Patterns in South Africa: Are Census Data of Any Value? *African Sociological Review* 5, no. 2:36–62.

————. 2002. Black South Africans *Do* Live in Nuclear Family *Households:* A Response to Russell. *Society in Transition* 33, no. 1:26–49.

Index

Afrobarometer survey, 369

AIDS: divisions, 370; inequality, 47, 333–336; policy response, 365; poverty, 336; prevention and treatment, 391–392, 395–396; unemployment, 296, 368

ANC (African National Congress), 30, 41, 64, 110, 189, 391, 394

apartheid: development model, 17; labour-market policy, 20, 22, 33, 35, 37–39, 137–141, 147–149; political policy, 18–19, 21, 46; principal features of, 19–20; social policy, 19–22, 37, 129–137, 149–157; understanding of, 18; *see also* distributional regime during apartheid, liberal approach, Marxist approach

Apprenticeship Act 1944, 138

Asian financial crisis, 350

ASSA2002 demographic model, 333

Australia, 8–10, 34, 36, 40, 82, 85

bantustans, *see* reserves

Basic Conditions of Employment Act 1997, 350

basic income grant (BIG), 48, 364, 374, 390–391, 393–398

BEE (black economic empowerment), 310, 343–345, 356, 365

Black Economic Empowerment Act 2003, 344

Black Economic Empowerment Commission, 344

Blacks (Urban Areas) Consolidation Act 1945, 103, 402 endnote 2

Bloemfontein, 111

BMR (Bureau of Market Research) surveys, 24, 111–112, 117–118, 120, 122

Bophuthatswana, 118, 175

Botha Committee, 170–171

brain drain, 306, 352

Brazil: agriculture, 220; employment rela-